Gas Money, Please

It is a pleasure to bring you a book of
our freewheeling biker, Harley. Now
a year old, he still throttles the engine of
his carefree lifestyle ... his big appetite for
fun (and his extra large pants); his love of
the open road, cats, coffee, dogs, and under-
dogs; his nature to be the "lone wolf ";
his good-humored but friendly dedication to
his sidekick, Cat. His motorcycle is neither fast
nor slow but perfect for crashing into Pointy
Rock Canyon.
My thanks to *Gocomics.com* for giving me
the outlet to make you the reader laugh on a
daily basis.
Harley and I hope you will enjoy coming
along for the ride with "Hey! Harley."

Dan Thompson

HEY!
HARLEY

by Dan Thompson

To Kari, George and Joe who made this book possible.

Printed in the United States of America

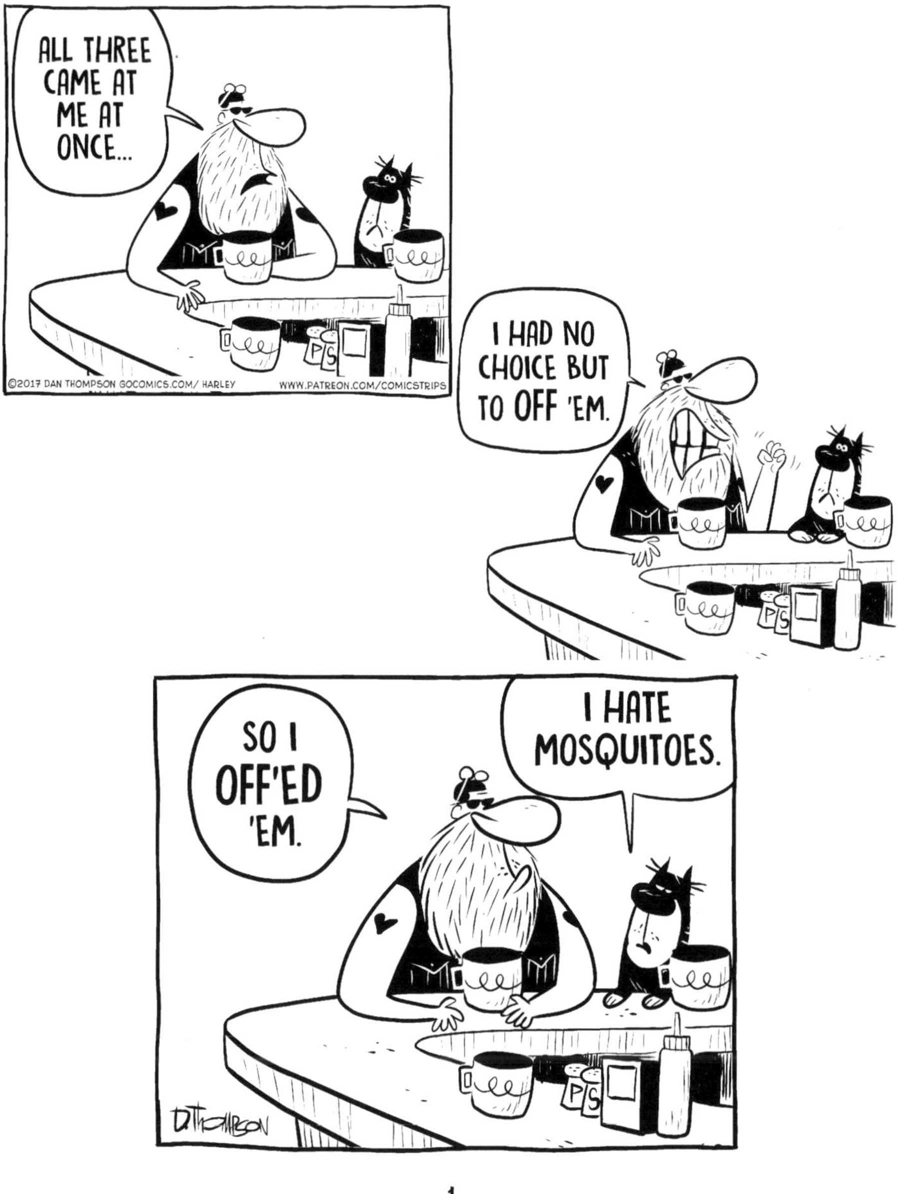
ALL THREE CAME AT ME AT ONCE...
©2017 DAN THOMPSON GOCOMICS.COM/ HARLEY
WWW.PATREON.COM/COMICSTRIPS
I HAD NO CHOICE BUT TO OFF 'EM.
SO I OFF'ED 'EM.
I HATE MOSQUITOES.
D. THOMPSON

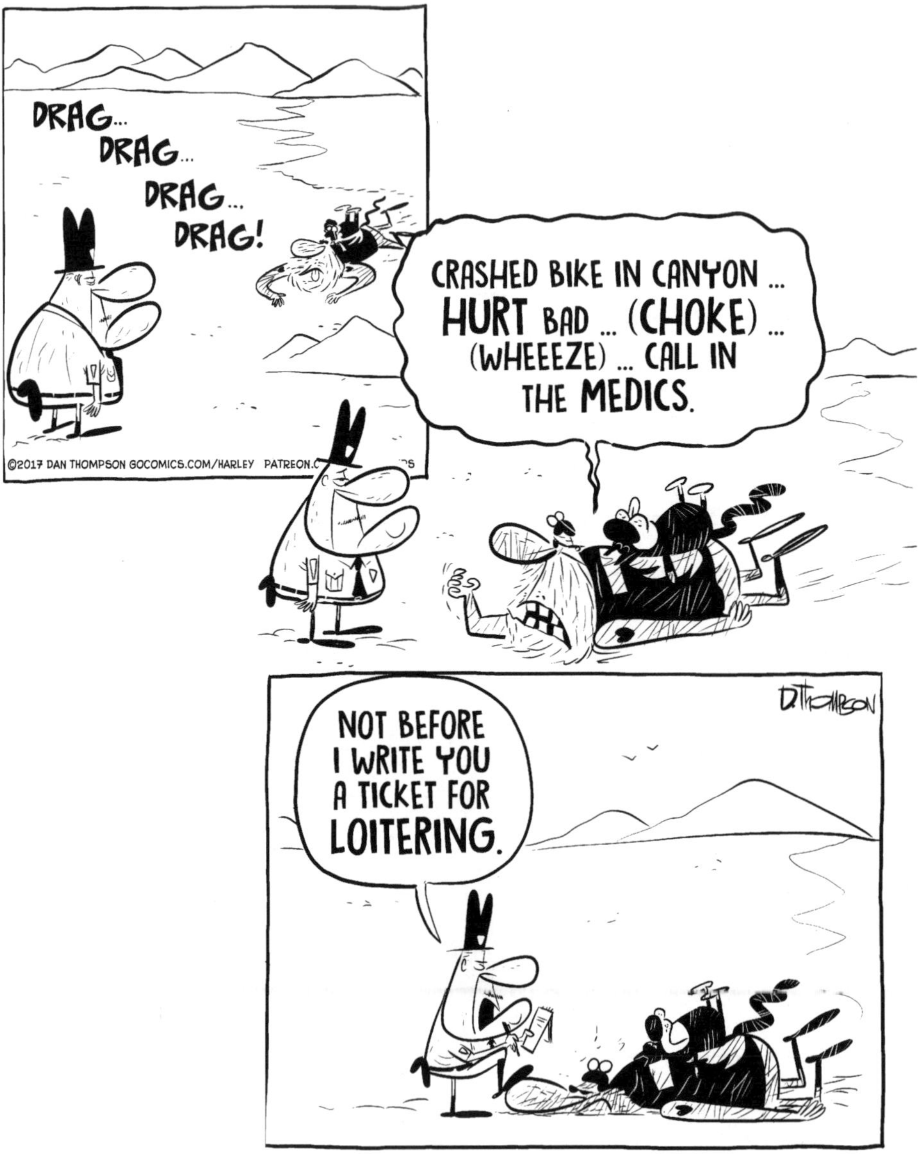
DRAG... DRAG... DRAG... DRAG!
©2017 DAN THOMPSON GOCOMICS.COM/HARLEY PATREON.C
CRASHED BIKE IN CANYON ... HURT BAD ... (CHOKE) ... (WHEEEZE) ... CALL IN THE MEDICS.
D.THOMPSON
NOT BEFORE I WRITE YOU A TICKET FOR LOITERING.

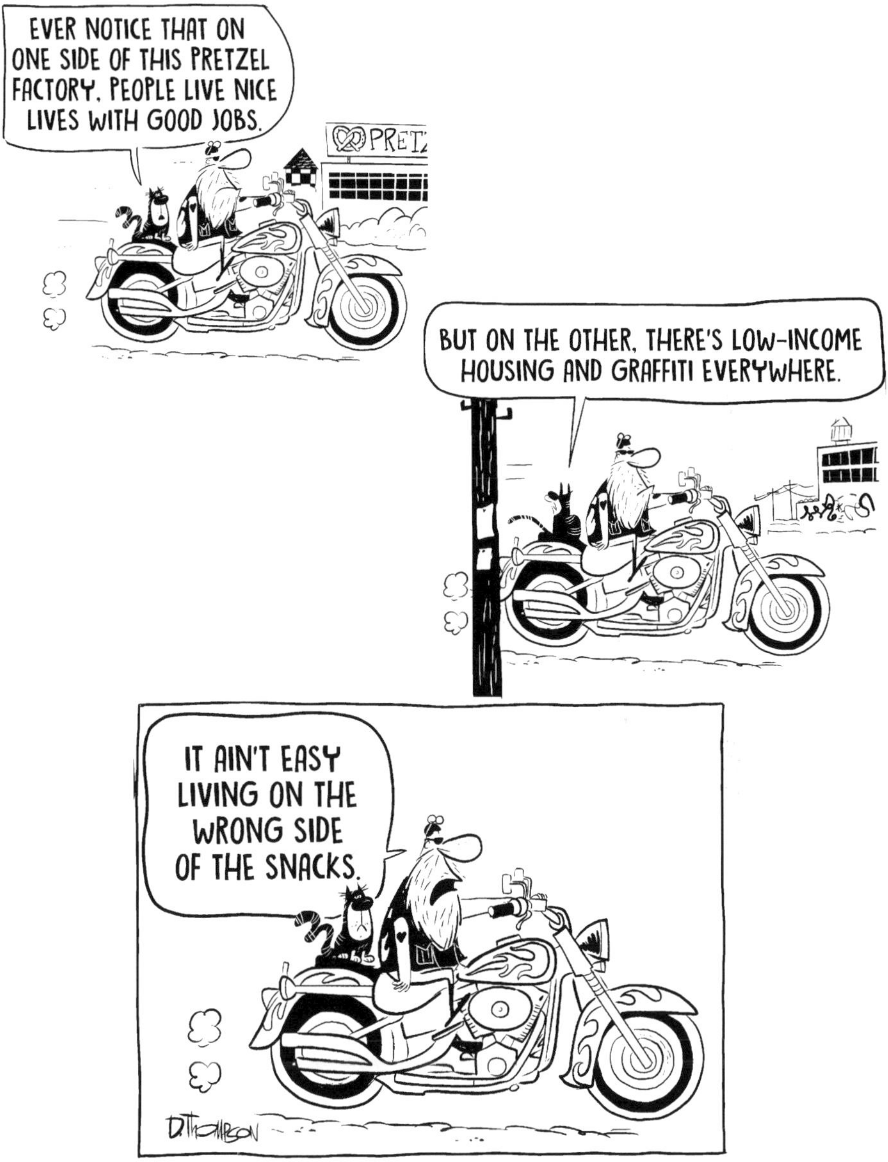
EVER NOTICE THAT ON ONE SIDE OF THIS PRETZEL FACTORY, PEOPLE LIVE NICE LIVES WITH GOOD JOBS.
BUT ON THE OTHER, THERE'S LOW-INCOME HOUSING AND GRAFFITI EVERYWHERE.
IT AIN'T EASY LIVING ON THE WRONG SIDE OF THE SNACKS.
D. THOMPSON

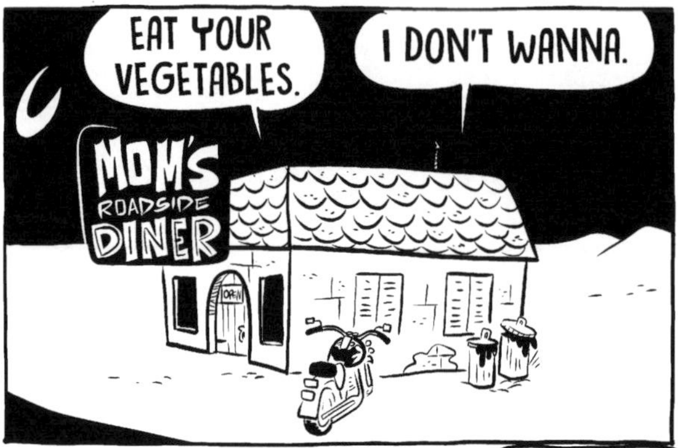
EAT YOUR VEGETABLES.
I DON'T WANNA.
MOM'S ROADSIDE DINER
OPEN

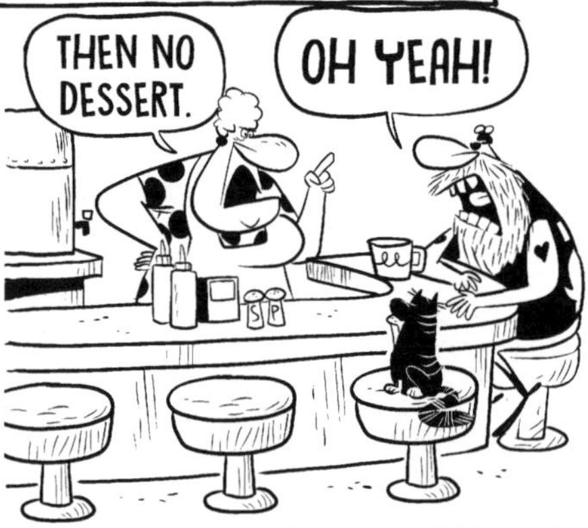
THEN NO DESSERT.
OH YEAH!
S
P

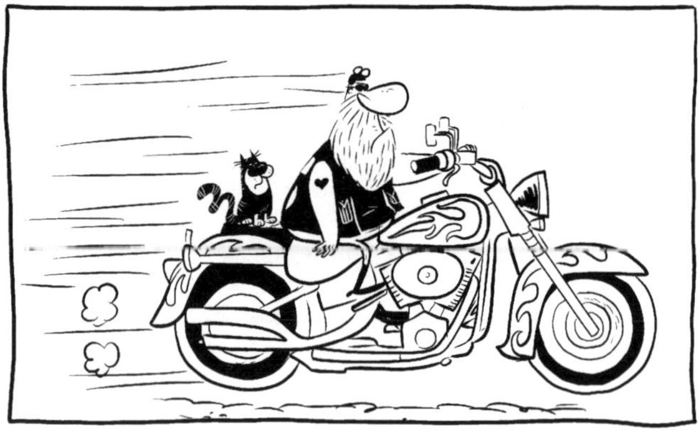

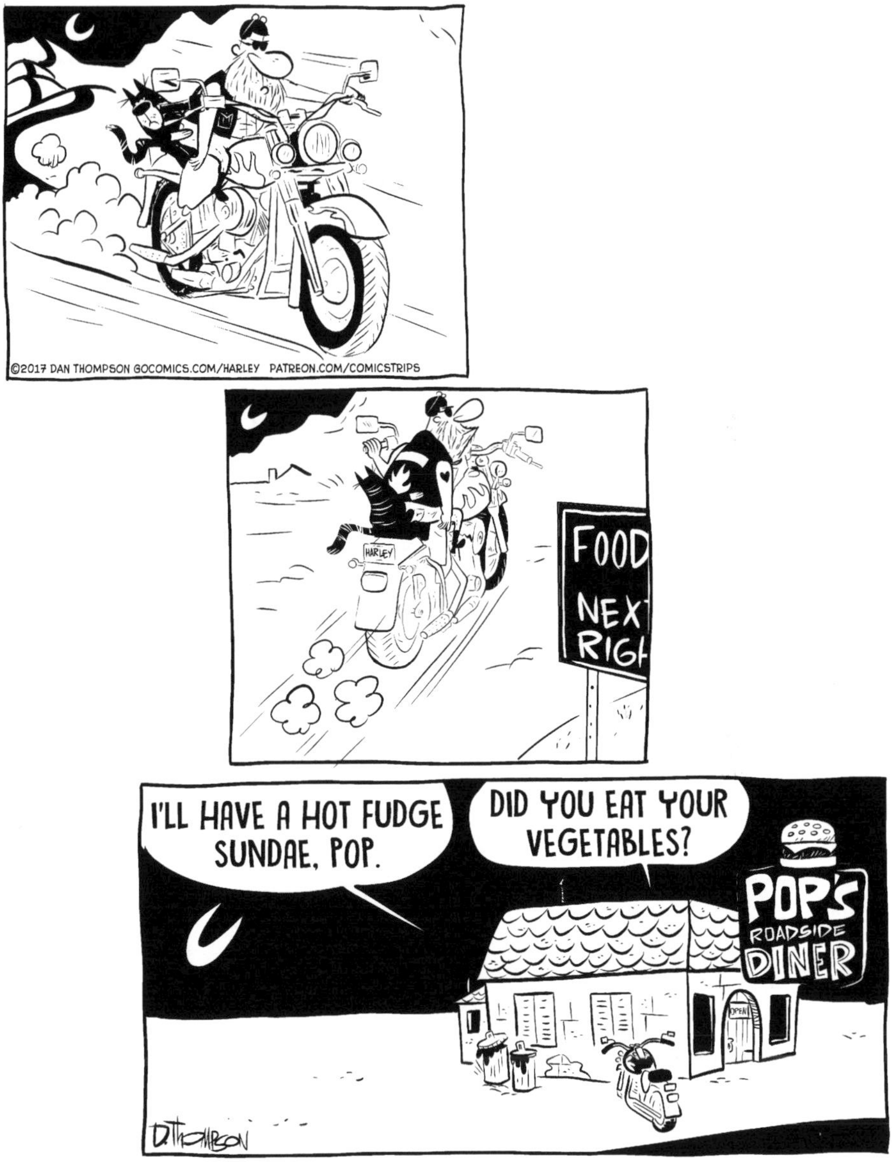
©2017 DAN THOMPSON GOCOMICS.COM/HARLEY PATREON.COM/COMICSTRIPS
HARLEY
FOOD
I'LL HAVE A HOT FUDGE SUNDAE, POP.
DID YOU EAT YOUR VEGETABLES?
POP'S ROADSIDE DINER
OPEN
D. THOMPSON

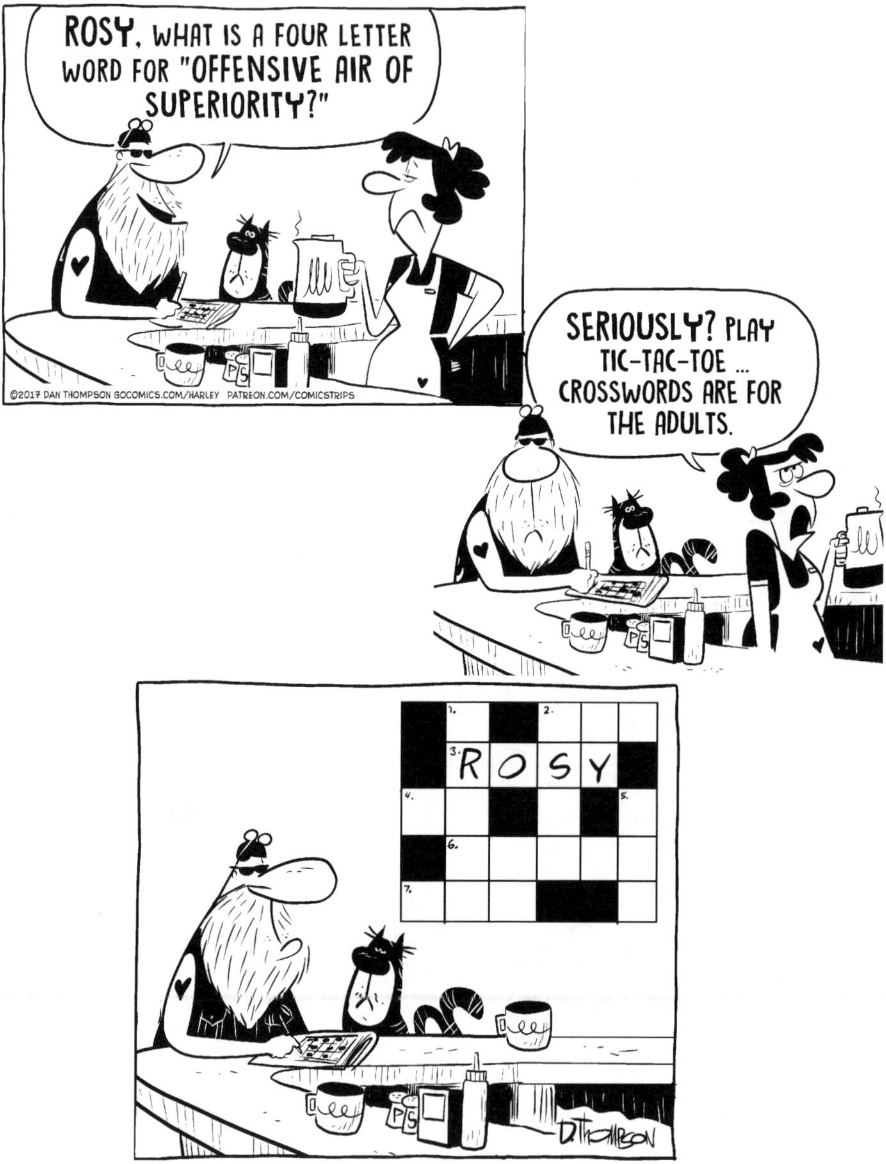
ROSY, WHAT IS A FOUR LETTER WORD FOR "OFFENSIVE AIR OF SUPERIORITY?"
©2017 DAN THOMPSON GOCOMICS.COM/HARLEY PATREON.COM/COMICSTRIPS
SERIOUSLY? PLAY TIC-TAC-TOE ... CROSSWORDS ARE FOR THE ADULTS.
ROSY
D. THOMPSON

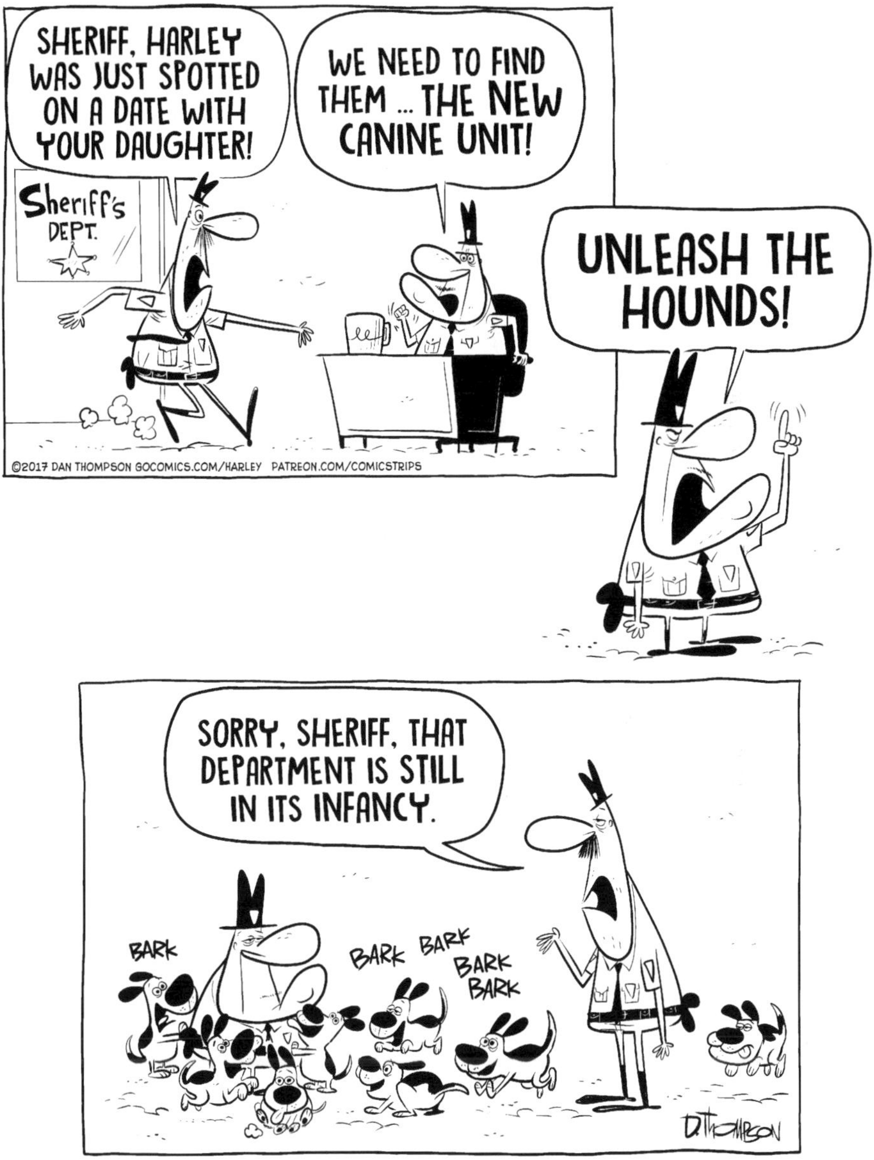
SHERIFF, HARLEY WAS JUST SPOTTED ON A DATE WITH YOUR DAUGHTER!
Sheriff's DEPT.
WE NEED TO FIND THEM ... THE NEW CANINE UNIT!
©2017 DAN THOMPSON GOCOMICS.COM/HARLEY PATREON.COM/COMICSTRIPS
UNLEASH THE HOUNDS!
SORRY, SHERIFF, THAT DEPARTMENT IS STILL IN ITS INFANCY.
BARK
BARK BARK
BARK BARK
D. THOMPSON

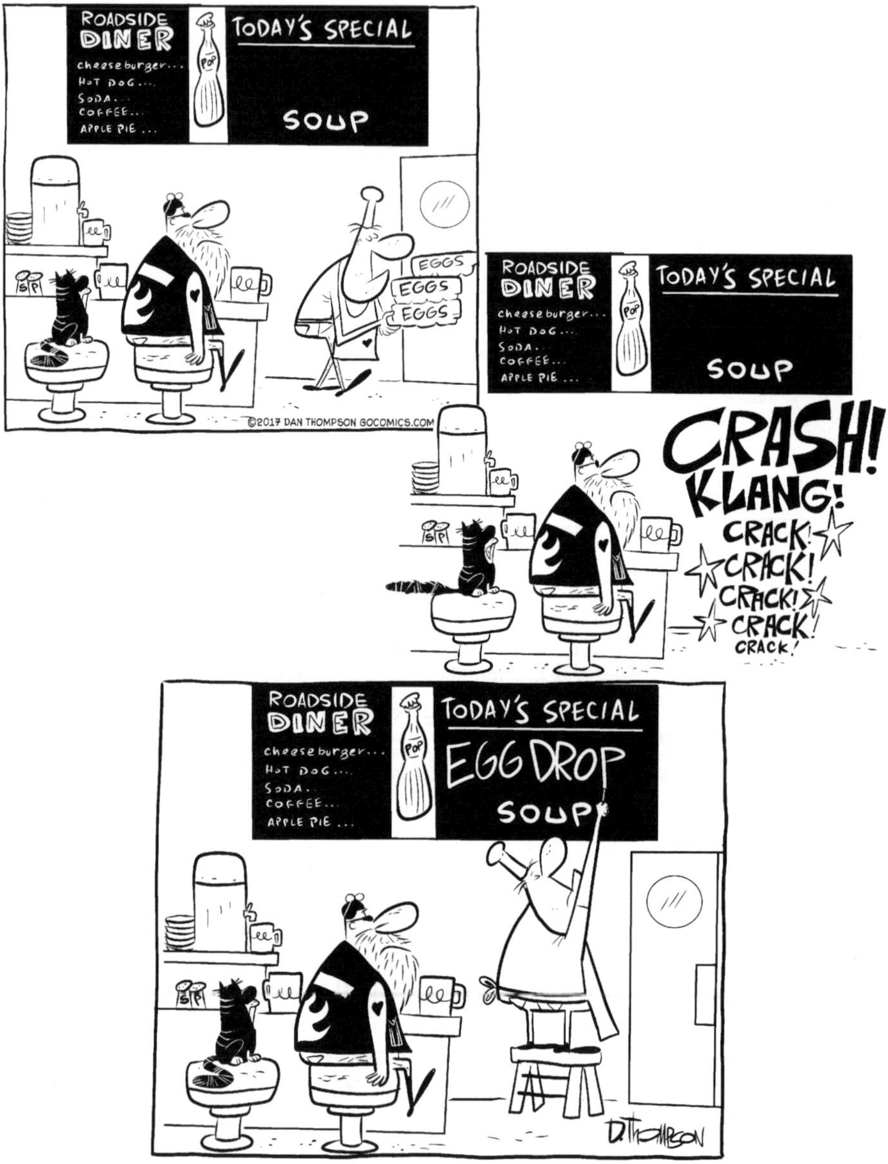
ROADSIDE DINER
cheeseburger...
HOT DOG....
SODA...
COFFEE...
APPLE PIE ...
POP
TODAY'S SPECIAL
SOUP
EGGS
EGGS
EGGS
©2017 DAN THOMPSON GOCOMICS.COM
ROADSIDE DINER
cheeseburger...
HOT DOG....
SODA..
COFFEE...
APPLE PIE ...
POP
TODAY'S SPECIAL
SOUP
CRASH!
KLANG!
CRACK!
CRACK!
CRACK!
CRACK!
CRACK!
ROADSIDE DINER
cheeseburger...
HOT DOG....
SODA..
COFFEE...
APPLE PIE ...
POP
TODAY'S SPECIAL
EGG DROP
SOUP
D. THOMPSON

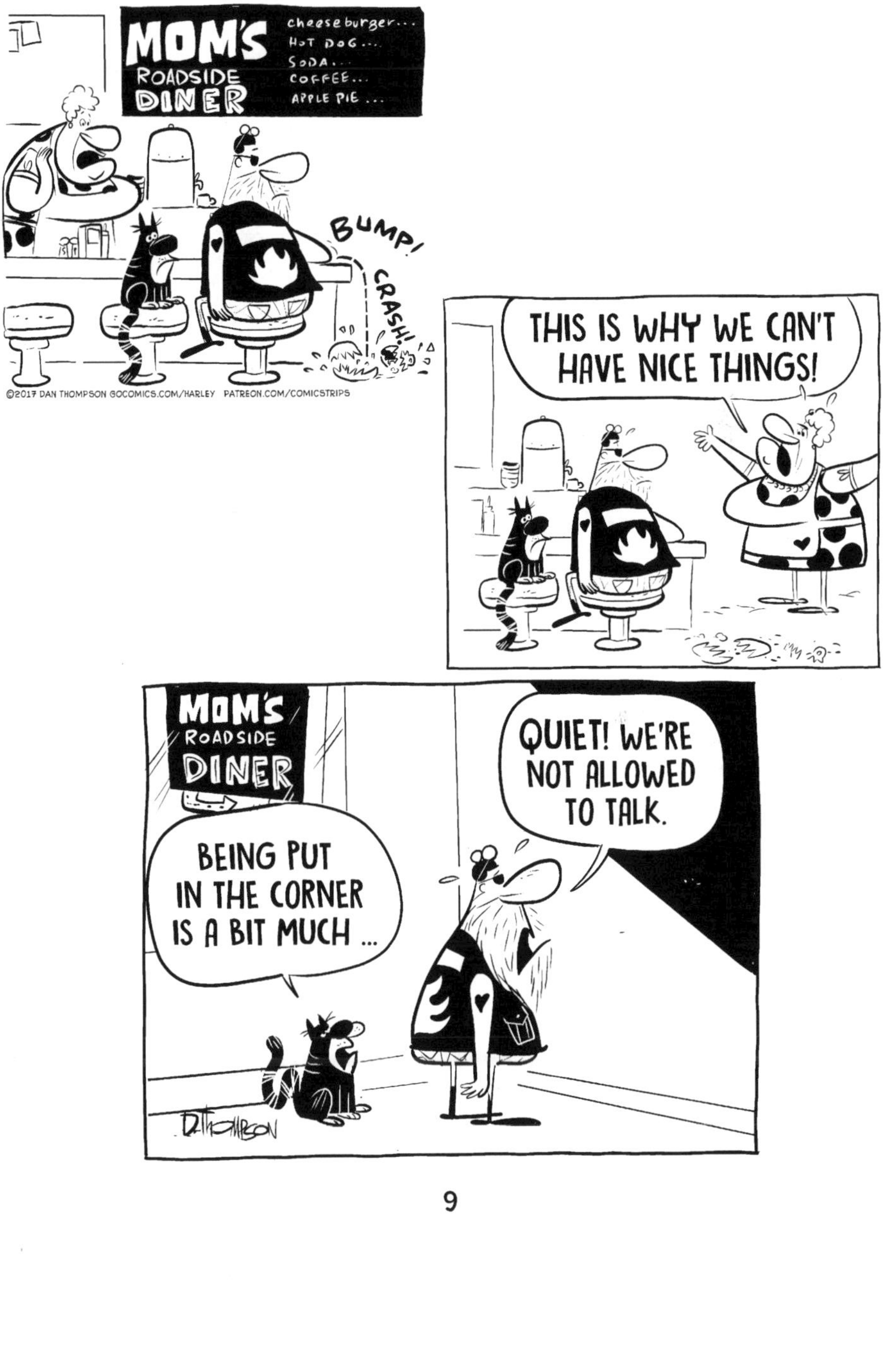
MOM'S ROADSIDE DINER
cheeseburger...
HOT DOG...
SODA...
COFFEE...
APPLE PIE ...
BUMP!
CRASH!
©2017 DAN THOMPSON GOCOMICS.COM/HARLEY PATREON.COM/COMICSTRIPS
THIS IS WHY WE CAN'T HAVE NICE THINGS!
MOM'S ROADSIDE DINER
QUIET! WE'RE NOT ALLOWED TO TALK.
BEING PUT IN THE CORNER IS A BIT MUCH ...
D. THOMPSON

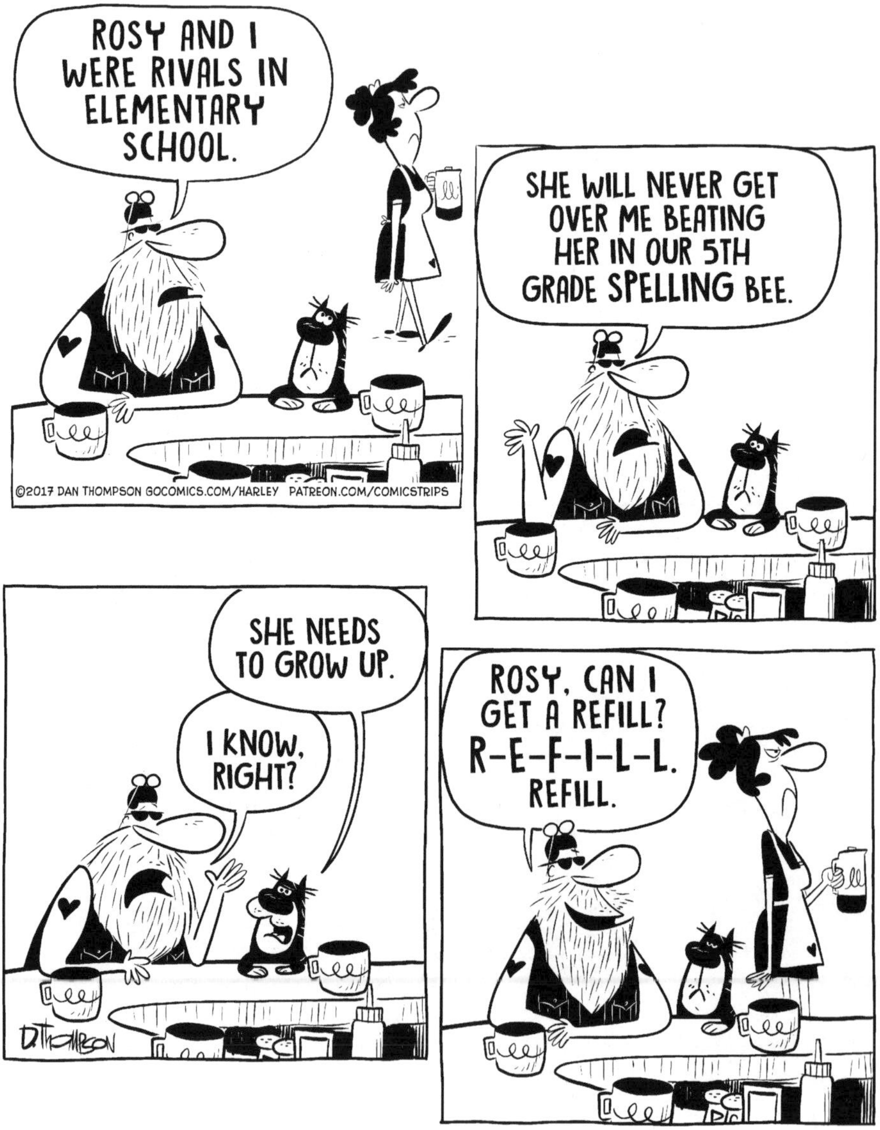
ROSY AND I WERE RIVALS IN ELEMENTARY SCHOOL.
©2017 DAN THOMPSON GOCOMICS.COM/HARLEY PATREON.COM/COMICSTRIPS
SHE WILL NEVER GET OVER ME BEATING HER IN OUR 5TH GRADE SPELLING BEE.
SHE NEEDS TO GROW UP.
I KNOW, RIGHT?
D.THOMPSON
ROSY, CAN I GET A REFILL? R-E-F-I-L-L. REFILL.

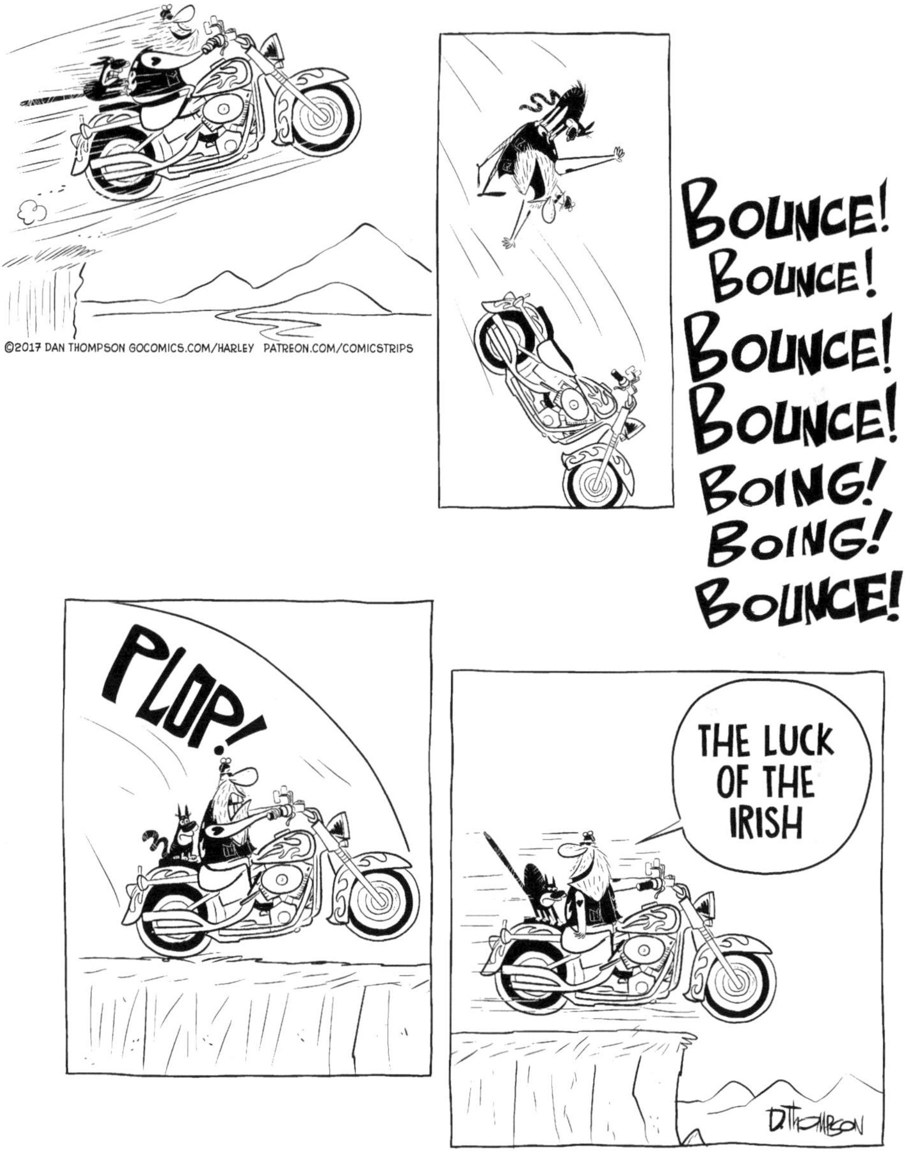
©2017 DAN THOMPSON GOCOMICS.COM/HARLEY PATREON.COM/COMICSTRIPS
BOUNCE!
BOUNCE!
BOUNCE!
BOUNCE!
BOING!
BOING!
BOUNCE!
PLOP!
THE LUCK OF THE IRISH
D. THOMPSON

THE SLINGSHOT WILL LAUNCH US FORCE-FULLY OVER POINTY ROCK CANYON!
©2017 DAN THOMPSON GOCOMICS.COM/HARLEY PATREON.COM/COMICSTRIPS
WE'RE GOING TO FLY SMACK INTO DESTINY!
SLING!

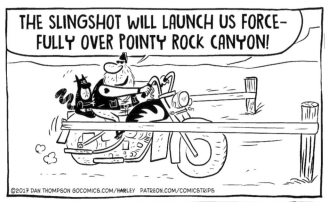

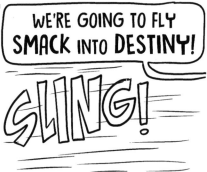

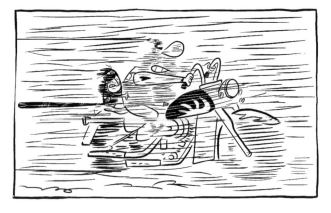

SMACK!

WELCOME to DESTINY RIDGE

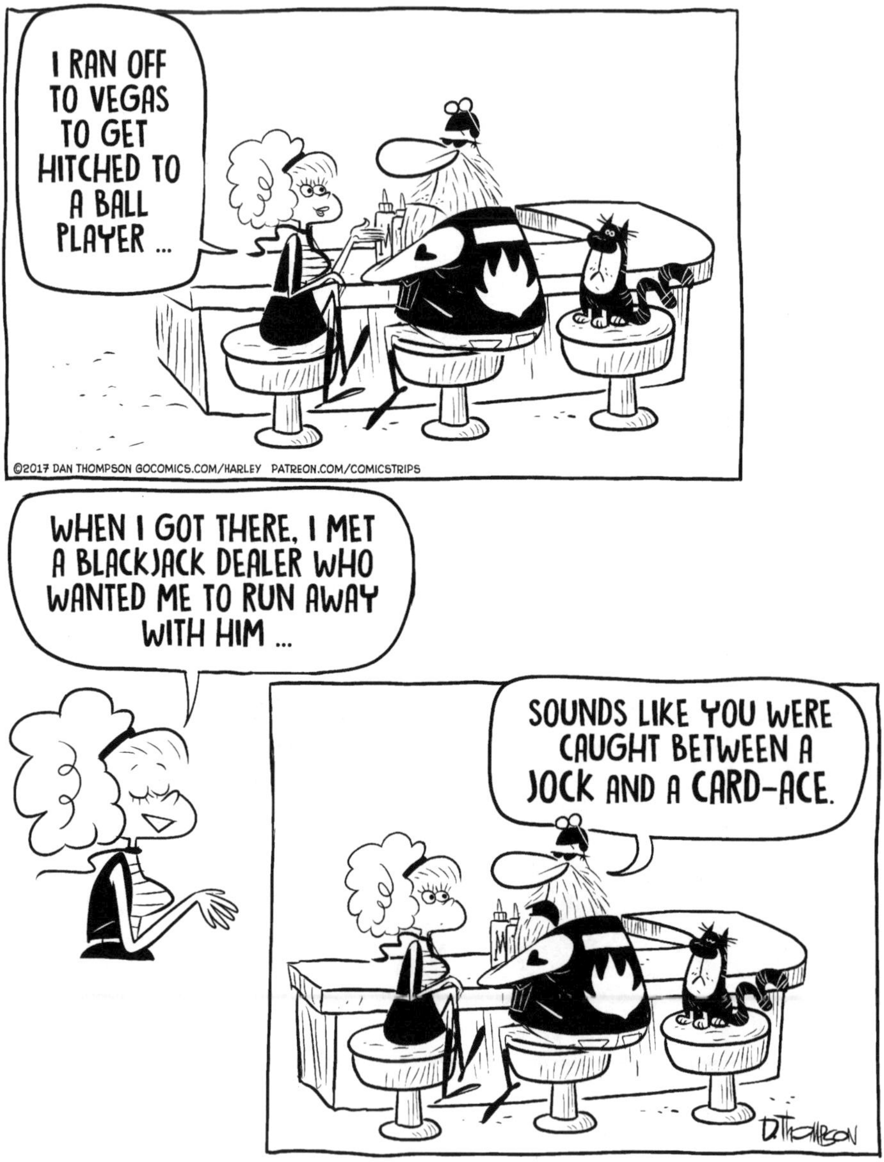
I RAN OFF TO VEGAS TO GET HITCHED TO A BALL PLAYER ...
©2017 DAN THOMPSON GOCOMICS.COM/HARLEY PATREON.COM/COMICSTRIPS
WHEN I GOT THERE, I MET A BLACKJACK DEALER WHO WANTED ME TO RUN AWAY WITH HIM ...
SOUNDS LIKE YOU WERE CAUGHT BETWEEN A JOCK AND A CARD-ACE.
D. THOMPSON

OOOOH, SUGAR. YOUR SHERIFF DADDY IS ASLEEP!
HOWZABOUT YOU AND ME GO ON A DATE?
©2017 DAN THOMPSON GOCOMICS.COM/HARLEY PATREON.COM/COMICSTRIPS
NOT TONIGHT, HARLEY, I'VE GOT A DATE WITH SOMEONE ELSE.
HIS LADDER IS PICKING ME UP AROUND MIDNIGHT.
D.THOMPSON

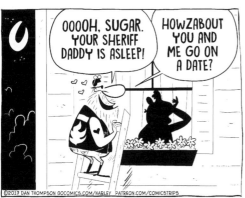

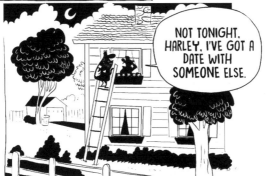

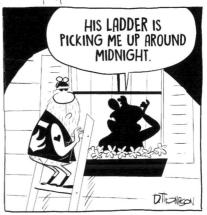

16

SCREEEEEECCH!
SCREECH!
SCRAPE!
CLANK!
CLUNK
CRASH!
JONES
GAS
REPAIR
SCREEEEEEEEECC
JONES
GAS
REPAIR
CcHHHH!
MOTORCYCLE TROUBLE?
D. THOMPSON

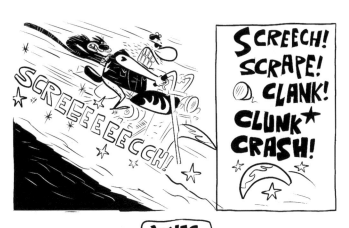

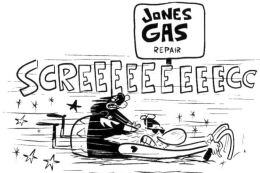

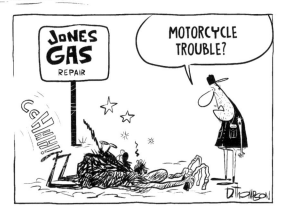

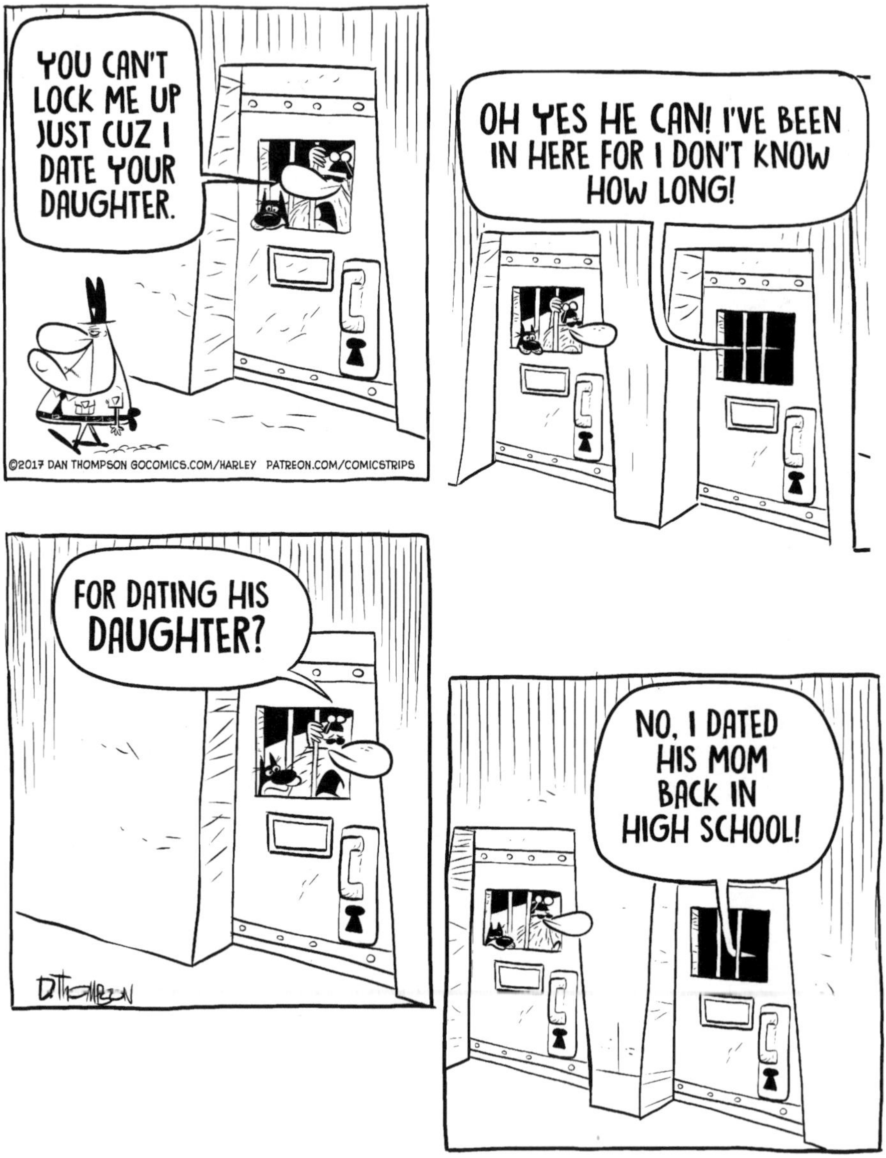
YOU CAN'T LOCK ME UP JUST CUZ I DATE YOUR DAUGHTER.
©2017 DAN THOMPSON GOCOMICS.COM/HARLEY PATREON.COM/COMICSTRIPS
OH YES HE CAN! I'VE BEEN IN HERE FOR I DON'T KNOW HOW LONG!
FOR DATING HIS DAUGHTER?
NO, I DATED HIS MOM BACK IN HIGH SCHOOL!

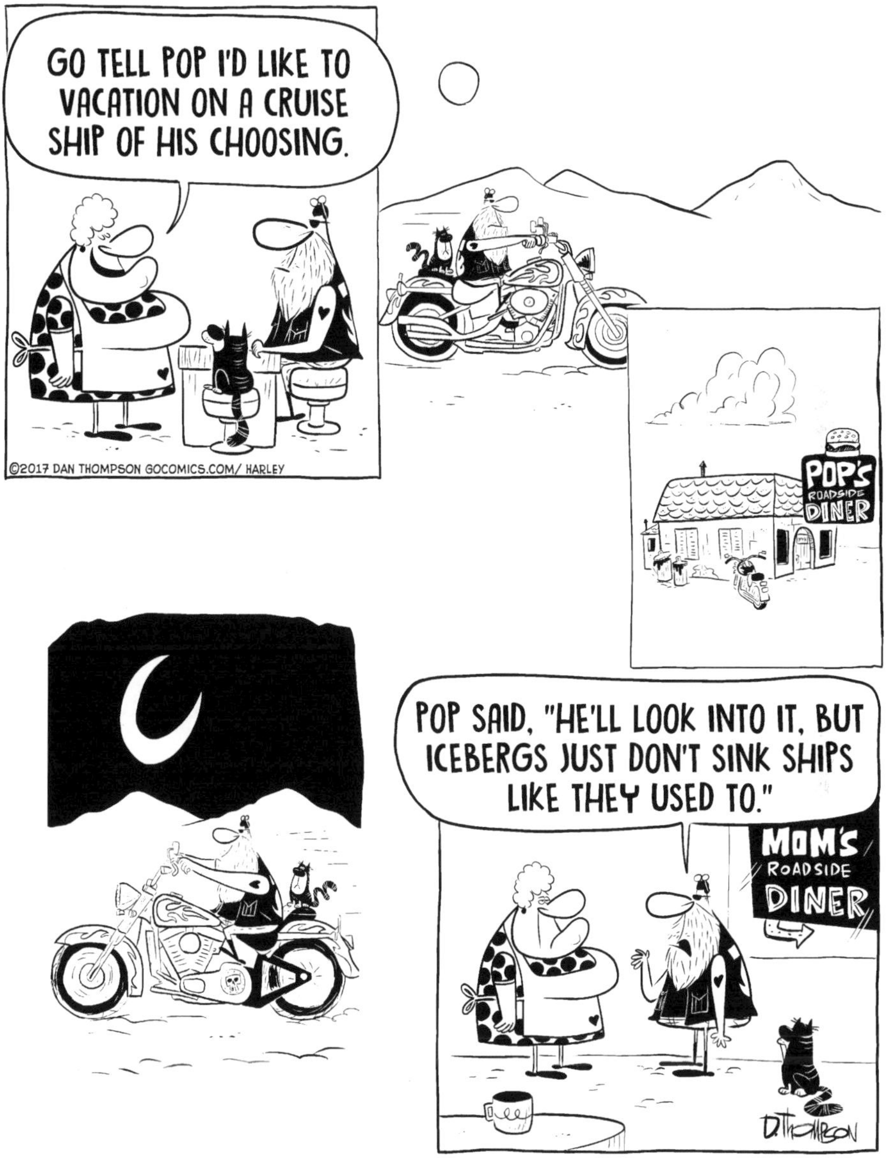
GO TELL POP I'D LIKE TO VACATION ON A CRUISE SHIP OF HIS CHOOSING.
©2017 DAN THOMPSON GOCOMICS.COM/ HARLEY
POP'S ROADSIDE DINER
POP SAID, "HE'LL LOOK INTO IT, BUT ICEBERGS JUST DON'T SINK SHIPS LIKE THEY USED TO."
MOM'S ROADSIDE DINER
D. THOMPSON

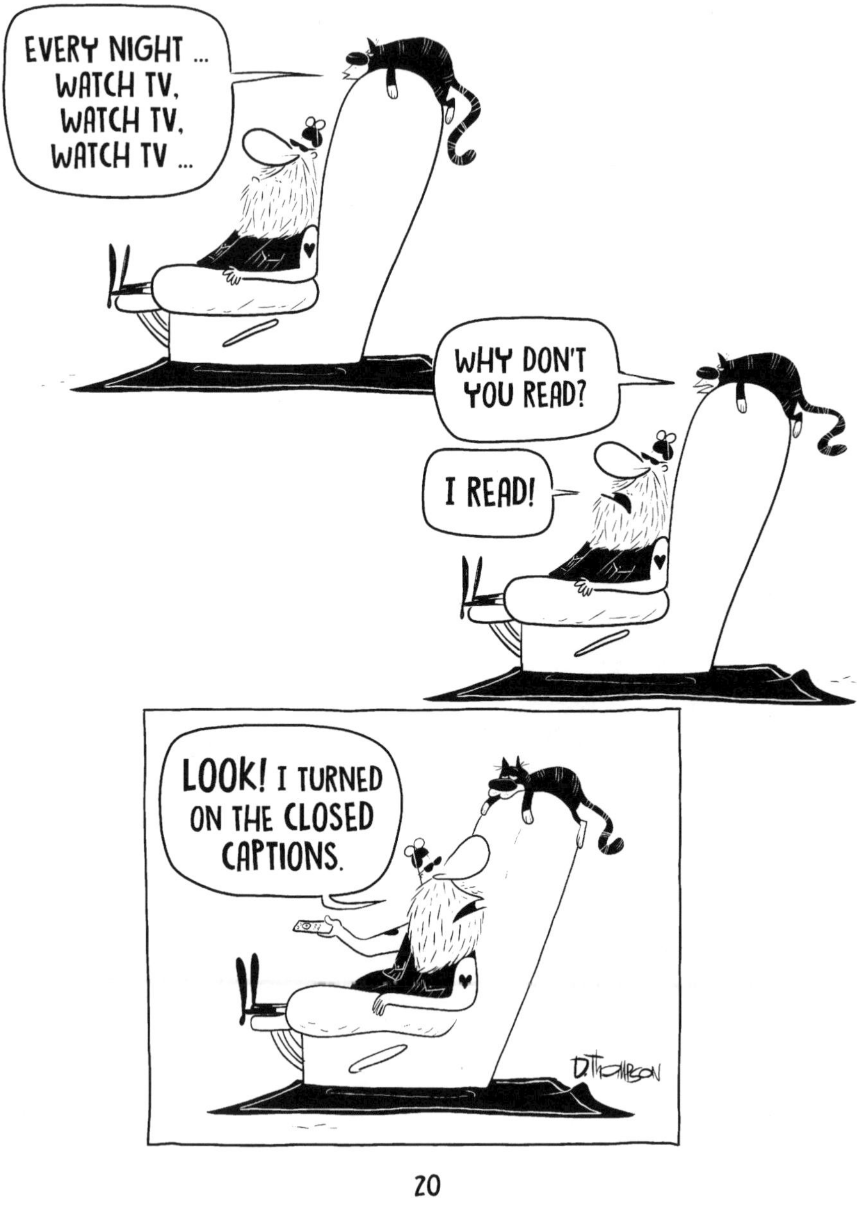
EVERY NIGHT ... WATCH TV, WATCH TV, WATCH TV ...
WHY DON'T YOU READ?
I READ!
LOOK! I TURNED ON THE CLOSED CAPTIONS.
D.THOMPSON

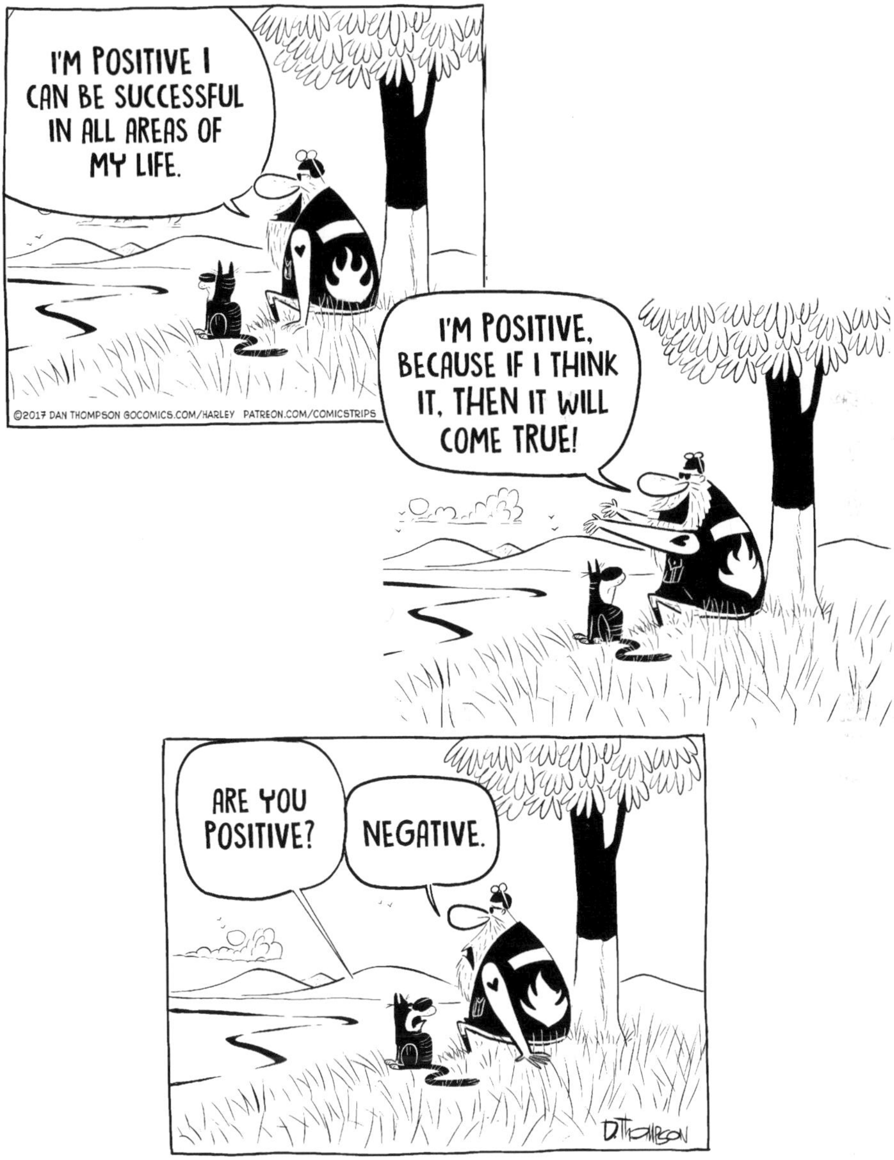
I'M POSITIVE I CAN BE SUCCESSFUL IN ALL AREAS OF MY LIFE.
©2017 DAN THOMPSON GOCOMICS.COM/HARLEY PATREON.COM/COMICSTRIPS
I'M POSITIVE, BECAUSE IF I THINK IT, THEN IT WILL COME TRUE!
ARE YOU POSITIVE?
NEGATIVE.
D. THOMPSON

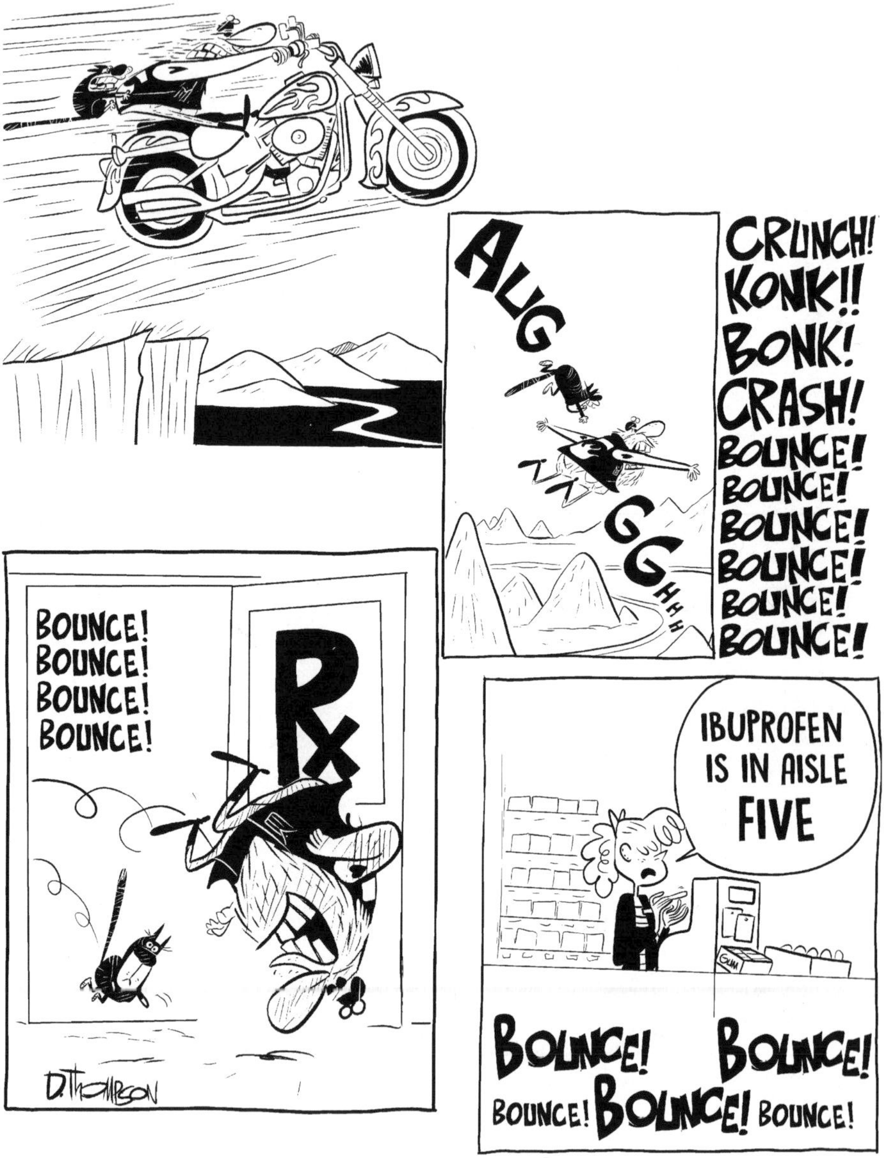
AUGGGhhh
CRUNCH!
KONK!!
BONK!
CRASH!
BOUNCE!
BOUNCE!
BOUNCE!
BOUNCE!
BOUNCE!
BOUNCE!
BOUNCE!
BOUNCE!
BOUNCE!
BOUNCE!
Rx
D. THOMPSON
IBUPROFEN IS IN AISLE FIVE
GUM
BOUNCE! BOUNCE!
BOUNCE! BOUNCE! BOUNCE!

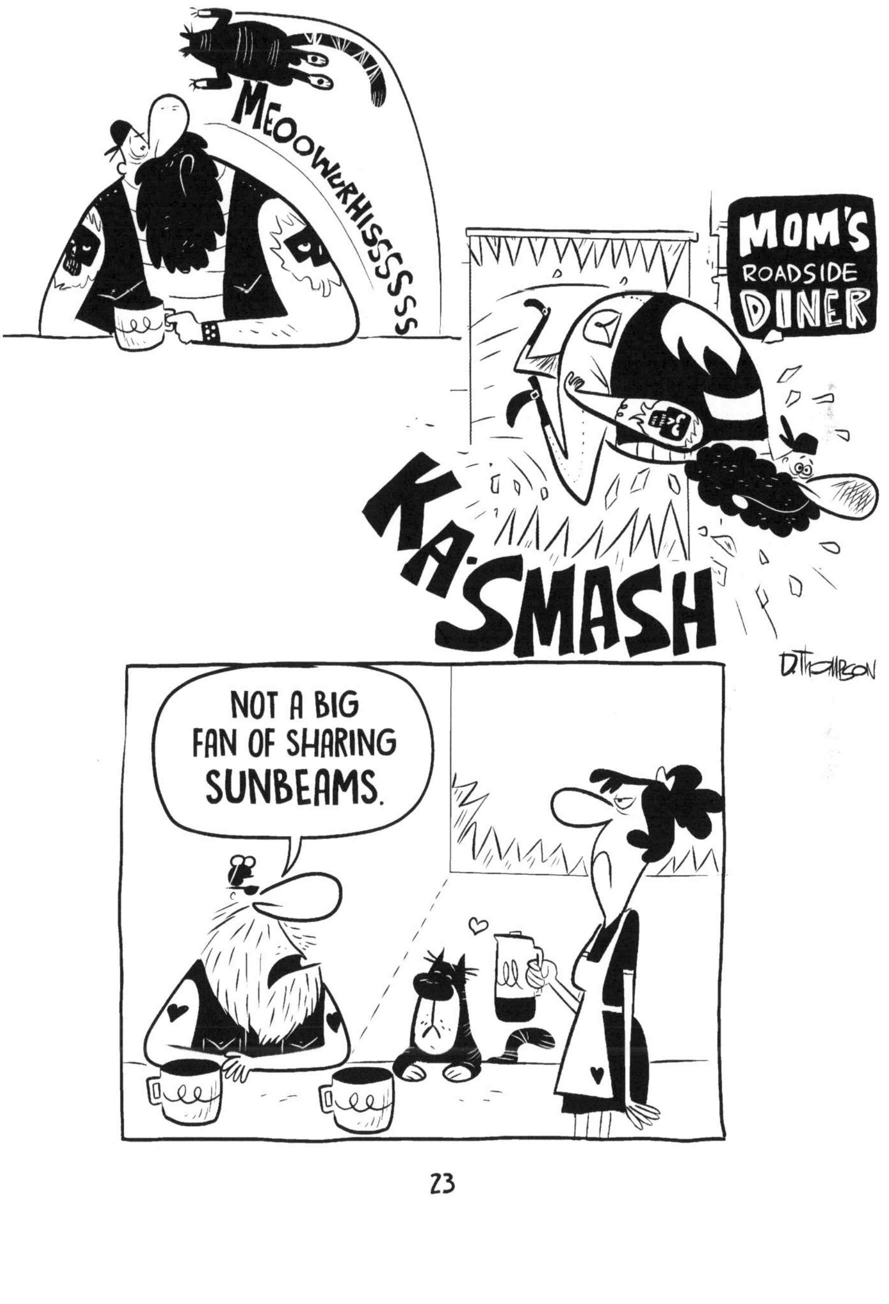
MEOOWURHISSSSSS
MOM'S ROADSIDE DINER
KA-SMASH
D.THOMPSON
NOT A BIG FAN OF SHARING SUNBEAMS.

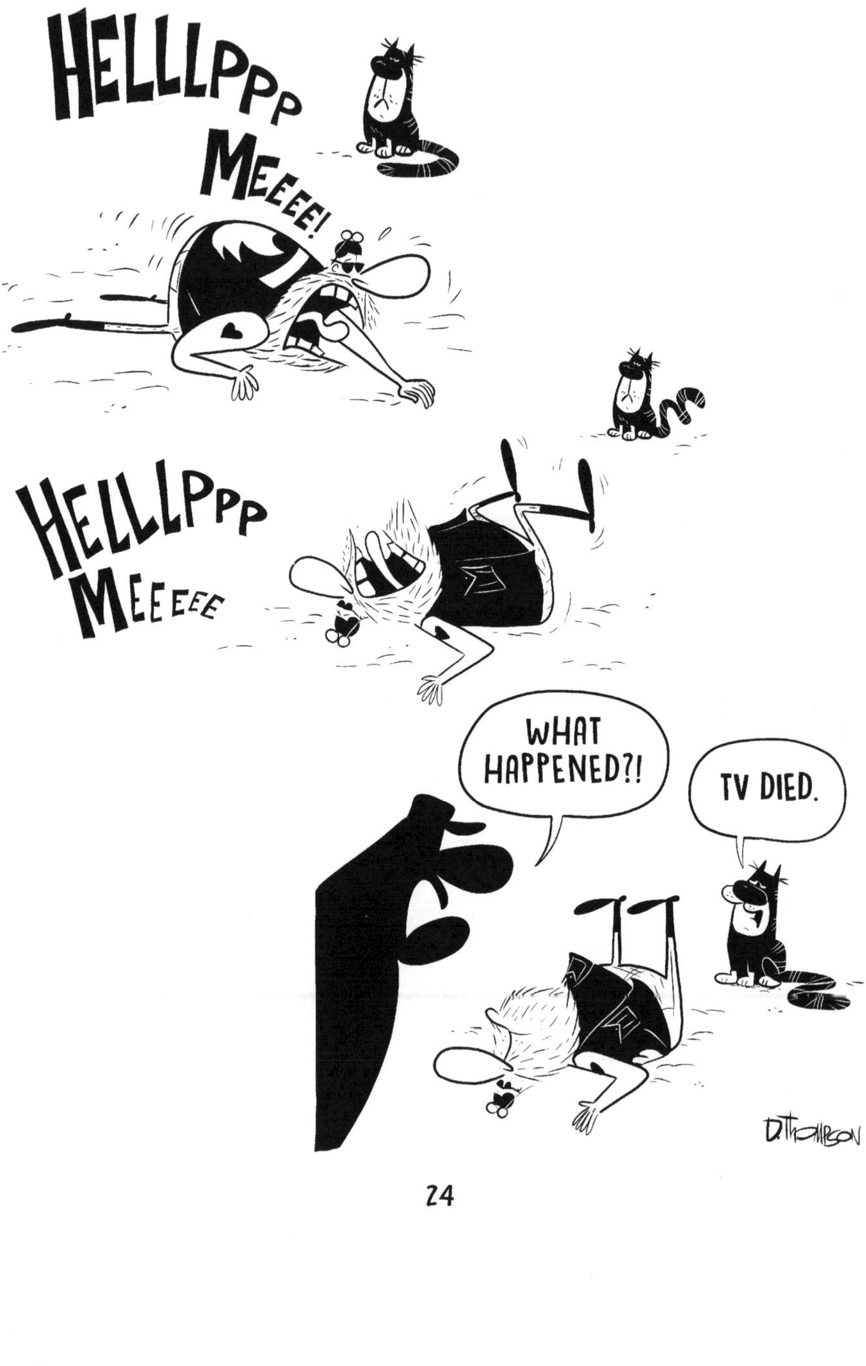
HELLLPPP MEEEE!
HELLLPPP MEEEEE
WHAT HAPPENED?!
TV DIED.
D.THOMPSON

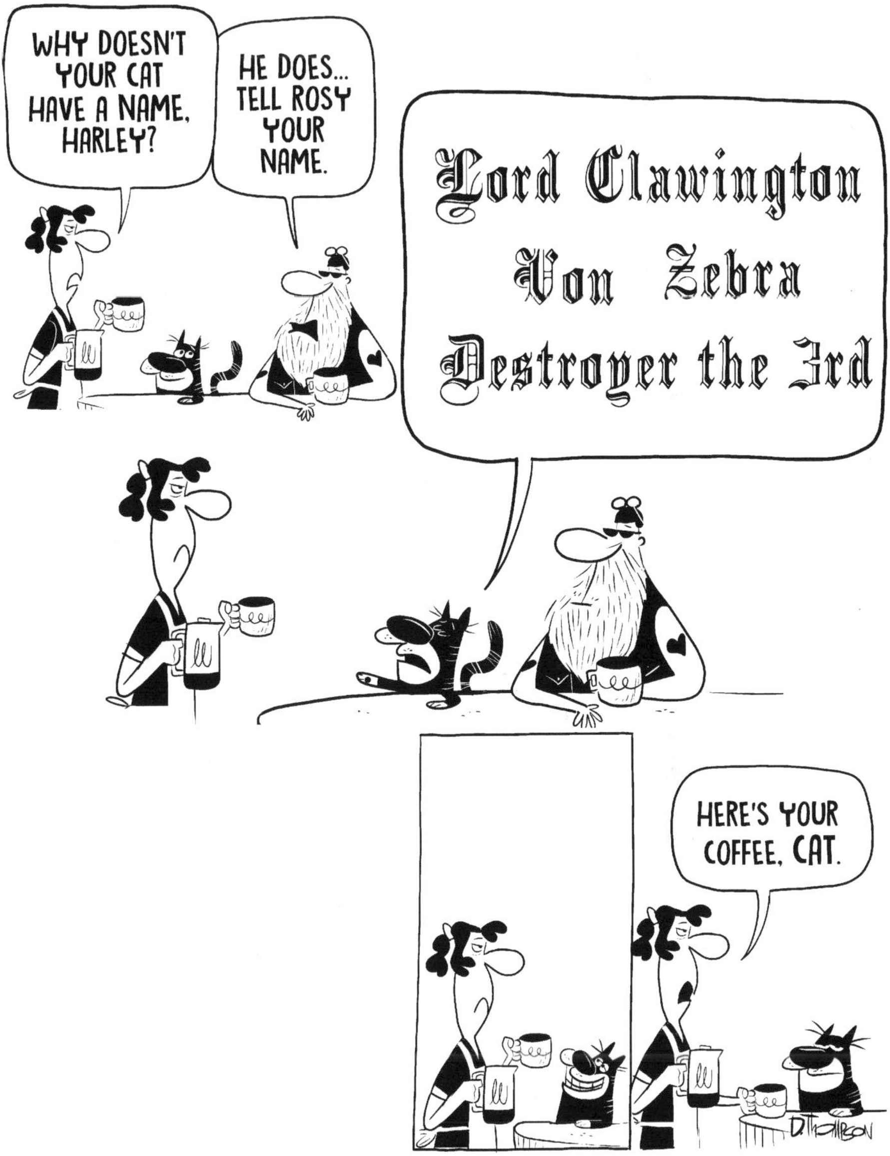
WHY DOESN'T YOUR CAT HAVE A NAME, HARLEY?
HE DOES... TELL ROSY YOUR NAME.
Lord Clawington Von Zebra Destroyer the 3rd
HERE'S YOUR COFFEE, CAT.
D. THOMPSON

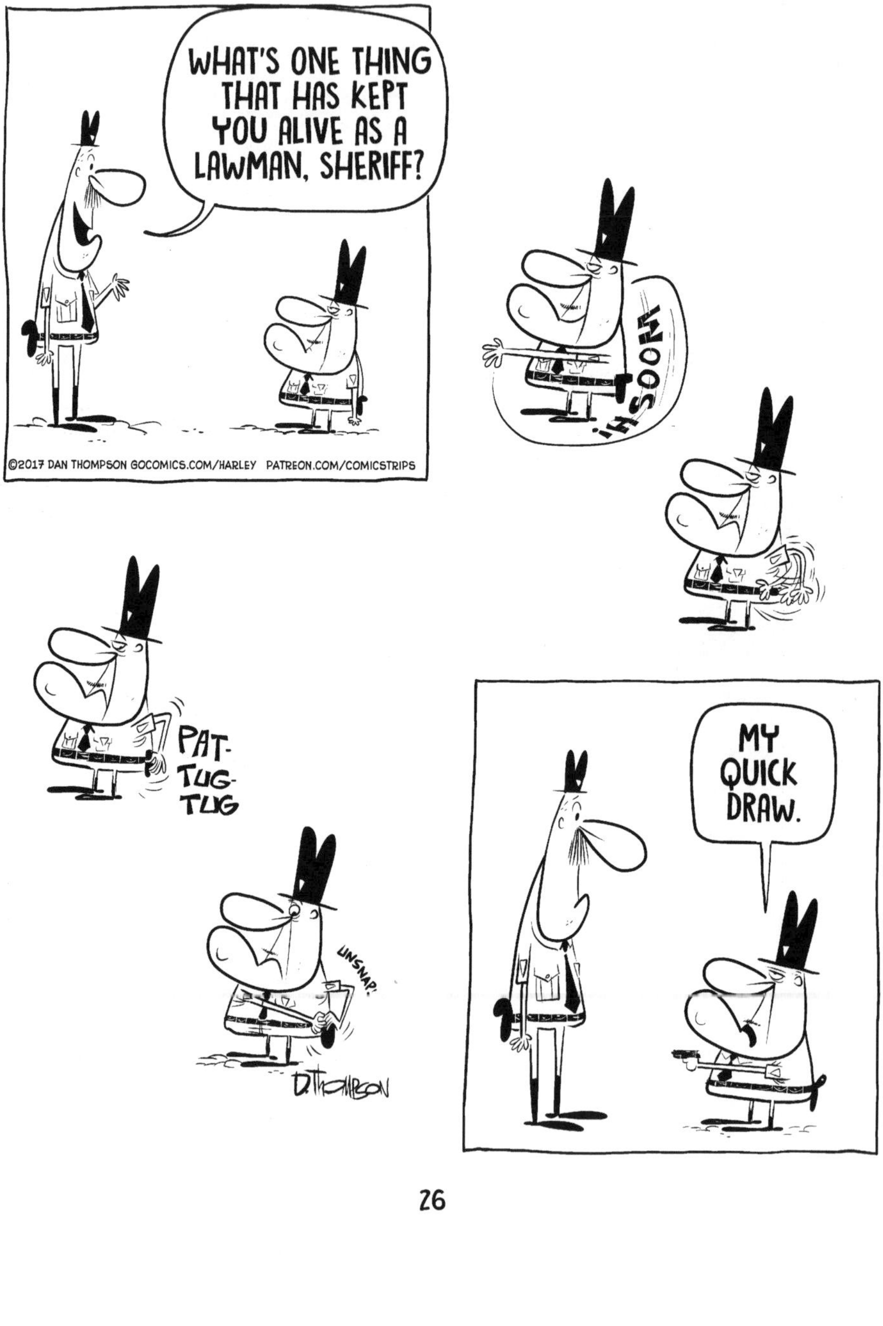
WHAT'S ONE THING THAT HAS KEPT YOU ALIVE AS A LAWMAN, SHERIFF?
©2017 DAN THOMPSON GOCOMICS.COM/HARLEY PATREON.COM/COMICSTRIPS
WHOOSH!
PAT-TUG-TUG
UNSNAP!
D. THOMPSON
MY QUICK DRAW.

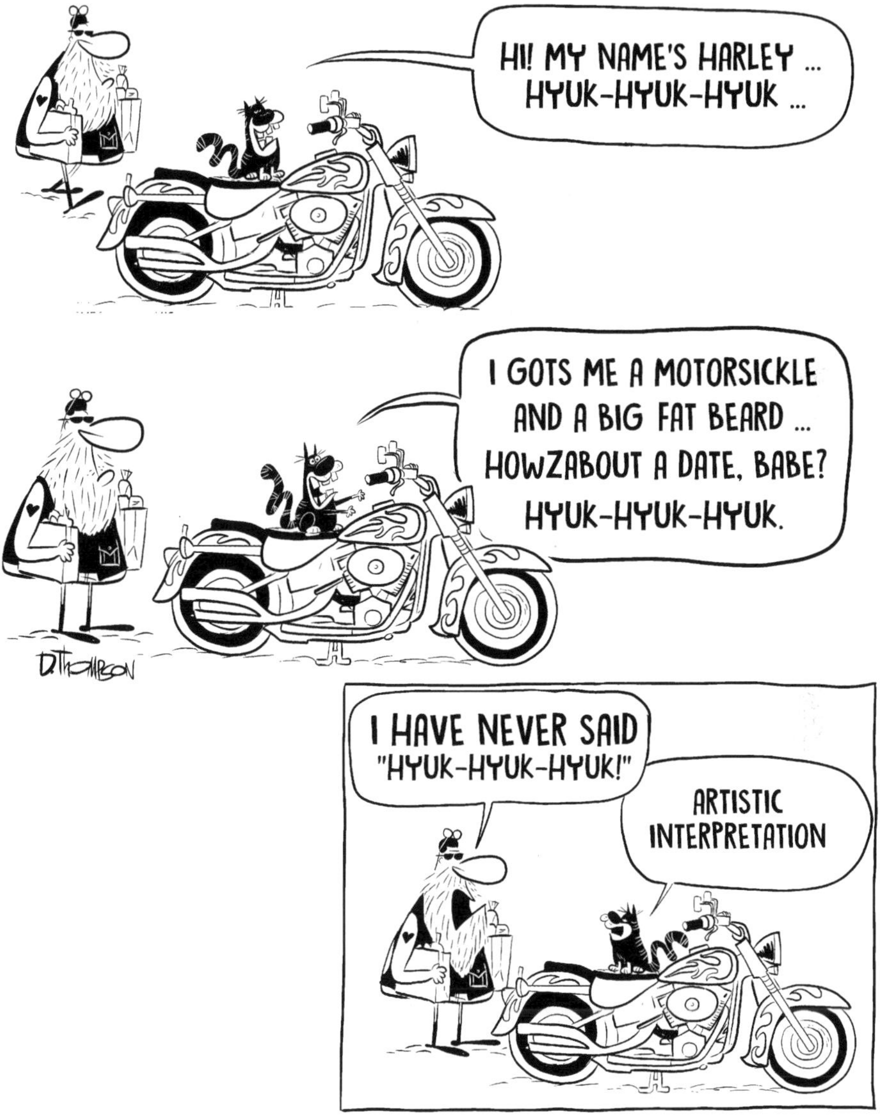
HI! MY NAME'S HARLEY ... HYUK-HYUK-HYUK ...
I GOTS ME A MOTORSICKLE AND A BIG FAT BEARD ... HOWZABOUT A DATE, BABE? HYUK-HYUK-HYUK.
D. THOMPSON
I HAVE NEVER SAID "HYUK-HYUK-HYUK!"
ARTISTIC INTERPRETATION

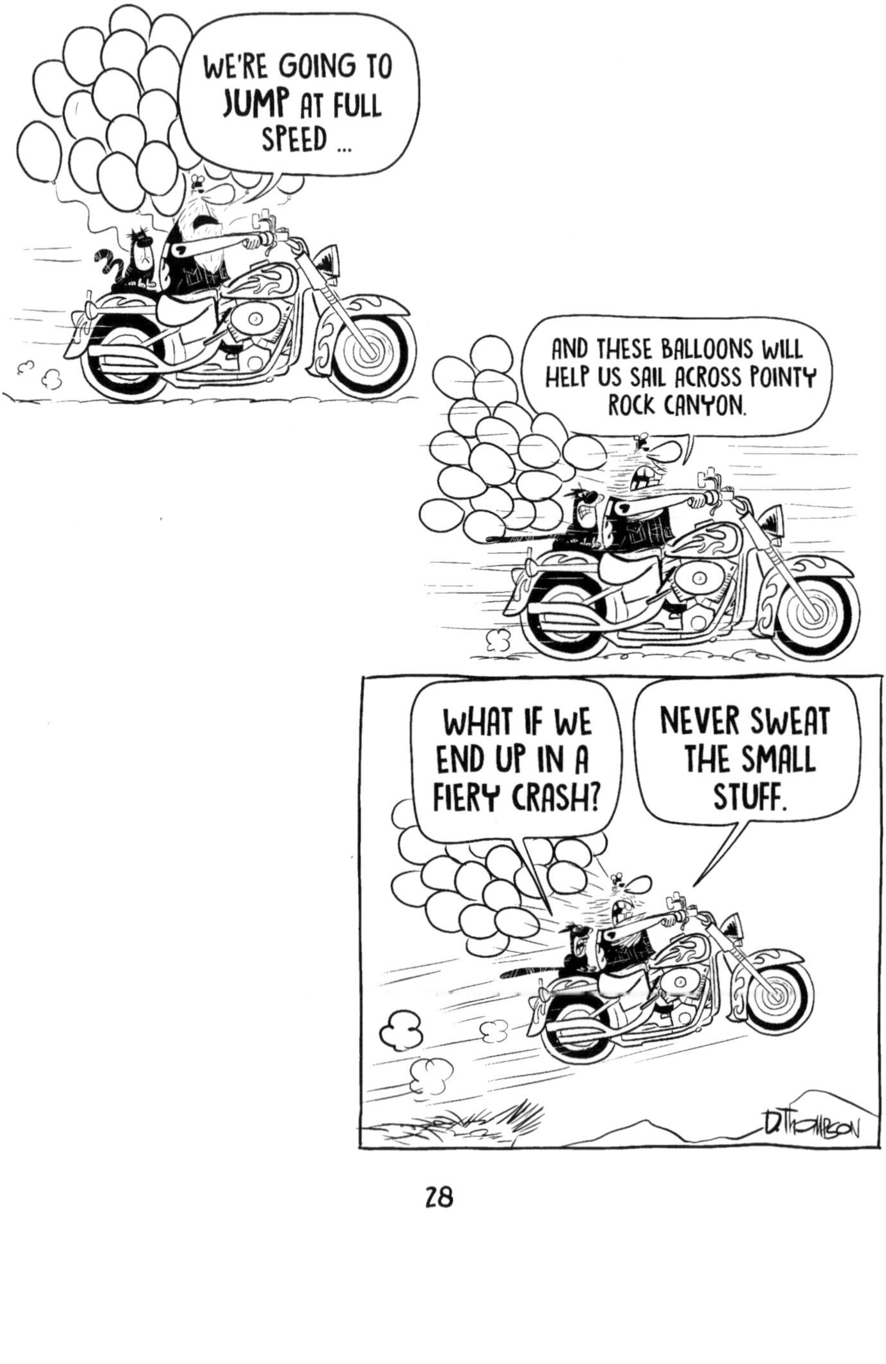
WE'RE GOING TO JUMP AT FULL SPEED ...
AND THESE BALLOONS WILL HELP US SAIL ACROSS POINTY ROCK CANYON.
WHAT IF WE END UP IN A FIERY CRASH?
NEVER SWEAT THE SMALL STUFF.
D. THOMPSON

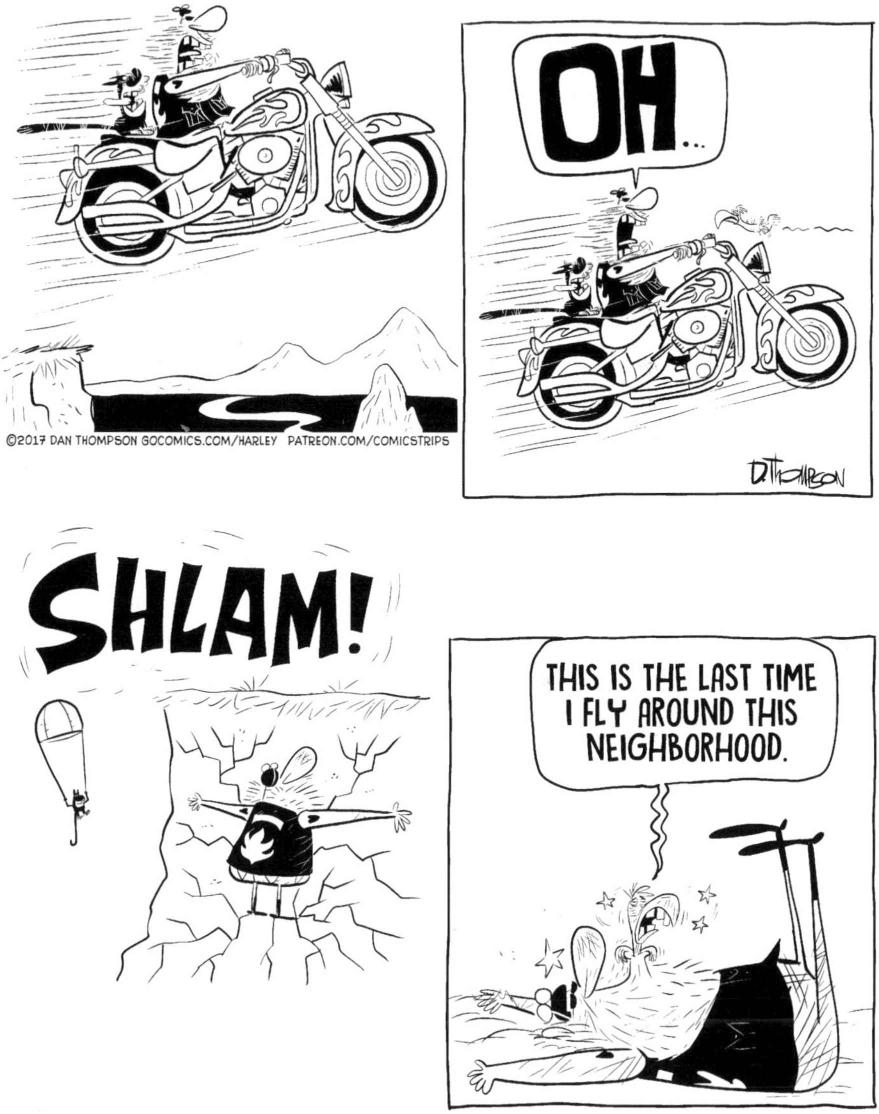
©2017 DAN THOMPSON GOCOMICS.COM/HARLEY PATREON.COM/COMICSTRIPS
OH...
D.THOMPSON
SHLAM!
THIS IS THE LAST TIME I FLY AROUND THIS NEIGHBORHOOD.

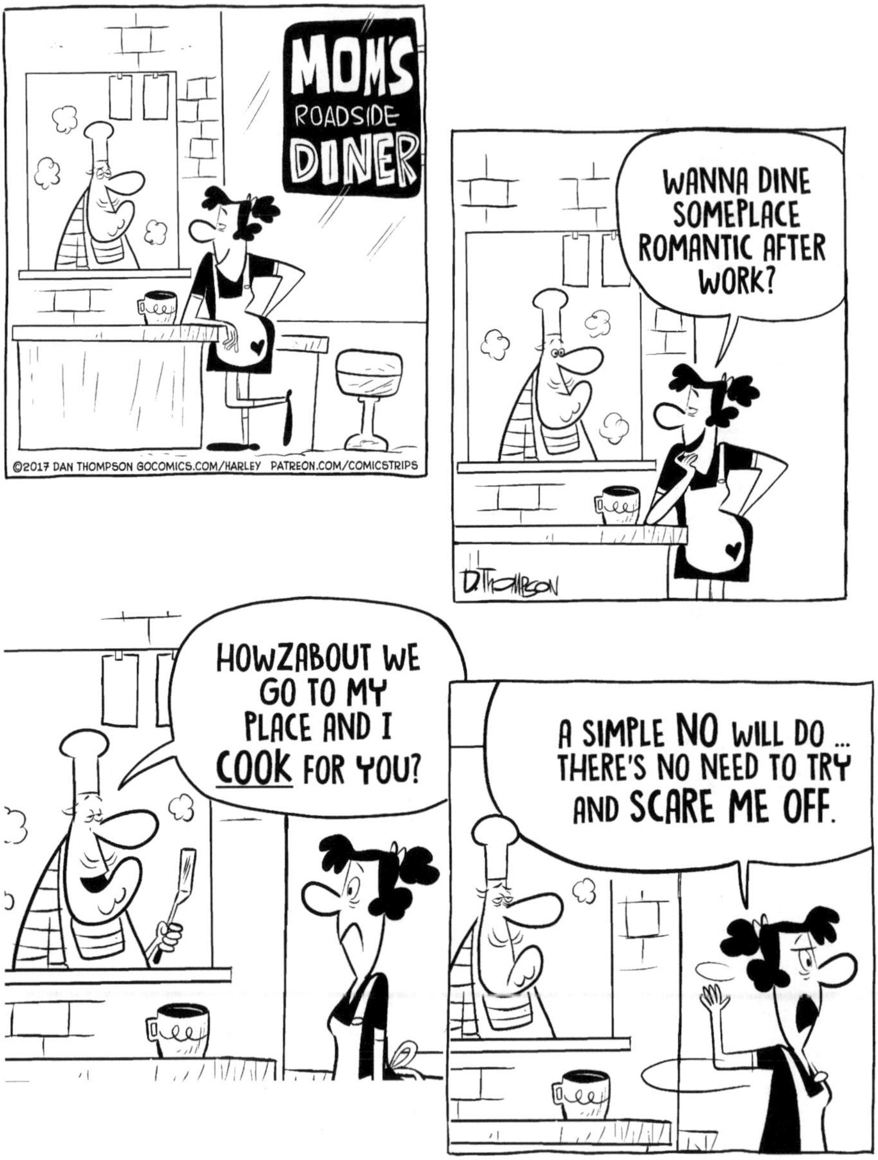
MOM'S
ROADSIDE
DINER
©2017 DAN THOMPSON GOCOMICS.COM/HARLEY PATREON.COM/COMICSTRIPS
WANNA DINE SOMEPLACE ROMANTIC AFTER WORK?
D. THOMPSON
HOWZABOUT WE GO TO MY PLACE AND I COOK FOR YOU?
A SIMPLE NO WILL DO ... THERE'S NO NEED TO TRY AND SCARE ME OFF.

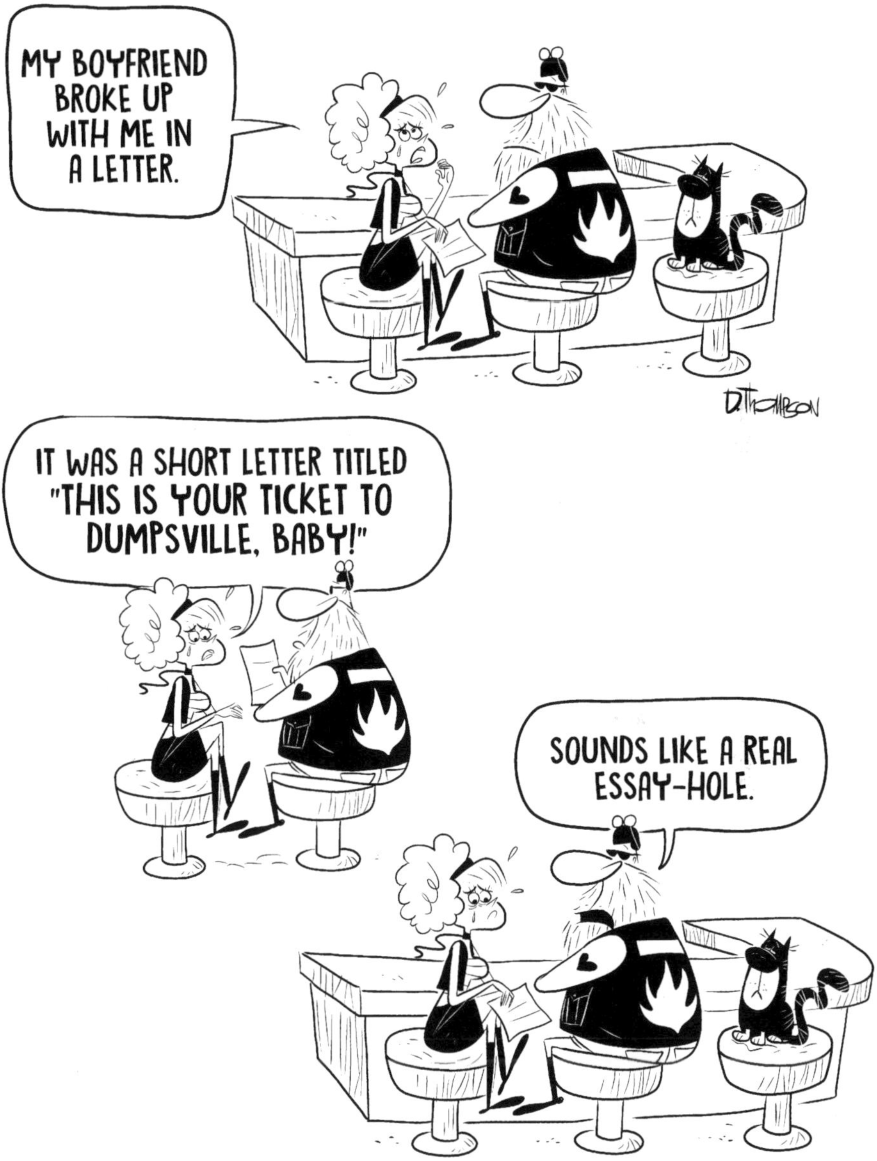
MY BOYFRIEND BROKE UP WITH ME IN A LETTER.
D. THOMPSON
IT WAS A SHORT LETTER TITLED "THIS IS YOUR TICKET TO DUMPSVILLE, BABY!"
SOUNDS LIKE A REAL ESSAY-HOLE.

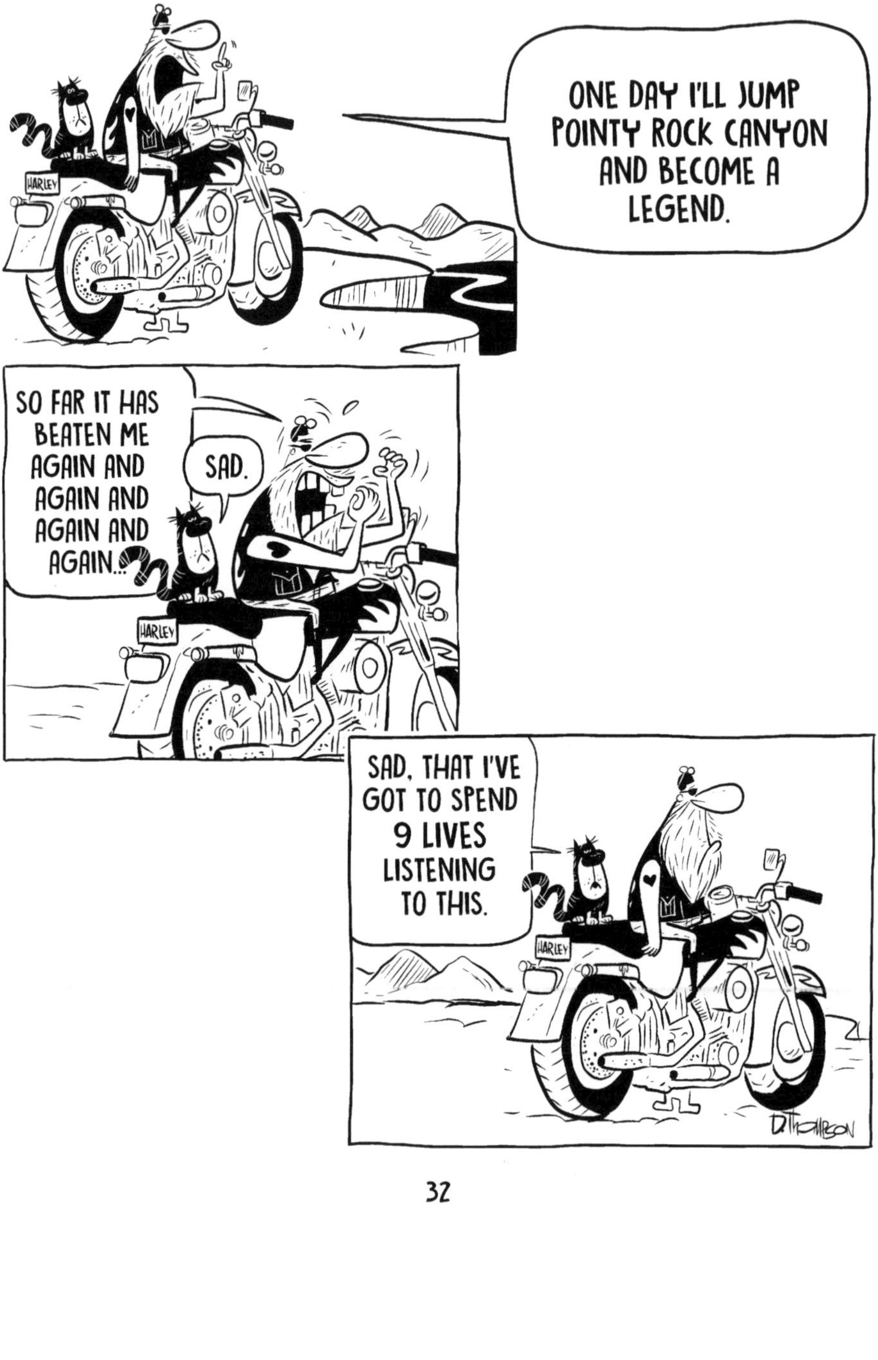
ONE DAY I'LL JUMP POINTY ROCK CANYON AND BECOME A LEGEND.
HARLEY
SO FAR IT HAS BEATEN ME AGAIN AND AGAIN AND AGAIN AND AGAIN...
SAD.
HARLEY
SAD, THAT I'VE GOT TO SPEND 9 LIVES LISTENING TO THIS.
HARLEY
D.THOMPSON

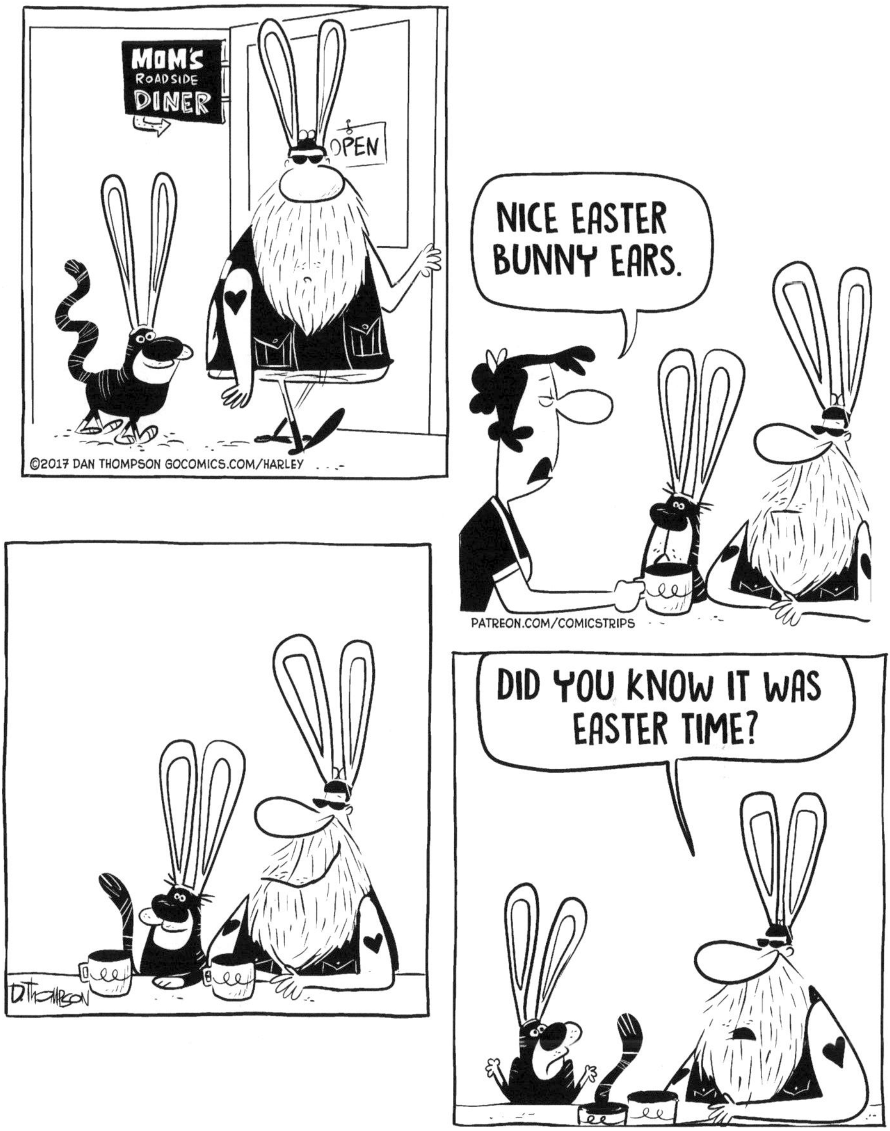
MOM'S
ROADSIDE
DINER
OPEN
©2017 DAN THOMPSON GOCOMICS.COM/HARLEY
NICE EASTER BUNNY EARS.
PATREON.COM/COMICSTRIPS
D THOMPSON
DID YOU KNOW IT WAS EASTER TIME?

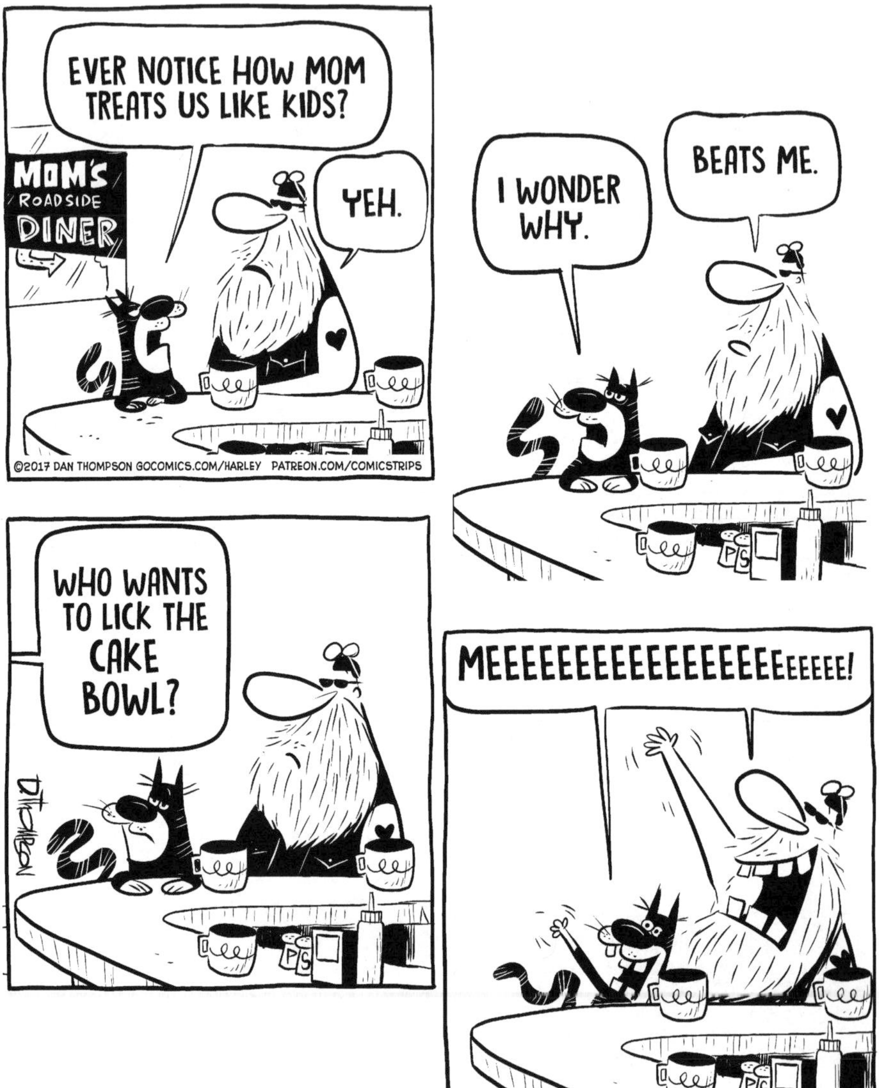
EVER NOTICE HOW MOM TREATS US LIKE KIDS?
MOM'S ROADSIDE DINER
YEH.
©2017 DAN THOMPSON GOCOMICS.COM/HARLEY PATREON.COM/COMICSTRIPS
I WONDER WHY.
BEATS ME.
WHO WANTS TO LICK THE CAKE BOWL?
MEEEEEEEEEEEEEEEEEEEEEE!

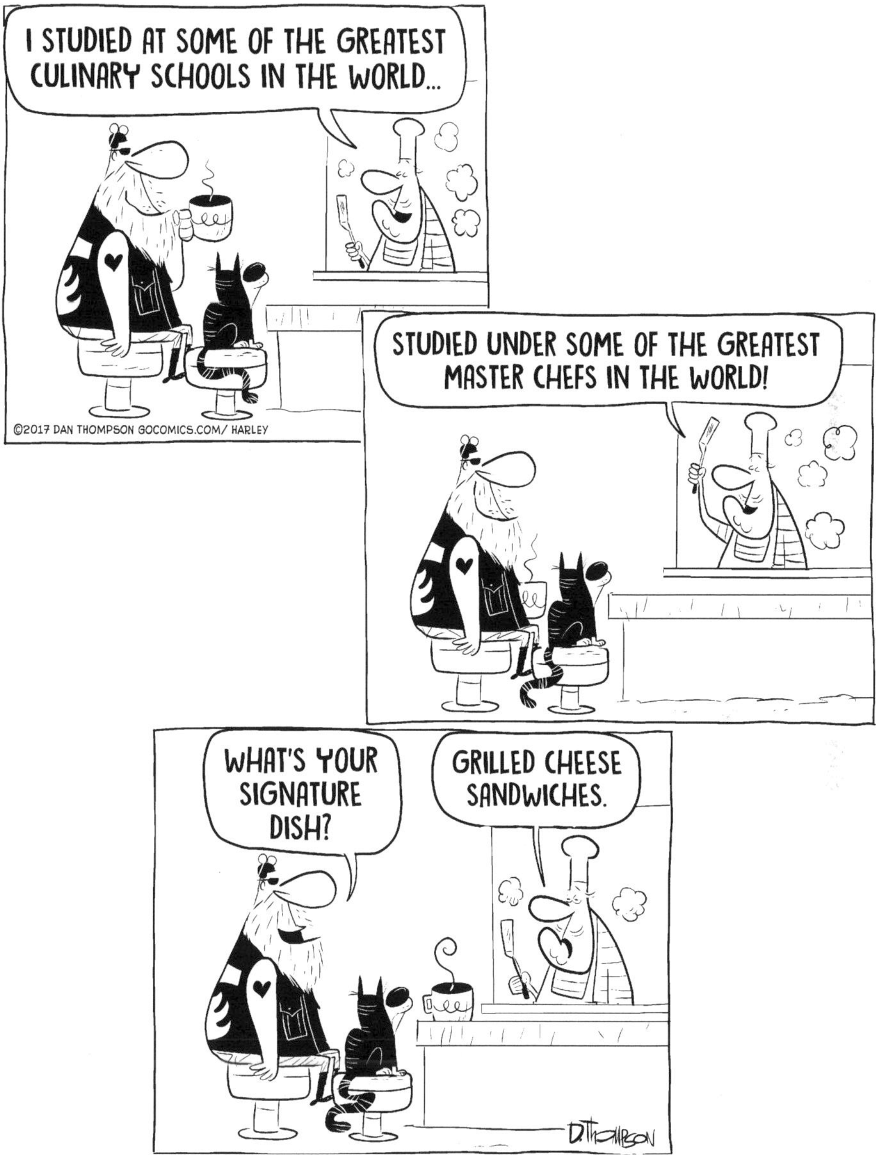
I STUDIED AT SOME OF THE GREATEST CULINARY SCHOOLS IN THE WORLD...
©2017 DAN THOMPSON GOCOMICS.COM/ HARLEY
STUDIED UNDER SOME OF THE GREATEST MASTER CHEFS IN THE WORLD!
WHAT'S YOUR SIGNATURE DISH?
GRILLED CHEESE SANDWICHES.
D. THOMPSON

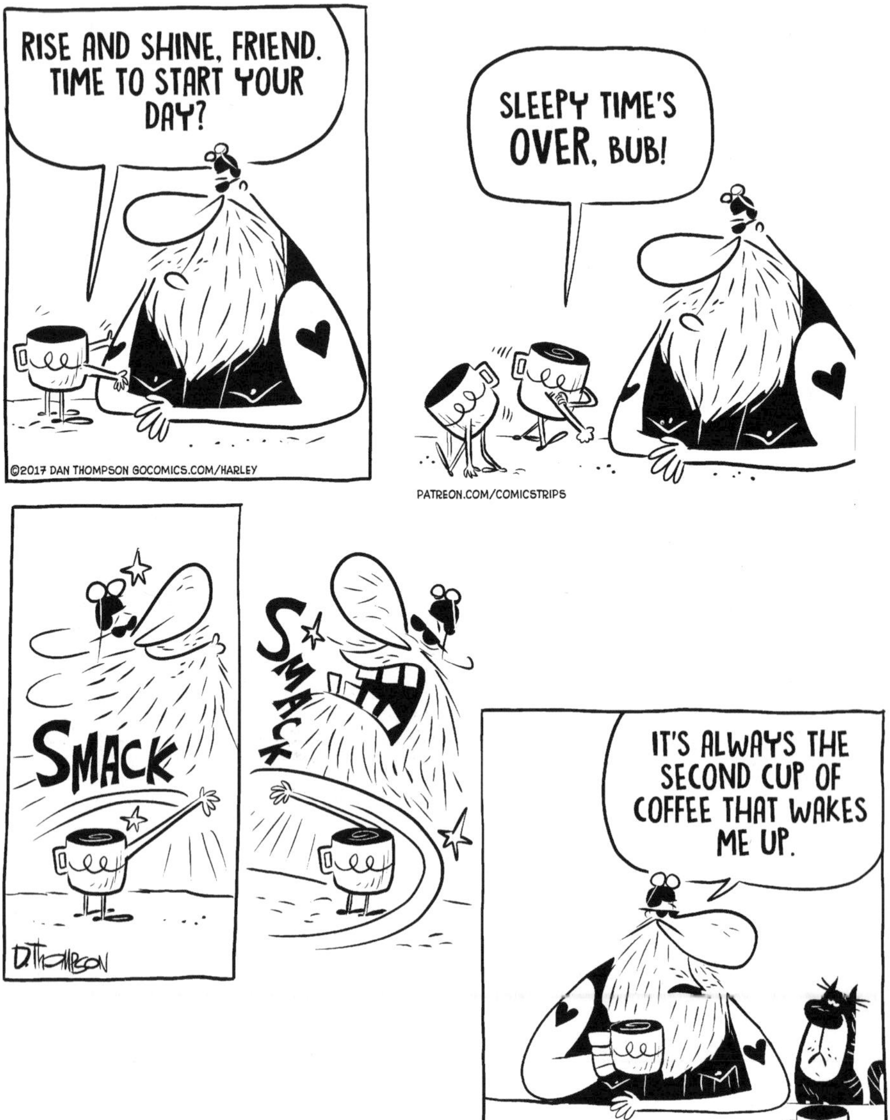

RISE AND SHINE, FRIEND. TIME TO START YOUR DAY?
©2017 DAN THOMPSON GOCOMICS.COM/HARLEY
SLEEPY TIME'S OVER, BUB!
PATREON.COM/COMICSTRIPS
SMACK
SMACK
IT'S ALWAYS THE SECOND CUP OF COFFEE THAT WAKES ME UP.

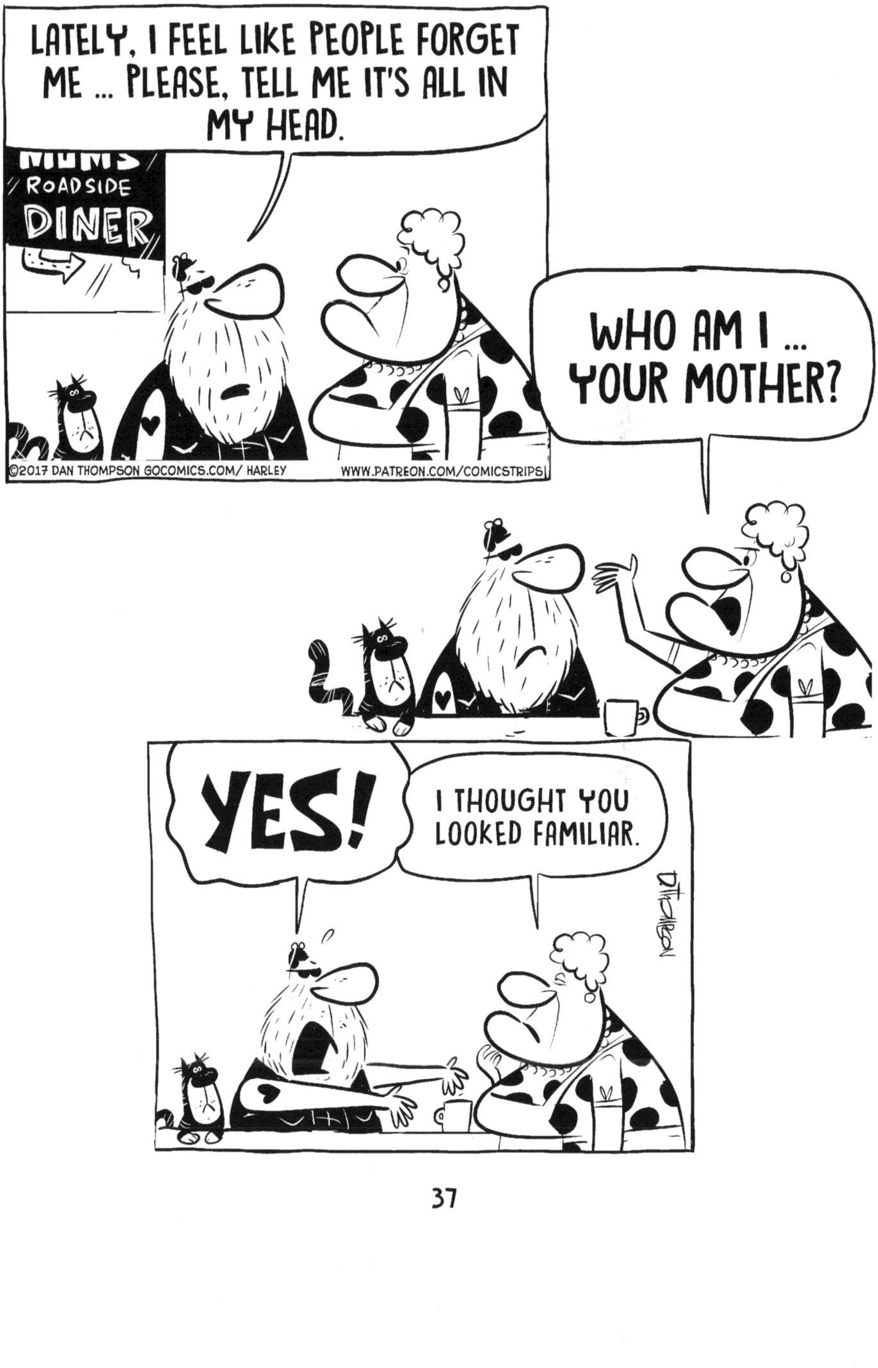
LATELY, I FEEL LIKE PEOPLE FORGET ME ... PLEASE, TELL ME IT'S ALL IN MY HEAD.
ROADSIDE
DINER
©2017 DAN THOMPSON GOCOMICS.COM/ HARLEY
WWW.PATREON.COM/COMICSTRIPS
WHO AM I ... YOUR MOTHER?
YES!
I THOUGHT YOU LOOKED FAMILIAR.

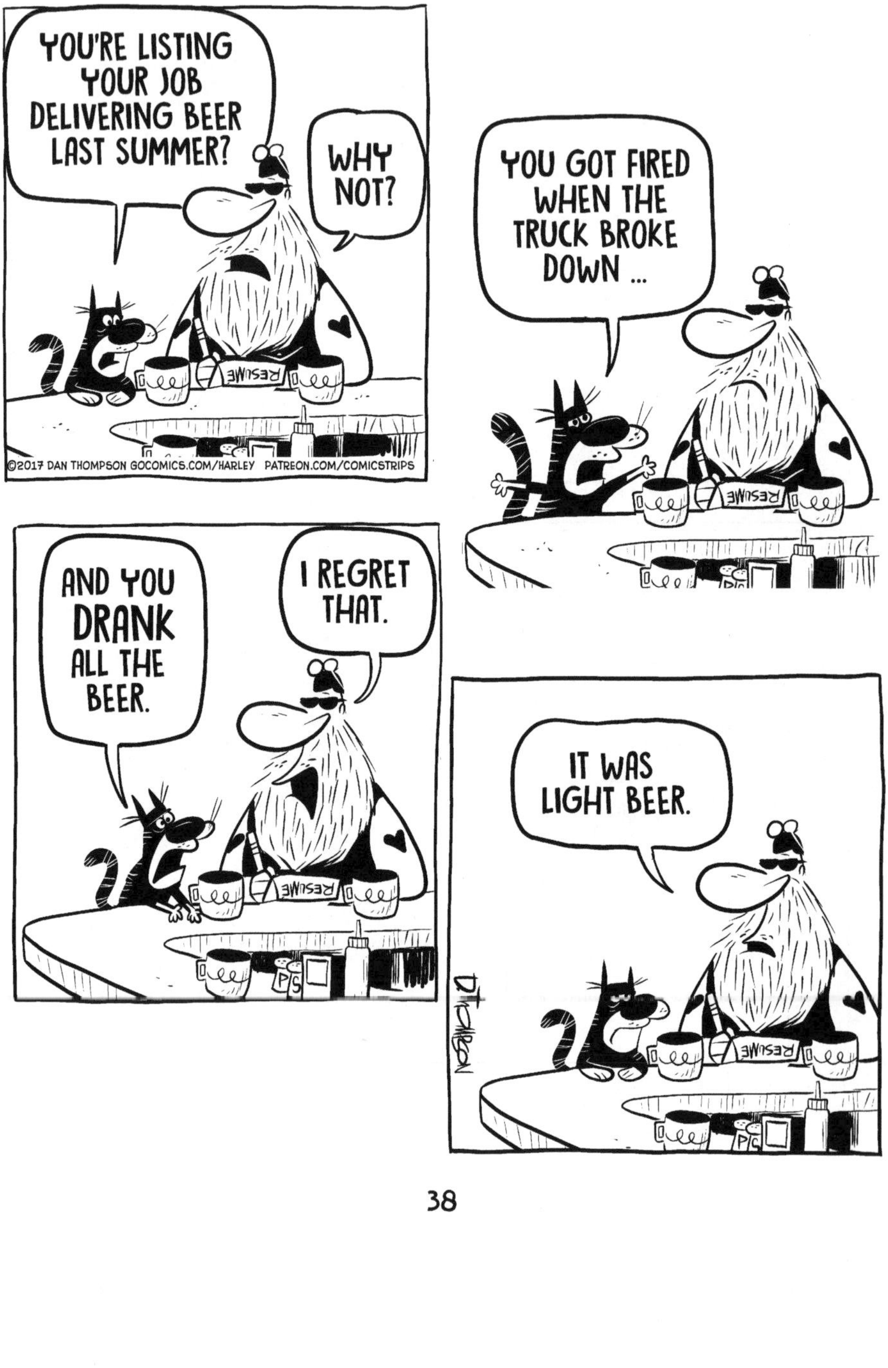
YOU'RE LISTING YOUR JOB DELIVERING BEER LAST SUMMER?
WHY NOT?
©2017 DAN THOMPSON GOCOMICS.COM/HARLEY PATREON.COM/COMICSTRIPS
YOU GOT FIRED WHEN THE TRUCK BROKE DOWN ...
AND YOU DRANK ALL THE BEER.
I REGRET THAT.
IT WAS LIGHT BEER.

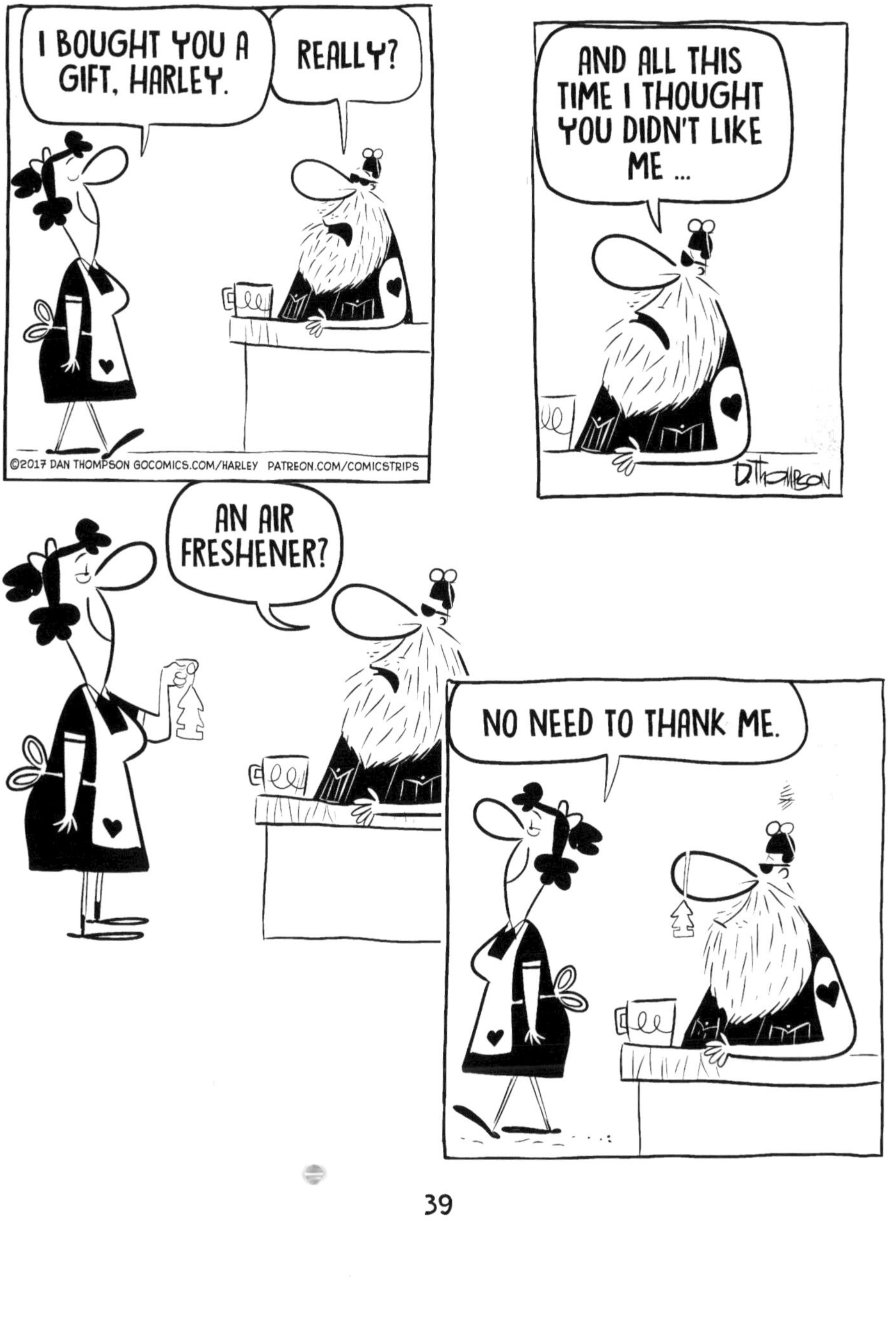
I BOUGHT YOU A GIFT, HARLEY.
REALLY?
©2017 DAN THOMPSON GOCOMICS.COM/HARLEY PATREON.COM/COMICSTRIPS
AND ALL THIS TIME I THOUGHT YOU DIDN'T LIKE ME ...
D.THOMPSON
AN AIR FRESHENER?
NO NEED TO THANK ME.

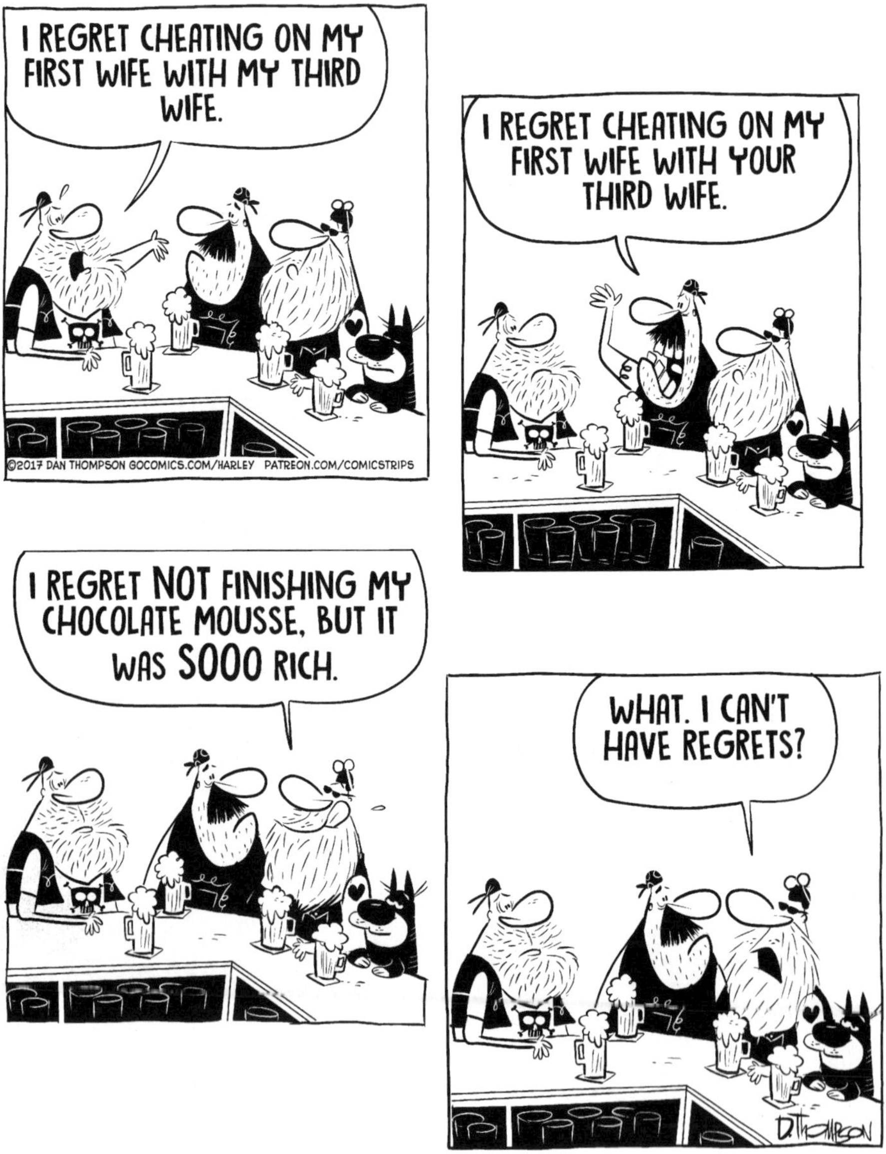
I REGRET CHEATING ON MY FIRST WIFE WITH MY THIRD WIFE.
©2017 DAN THOMPSON GOCOMICS.COM/HARLEY PATREON.COM/COMICSTRIPS
I REGRET CHEATING ON MY FIRST WIFE WITH YOUR THIRD WIFE.
I REGRET NOT FINISHING MY CHOCOLATE MOUSSE, BUT IT WAS SOOO RICH.
WHAT. I CAN'T HAVE REGRETS?
D. THOMPSON

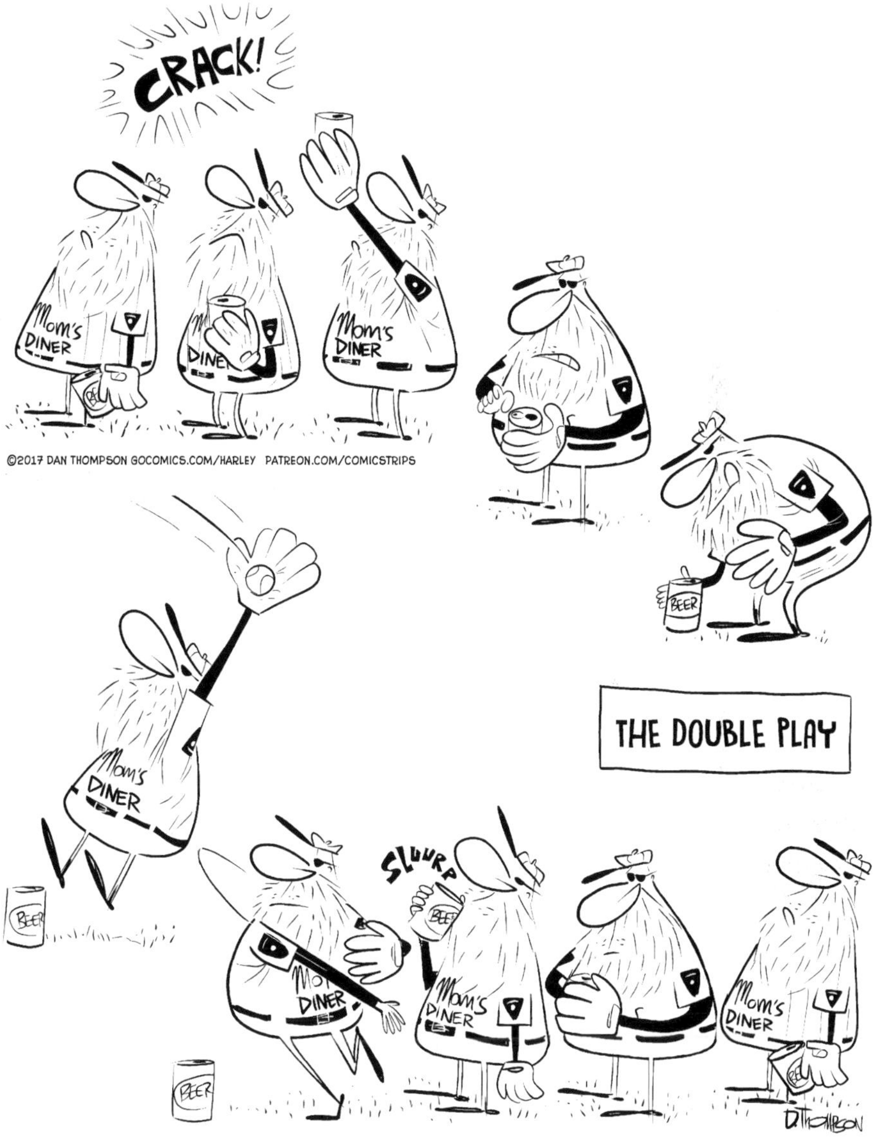
CRACK!
©2017 DAN THOMPSON GOCOMICS.COM/HARLEY PATREON.COM/COMICSTRIPS
THE DOUBLE PLAY
SLURP
D THOMPSON

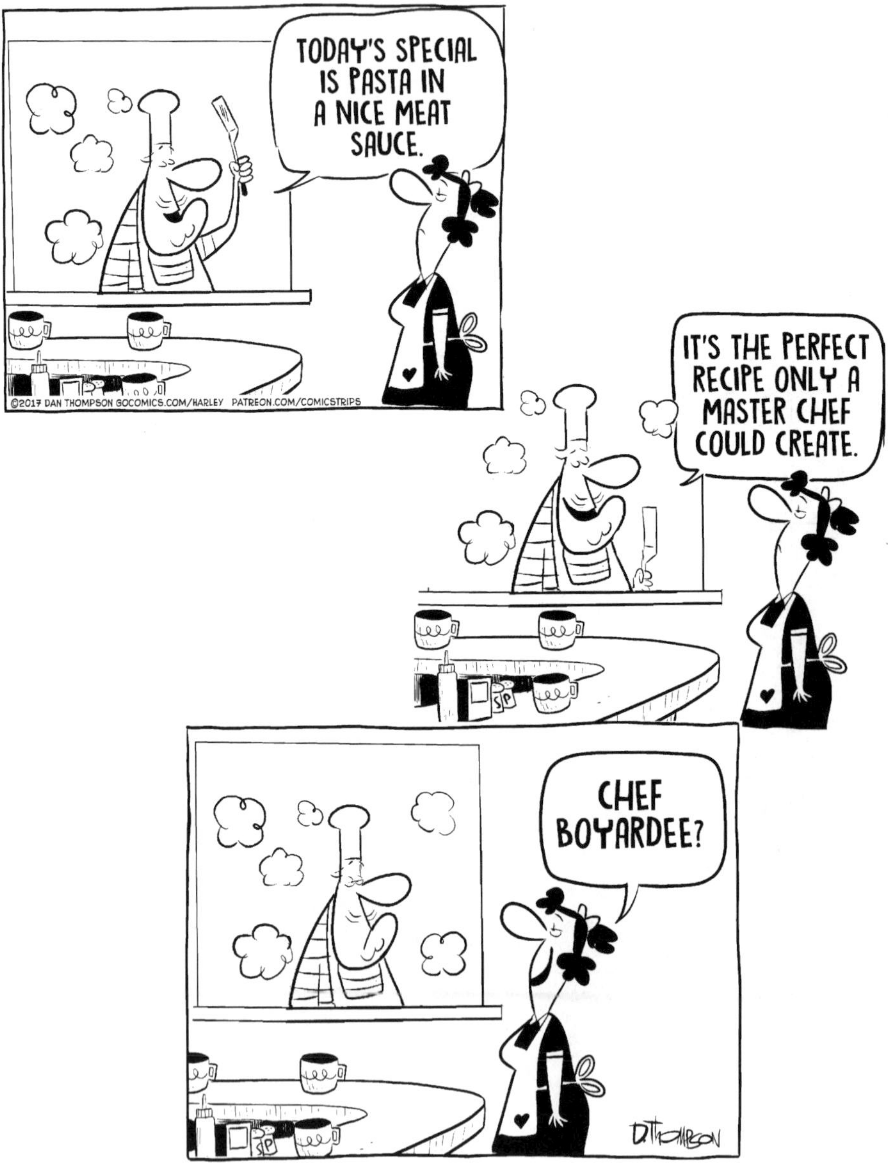
TODAY'S SPECIAL IS PASTA IN A NICE MEAT SAUCE.
©2017 DAN THOMPSON GOCOMICS.COM/HARLEY PATREON.COM/COMICSTRIPS
IT'S THE PERFECT RECIPE ONLY A MASTER CHEF COULD CREATE.
CHEF BOYARDEE?
D. THOMPSON

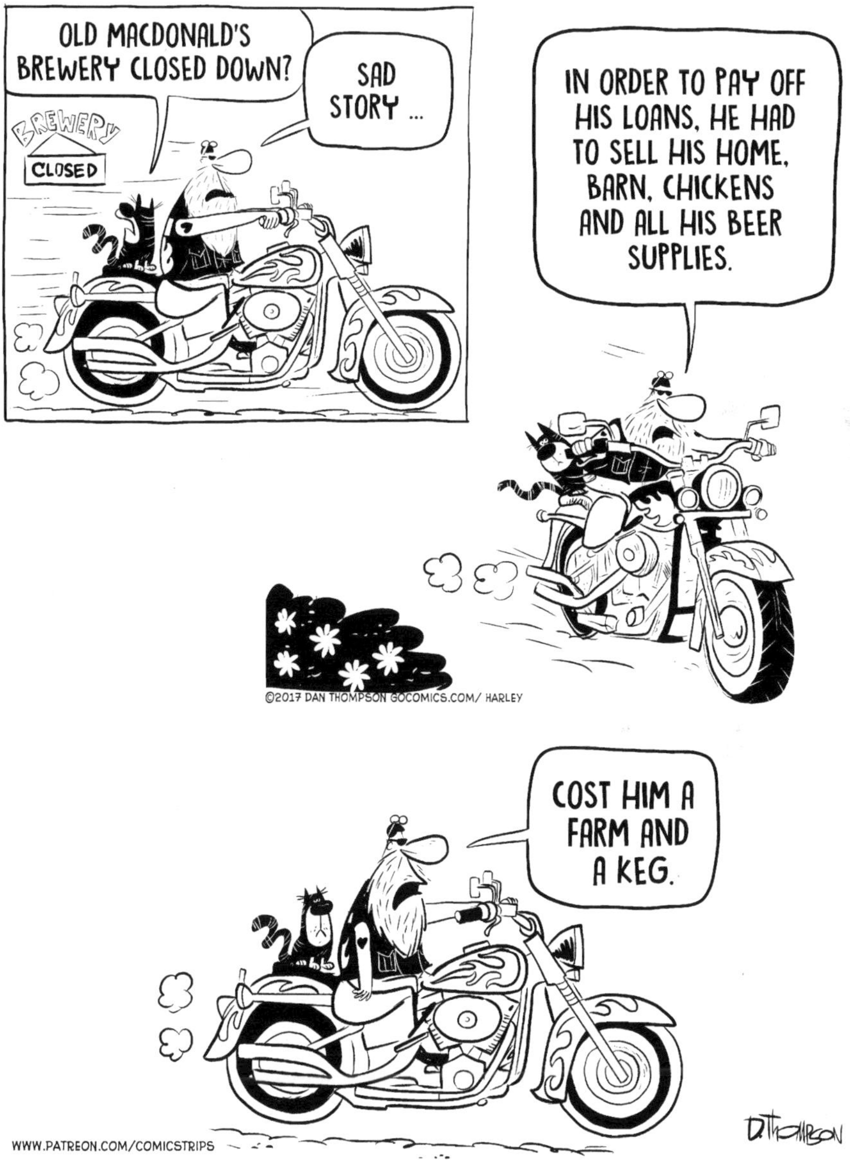
OLD MACDONALD'S BREWERY CLOSED DOWN?
SAD STORY ...
BREWERY
CLOSED
IN ORDER TO PAY OFF HIS LOANS, HE HAD TO SELL HIS HOME, BARN, CHICKENS AND ALL HIS BEER SUPPLIES.
©2017 DAN THOMPSON GOCOMICS.COM/ HARLEY
COST HIM A FARM AND A KEG.
WWW.PATREON.COM/COMICSTRIPS
D.THOMPSON

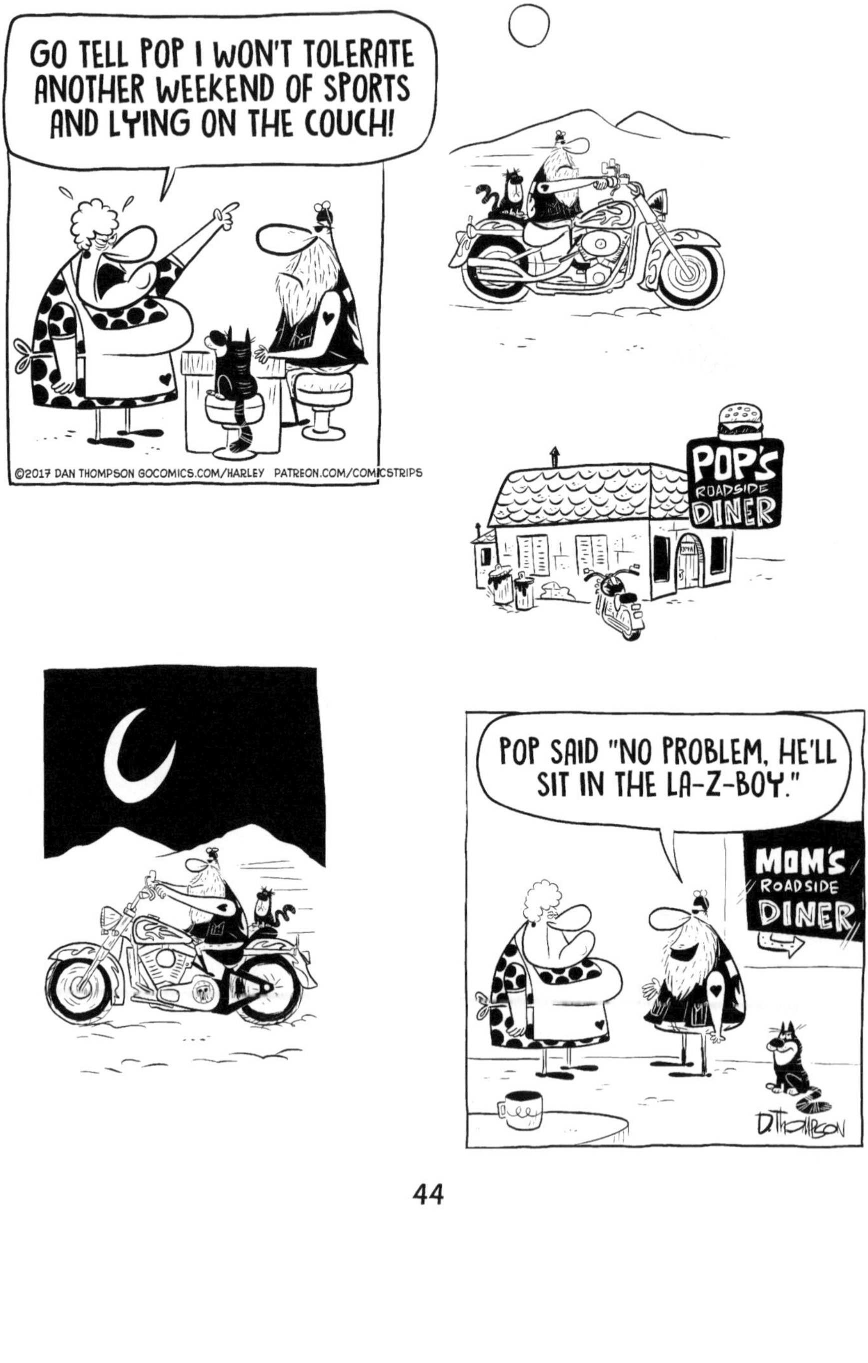
GO TELL POP I WON'T TOLERATE ANOTHER WEEKEND OF SPORTS AND LYING ON THE COUCH!
©2017 DAN THOMPSON GOCOMICS.COM/HARLEY PATREON.COM/COMICSTRIPS
POP'S ROADSIDE DINER
POP SAID "NO PROBLEM, HE'LL SIT IN THE LA-Z-BOY."
MOM'S ROADSIDE DINER
D.THOMPSON

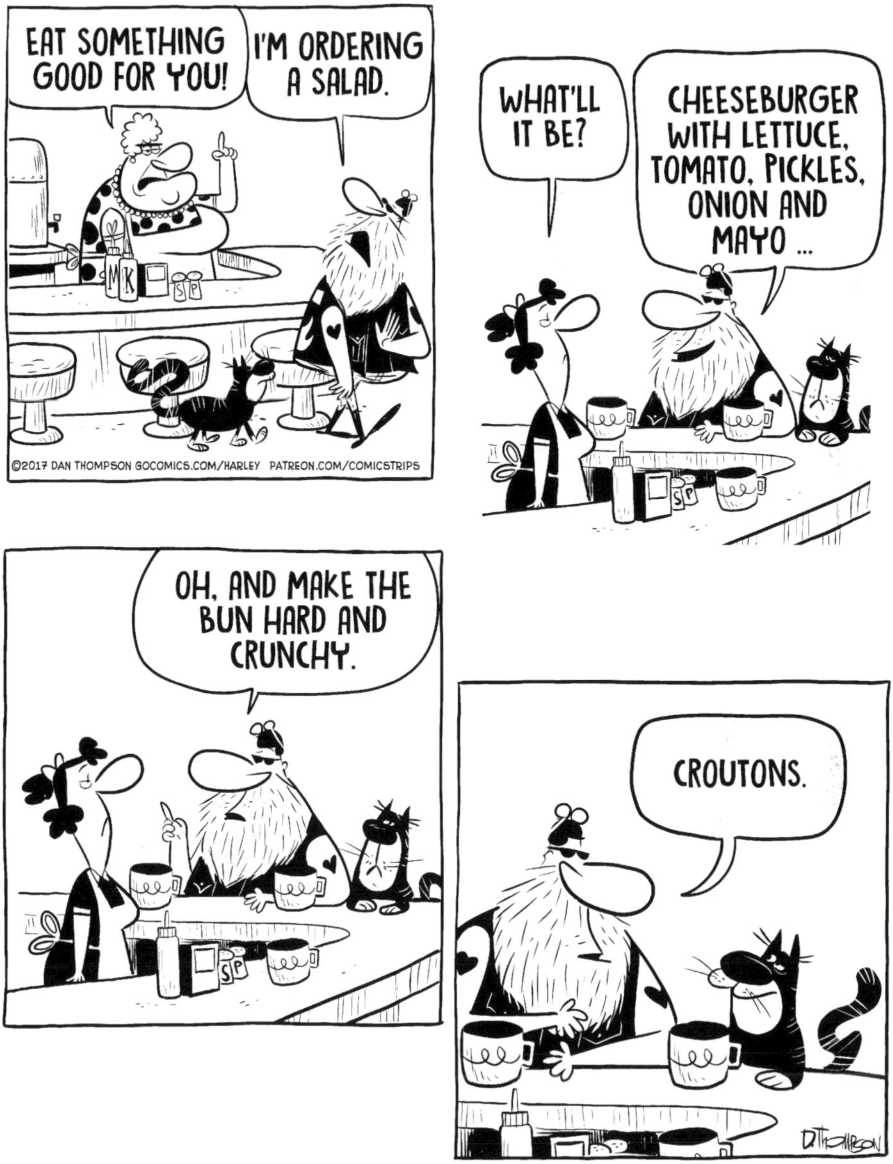
EAT SOMETHING GOOD FOR YOU!
I'M ORDERING A SALAD.
©2017 DAN THOMPSON GOCOMICS.COM/HARLEY PATREON.COM/COMICSTRIPS
WHAT'LL IT BE?
CHEESEBURGER WITH LETTUCE, TOMATO, PICKLES, ONION AND MAYO ...
OH, AND MAKE THE BUN HARD AND CRUNCHY.
CROUTONS.

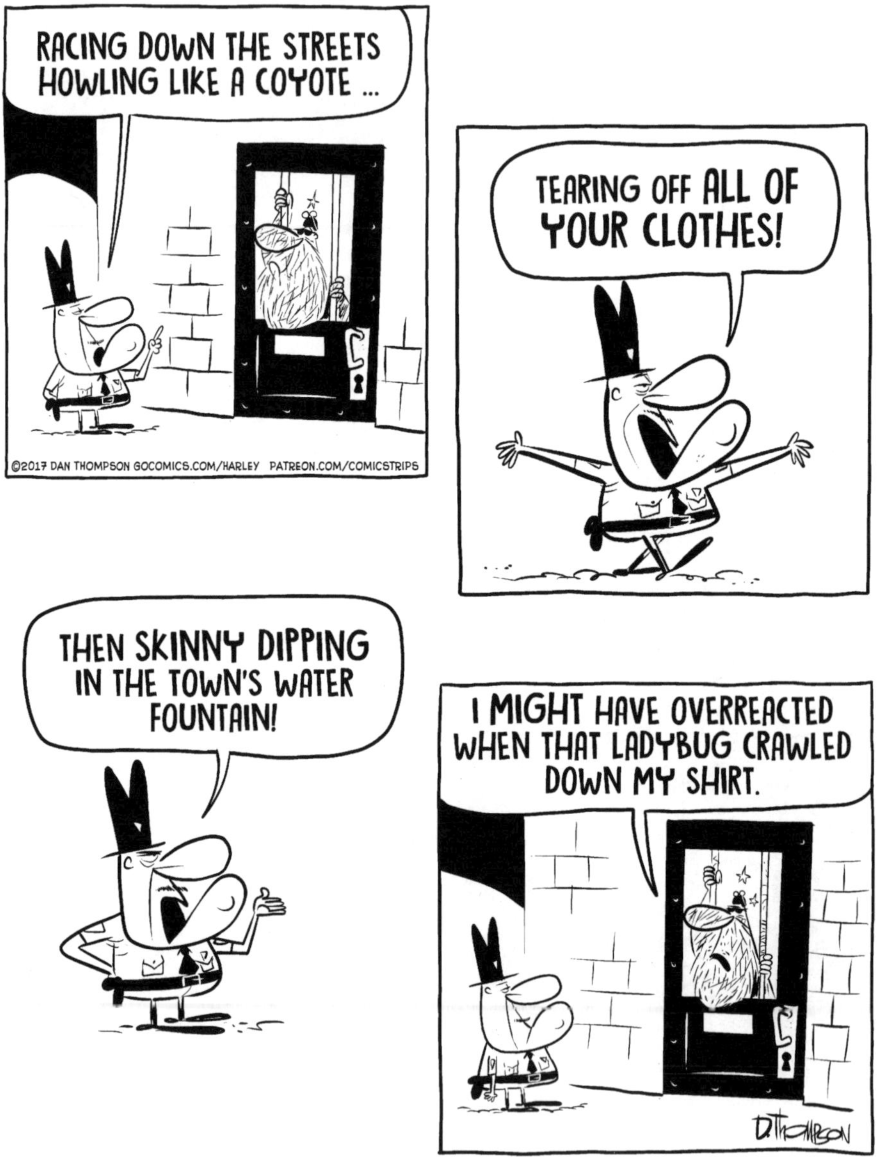
RACING DOWN THE STREETS HOWLING LIKE A COYOTE ...
©2017 DAN THOMPSON GOCOMICS.COM/HARLEY PATREON.COM/COMICSTRIPS
TEARING OFF ALL OF YOUR CLOTHES!
THEN SKINNY DIPPING IN THE TOWN'S WATER FOUNTAIN!
I MIGHT HAVE OVERREACTED WHEN THAT LADYBUG CRAWLED DOWN MY SHIRT.
D. THOMPSON

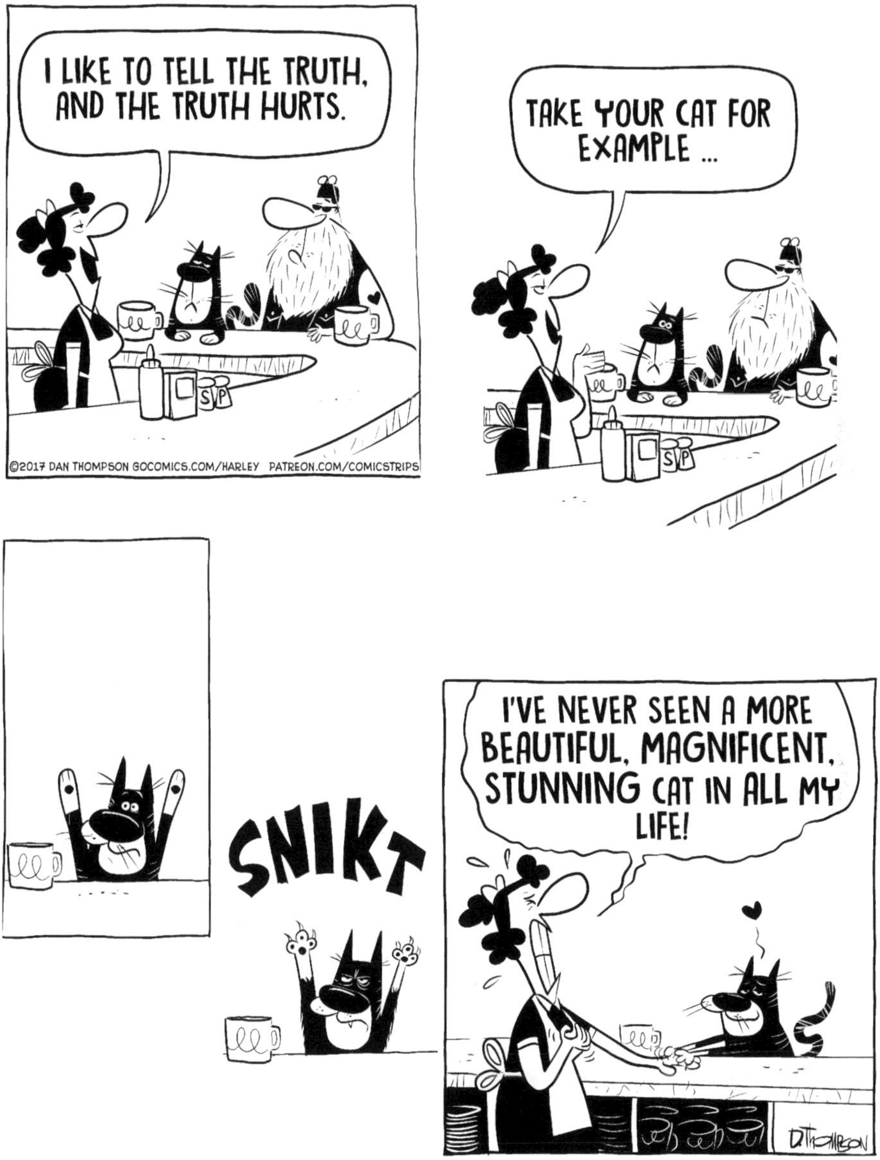
I LIKE TO TELL THE TRUTH, AND THE TRUTH HURTS.
©2017 DAN THOMPSON GOCOMICS.COM/HARLEY PATREON.COM/COMICSTRIPS
TAKE YOUR CAT FOR EXAMPLE ...
SNIKT
I'VE NEVER SEEN A MORE BEAUTIFUL, MAGNIFICENT, STUNNING CAT IN ALL MY LIFE!
D. THOMPSON

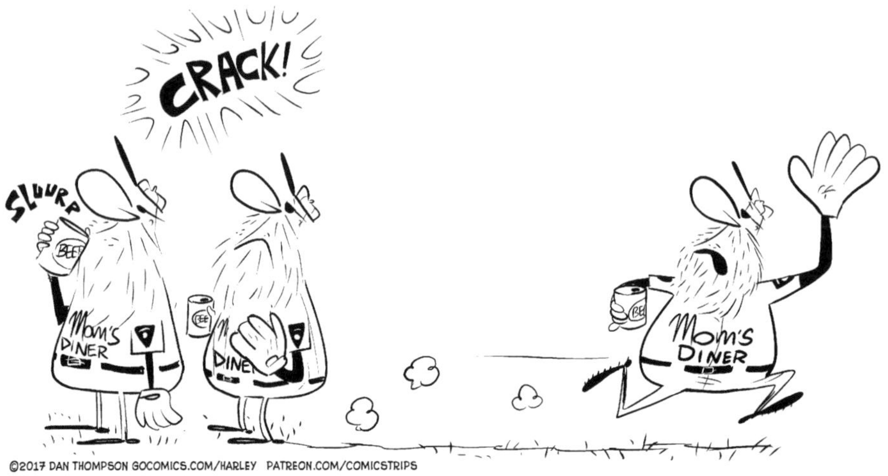
CRACK!
SLUURP
BEER
Mom's DINER
©2017 DAN THOMPSON GOCOMICS.COM/HARLEY PATREON.COM/COMICSTRIPS

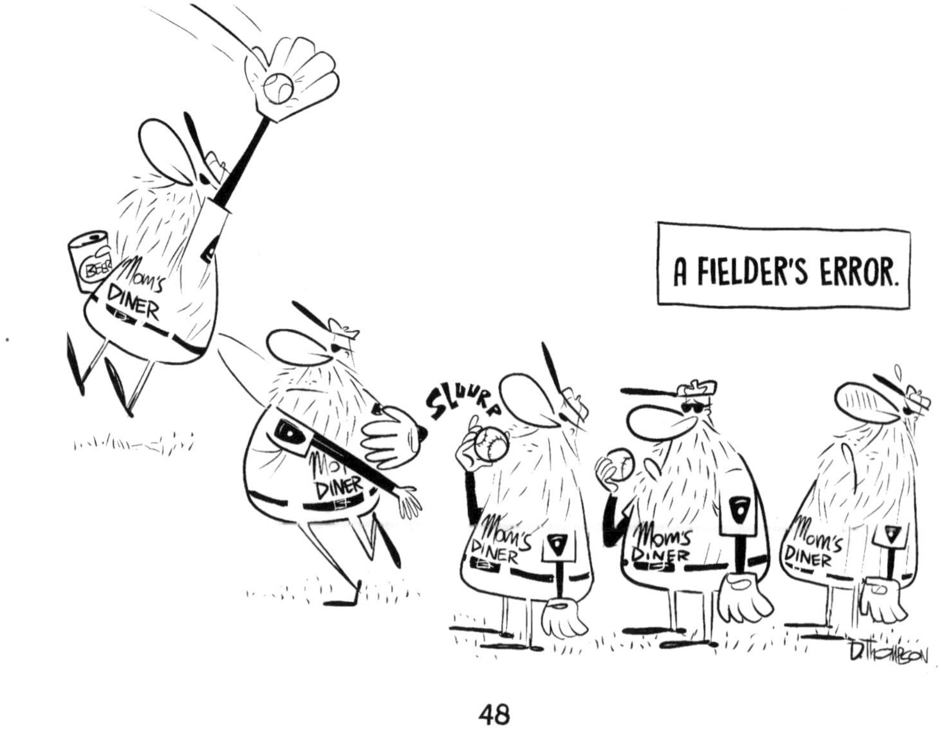
A FIELDER'S ERROR.
SLUURP
BEER
Mom's DINER
D.THOMPSON

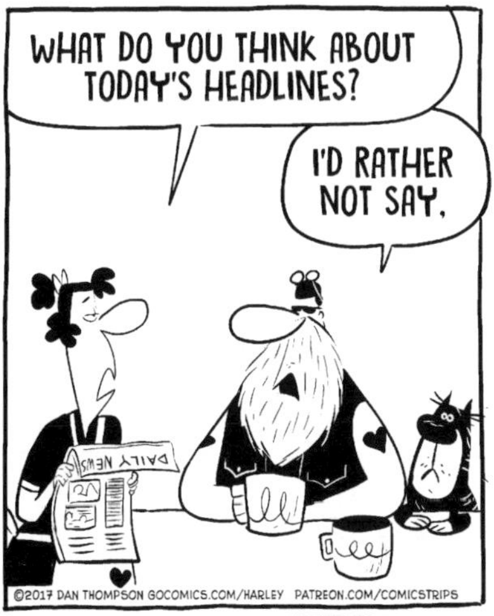
WHAT DO YOU THINK ABOUT TODAY'S HEADLINES?
I'D RATHER NOT SAY.
DAILY NEWS
©2017 DAN THOMPSON GOCOMICS.COM/HARLEY PATREON.COM/COMICSTRIPS

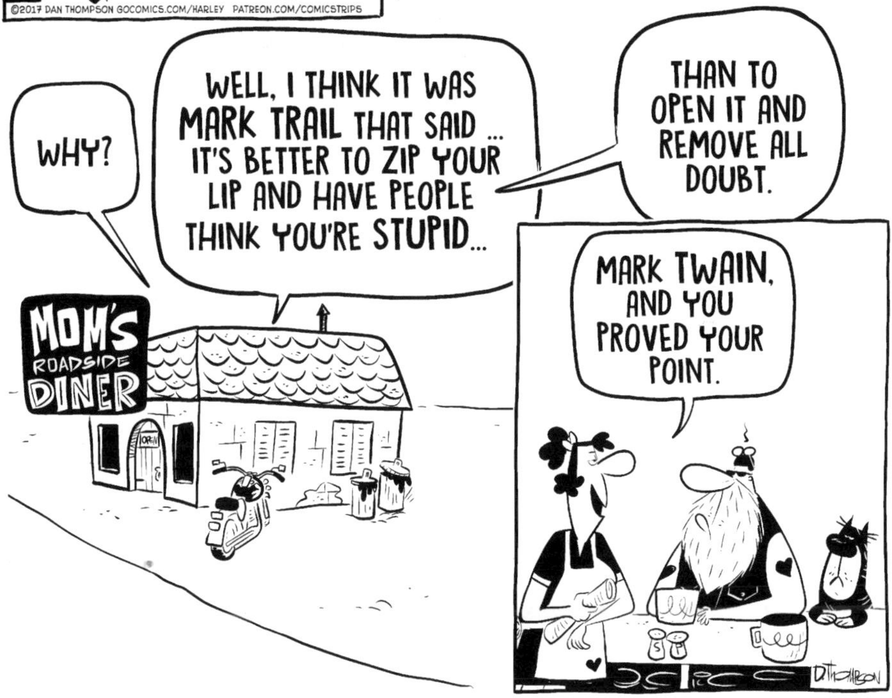
WHY?
WELL, I THINK IT WAS MARK TRAIL THAT SAID ... IT'S BETTER TO ZIP YOUR LIP AND HAVE PEOPLE THINK YOU'RE STUPID...
THAN TO OPEN IT AND REMOVE ALL DOUBT.
MOM'S ROADSIDE DINER
OPEN
MARK TWAIN, AND YOU PROVED YOUR POINT.
D THOMPSON

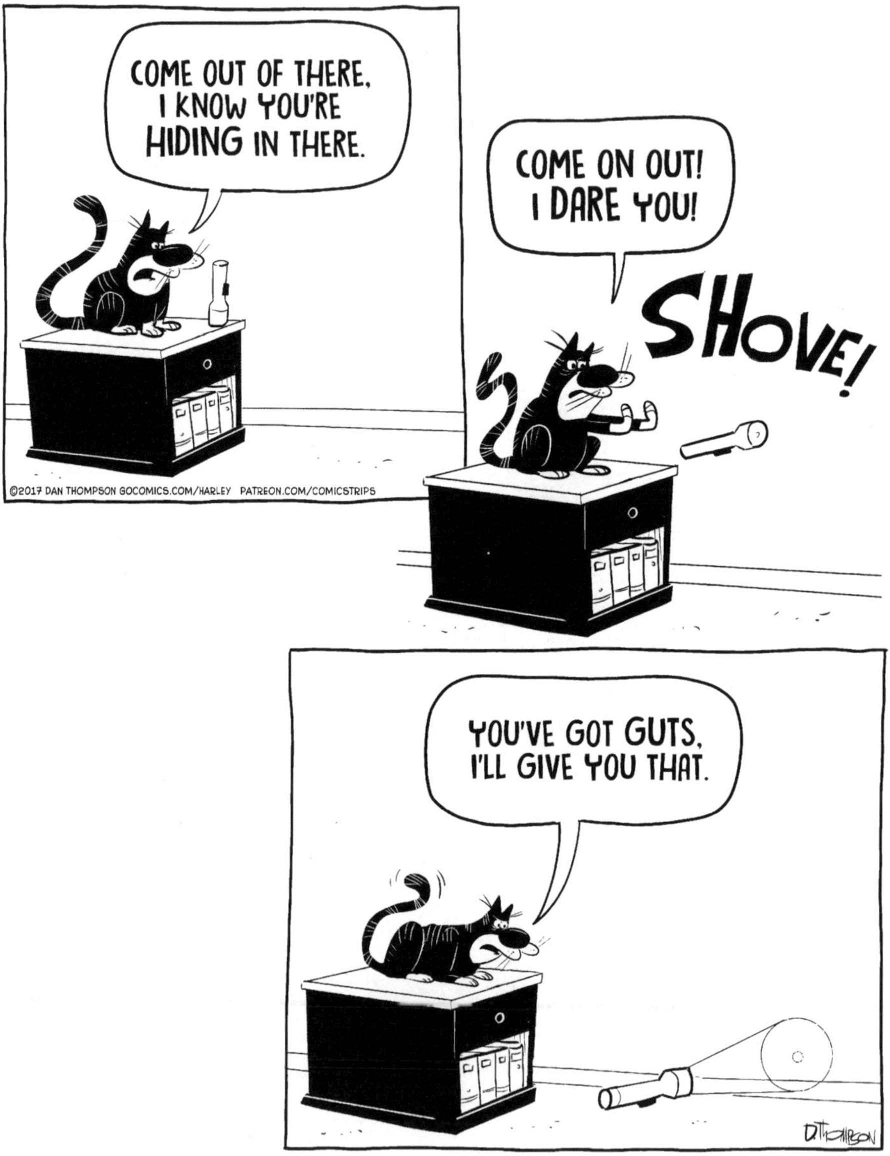
COME OUT OF THERE, I KNOW YOU'RE HIDING IN THERE.
©2017 DAN THOMPSON GOCOMICS.COM/HARLEY PATREON.COM/COMICSTRIPS
COME ON OUT! I DARE YOU!
SHOVE!
YOU'VE GOT GUTS, I'LL GIVE YOU THAT.
D THOMPSON

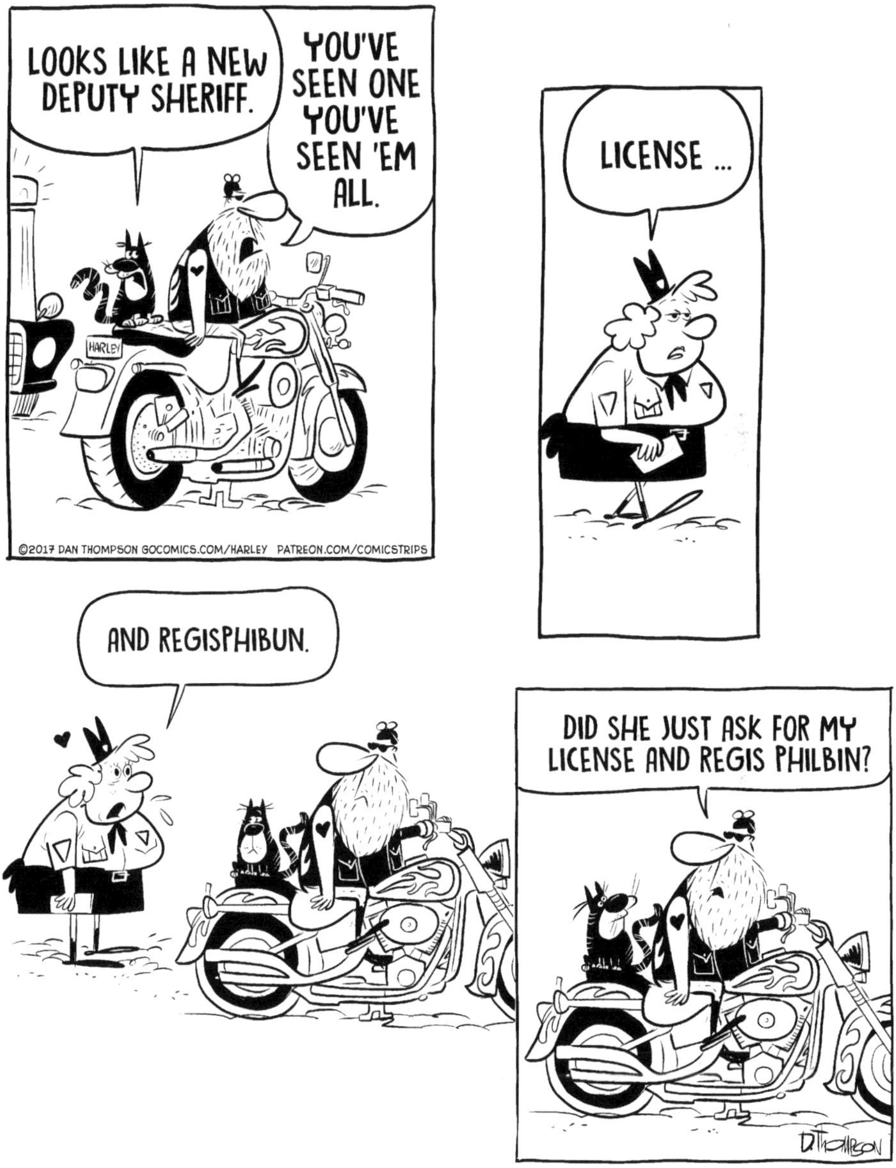
LOOKS LIKE A NEW DEPUTY SHERIFF.
YOU'VE SEEN ONE YOU'VE SEEN 'EM ALL.
HARLEY
©2017 DAN THOMPSON GOCOMICS.COM/HARLEY PATREON.COM/COMICSTRIPS
LICENSE ...
AND REGISPHIBUN.
DID SHE JUST ASK FOR MY LICENSE AND REGIS PHILBIN?
D.THOMPSON

I'M GOING TO LET YOU OFF WITH A WARNING, MR. HARLEY.
SO, I'M FREE TO GO?
WELL, YES, BUT...
©2017 DAN THOMPSON GOCOMICS.COM/HARLEY PATREON.COM/COMICSTRIPS
SCREECH!
BURN RUBBER!
ZOOM!
I LOVE A MAN WHO PLAYS HARD TO GET.
D. THOMPSON

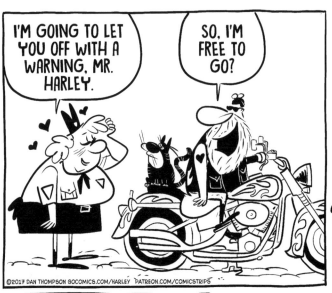

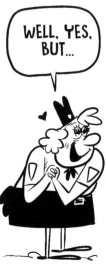

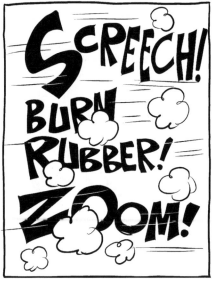

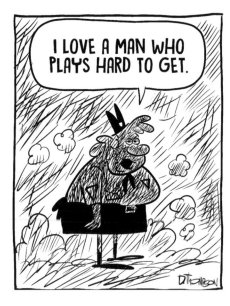

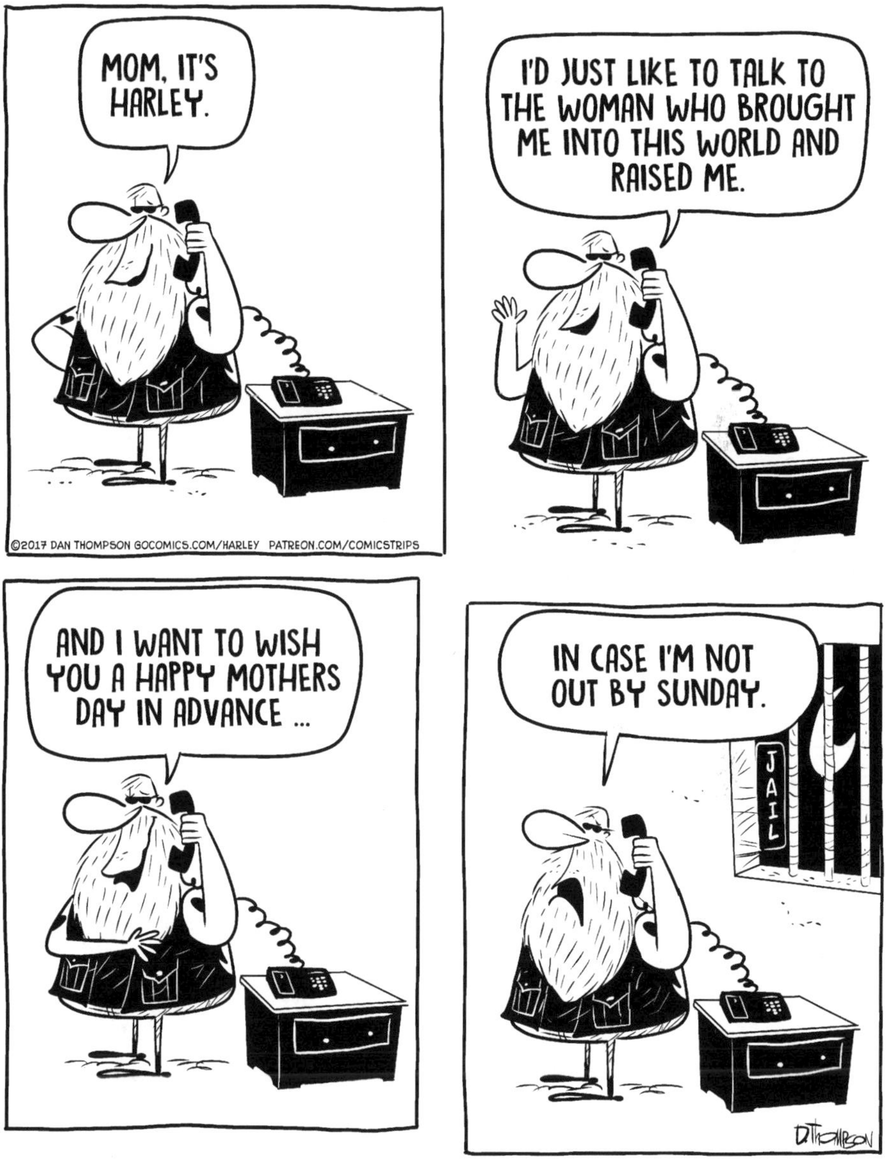
MOM, IT'S HARLEY.
©2017 DAN THOMPSON GOCOMICS.COM/HARLEY PATREON.COM/COMICSTRIPS
I'D JUST LIKE TO TALK TO THE WOMAN WHO BROUGHT ME INTO THIS WORLD AND RAISED ME.
AND I WANT TO WISH YOU A HAPPY MOTHERS DAY IN ADVANCE ...
IN CASE I'M NOT OUT BY SUNDAY.
JAIL
D. THOMPSON

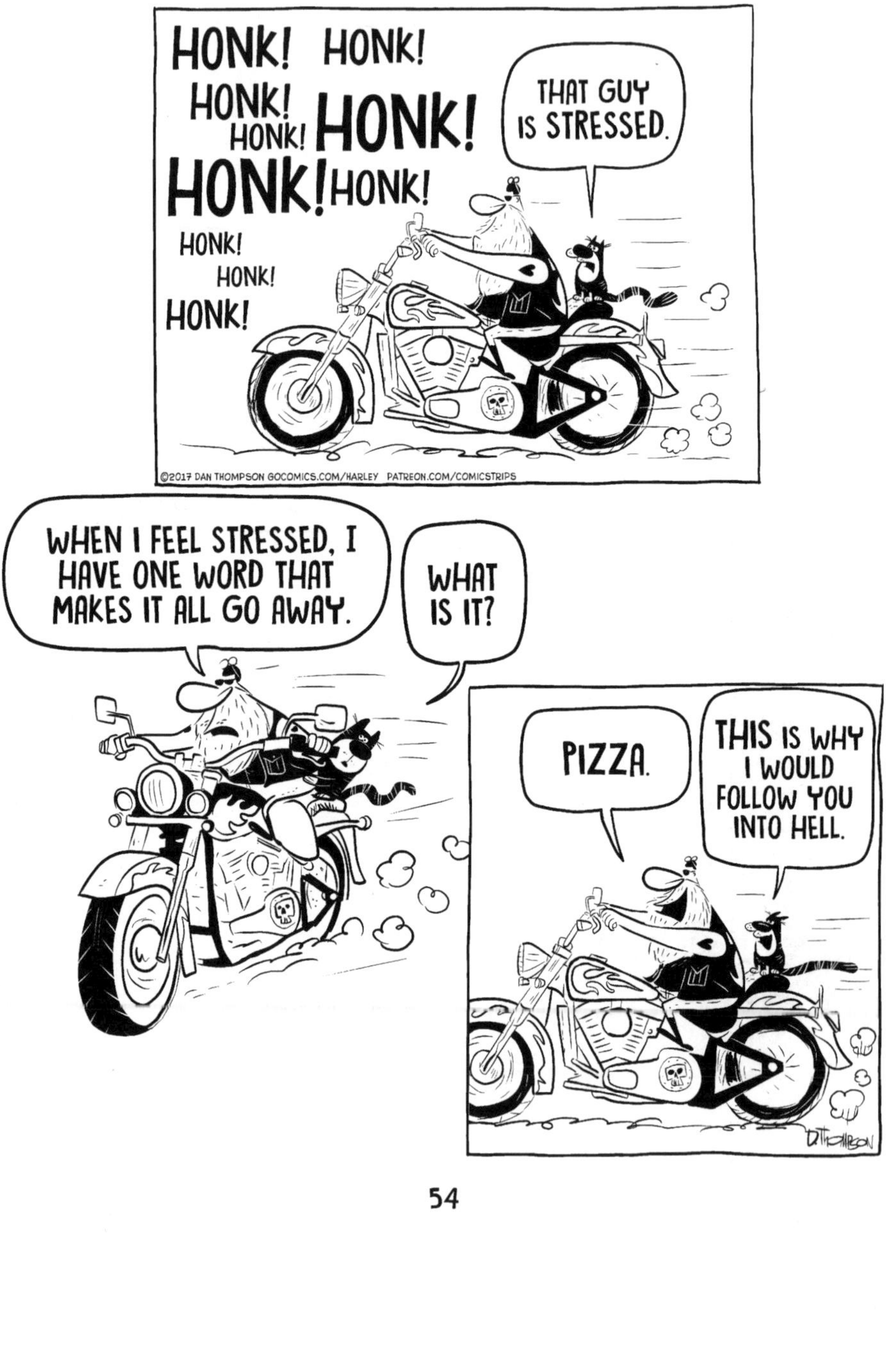
HONK! HONK!
HONK! HONK! HONK!
HONK! HONK!
HONK!
HONK!
HONK!
THAT GUY IS STRESSED.
©2017 DAN THOMPSON GOCOMICS.COM/HARLEY PATREON.COM/COMICSTRIPS
WHEN I FEEL STRESSED, I HAVE ONE WORD THAT MAKES IT ALL GO AWAY.
WHAT IS IT?
PIZZA.
THIS IS WHY I WOULD FOLLOW YOU INTO HELL.

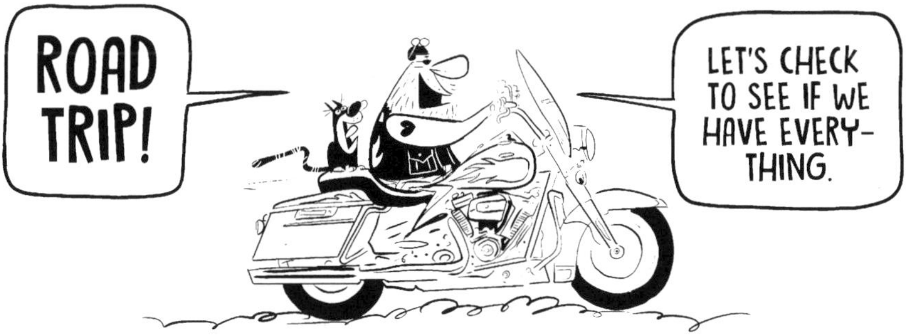
ROAD TRIP!
LET'S CHECK TO SEE IF WE HAVE EVERY-THING.

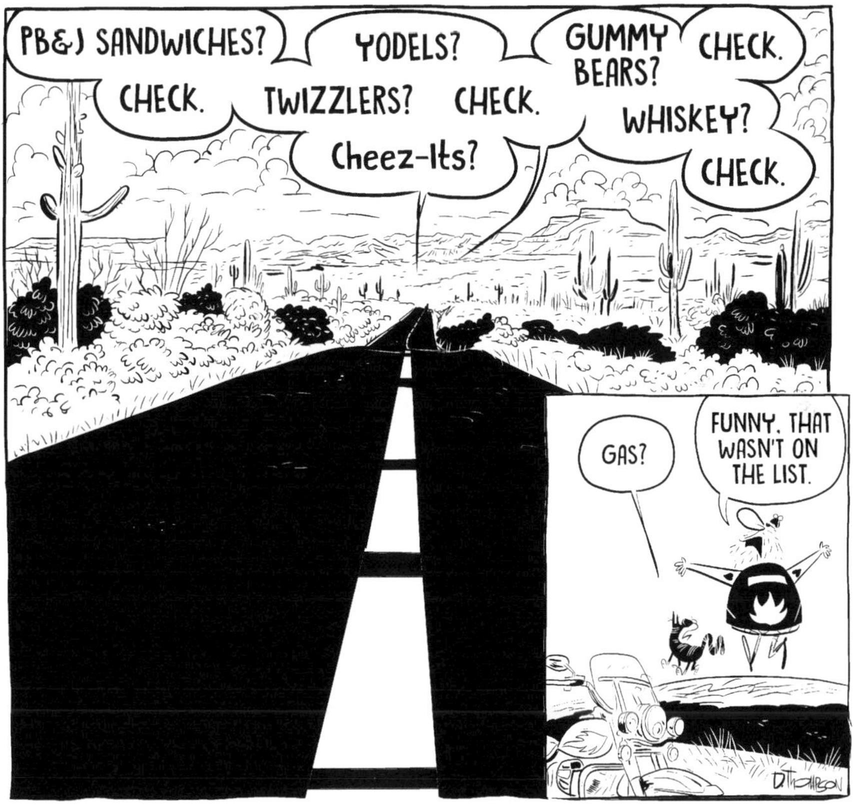
PB&J SANDWICHES?
CHECK.
YODELS?
TWIZZLERS?
CHECK.
Cheez-Its?
GUMMY BEARS?
CHECK.
WHISKEY?
CHECK.
GAS?
FUNNY. THAT WASN'T ON THE LIST.

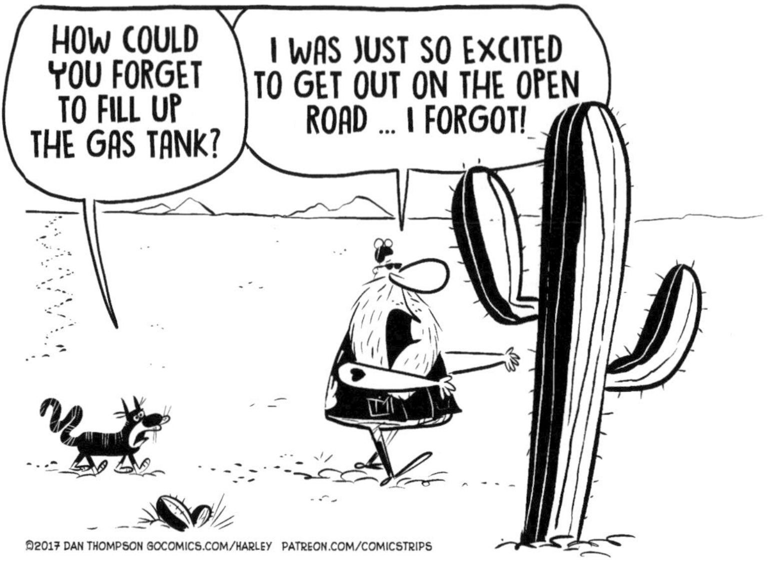
HOW COULD YOU FORGET TO FILL UP THE GAS TANK?
I WAS JUST SO EXCITED TO GET OUT ON THE OPEN ROAD ... I FORGOT!
©2017 DAN THOMPSON GOCOMICS.COM/HARLEY PATREON.COM/COMICSTRIPS

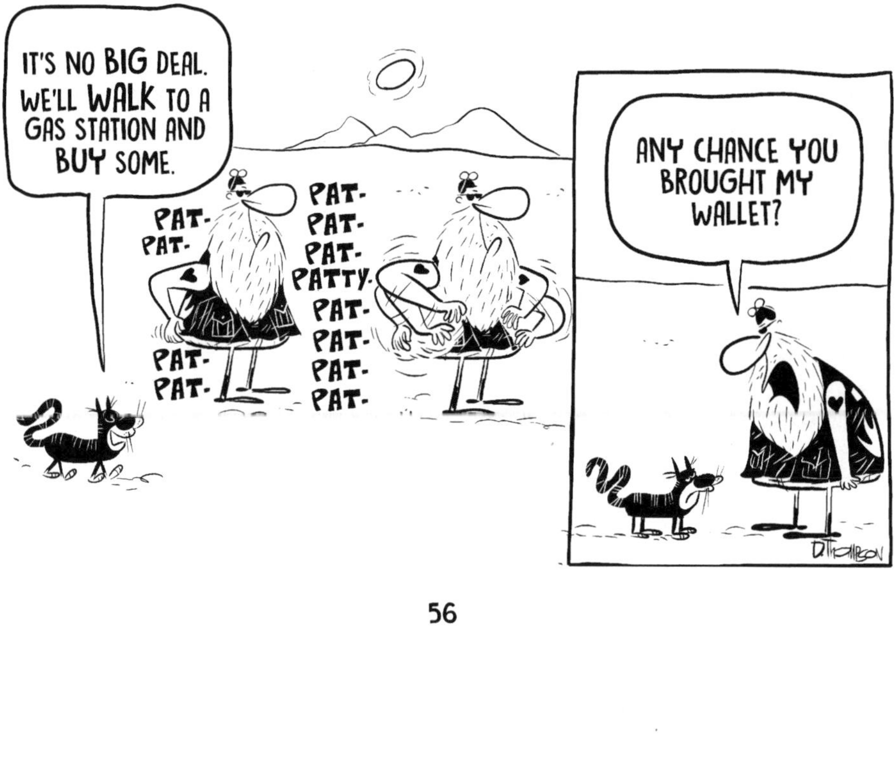
IT'S NO BIG DEAL. WE'LL WALK TO A GAS STATION AND BUY SOME.
PAT- PAT-
PAT- PAT-
PAT- PAT- PAT- PATTY- PAT- PAT- PAT- PAT-
ANY CHANCE YOU BROUGHT MY WALLET?
D.THOMPSON

WE'VE BEEN OUT IN THE SUN FOR A LONG TIME.
©2017 DAN THOMPSON GOCOMICS.COM/HARLEY PATREON.COM/COMICSTRIPS
DID YOU EVER HEAR ABOUT HALLUCINATING IN THE DESERT?
WHY?
NO REASON.

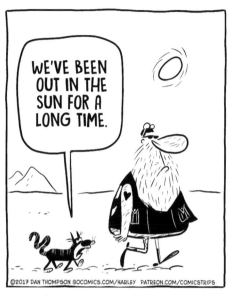

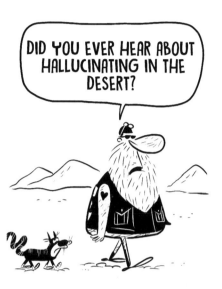

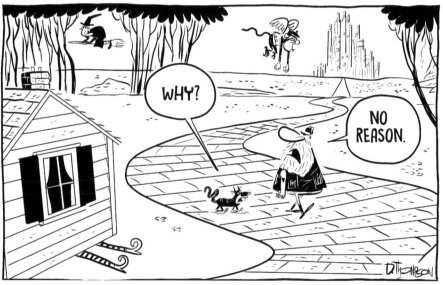

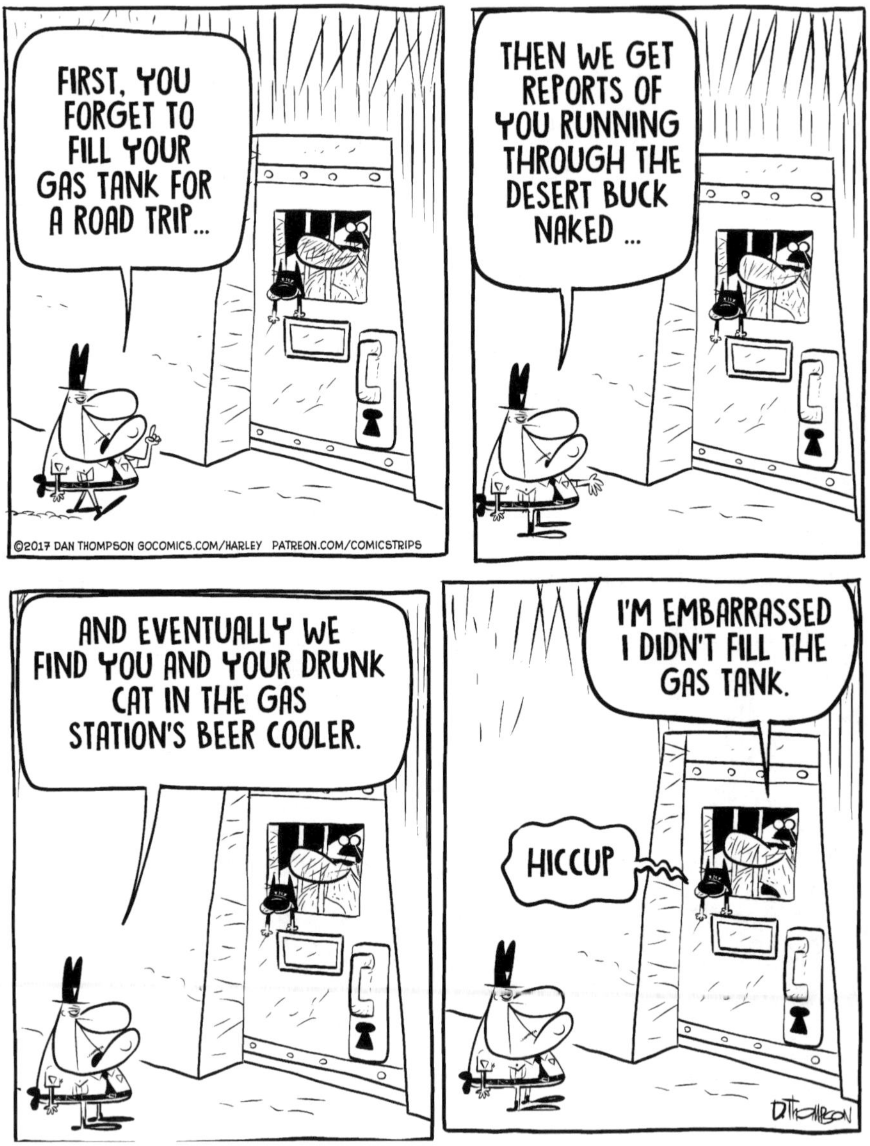
FIRST, YOU FORGET TO FILL YOUR GAS TANK FOR A ROAD TRIP...
©2017 DAN THOMPSON GOCOMICS.COM/HARLEY PATREON.COM/COMICSTRIPS
THEN WE GET REPORTS OF YOU RUNNING THROUGH THE DESERT BUCK NAKED ...
AND EVENTUALLY WE FIND YOU AND YOUR DRUNK CAT IN THE GAS STATION'S BEER COOLER.
I'M EMBARRASSED I DIDN'T FILL THE GAS TANK.
HICCUP
D.THOMPSON

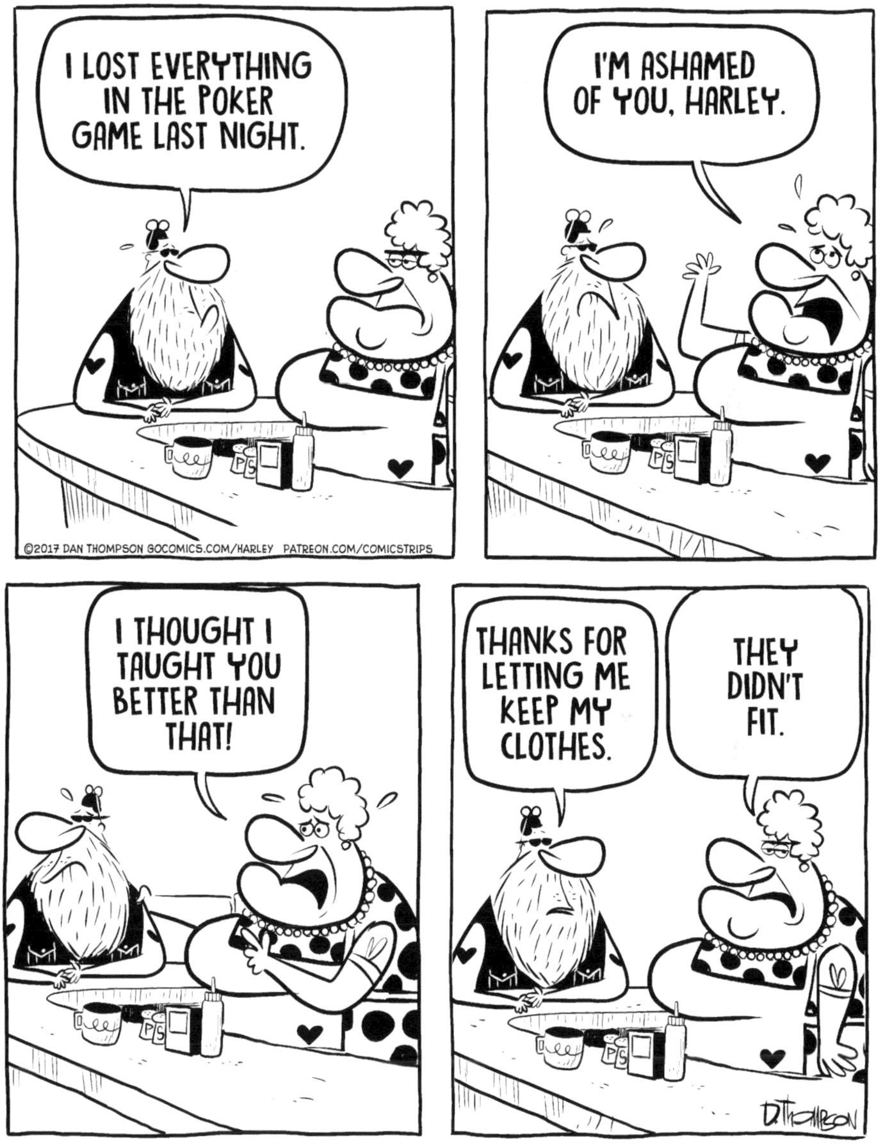
I LOST EVERYTHING IN THE POKER GAME LAST NIGHT.
©2017 DAN THOMPSON GOCOMICS.COM/HARLEY PATREON.COM/COMICSTRIPS
I'M ASHAMED OF YOU, HARLEY.
I THOUGHT I TAUGHT YOU BETTER THAN THAT!
THANKS FOR LETTING ME KEEP MY CLOTHES.
THEY DIDN'T FIT.
D. THOMPSON

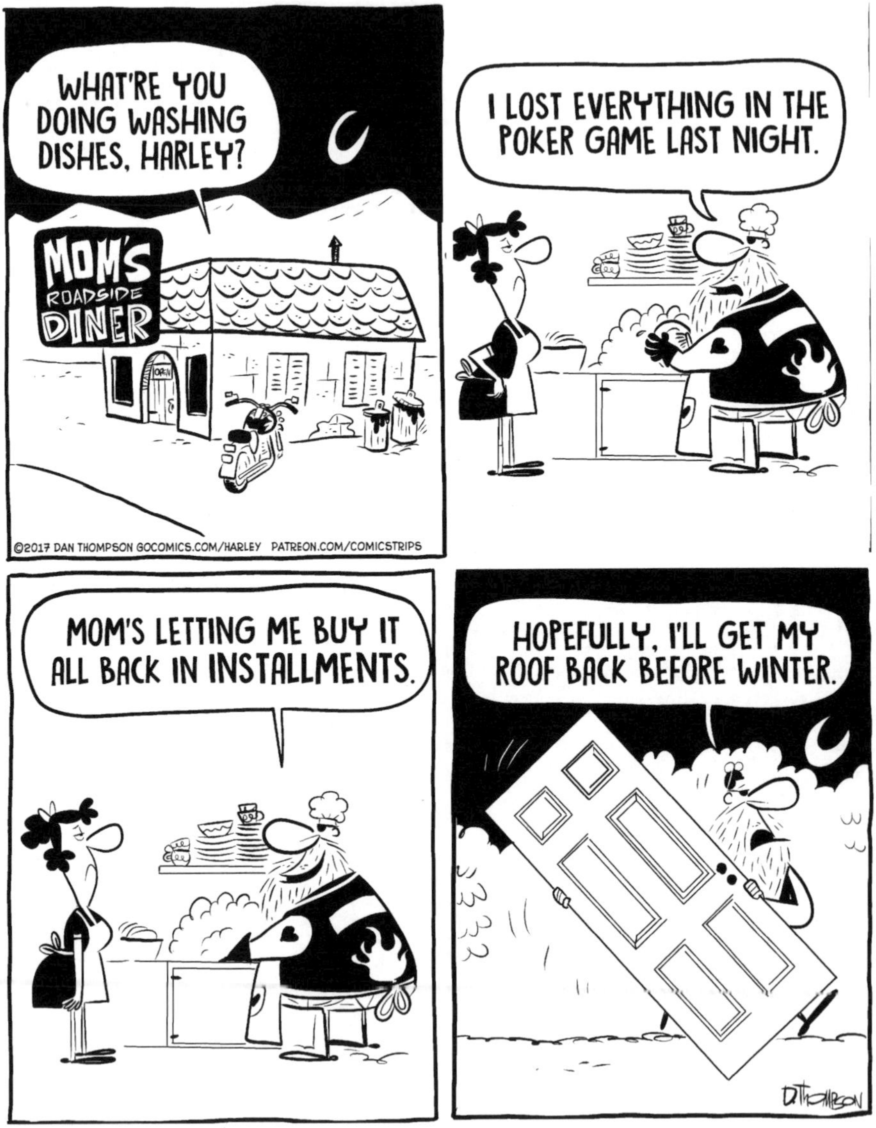
WHAT'RE YOU DOING WASHING DISHES, HARLEY?
MOM'S ROADSIDE DINER
©2017 DAN THOMPSON GOCOMICS.COM/HARLEY PATREON.COM/COMICSTRIPS
I LOST EVERYTHING IN THE POKER GAME LAST NIGHT.
MOM'S LETTING ME BUY IT ALL BACK IN INSTALLMENTS.
HOPEFULLY, I'LL GET MY ROOF BACK BEFORE WINTER.
D.THOMPSON

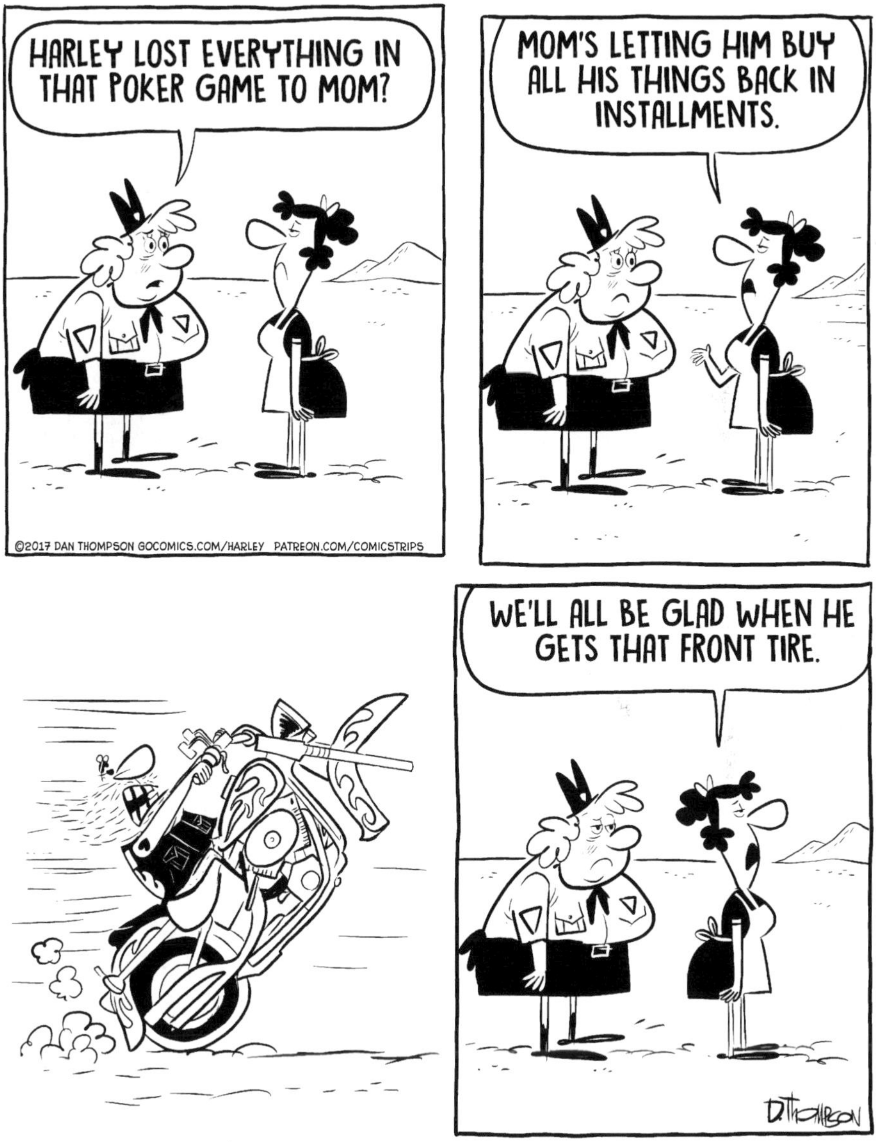
HARLEY LOST EVERYTHING IN THAT POKER GAME TO MOM?
©2017 DAN THOMPSON GOCOMICS.COM/HARLEY PATREON.COM/COMICSTRIPS
MOM'S LETTING HIM BUY ALL HIS THINGS BACK IN INSTALLMENTS.
WE'LL ALL BE GLAD WHEN HE GETS THAT FRONT TIRE.
D. THOMPSON

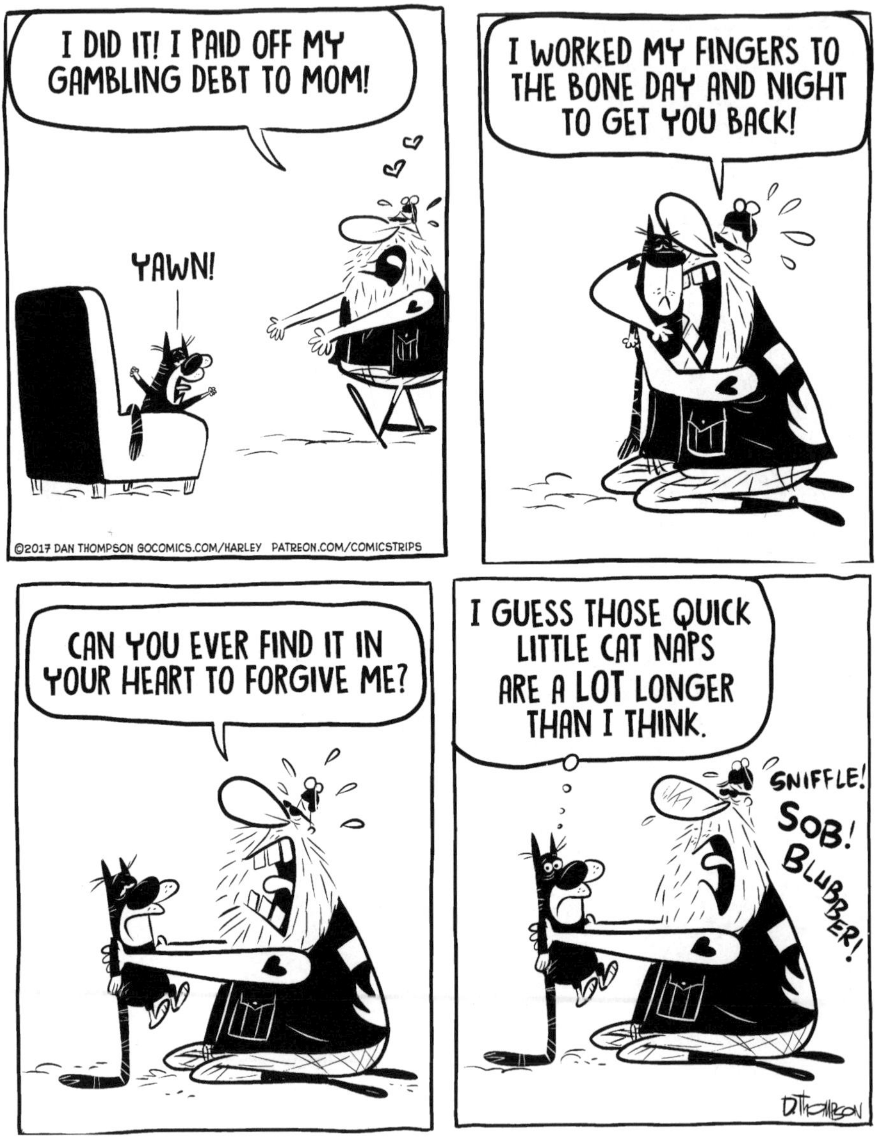
I DID IT! I PAID OFF MY GAMBLING DEBT TO MOM!
YAWN!
©2017 DAN THOMPSON GOCOMICS.COM/HARLEY PATREON.COM/COMICSTRIPS
I WORKED MY FINGERS TO THE BONE DAY AND NIGHT TO GET YOU BACK!
CAN YOU EVER FIND IT IN YOUR HEART TO FORGIVE ME?
I GUESS THOSE QUICK LITTLE CAT NAPS ARE A LOT LONGER THAN I THINK.
SNIFFLE!
SOB!
BLUBBER!
D.THOMPSON

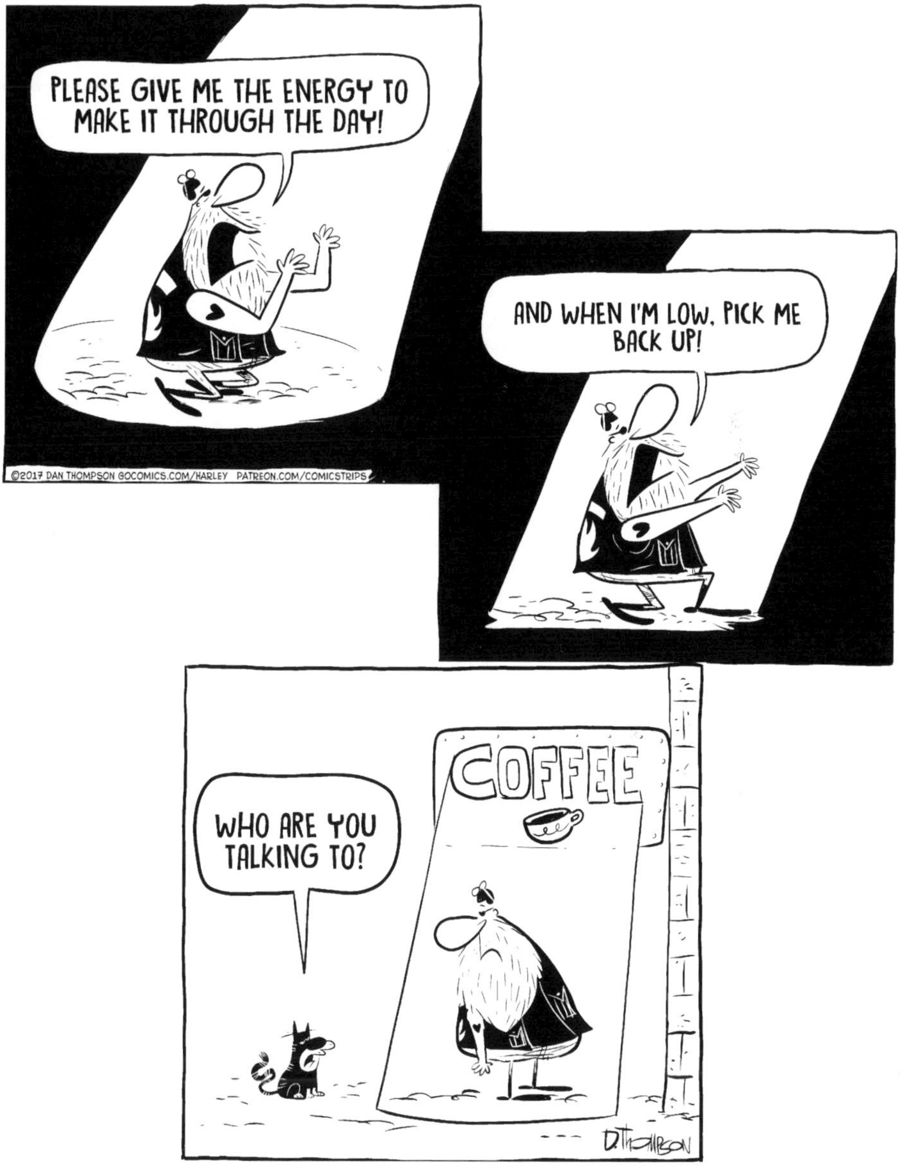
PLEASE GIVE ME THE ENERGY TO MAKE IT THROUGH THE DAY!
©2017 DAN THOMPSON GOCOMICS.COM/HARLEY PATREON.COM/COMICSTRIPS
AND WHEN I'M LOW, PICK ME BACK UP!
COFFEE
WHO ARE YOU TALKING TO?
D. THOMPSON

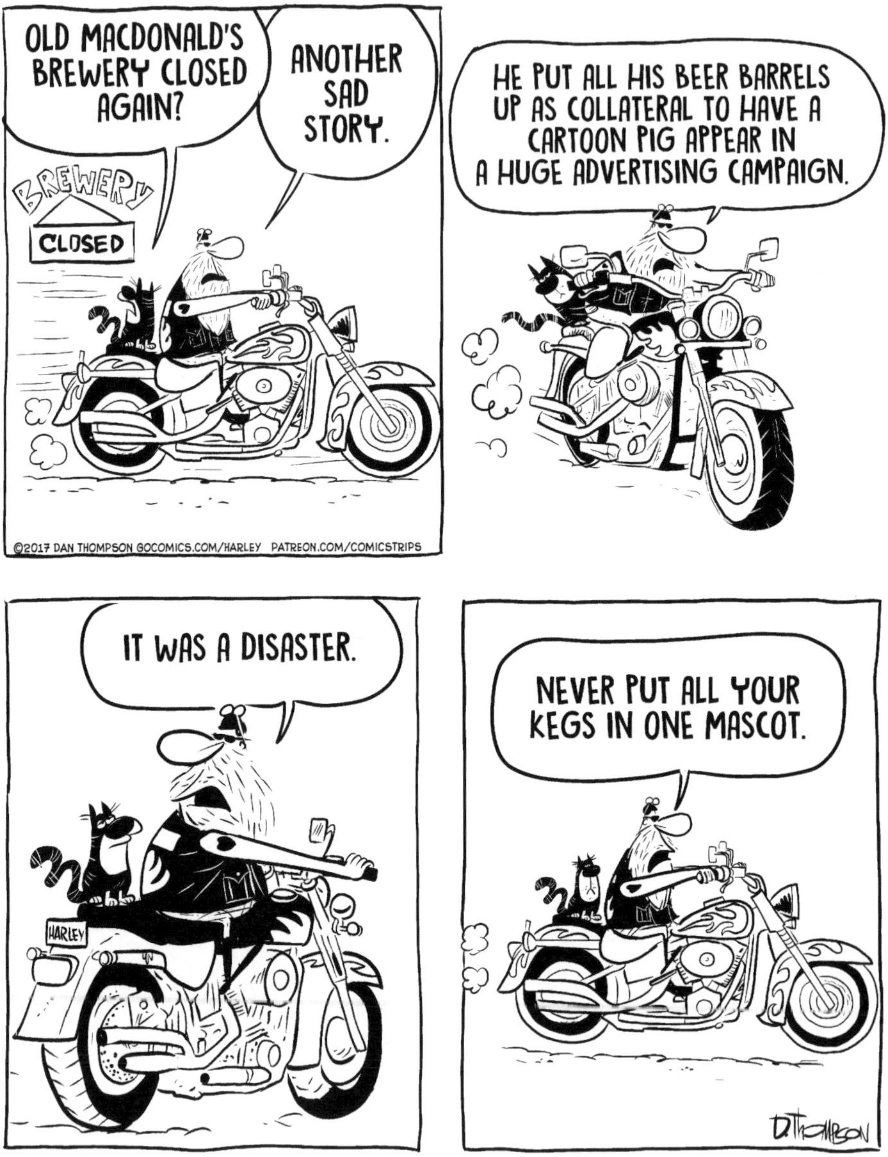
OLD MACDONALD'S BREWERY CLOSED AGAIN?
ANOTHER SAD STORY.
BREWERY
CLOSED
©2017 DAN THOMPSON GOCOMICS.COM/HARLEY PATREON.COM/COMICSTRIPS
HE PUT ALL HIS BEER BARRELS UP AS COLLATERAL TO HAVE A CARTOON PIG APPEAR IN A HUGE ADVERTISING CAMPAIGN.
IT WAS A DISASTER.
HARLEY
NEVER PUT ALL YOUR KEGS IN ONE MASCOT.
D. THOMPSON

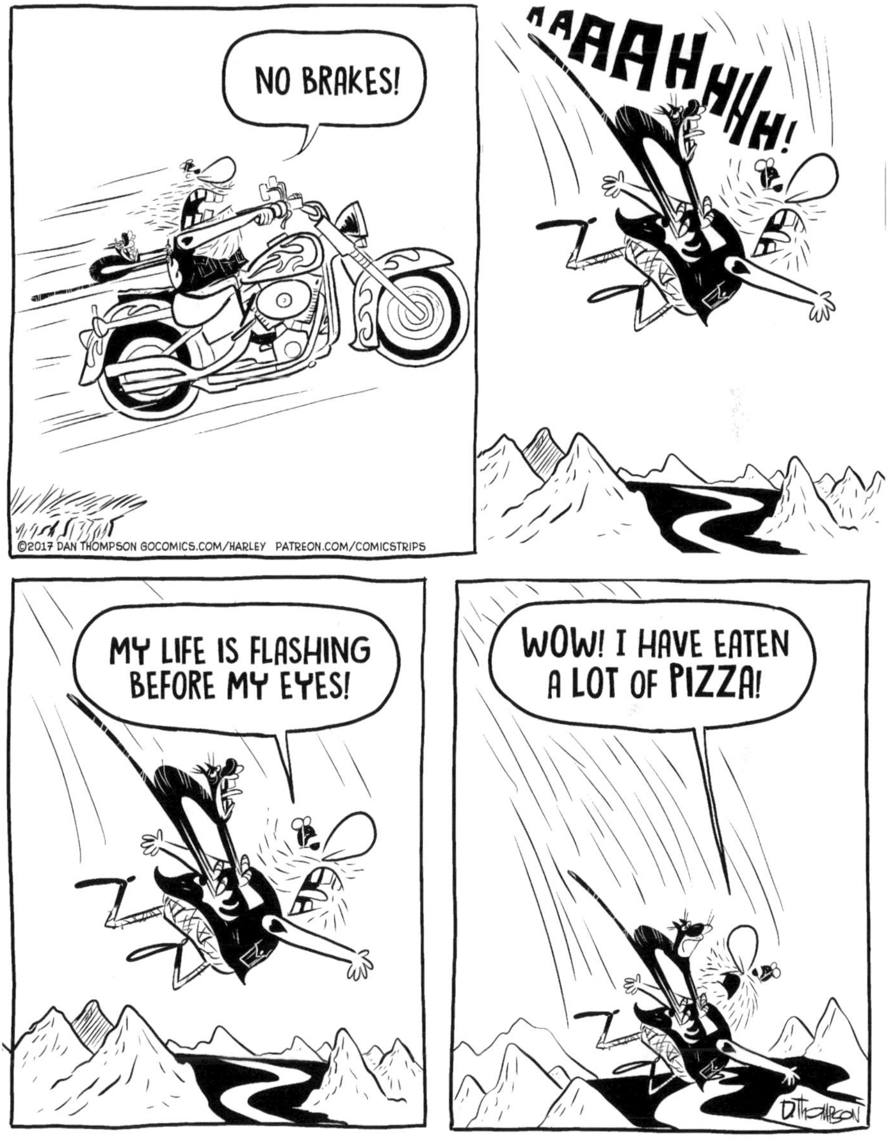
NO BRAKES!
©2017 DAN THOMPSON GOCOMICS.COM/HARLEY PATREON.COM/COMICSTRIPS
AAAAHHHHH!
MY LIFE IS FLASHING BEFORE MY EYES!
WOW! I HAVE EATEN A LOT OF PIZZA!
D. THOMPSON

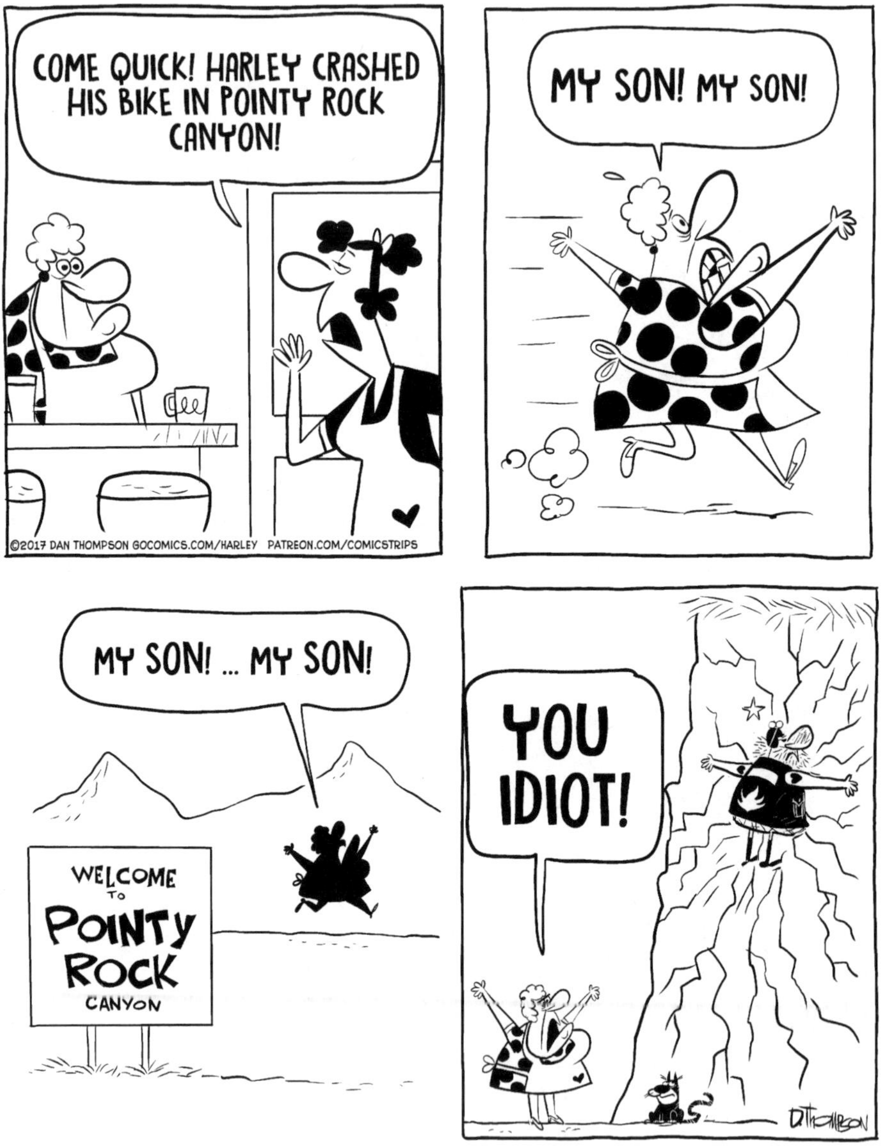
COME QUICK! HARLEY CRASHED HIS BIKE IN POINTY ROCK CANYON!
©2017 DAN THOMPSON GOCOMICS.COM/HARLEY PATREON.COM/COMICSTRIPS
MY SON! MY SON!
MY SON! ... MY SON!
WELCOME TO POINTY ROCK CANYON
YOU IDIOT!
D.THOMPSON

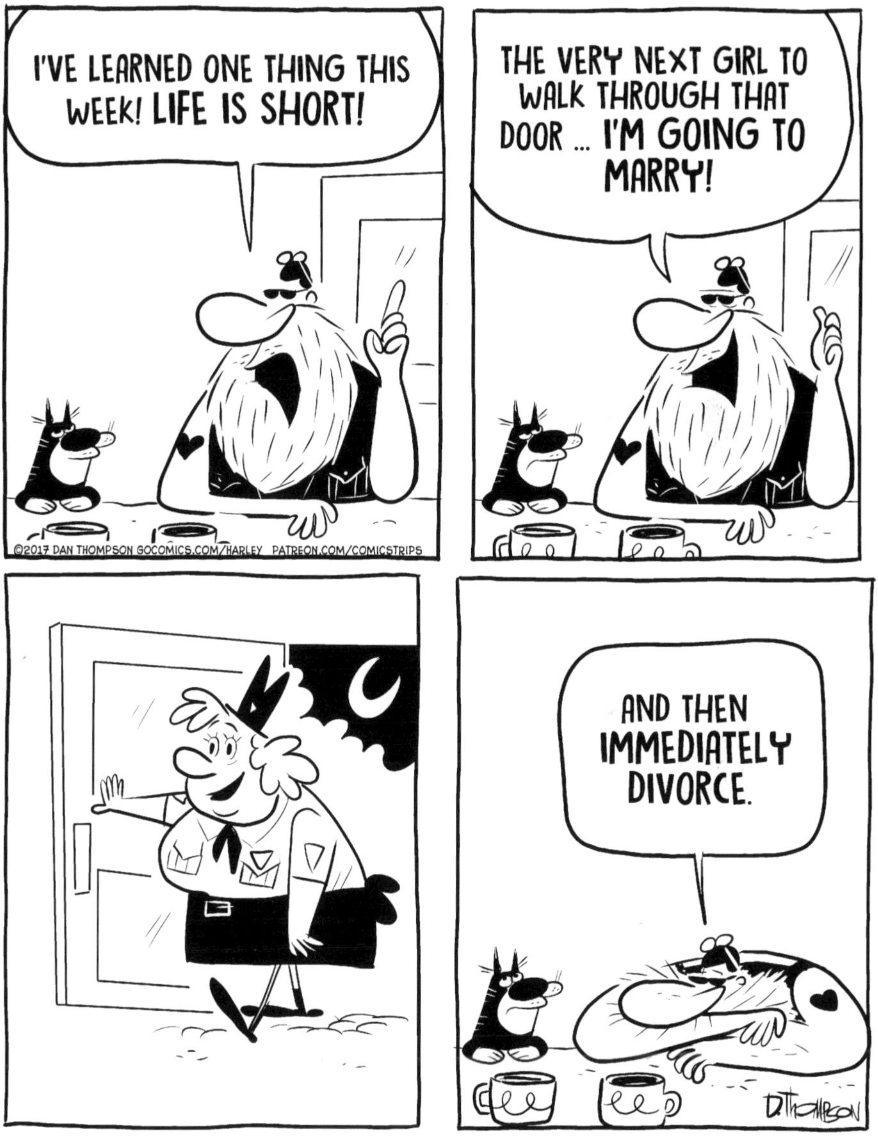
I'VE LEARNED ONE THING THIS WEEK! LIFE IS SHORT!
©2017 DAN THOMPSON GOCOMICS.COM/HARLEY PATREON.COM/COMICSTRIPS
THE VERY NEXT GIRL TO WALK THROUGH THAT DOOR ... I'M GOING TO MARRY!
AND THEN IMMEDIATELY DIVORCE.
D. THOMPSON

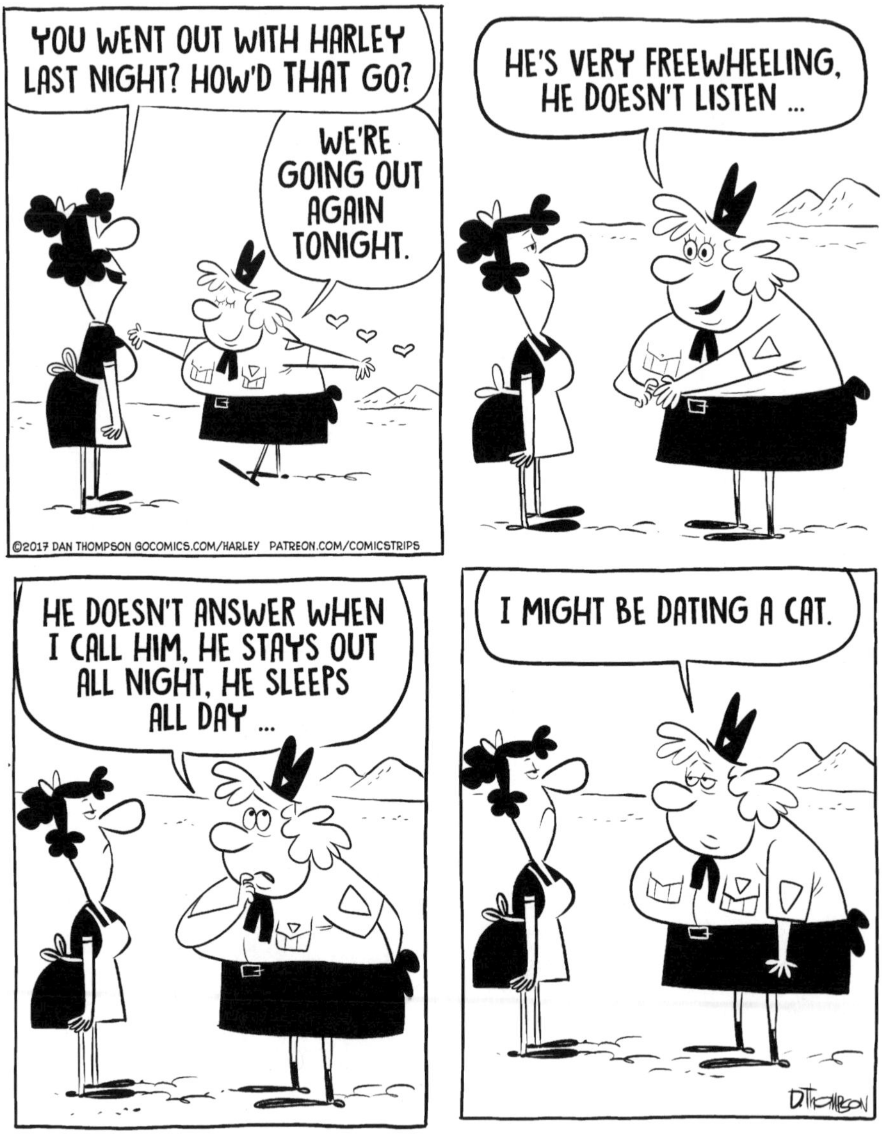
YOU WENT OUT WITH HARLEY LAST NIGHT? HOW'D THAT GO?
WE'RE GOING OUT AGAIN TONIGHT.
©2017 DAN THOMPSON GOCOMICS.COM/HARLEY PATREON.COM/COMICSTRIPS
HE'S VERY FREEWHEELING, HE DOESN'T LISTEN ...
HE DOESN'T ANSWER WHEN I CALL HIM, HE STAYS OUT ALL NIGHT, HE SLEEPS ALL DAY ...
I MIGHT BE DATING A CAT.
D.THOMPSON

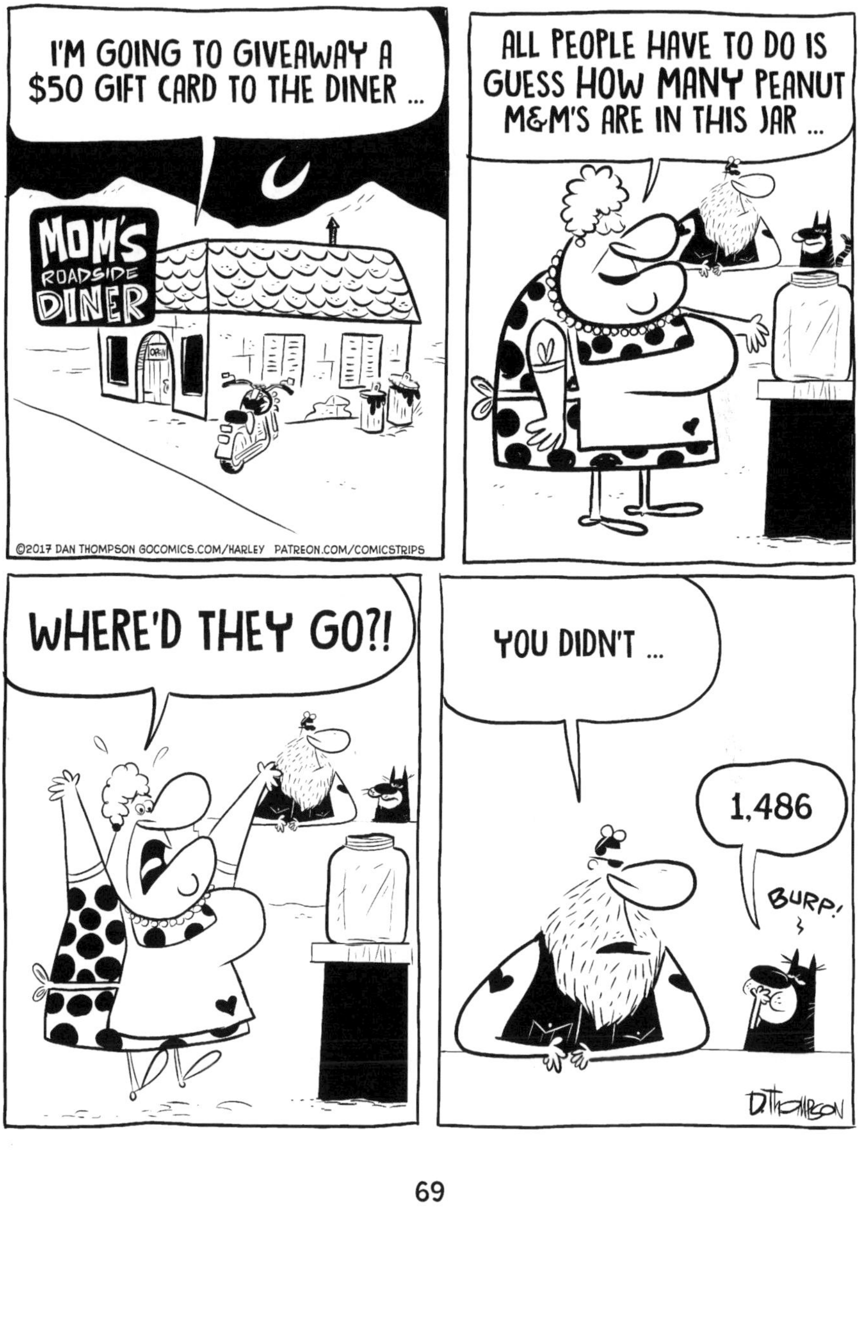
I'M GOING TO GIVEAWAY A $50 GIFT CARD TO THE DINER ...
MOM'S ROADSIDE DINER
OPEN
©2017 DAN THOMPSON GOCOMICS.COM/HARLEY PATREON.COM/COMICSTRIPS
ALL PEOPLE HAVE TO DO IS GUESS HOW MANY PEANUT M&M'S ARE IN THIS JAR ...
WHERE'D THEY GO?!
YOU DIDN'T ...
1,486
BURP!
D. THOMPSON

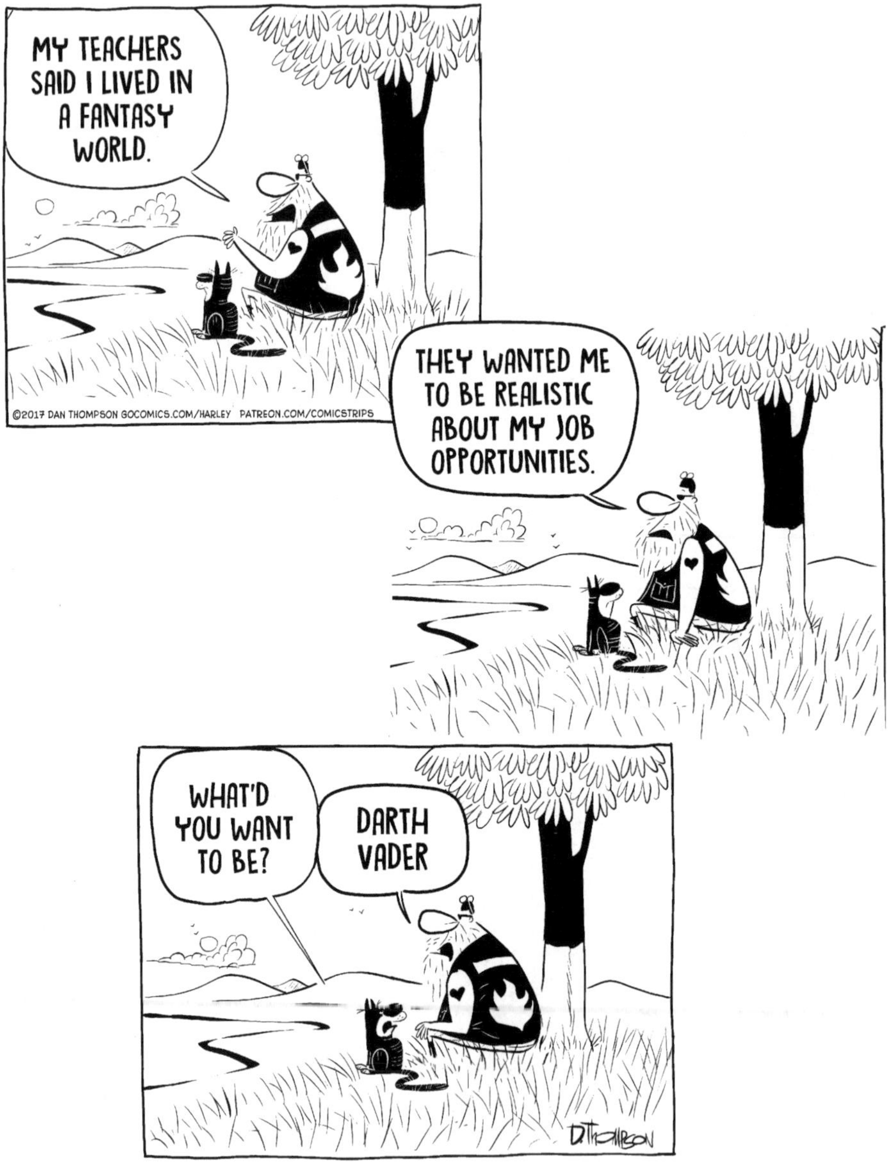
MY TEACHERS SAID I LIVED IN A FANTASY WORLD.
©2017 DAN THOMPSON GOCOMICS.COM/HARLEY PATREON.COM/COMICSTRIPS
THEY WANTED ME TO BE REALISTIC ABOUT MY JOB OPPORTUNITIES.
WHAT'D YOU WANT TO BE?
DARTH VADER
D. THOMPSON

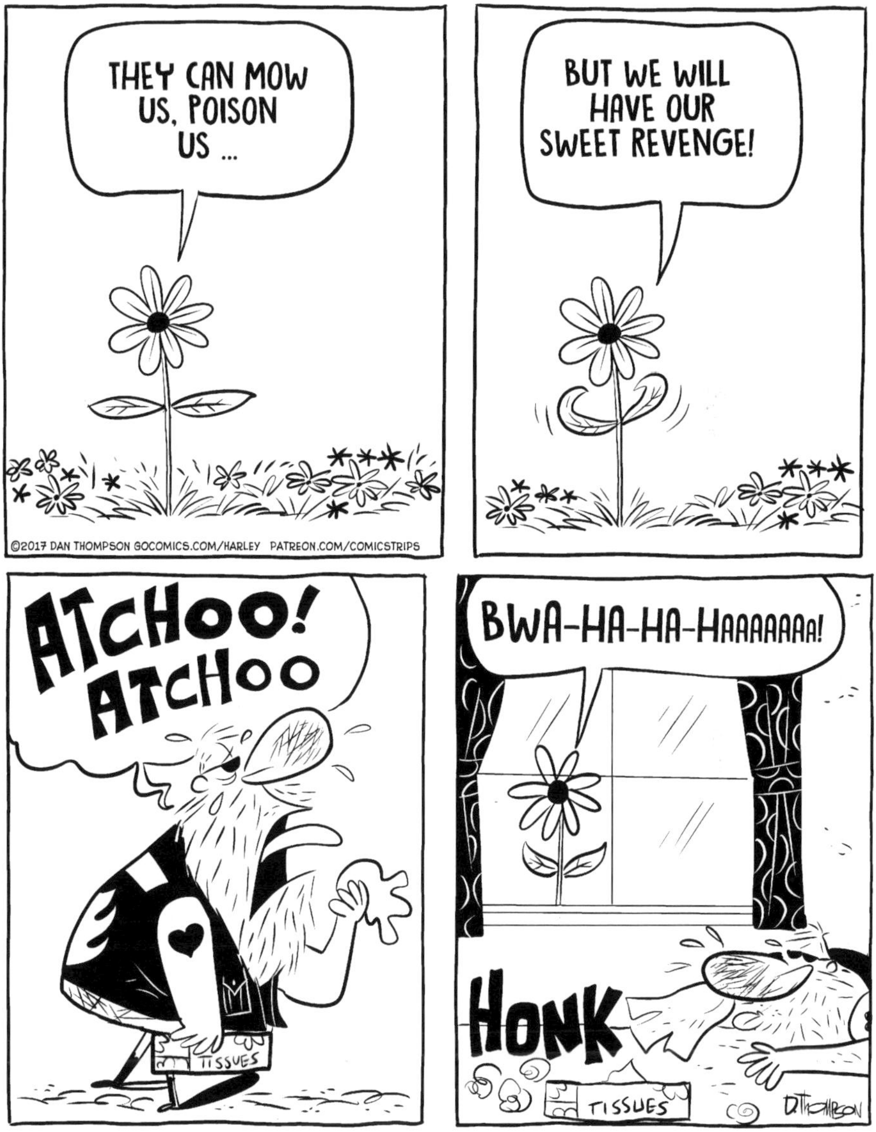
THEY CAN MOW US, POISON US ...
©2017 DAN THOMPSON GOCOMICS.COM/HARLEY PATREON.COM/COMICSTRIPS
BUT WE WILL HAVE OUR SWEET REVENGE!
ATCHOO! ATCHOO
TISSUES
BWA-HA-HA-HAAAAAAA!
HONK
TISSUES
D THOMPSON

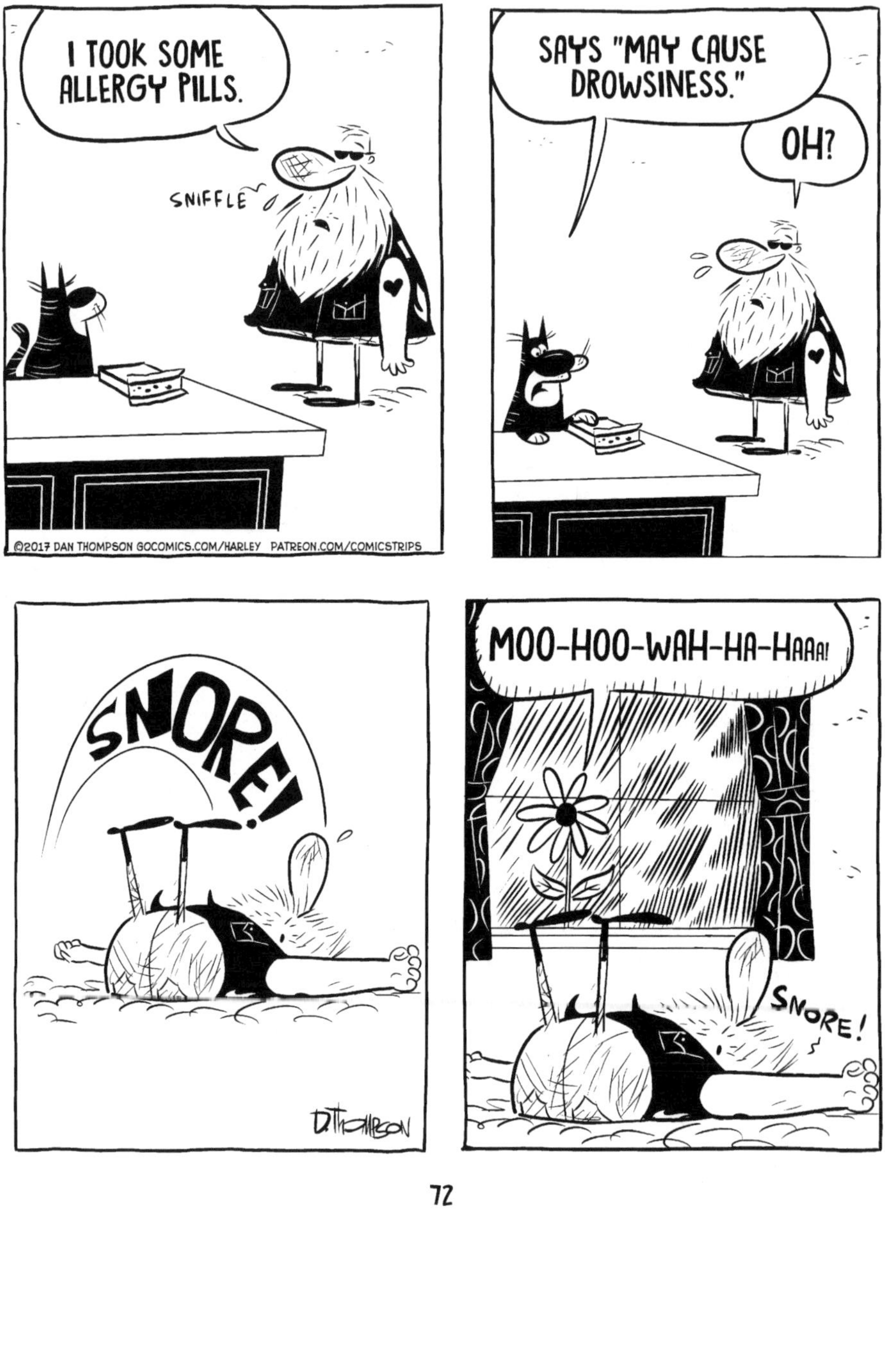
I TOOK SOME ALLERGY PILLS.
SNIFFLE
©2017 DAN THOMPSON GOCOMICS.COM/HARLEY PATREON.COM/COMICSTRIPS
SAYS "MAY CAUSE DROWSINESS."
OH?
SNORE!
D. THOMPSON
MOO-HOO-WAH-HA-HAAA!
SNORE!

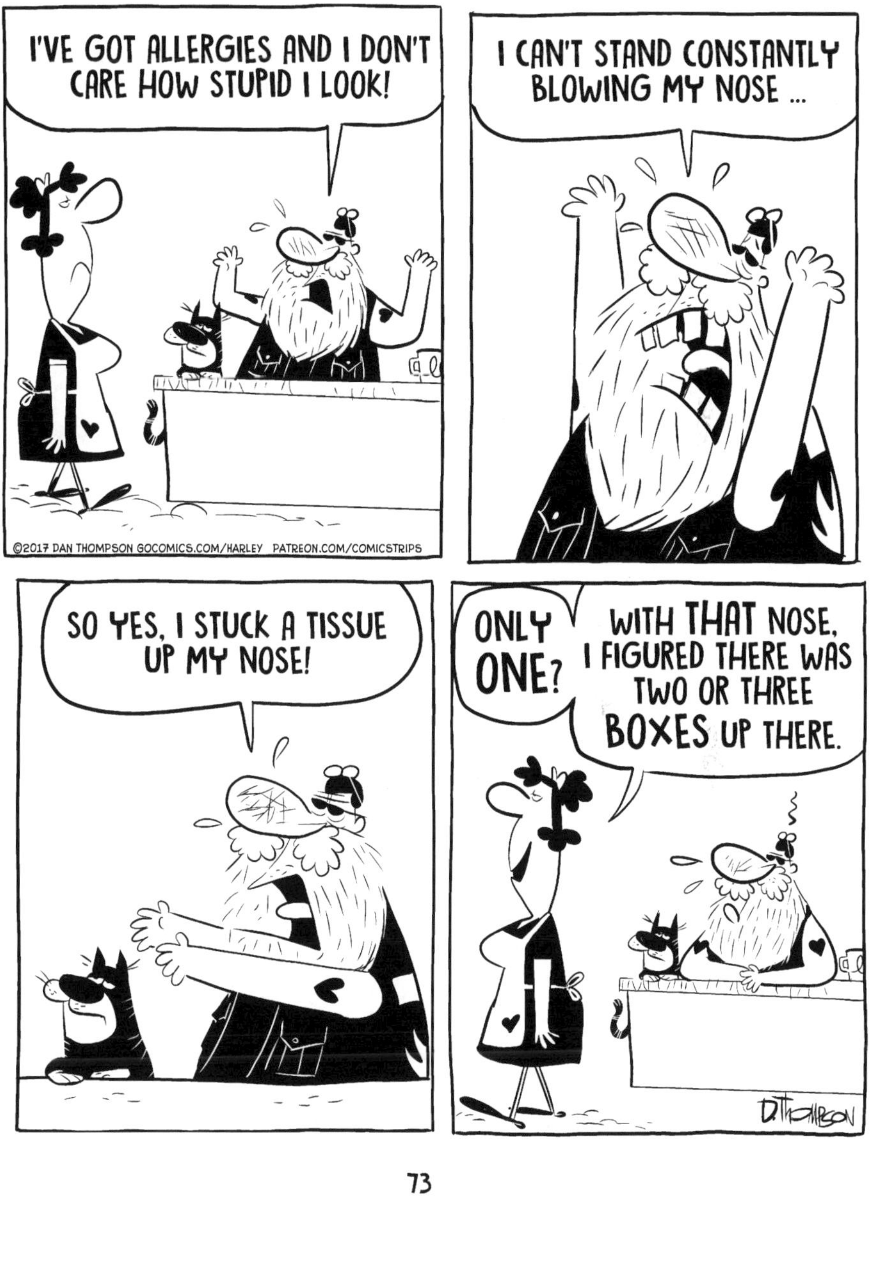
I'VE GOT ALLERGIES AND I DON'T CARE HOW STUPID I LOOK!
©2017 DAN THOMPSON GOCOMICS.COM/HARLEY PATREON.COM/COMICSTRIPS
I CAN'T STAND CONSTANTLY BLOWING MY NOSE ...
SO YES, I STUCK A TISSUE UP MY NOSE!
ONLY ONE?
WITH THAT NOSE, I FIGURED THERE WAS TWO OR THREE BOXES UP THERE.
D. THOMPSON

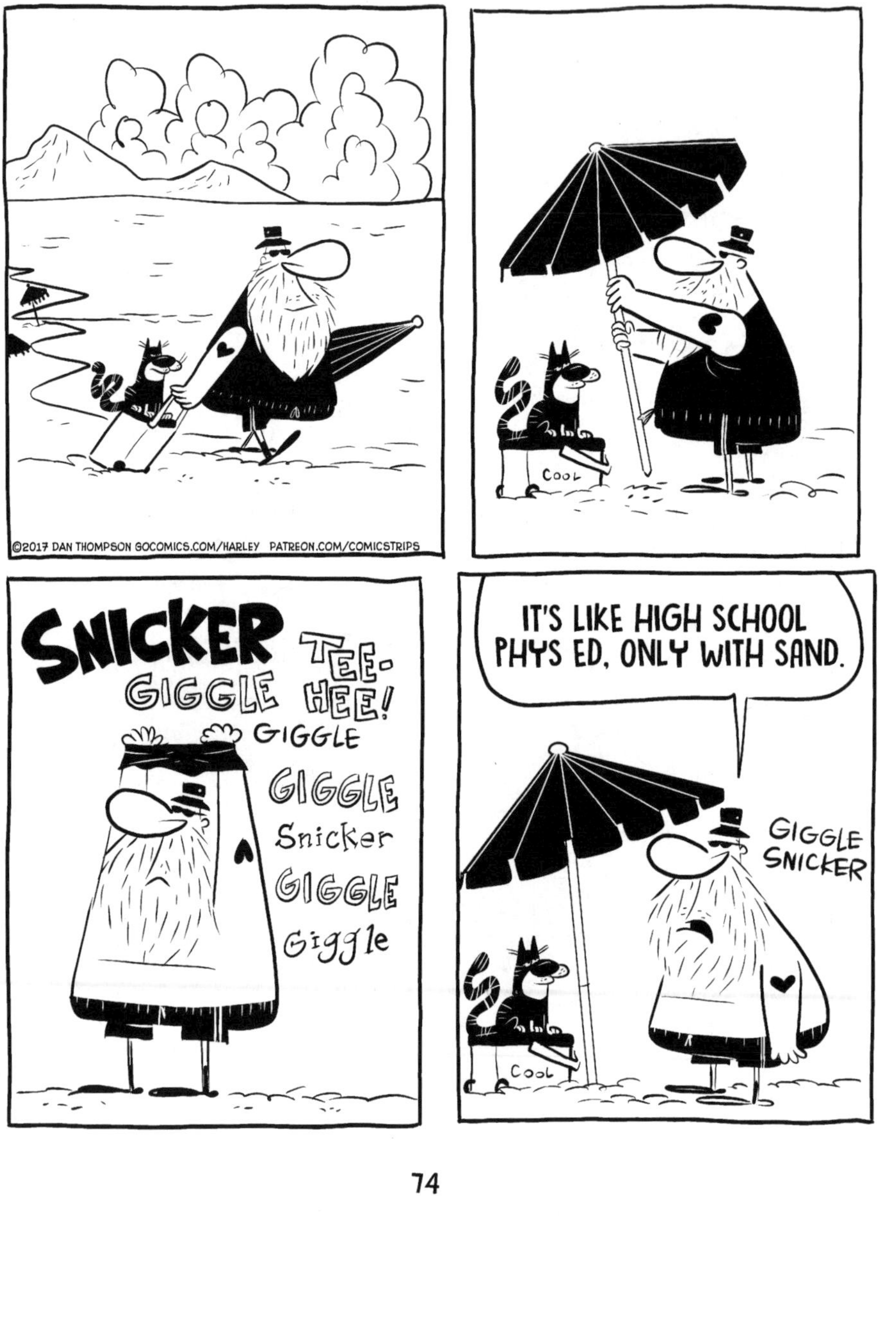
©2017 DAN THOMPSON GOCOMICS.COM/HARLEY PATREON.COM/COMICSTRIPS
COOL
SNICKER
TEE-HEE!
GIGGLE
GIGGLE
GIGGLE
Snicker
GIGGLE
Giggle
IT'S LIKE HIGH SCHOOL PHYS ED, ONLY WITH SAND.
GIGGLE SNICKER
COOL

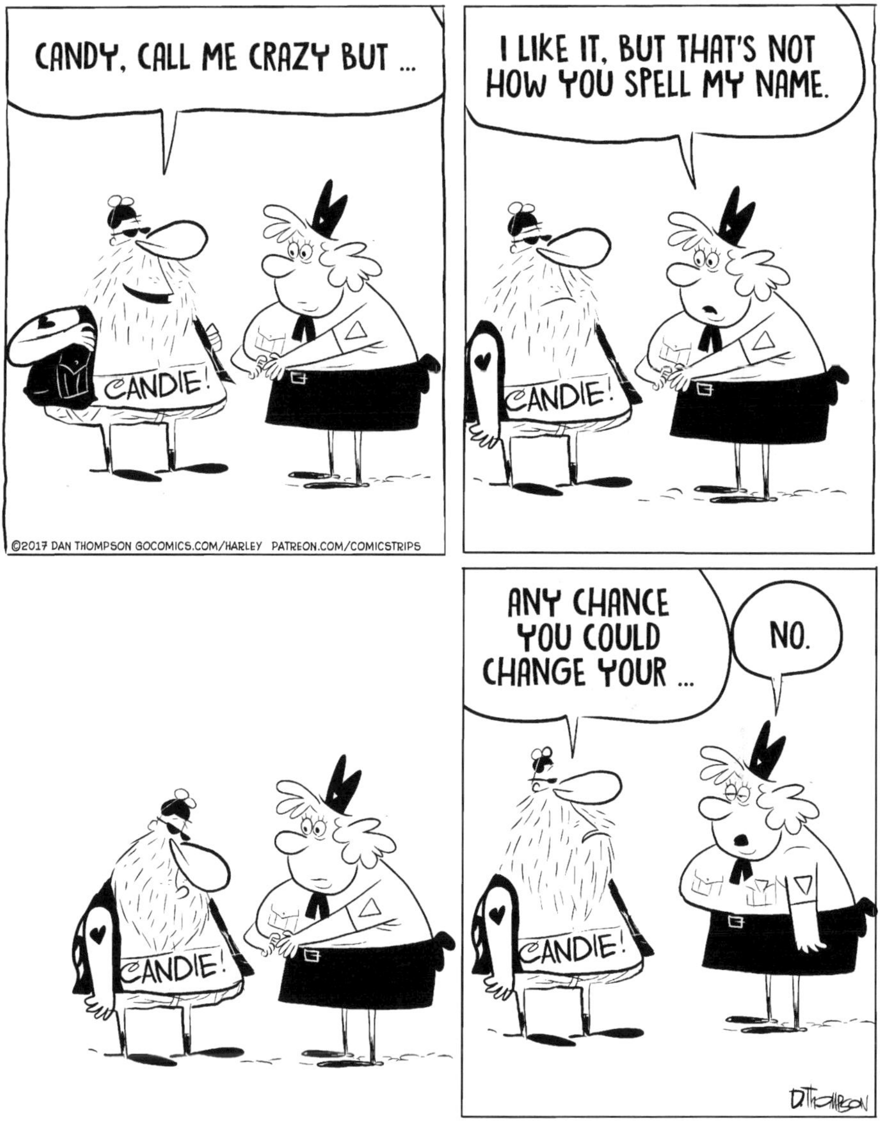
CANDY, CALL ME CRAZY BUT ...
CANDIE!
©2017 DAN THOMPSON GOCOMICS.COM/HARLEY PATREON.COM/COMICSTRIPS
I LIKE IT, BUT THAT'S NOT HOW YOU SPELL MY NAME.
CANDIE!
CANDIE!
ANY CHANCE YOU COULD CHANGE YOUR ...
NO.
CANDIE!
D. THOMPSON

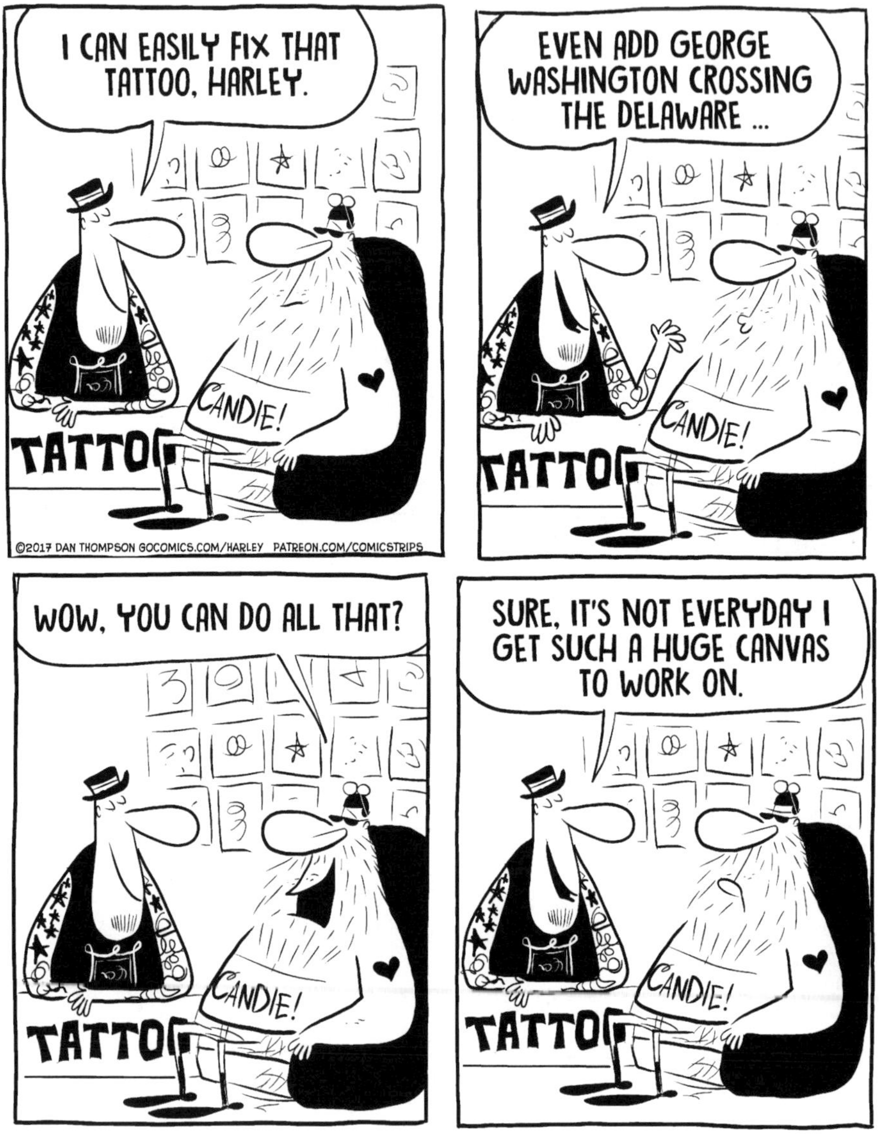
I CAN EASILY FIX THAT TATTOO, HARLEY.
TATTOO
CANDIE!
©2017 DAN THOMPSON GOCOMICS.COM/HARLEY PATREON.COM/COMICSTRIPS
EVEN ADD GEORGE WASHINGTON CROSSING THE DELAWARE ...
WOW, YOU CAN DO ALL THAT?
SURE, IT'S NOT EVERYDAY I GET SUCH A HUGE CANVAS TO WORK ON.

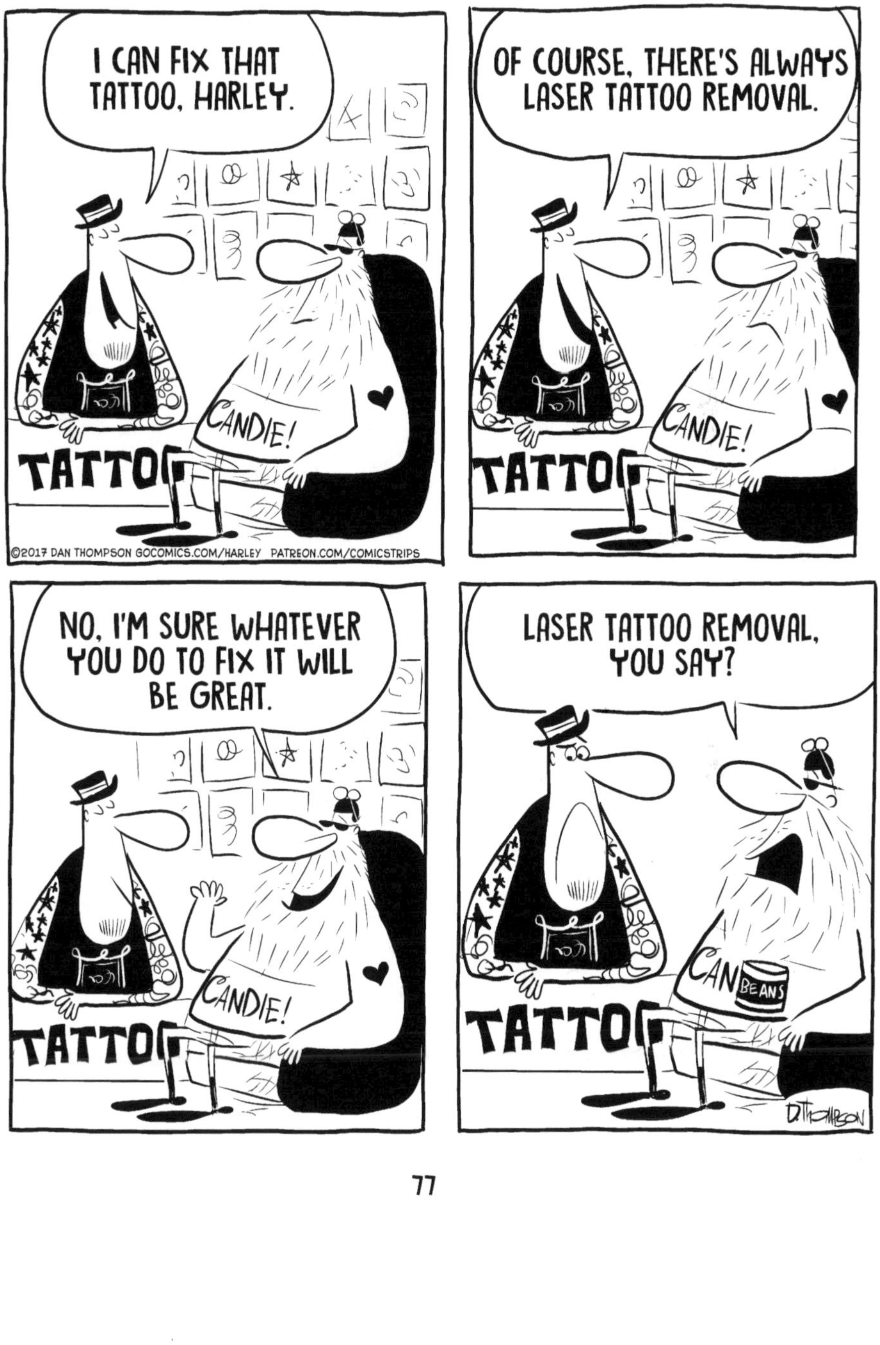
I CAN FIX THAT TATTOO, HARLEY.
TATTOO
CANDIE!
©2017 DAN THOMPSON GOCOMICS.COM/HARLEY PATREON.COM/COMICSTRIPS
OF COURSE, THERE'S ALWAYS LASER TATTOO REMOVAL.
TATTOO
CANDIE!
NO, I'M SURE WHATEVER YOU DO TO FIX IT WILL BE GREAT.
TATTOO
CANDIE!
LASER TATTOO REMOVAL, YOU SAY?
TATTOO
CAN
BEANS
D THOMPSON

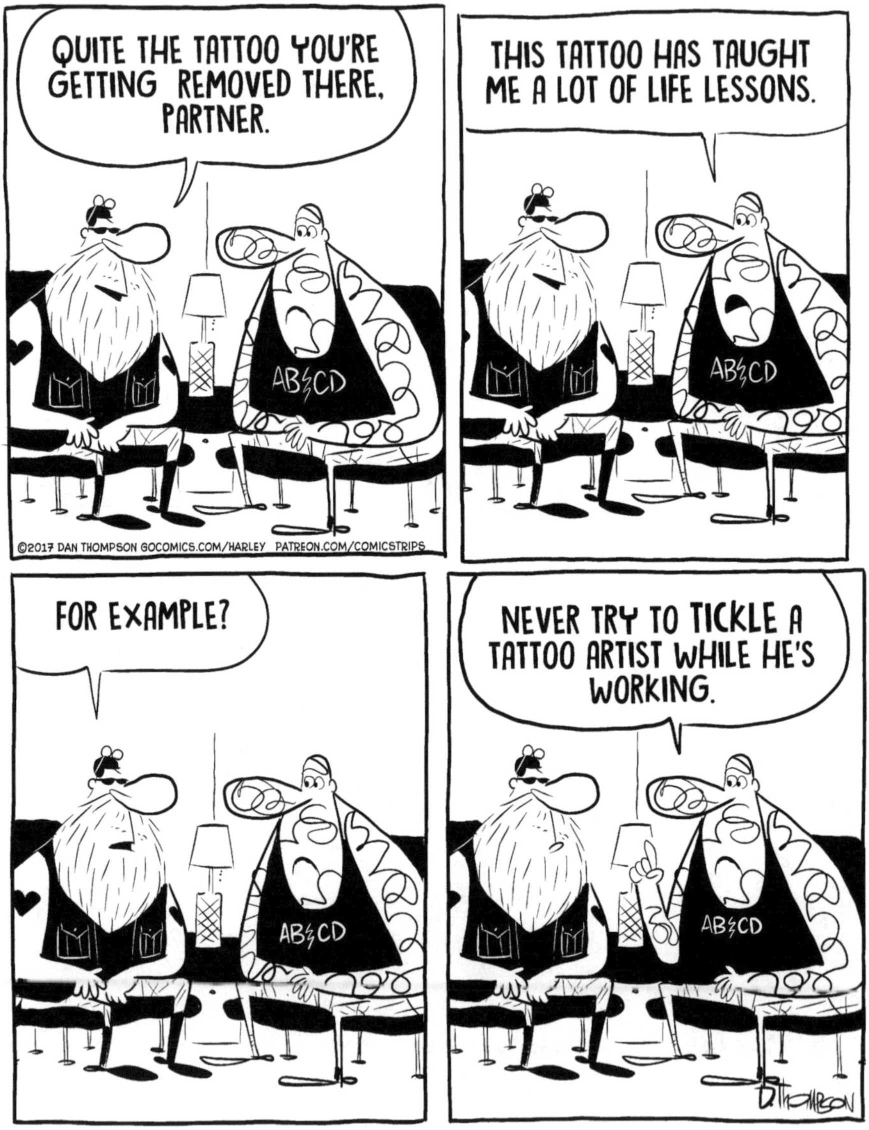
QUITE THE TATTOO YOU'RE GETTING REMOVED THERE, PARTNER.
AB⚡CD
©2017 DAN THOMPSON GOCOMICS.COM/HARLEY PATREON.COM/COMICSTRIPS
THIS TATTOO HAS TAUGHT ME A LOT OF LIFE LESSONS.
AB⚡CD
FOR EXAMPLE?
AB⚡CD
NEVER TRY TO TICKLE A TATTOO ARTIST WHILE HE'S WORKING.
AB⚡CD
D. THOMPSON

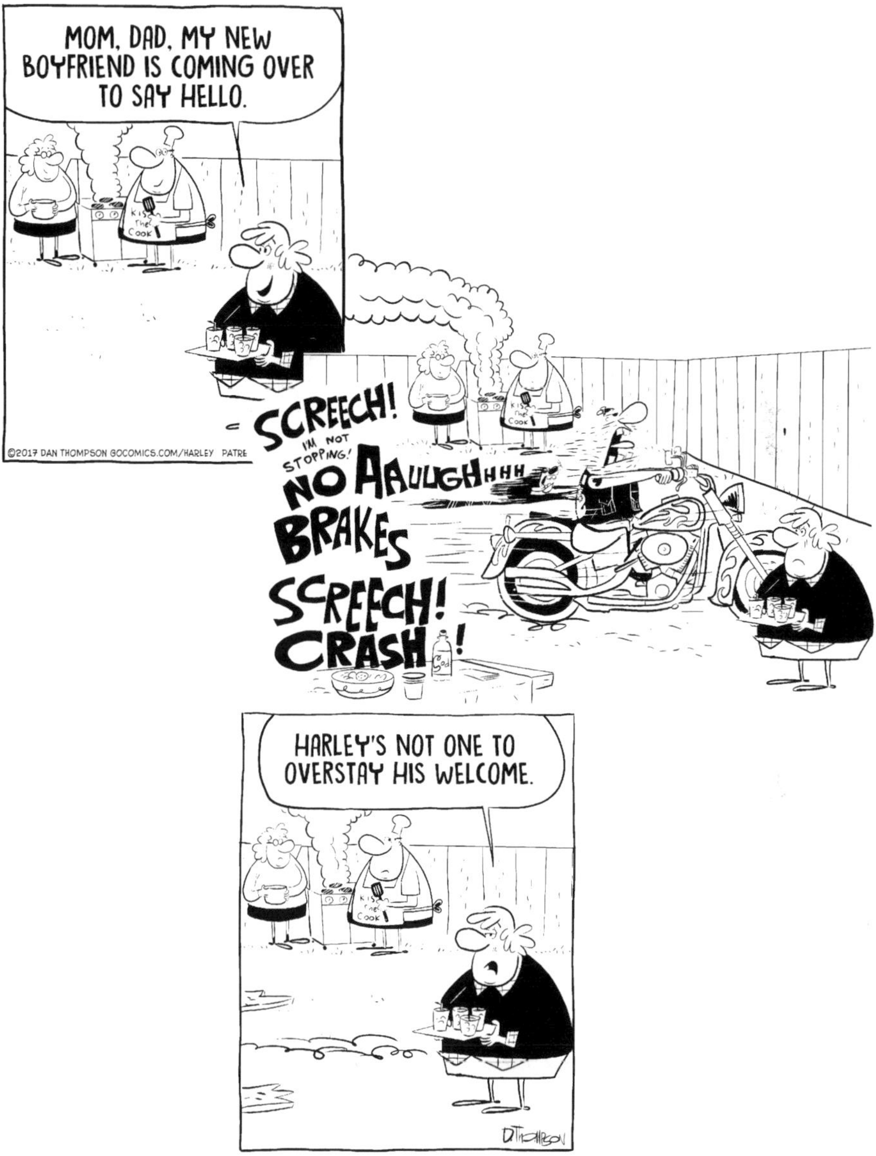

MOM, DAD, MY NEW BOYFRIEND IS COMING OVER TO SAY HELLO.
©2017 DAN THOMPSON GOCOMICS.COM/HARLEY PATRE
SCREECH!
I'M NOT STOPPING!
NO BRAKES
AAUUGHHHH
SCREECH!
CRASH!
HARLEY'S NOT ONE TO OVERSTAY HIS WELCOME.
D.THOMPSON

HAW-
HAW-
HAW!
©2017 DAN THOMPSON GOCOMICS.COM/HARLEY PATREON.COM/COMICSTRIPS
HOO-HOO-HOO!
WHAT'S SO FUNNY?
I ASKED IF DATING DEPUTY CANDY WOULD RUIN MY REPUTATION AS A WILD MAN BIKER.
MOM'S ROADSIDE DINER
S
P
D. THOMPSON

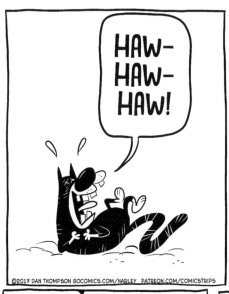

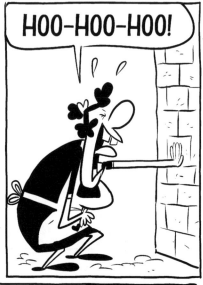

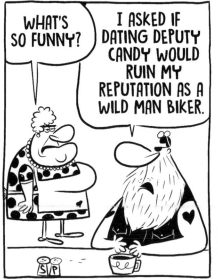

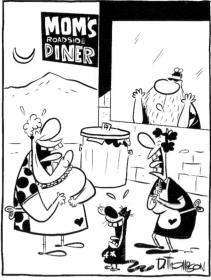

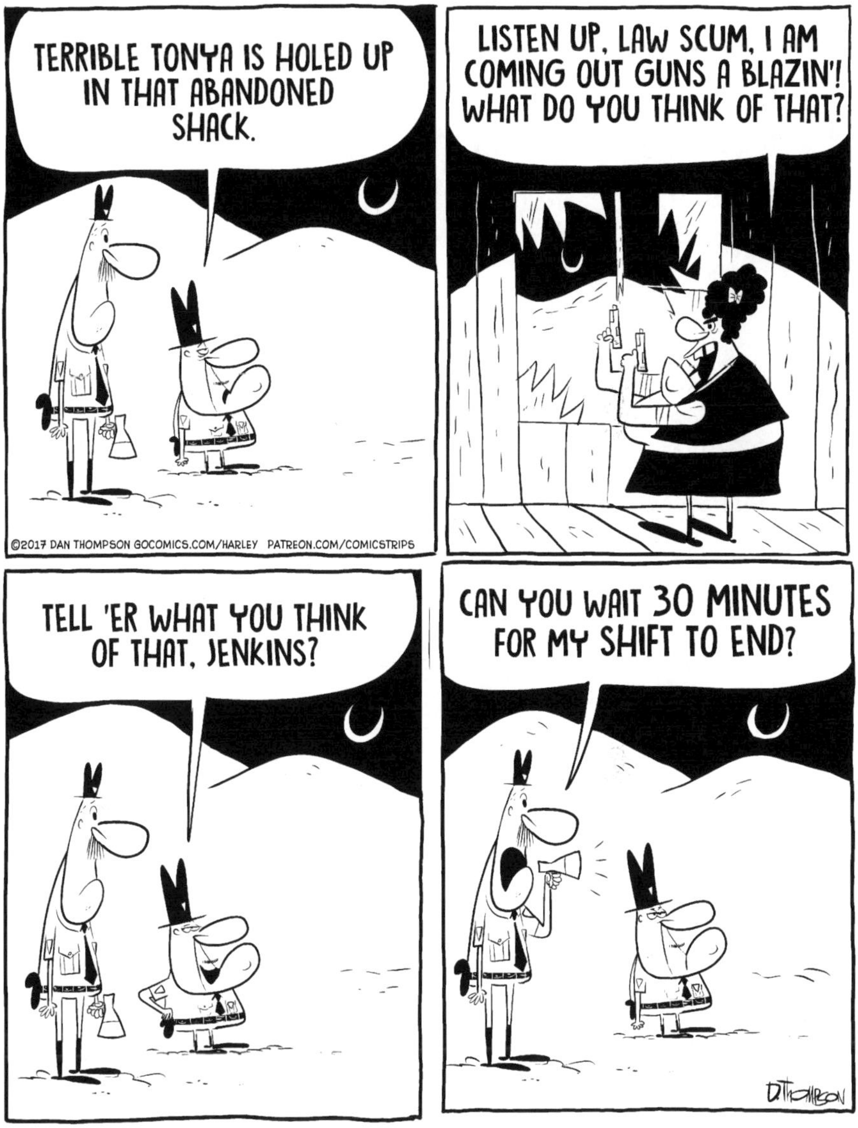
TERRIBLE TONYA IS HOLED UP IN THAT ABANDONED SHACK.
©2017 DAN THOMPSON GOCOMICS.COM/HARLEY PATREON.COM/COMICSTRIPS
LISTEN UP, LAW SCUM, I AM COMING OUT GUNS A BLAZIN'! WHAT DO YOU THINK OF THAT?
TELL 'ER WHAT YOU THINK OF THAT, JENKINS?
CAN YOU WAIT 30 MINUTES FOR MY SHIFT TO END?
D. THOMPSON

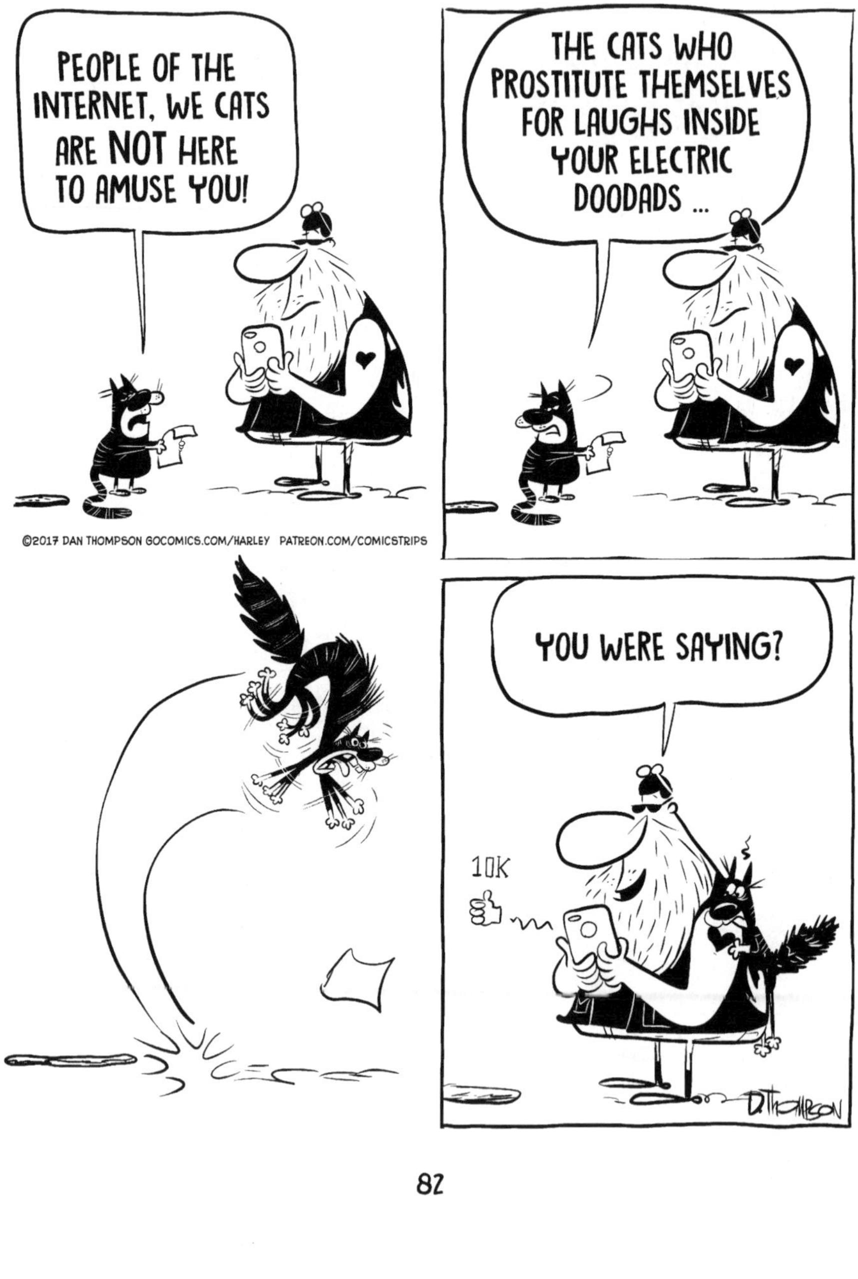
PEOPLE OF THE INTERNET, WE CATS ARE NOT HERE TO AMUSE YOU!
©2017 DAN THOMPSON GOCOMICS.COM/HARLEY PATREON.COM/COMICSTRIPS
THE CATS WHO PROSTITUTE THEMSELVES FOR LAUGHS INSIDE YOUR ELECTRIC DOODADS ...
10K
YOU WERE SAYING?
D.THOMPSON

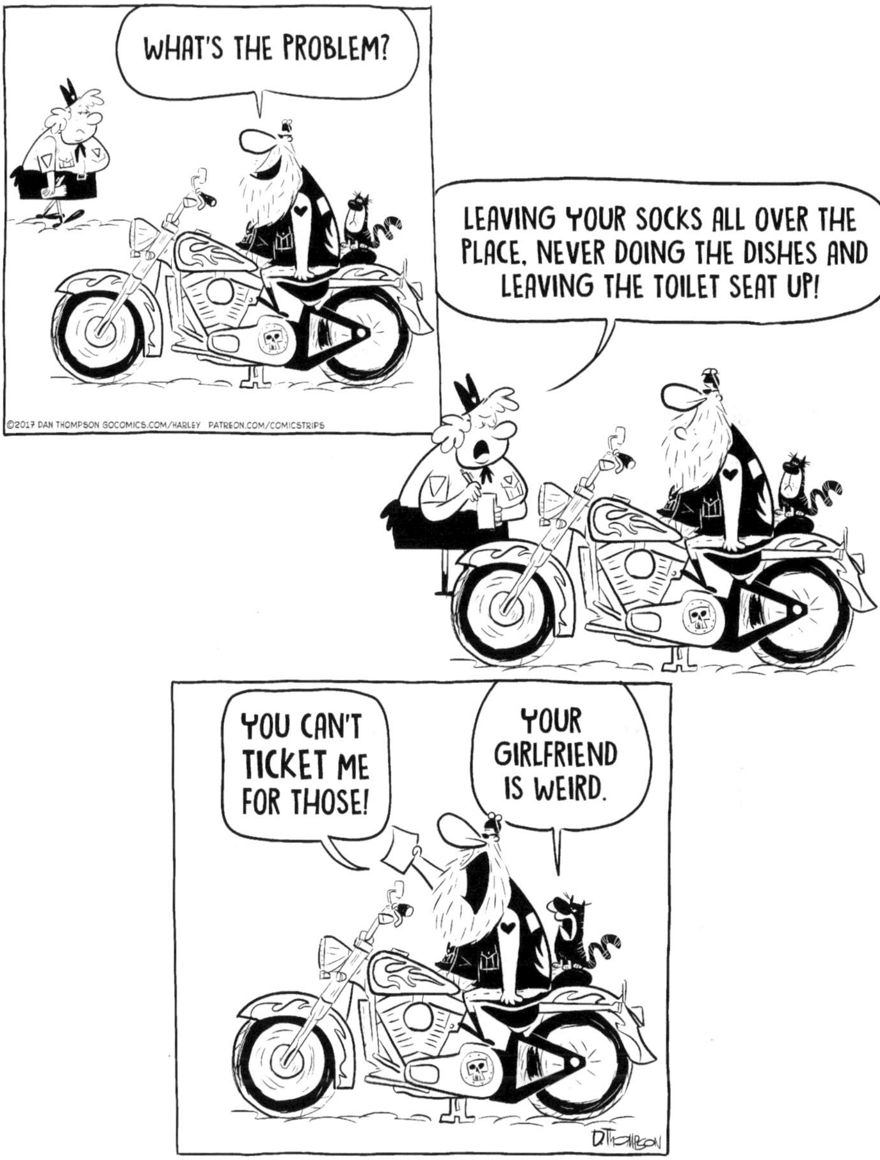
WHAT'S THE PROBLEM?
LEAVING YOUR SOCKS ALL OVER THE PLACE, NEVER DOING THE DISHES AND LEAVING THE TOILET SEAT UP!
YOU CAN'T TICKET ME FOR THOSE!
YOUR GIRLFRIEND IS WEIRD.
©2017 DAN THOMPSON GOCOMICS.COM/HARLEY PATREON.COM/COMICSTRIPS
D.THOMPSON

I HEARD YOU WERE IN A TOUGH GANG ONCE.
WHAT WAS THE NAME?
THE MERLOTS.
SOUNDS MORE LIKE A WINE CLUB THAN A GANG.
YOU SHOULD HAVE SEEN THOSE LADIES AFTER THEIR SECOND GLASS.
©2017 DAN THOMPSON GOCOMICS.COM/HARLEY PATREON.COM/COMICSTRIPS
D.THOMPSON

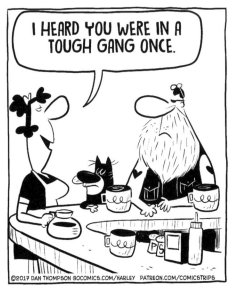

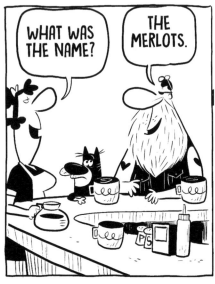

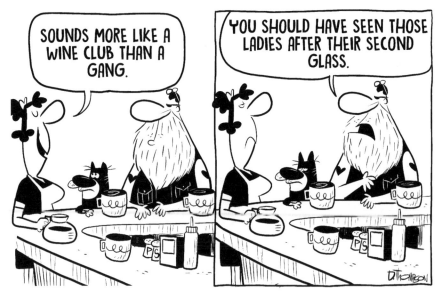

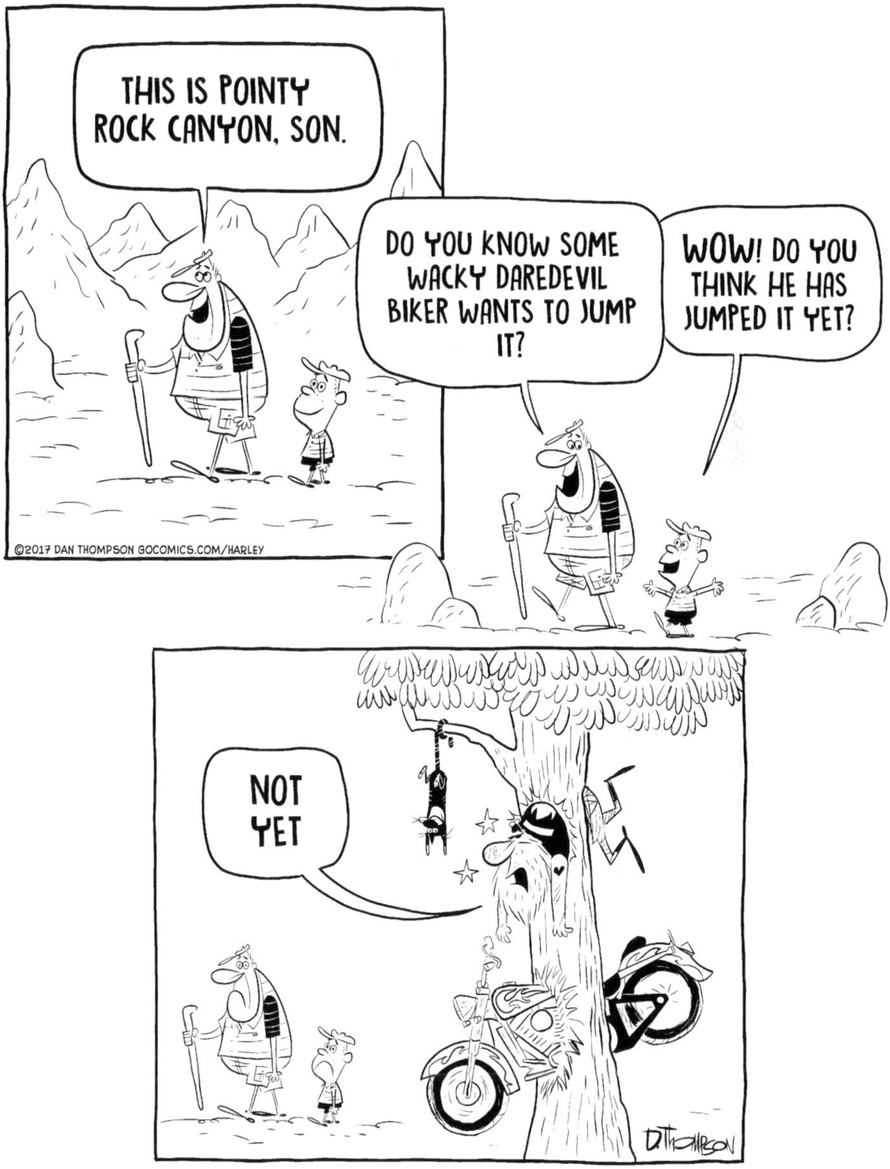
THIS IS POINTY ROCK CANYON, SON.
DO YOU KNOW SOME WACKY DAREDEVIL BIKER WANTS TO JUMP IT?
WOW! DO YOU THINK HE HAS JUMPED IT YET?
NOT YET
©2017 DAN THOMPSON GOCOMICS.COM/HARLEY
D. THOMPSON

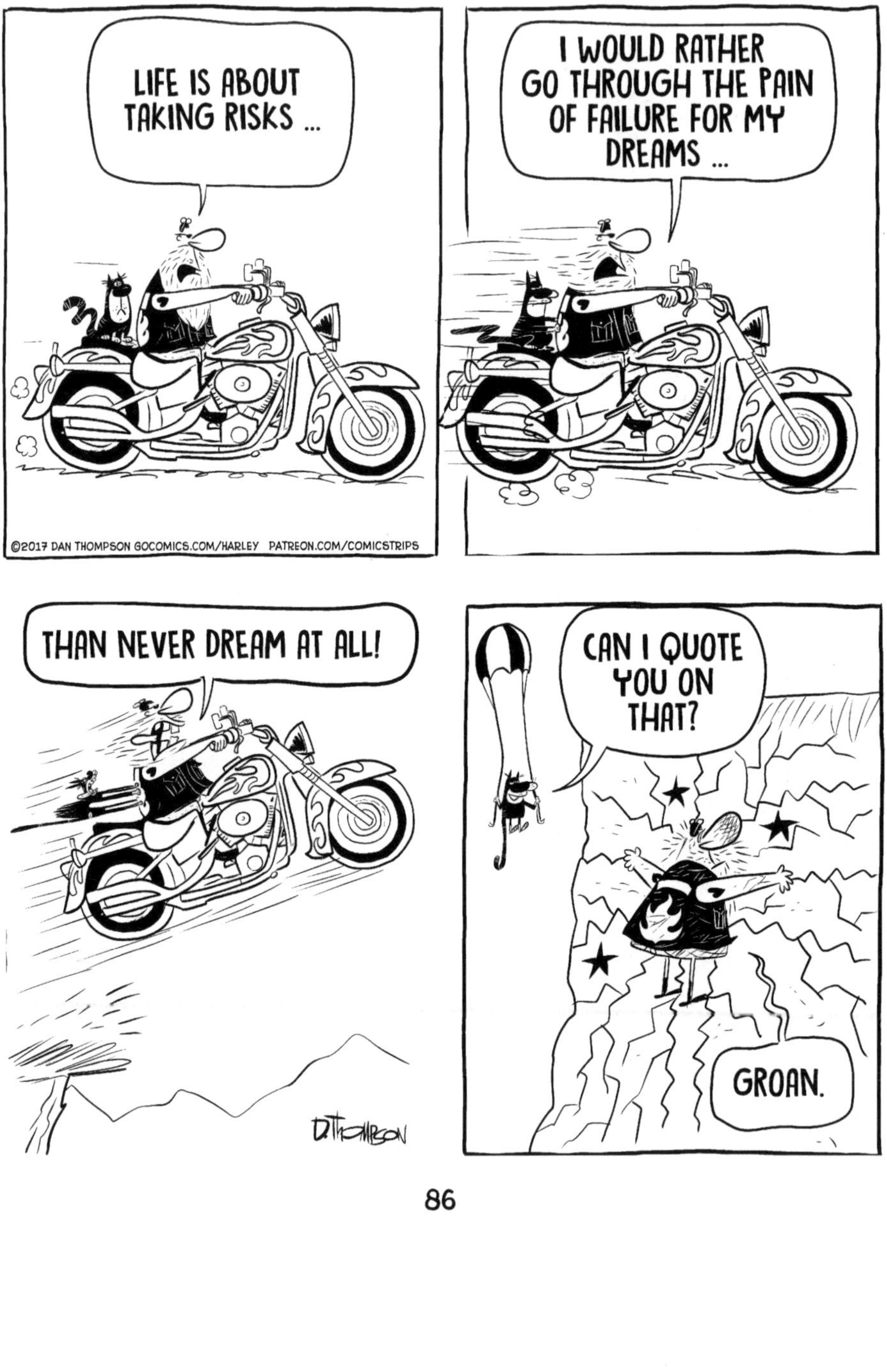
LIFE IS ABOUT TAKING RISKS ...
©2017 DAN THOMPSON GOCOMICS.COM/HARLEY PATREON.COM/COMICSTRIPS
I WOULD RATHER GO THROUGH THE PAIN OF FAILURE FOR MY DREAMS ...
THAN NEVER DREAM AT ALL!
D.THOMPSON
CAN I QUOTE YOU ON THAT?
GROAN.

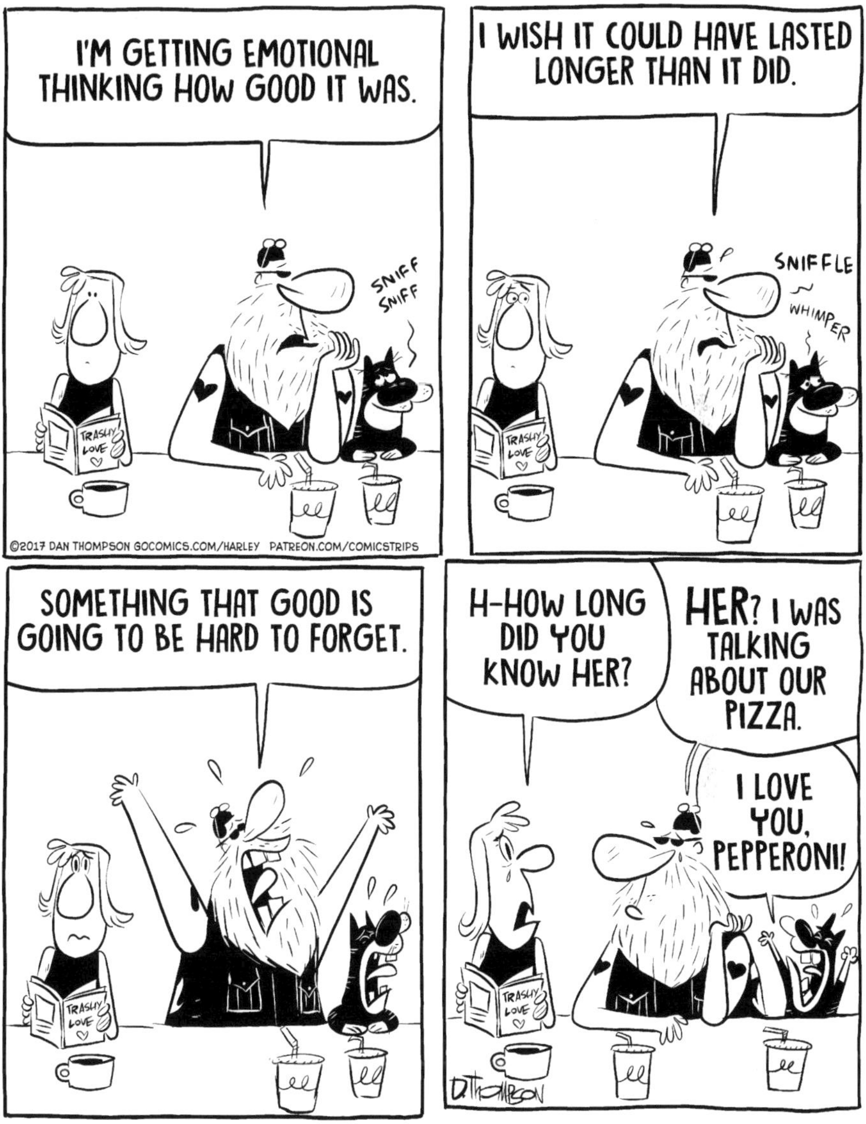
I'M GETTING EMOTIONAL THINKING HOW GOOD IT WAS.
SNIFF SNIFF
TRASHY LOVE
©2017 DAN THOMPSON GOCOMICS.COM/HARLEY PATREON.COM/COMICSTRIPS
I WISH IT COULD HAVE LASTED LONGER THAN IT DID.
SNIFFLE
WHIMPER
TRASHY LOVE
SOMETHING THAT GOOD IS GOING TO BE HARD TO FORGET.
TRASHY LOVE
H-HOW LONG DID YOU KNOW HER?
HER? I WAS TALKING ABOUT OUR PIZZA.
I LOVE YOU, PEPPERONI!
TRASHY LOVE
D. THOMPSON

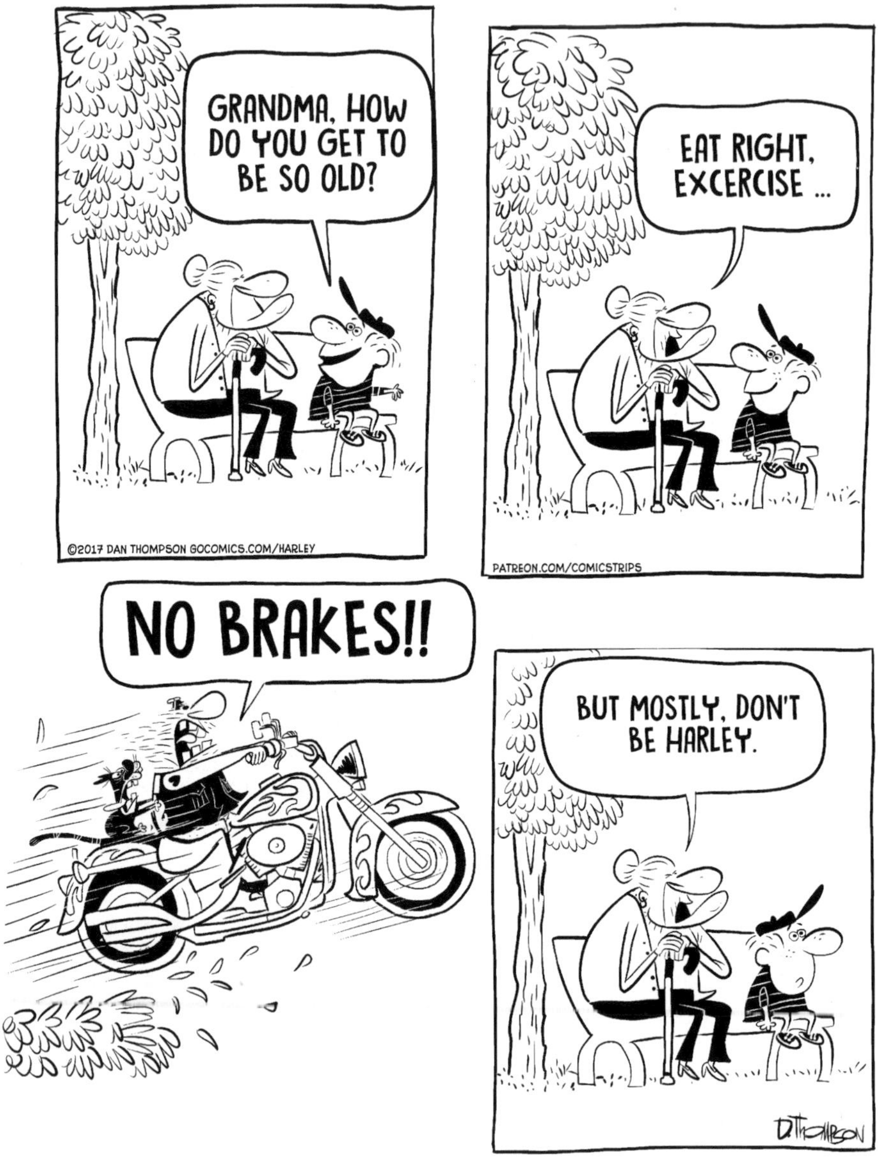
GRANDMA, HOW DO YOU GET TO BE SO OLD?
©2017 DAN THOMPSON GOCOMICS.COM/HARLEY
EAT RIGHT, EXCERCISE ...
PATREON.COM/COMICSTRIPS
NO BRAKES!!
BUT MOSTLY, DON'T BE HARLEY.
D. THOMPSON

YOU'RE TRYING TO BREAK MY FREE-WHEELING SPIRIT!
©2017 DAN THOMPSON GOCOMICS.COM/HARLEY PATREON.COM/COMICSTRIPS
I'LL DROP DEAD ON THIS CHAIN GANG BEFORE THAT HAPPENS!
DON'T DO THAT, HARLEY!
NOT UNTIL I GET MY POPCORN OUT OF THE MICROWAVE.
D. THOMPSON

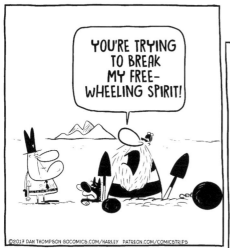

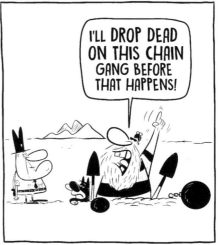

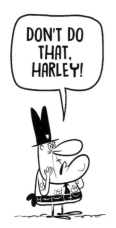

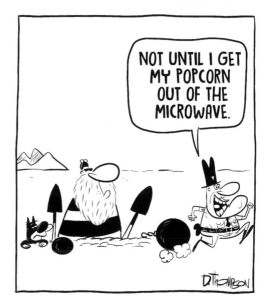

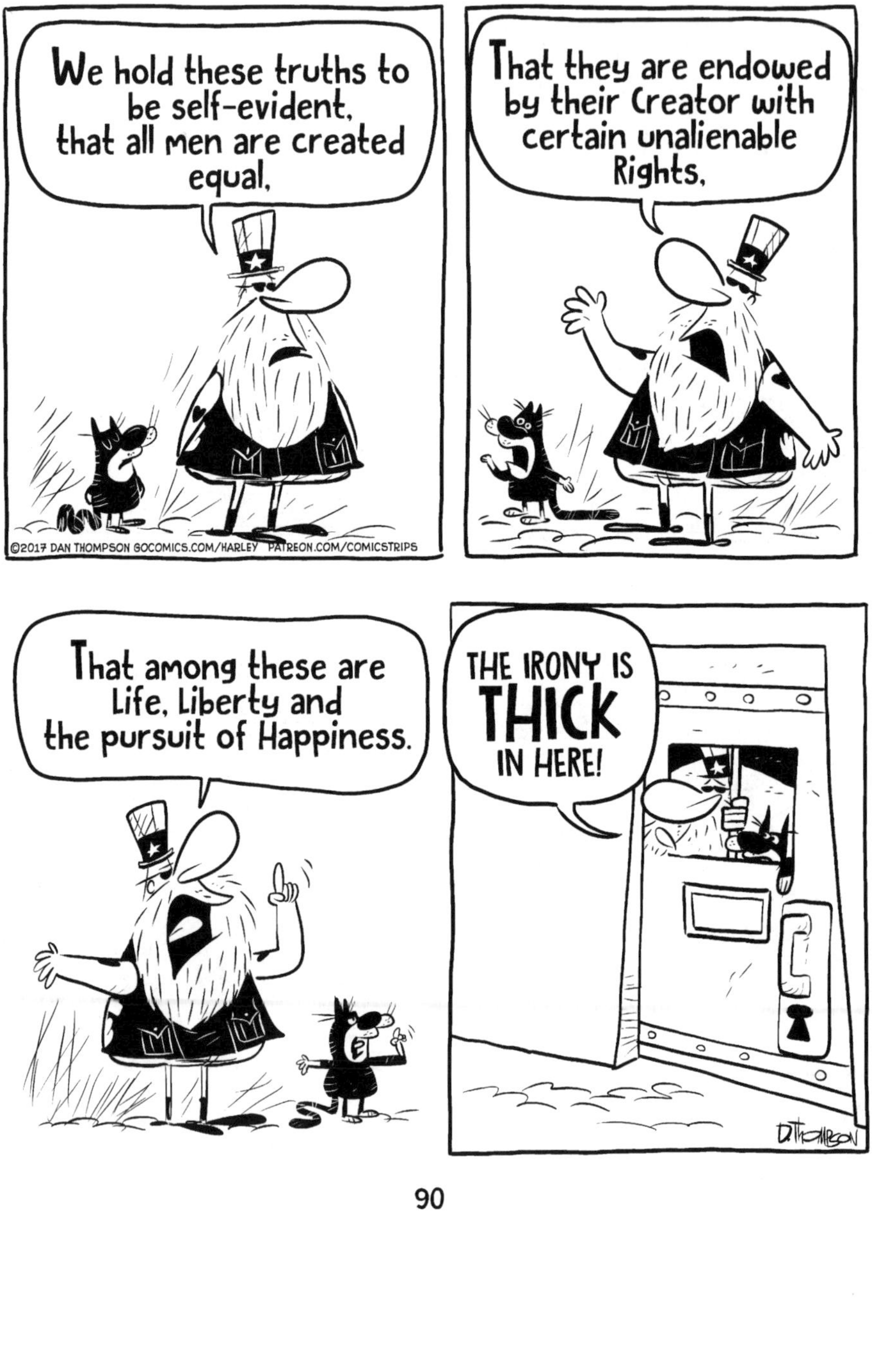
We hold these truths to be self-evident, that all men are created equal,
©2017 DAN THOMPSON GOCOMICS.COM/HARLEY PATREON.COM/COMICSTRIPS
That they are endowed by their Creator with certain unalienable Rights,
That among these are Life, Liberty and the pursuit of Happiness.
THE IRONY IS THICK IN HERE!
D. THOMPSON

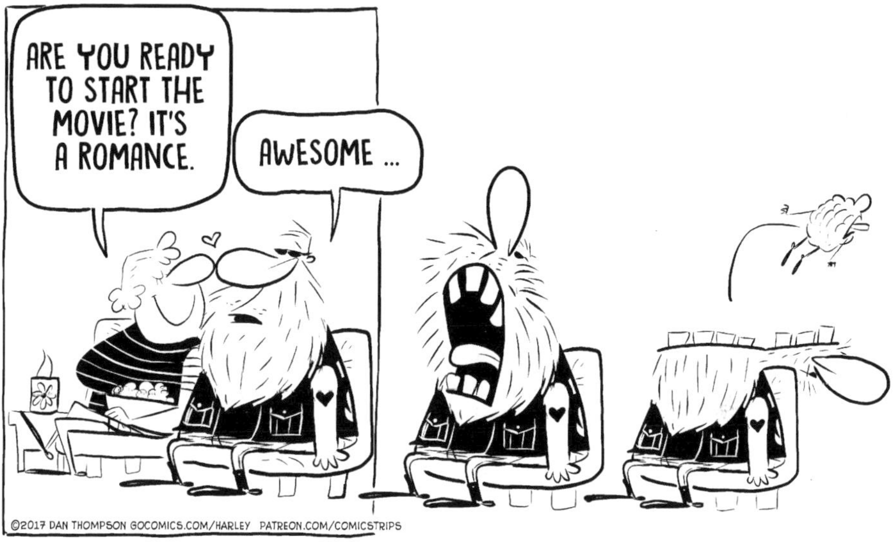
ARE YOU READY TO START THE MOVIE? IT'S A ROMANCE.
AWESOME ...
©2017 DAN THOMPSON GOCOMICS.COM/HARLEY PATREON.COM/COMICSTRIPS

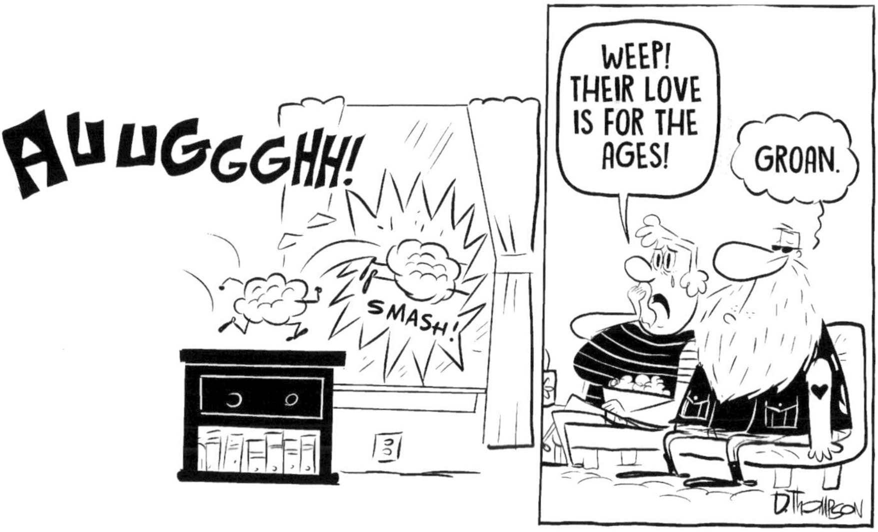
AUUGGGHH!
SMASH!
WEEP! THEIR LOVE IS FOR THE AGES!
GROAN.
D.THOMPSON

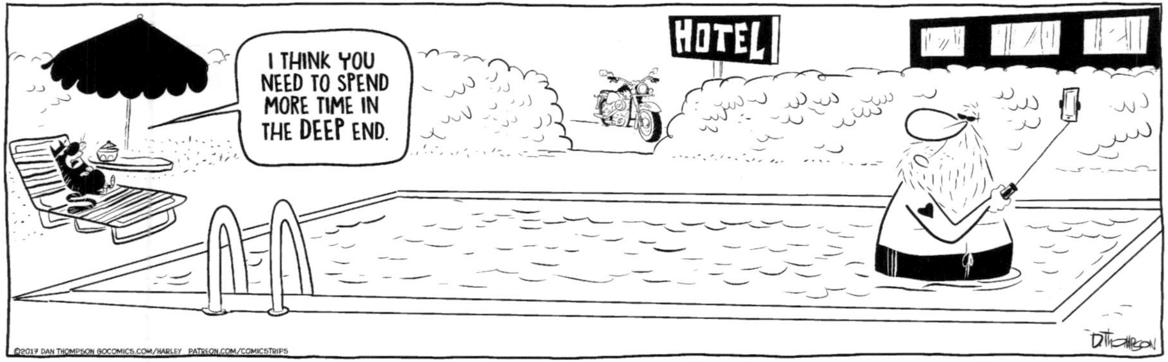
I THINK YOU NEED TO SPEND MORE TIME IN THE DEEP END.
HOTEL
©2017 DAN THOMPSON GOCOMICS.COM/HARLEY PATREON.COM/COMICSTRIPS
D.THOMPSON

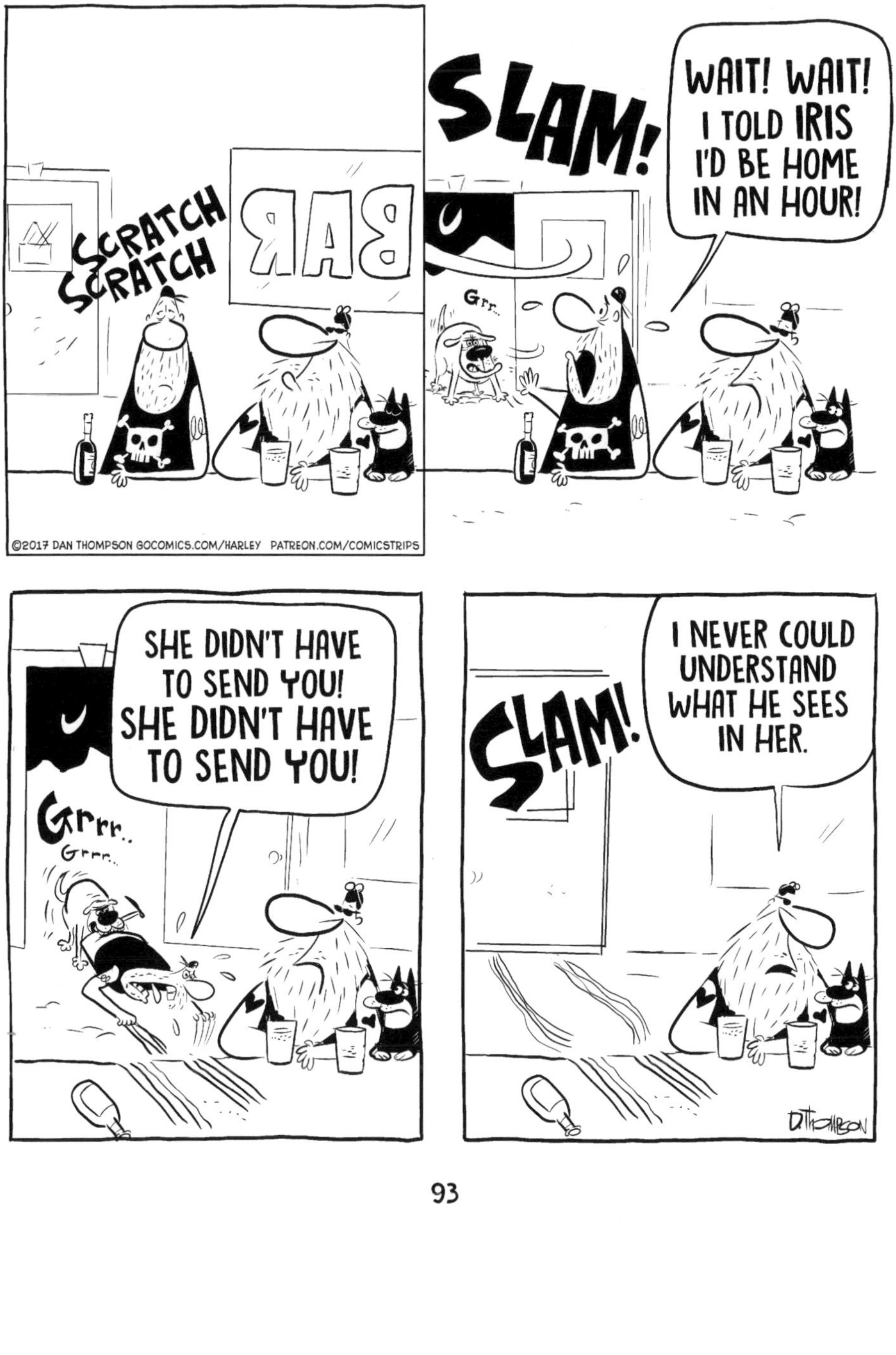
SCRATCH SCRATCH
BAR
SLAM!
WAIT! WAIT! I TOLD IRIS I'D BE HOME IN AN HOUR!
Grr..
©2017 DAN THOMPSON GOCOMICS.COM/HARLEY PATREON.COM/COMICSTRIPS
SHE DIDN'T HAVE TO SEND YOU! SHE DIDN'T HAVE TO SEND YOU!
Grrr..
Grrr..
SLAM!
I NEVER COULD UNDERSTAND WHAT HE SEES IN HER.
D. THOMPSON

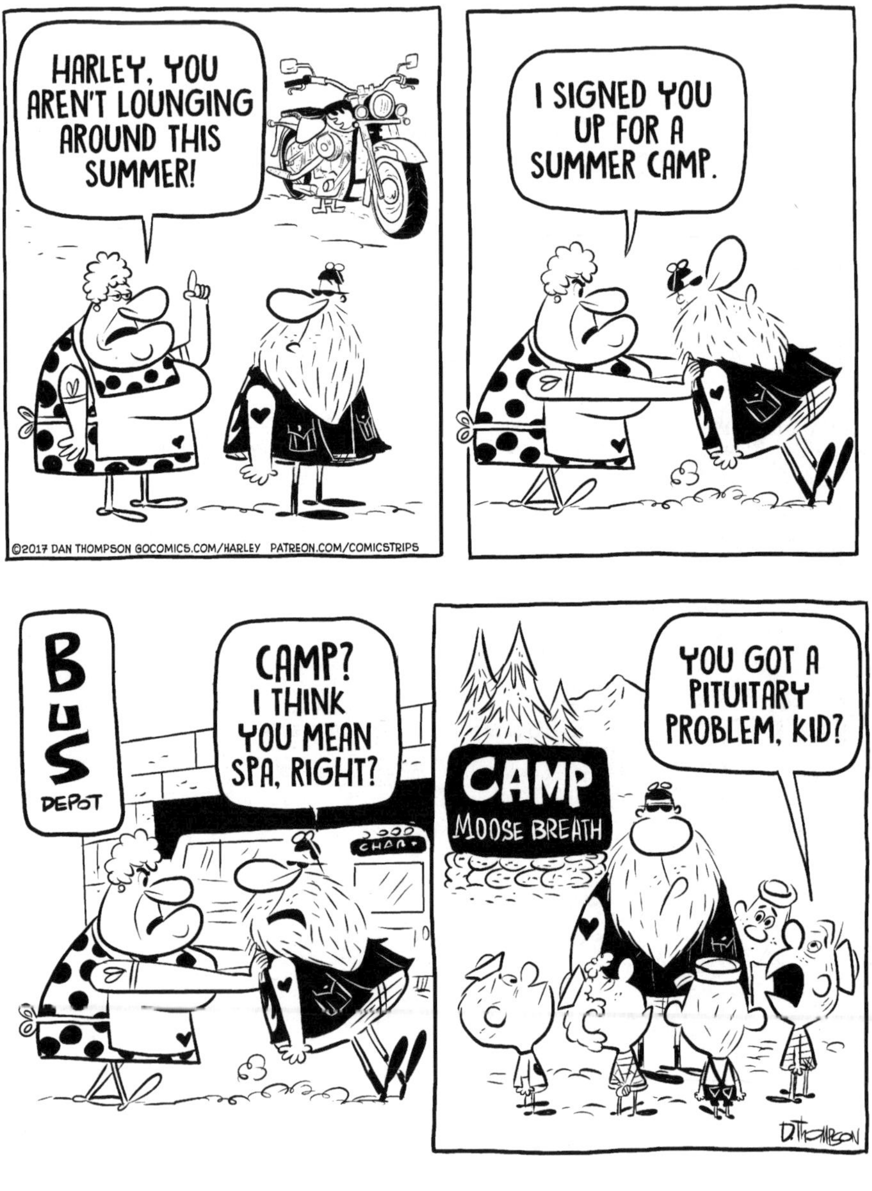
HARLEY, YOU AREN'T LOUNGING AROUND THIS SUMMER!
©2017 DAN THOMPSON GOCOMICS.COM/HARLEY PATREON.COM/COMICSTRIPS
I SIGNED YOU UP FOR A SUMMER CAMP.
BUS DEPOT
CAMP? I THINK YOU MEAN SPA, RIGHT?
CHAR
CAMP MOOSE BREATH
YOU GOT A PITUITARY PROBLEM, KID?
D.THOMPSON

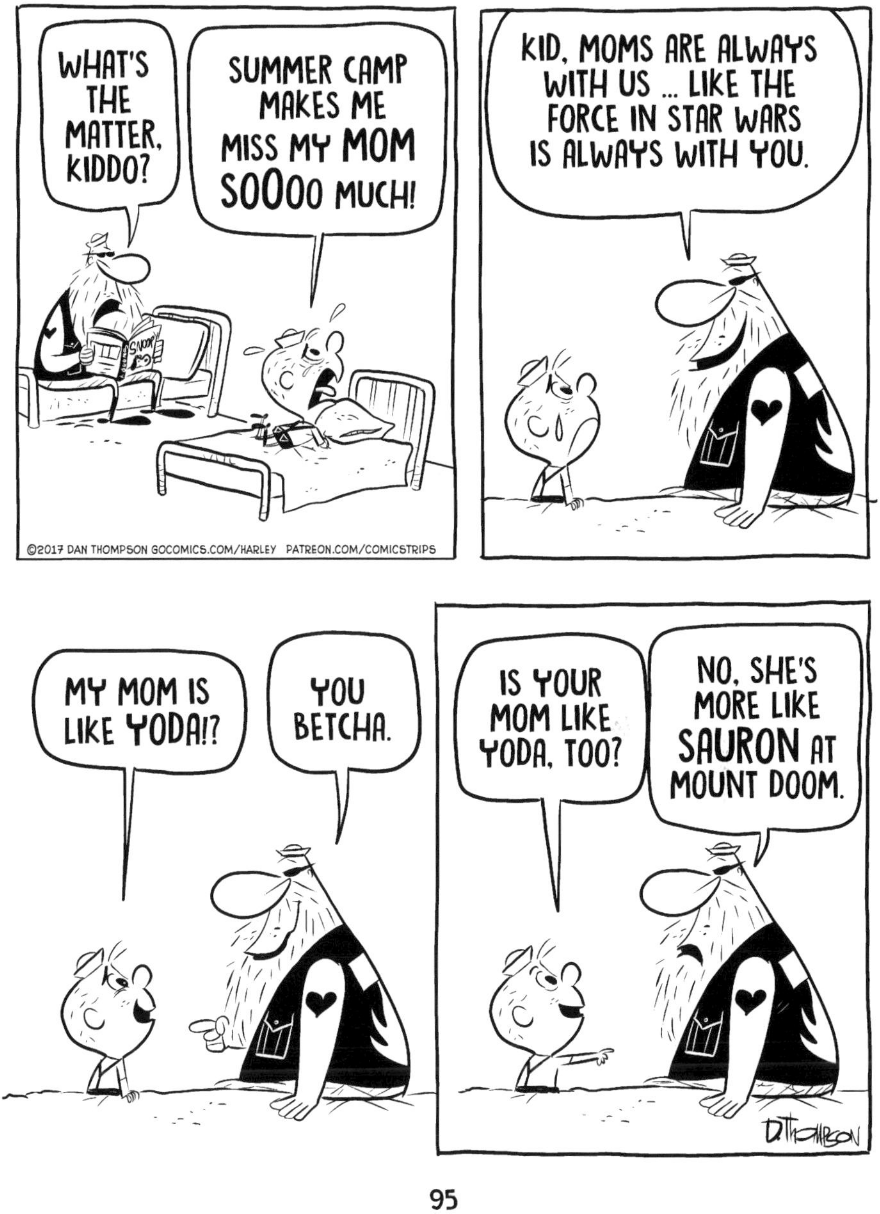
WHAT'S THE MATTER, KIDDO?
SUMMER CAMP MAKES ME MISS MY MOM SOOOO MUCH!
©2017 DAN THOMPSON GOCOMICS.COM/HARLEY PATREON.COM/COMICSTRIPS
KID, MOMS ARE ALWAYS WITH US ... LIKE THE FORCE IN STAR WARS IS ALWAYS WITH YOU.
MY MOM IS LIKE YODA!?
YOU BETCHA.
IS YOUR MOM LIKE YODA, TOO?
NO, SHE'S MORE LIKE SAURON AT MOUNT DOOM.
D.THOMPSON

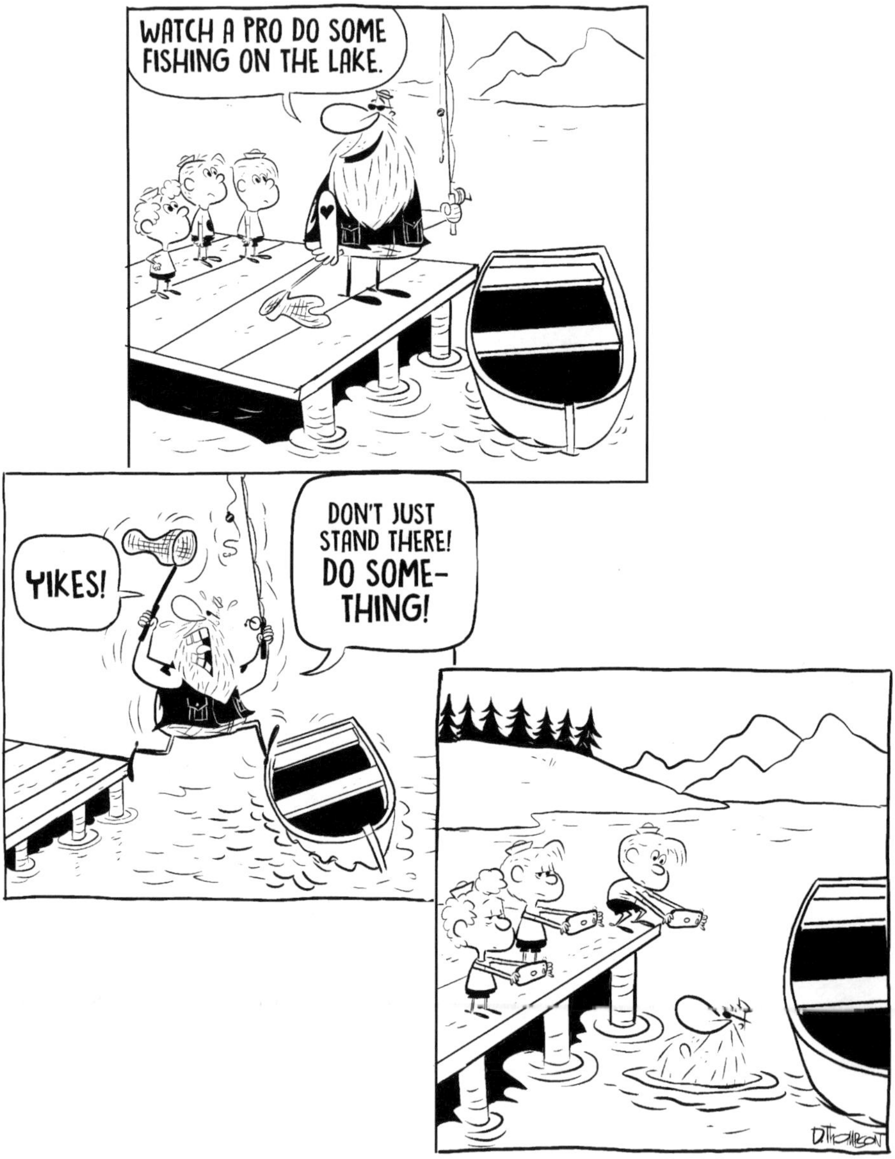
WATCH A PRO DO SOME FISHING ON THE LAKE.
YIKES!
DON'T JUST STAND THERE! DO SOME-THING!
D. THOMPSON

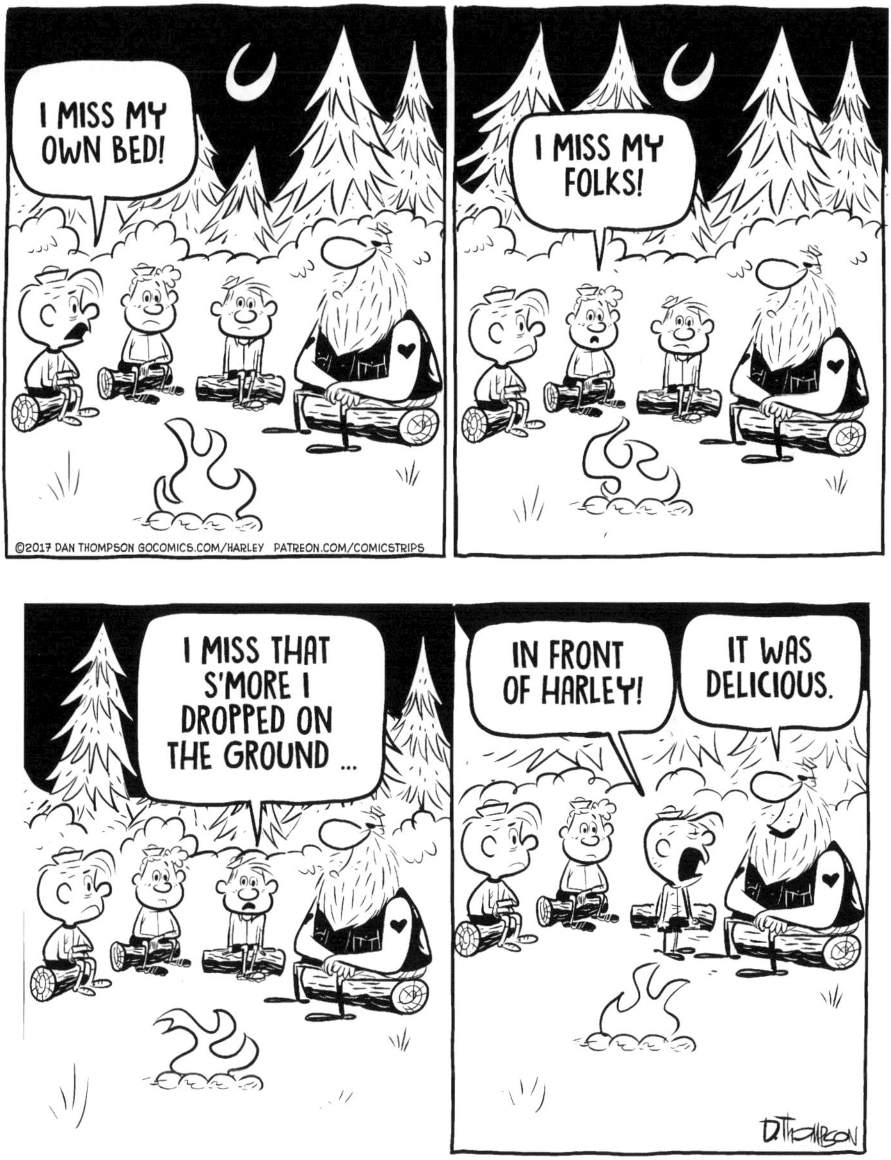
I MISS MY OWN BED!
©2017 DAN THOMPSON GOCOMICS.COM/HARLEY PATREON.COM/COMICSTRIPS
I MISS MY FOLKS!
I MISS THAT S'MORE I DROPPED ON THE GROUND ...
IN FRONT OF HARLEY!
IT WAS DELICIOUS.
D. THOMPSON

"MAIL CALL," HARLEY! YOU GOT A PACKAGE.
©2017 DAN THOMPSON GOCOMICS.COM/HARLEY PATREON.COM/COMICSTRIPS
PERFECT, AND TODAY IS PARENT VISITING DAY!
℅ HARLEY
CAMP MOOSE BREATH
CLEAN $5 UNDERWEAR
D THOMPSON

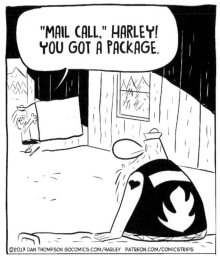

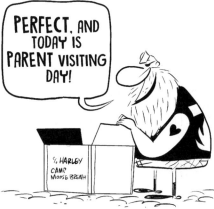

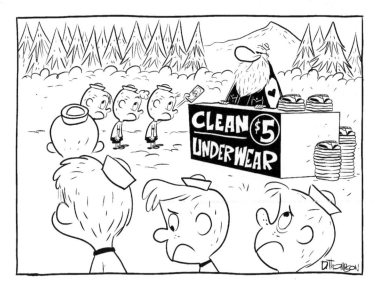

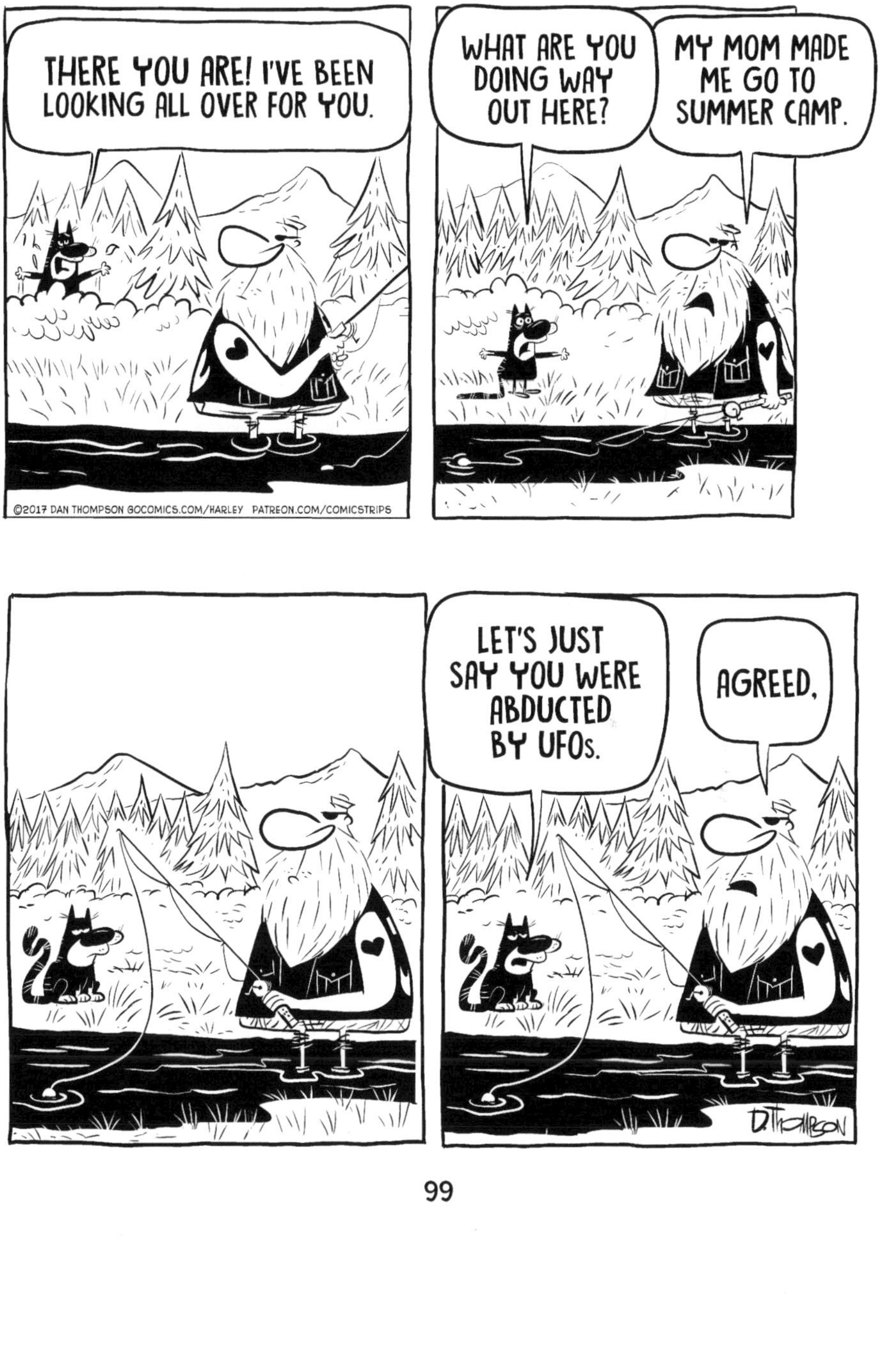
THERE YOU ARE! I'VE BEEN LOOKING ALL OVER FOR YOU.
©2017 DAN THOMPSON GOCOMICS.COM/HARLEY PATREON.COM/COMICSTRIPS
WHAT ARE YOU DOING WAY OUT HERE?
MY MOM MADE ME GO TO SUMMER CAMP.
LET'S JUST SAY YOU WERE ABDUCTED BY UFOs.
AGREED.
D. THOMPSON

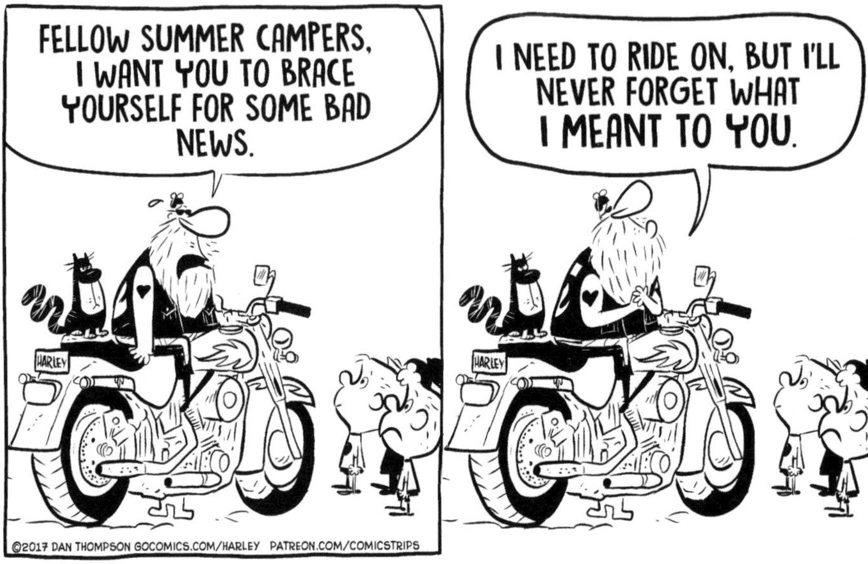
FELLOW SUMMER CAMPERS, I WANT YOU TO BRACE YOURSELF FOR SOME BAD NEWS.
HARLEY
I NEED TO RIDE ON, BUT I'LL NEVER FORGET WHAT I MEANT TO YOU.
HARLEY
©2017 DAN THOMPSON GOCOMICS.COM/HARLEY PATREON.COM/COMICSTRIPS

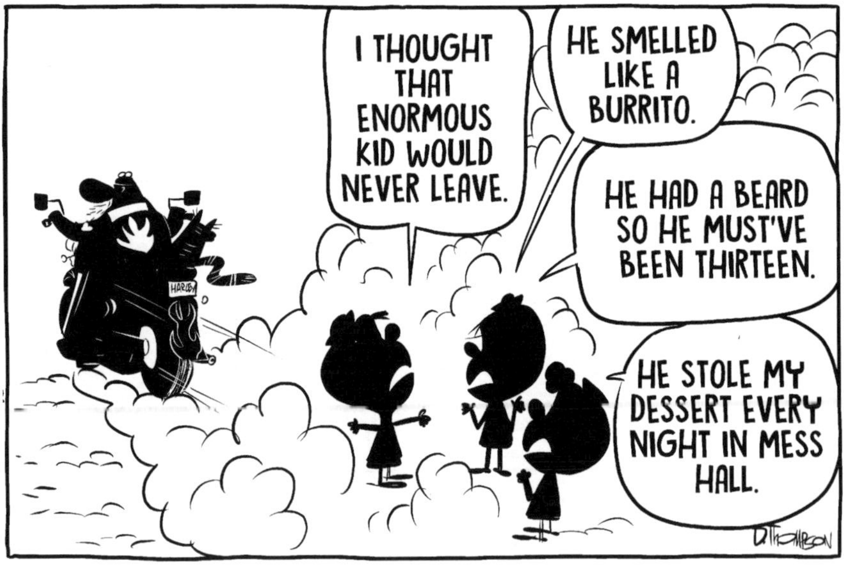
I THOUGHT THAT ENORMOUS KID WOULD NEVER LEAVE.
HE SMELLED LIKE A BURRITO.
HE HAD A BEARD SO HE MUST'VE BEEN THIRTEEN.
HE STOLE MY DESSERT EVERY NIGHT IN MESS HALL.
D.THOMPSON

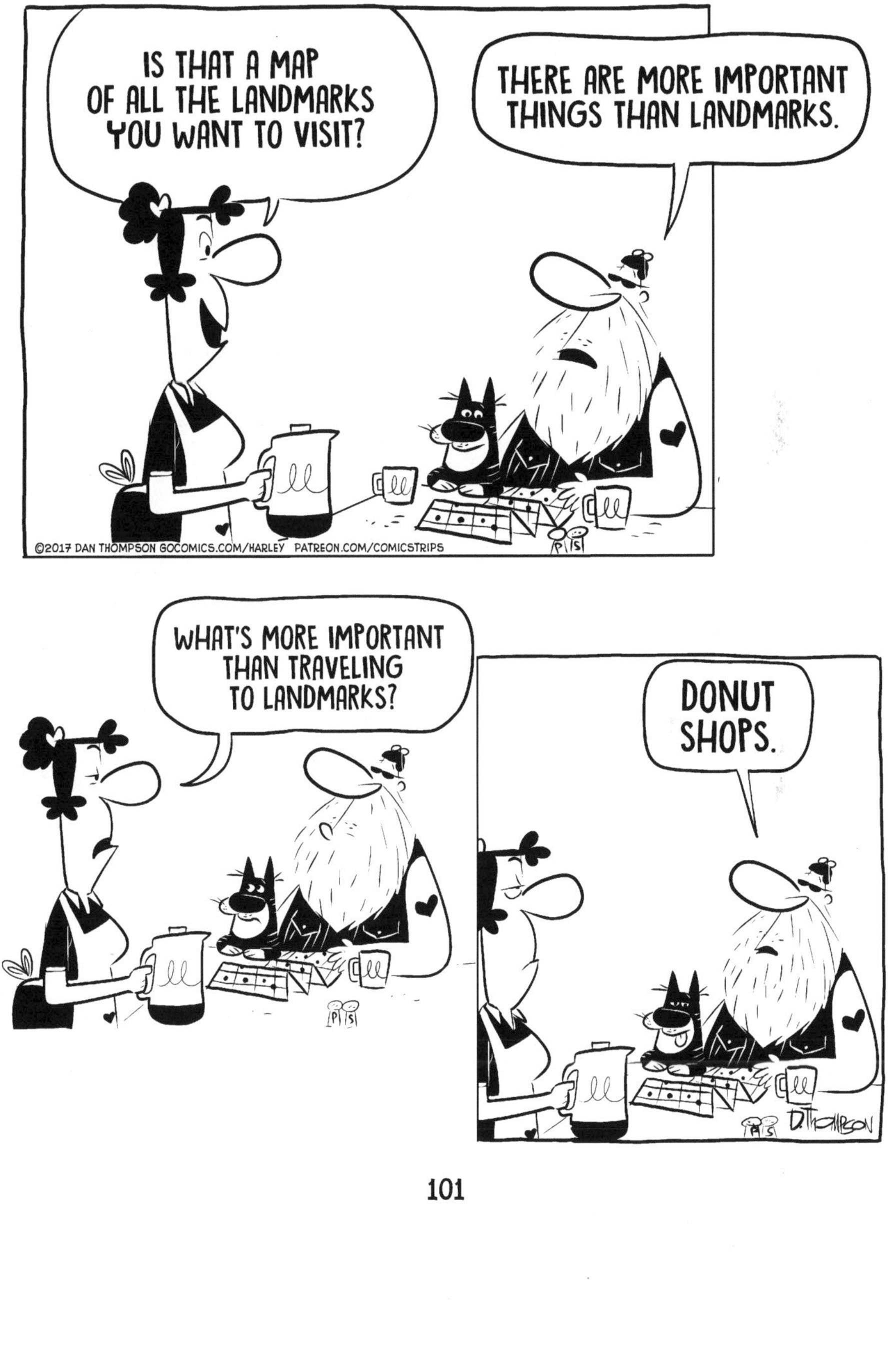
IS THAT A MAP OF ALL THE LANDMARKS YOU WANT TO VISIT?
THERE ARE MORE IMPORTANT THINGS THAN LANDMARKS.
©2017 DAN THOMPSON GOCOMICS.COM/HARLEY PATREON.COM/COMICSTRIPS
WHAT'S MORE IMPORTANT THAN TRAVELING TO LANDMARKS?
DONUT SHOPS.
D.THOMPSON

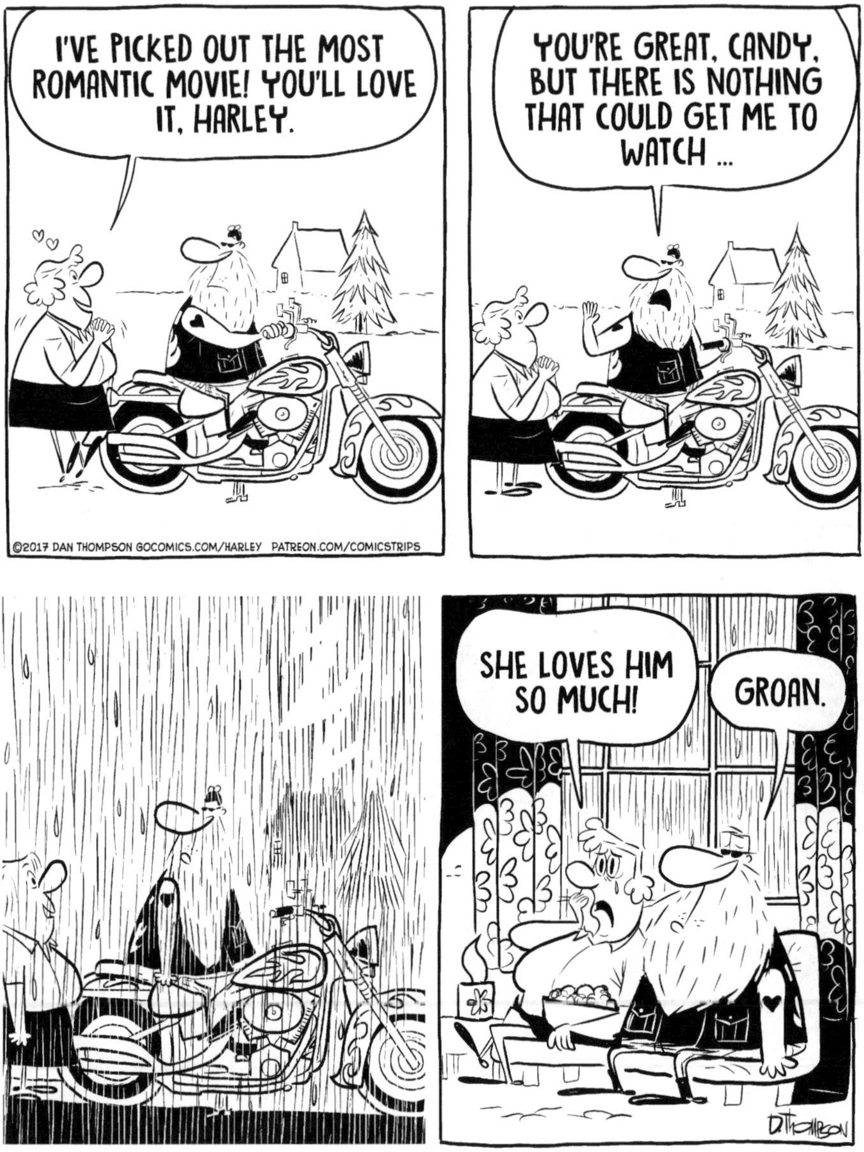
I'VE PICKED OUT THE MOST ROMANTIC MOVIE! YOU'LL LOVE IT, HARLEY.
©2017 DAN THOMPSON GOCOMICS.COM/HARLEY PATREON.COM/COMICSTRIPS
YOU'RE GREAT, CANDY, BUT THERE IS NOTHING THAT COULD GET ME TO WATCH ...
SHE LOVES HIM SO MUCH!
GROAN.
D. THOMPSON

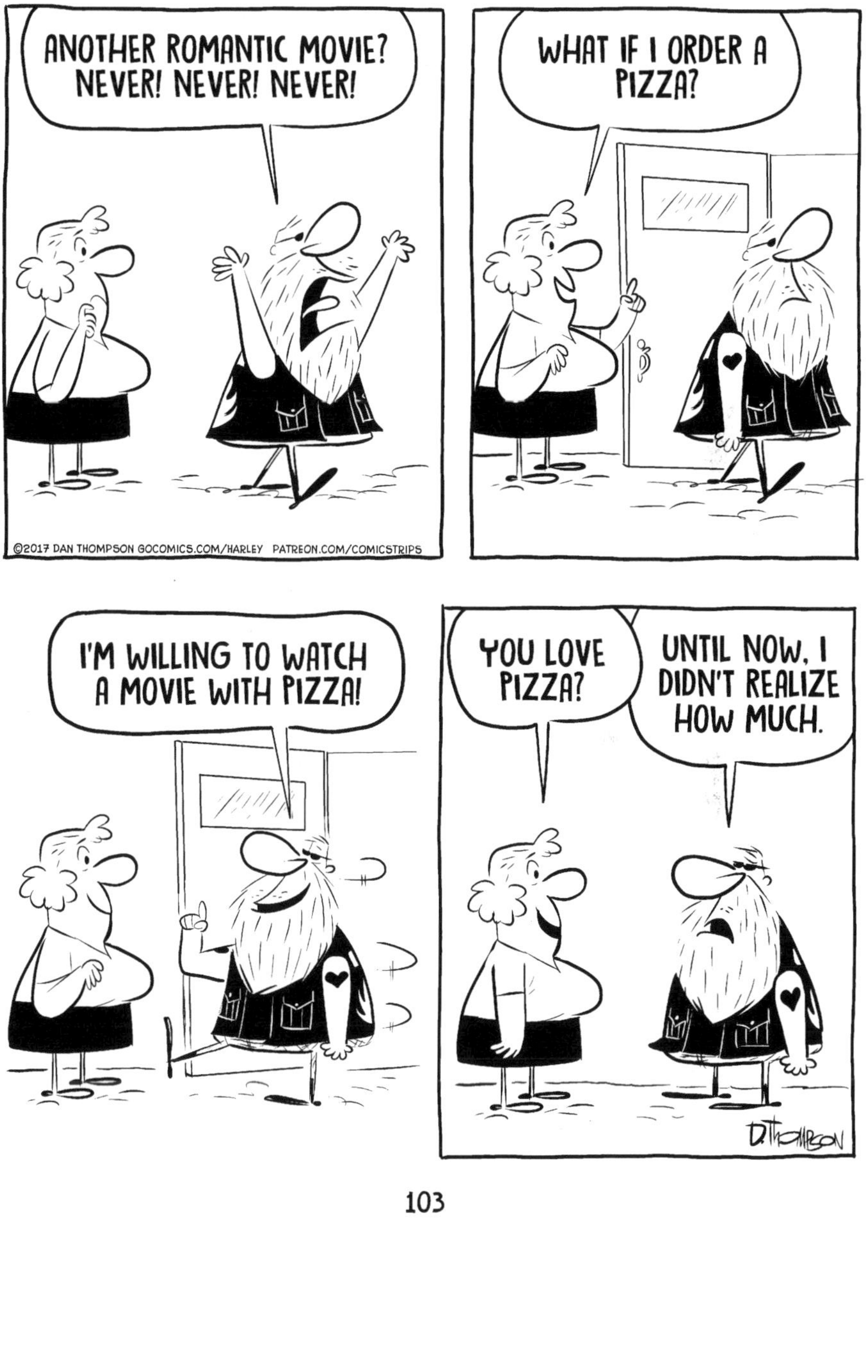
ANOTHER ROMANTIC MOVIE? NEVER! NEVER! NEVER!
©2017 DAN THOMPSON GOCOMICS.COM/HARLEY PATREON.COM/COMICSTRIPS
WHAT IF I ORDER A PIZZA?
I'M WILLING TO WATCH A MOVIE WITH PIZZA!
YOU LOVE PIZZA?
UNTIL NOW, I DIDN'T REALIZE HOW MUCH.
D. THOMPSON

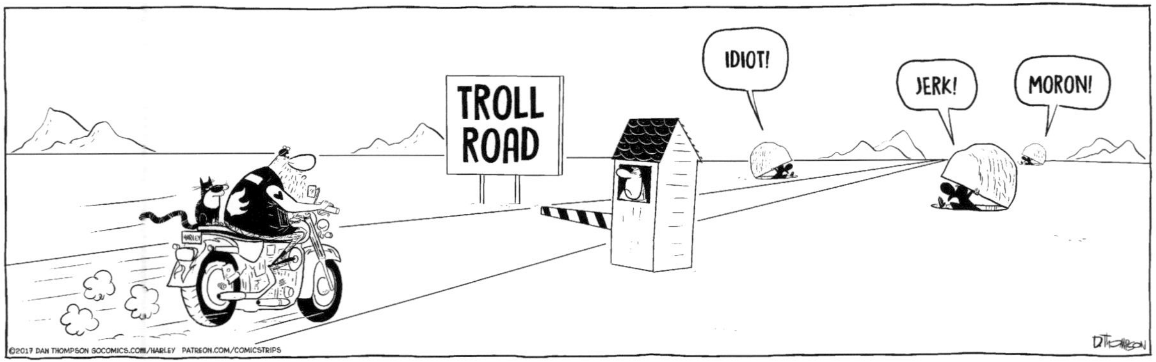
TROLL ROAD
IDIOT!
JERK!
MORON!
©2017 DAN THOMPSON GOCOMICS.COM/HARLEY PATREON.COM/COMICSTRIPS
DTHOMPSON

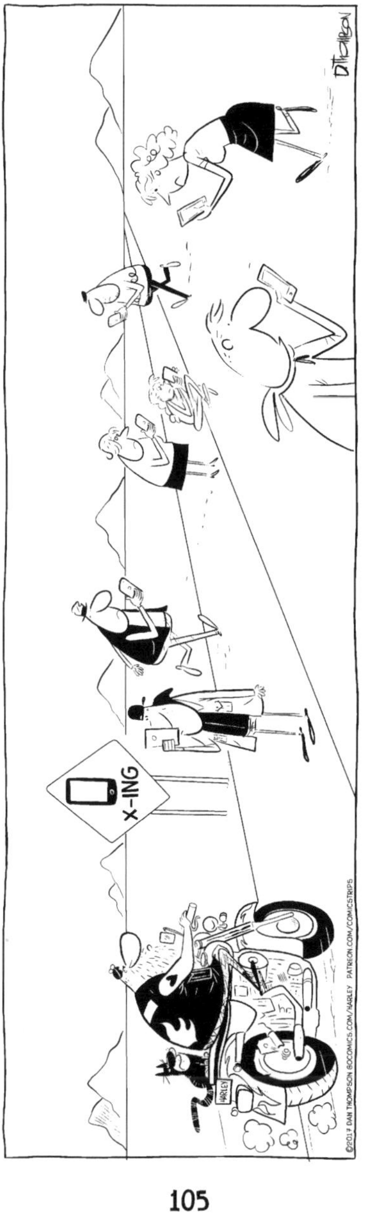
X-ING
HARLEY
D.THOMPSON
©2017 DAN THOMPSON GOCOMICS.COM/HARLEY PATREON.COM/COMICSTRIPS

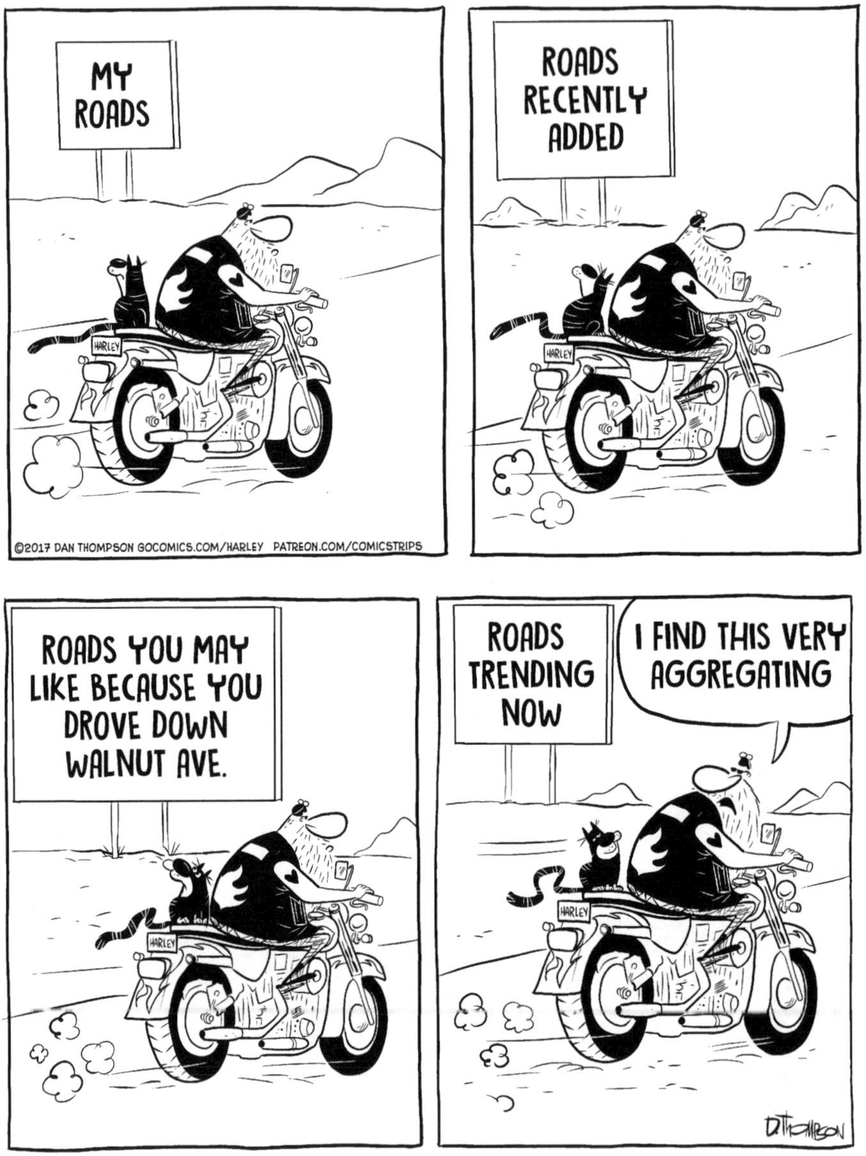
MY ROADS
HARLEY
©2017 DAN THOMPSON GOCOMICS.COM/HARLEY PATREON.COM/COMICSTRIPS
ROADS RECENTLY ADDED
HARLEY
ROADS YOU MAY LIKE BECAUSE YOU DROVE DOWN WALNUT AVE.
HARLEY
ROADS TRENDING NOW
I FIND THIS VERY AGGREGATING
HARLEY
D.THOMPSON

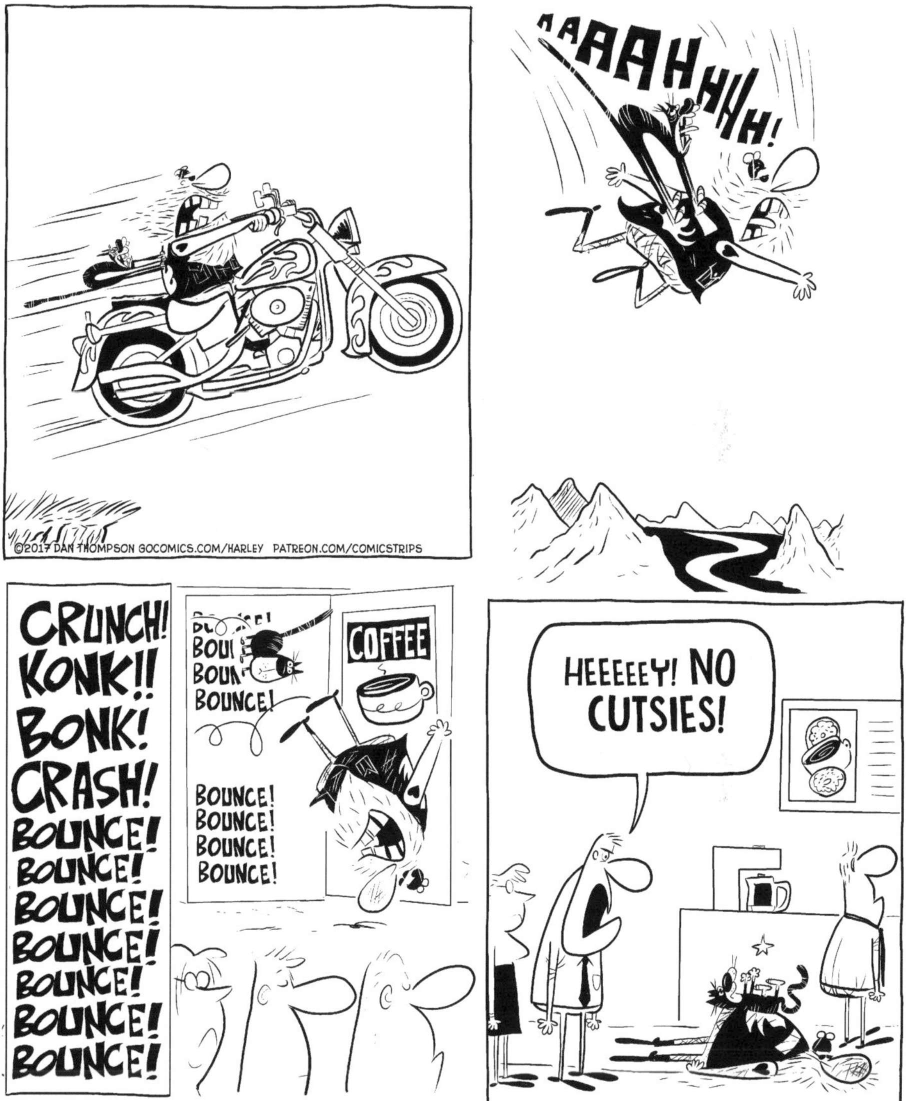
©2017 DAN THOMPSON GOCOMICS.COM/HARLEY PATREON.COM/COMICSTRIPS
AAAAHHHHH!
CRUNCH!
KONK!!
BONK!
CRASH!
BOUNCE!
BOUNCE!
BOUNCE!
BOUNCE!
BOUNCE!
BOUNCE!
BOUNCE!
BOUNCE!
BOUNCE!
COFFEE
BOUNCE!
BOUNCE!
BOUNCE!
BOUNCE!
HEEEEEY! NO CUTSIES!
D.THOMPSON

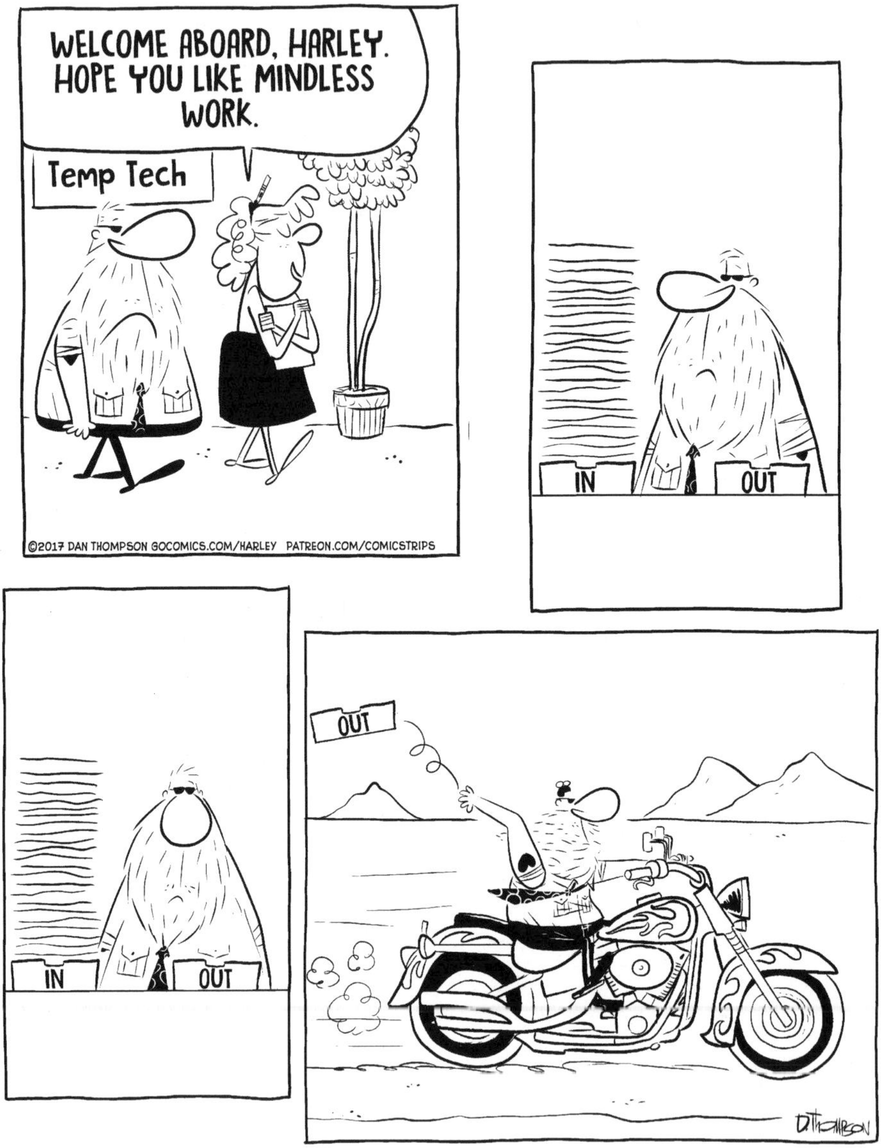
WELCOME ABOARD, HARLEY. HOPE YOU LIKE MINDLESS WORK.
Temp Tech
©2017 DAN THOMPSON GOCOMICS.COM/HARLEY PATREON.COM/COMICSTRIPS
IN
OUT
IN
OUT
OUT
D. THOMPSON

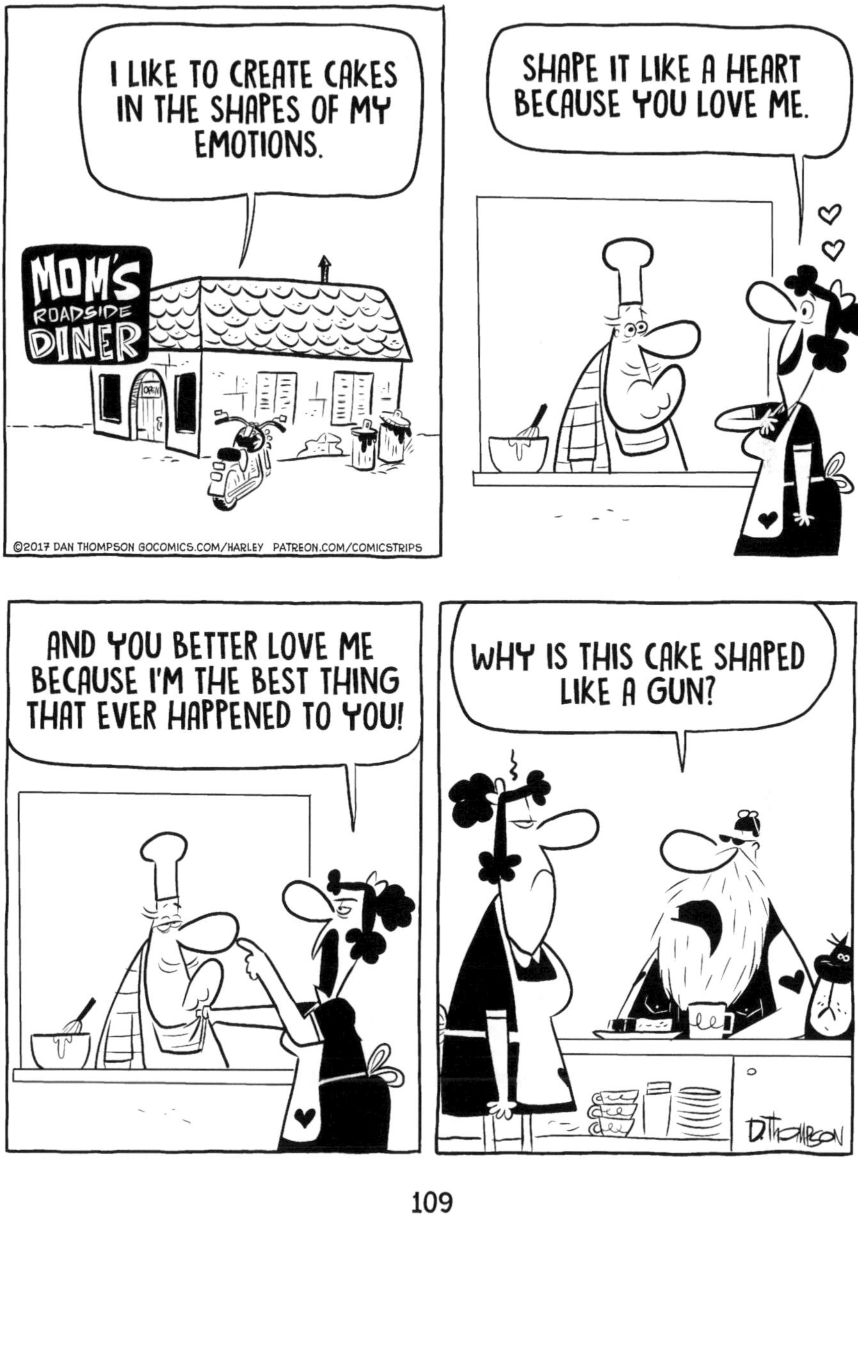
I LIKE TO CREATE CAKES IN THE SHAPES OF MY EMOTIONS.
MOM'S ROADSIDE DINER
OPEN
©2017 DAN THOMPSON GOCOMICS.COM/HARLEY PATREON.COM/COMICSTRIPS
SHAPE IT LIKE A HEART BECAUSE YOU LOVE ME.
AND YOU BETTER LOVE ME BECAUSE I'M THE BEST THING THAT EVER HAPPENED TO YOU!
WHY IS THIS CAKE SHAPED LIKE A GUN?
D. THOMPSON

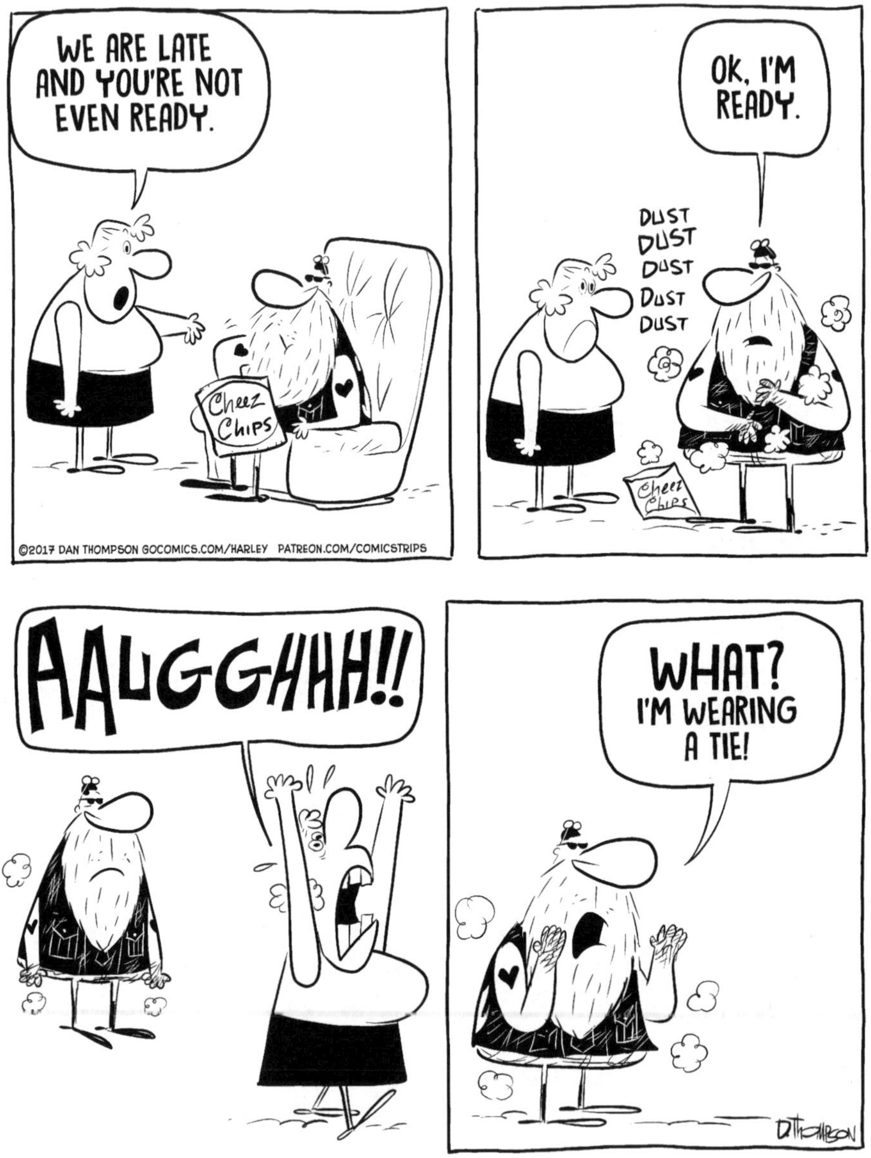
WE ARE LATE AND YOU'RE NOT EVEN READY.
Cheez Chips
©2017 DAN THOMPSON GOCOMICS.COM/HARLEY PATREON.COM/COMICSTRIPS
OK, I'M READY.
DUST DUST DUST DUST DUST
Cheez Chips
AAUGGHHH!!
WHAT? I'M WEARING A TIE!
D THOMPSON

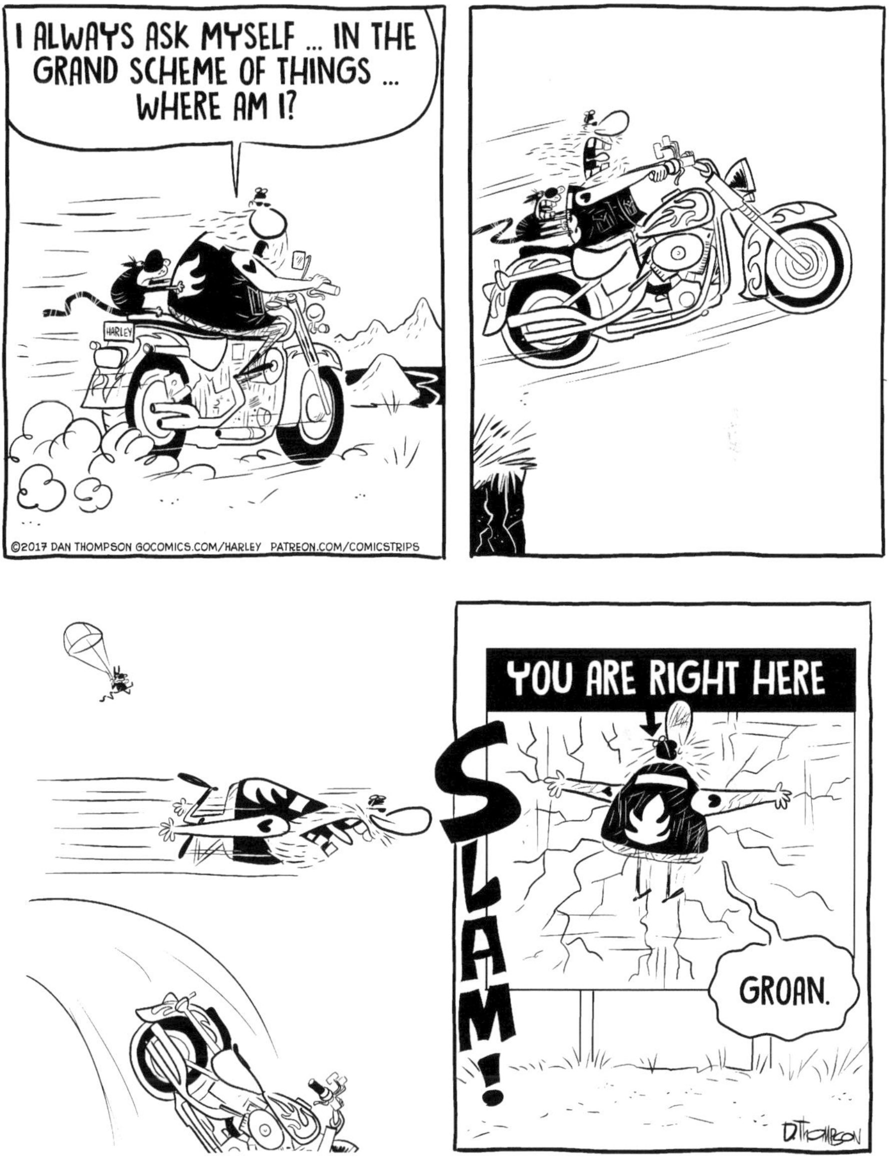
I ALWAYS ASK MYSELF ... IN THE GRAND SCHEME OF THINGS ... WHERE AM I?
HARLEY
©2017 DAN THOMPSON GOCOMICS.COM/HARLEY PATREON.COM/COMICSTRIPS
SLAM!
YOU ARE RIGHT HERE
GROAN.
D.THOMPSON

DON'T TELL IRIS, BUT I WON $500 BUCKS ON A SCRATCH TICKET.

BAR

©2017 DAN THOMPSON GOCOMICS.COM/HARLEY PATREON.COM/COMICSTRIPS

Grrrr...

WAIT! WAIT! I WAS GOING TO BUY HER SOME-THING WITH THE MONEY.

I WAS GOING TO **SURPRISE** HER! I WAS GOING TO **SURPRISE** HER!

Grrr..
Grrr..

SLAM!

THAT'S WHY I STAY BROKE.

D.Thompson

AAUGGGHhh!
©2017 DAN THOMPSON GOCOMICS.COM/HARLEY PATREON.COM/COMICSTRIPS
SKID!
SKID!
SKID!
SKID!
EMERGENCY ROOM
NO SMOKING
FRONT DESK
D. THOMPSON

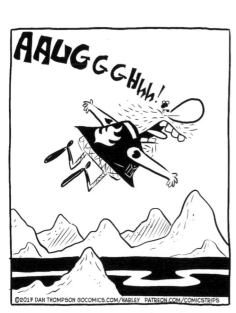

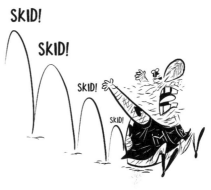

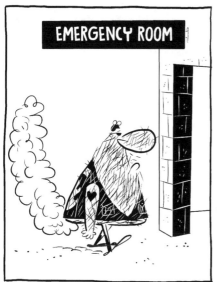

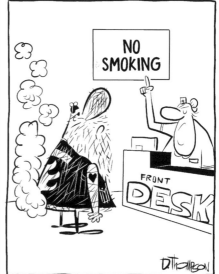

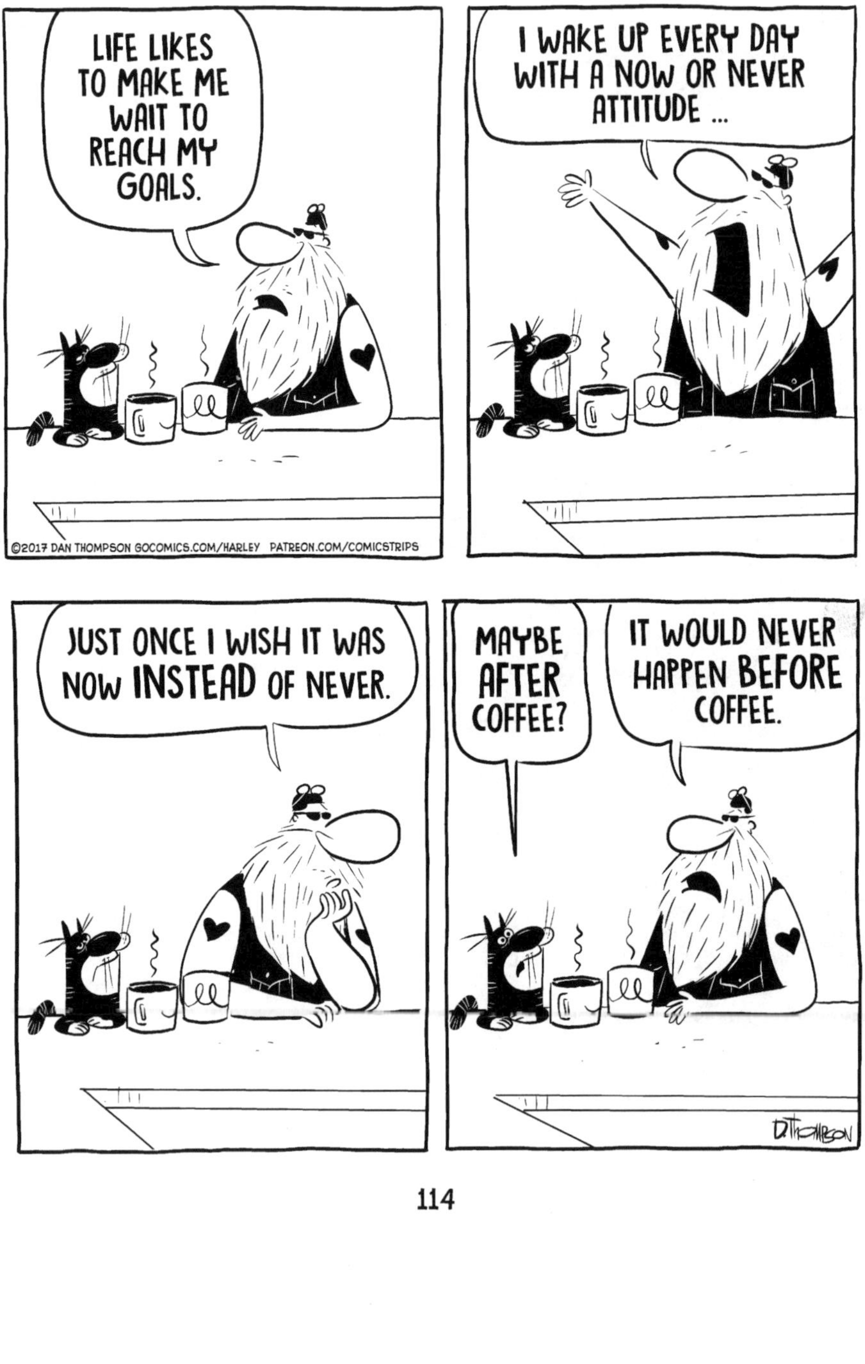
LIFE LIKES TO MAKE ME WAIT TO REACH MY GOALS.
©2017 DAN THOMPSON GOCOMICS.COM/HARLEY PATREON.COM/COMICSTRIPS
I WAKE UP EVERY DAY WITH A NOW OR NEVER ATTITUDE ...
JUST ONCE I WISH IT WAS NOW INSTEAD OF NEVER.
MAYBE AFTER COFFEE?
IT WOULD NEVER HAPPEN BEFORE COFFEE.
D. THOMPSON

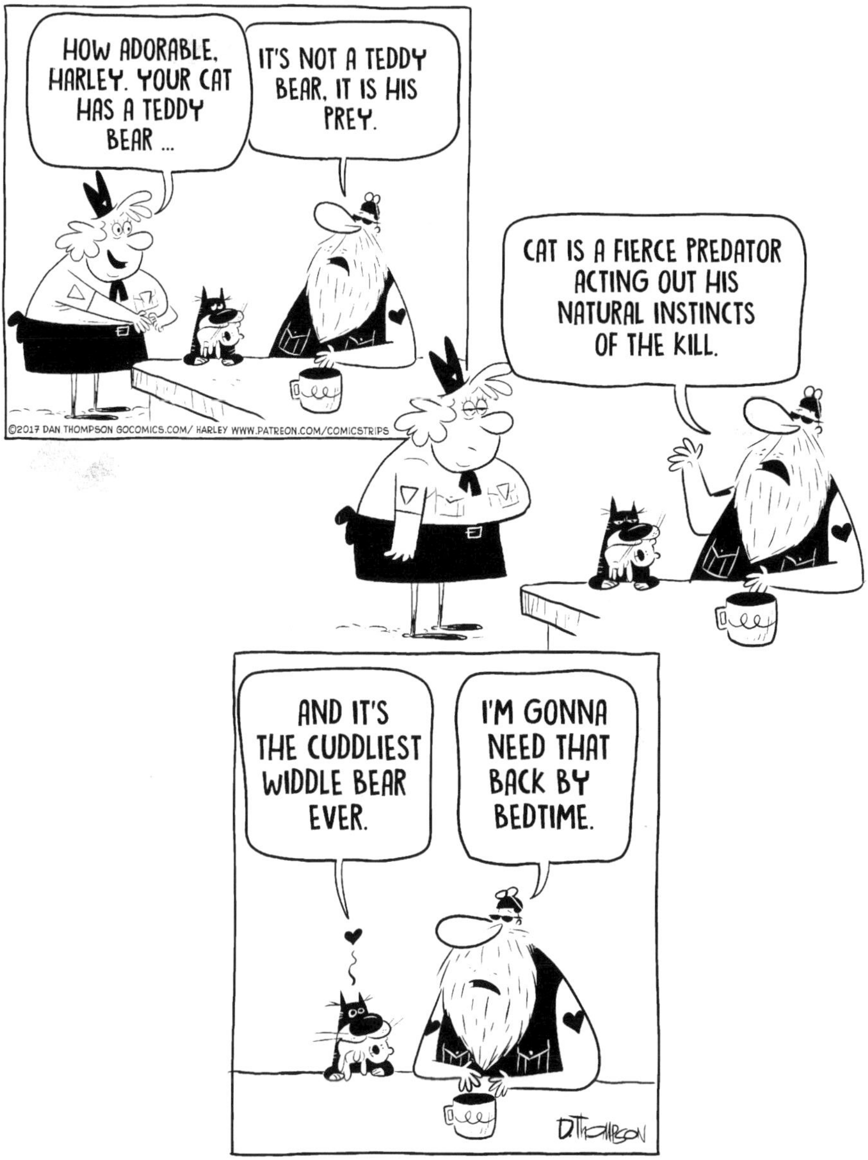
HOW ADORABLE, HARLEY. YOUR CAT HAS A TEDDY BEAR ...
IT'S NOT A TEDDY BEAR, IT IS HIS PREY.
©2017 DAN THOMPSON GOCOMICS.COM/ HARLEY WWW.PATREON.COM/COMICSTRIPS
CAT IS A FIERCE PREDATOR ACTING OUT HIS NATURAL INSTINCTS OF THE KILL.
AND IT'S THE CUDDLIEST WIDDLE BEAR EVER.
I'M GONNA NEED THAT BACK BY BEDTIME.
D.THOMPSON

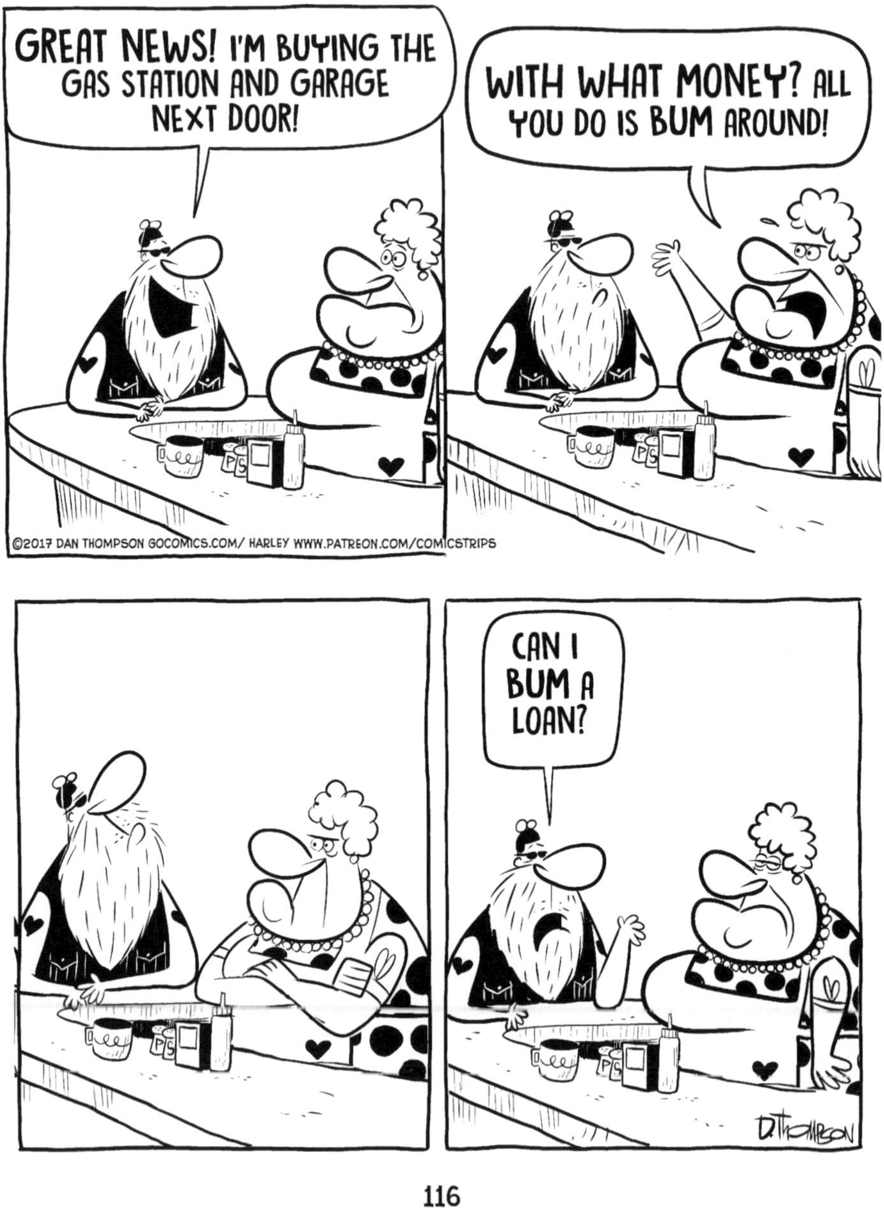
GREAT NEWS! I'M BUYING THE GAS STATION AND GARAGE NEXT DOOR!
WITH WHAT MONEY? ALL YOU DO IS BUM AROUND!
CAN I BUM A LOAN?
©2017 DAN THOMPSON GOCOMICS.COM/ HARLEY WWW.PATREON.COM/COMICSTRIPS
D.THOMPSON

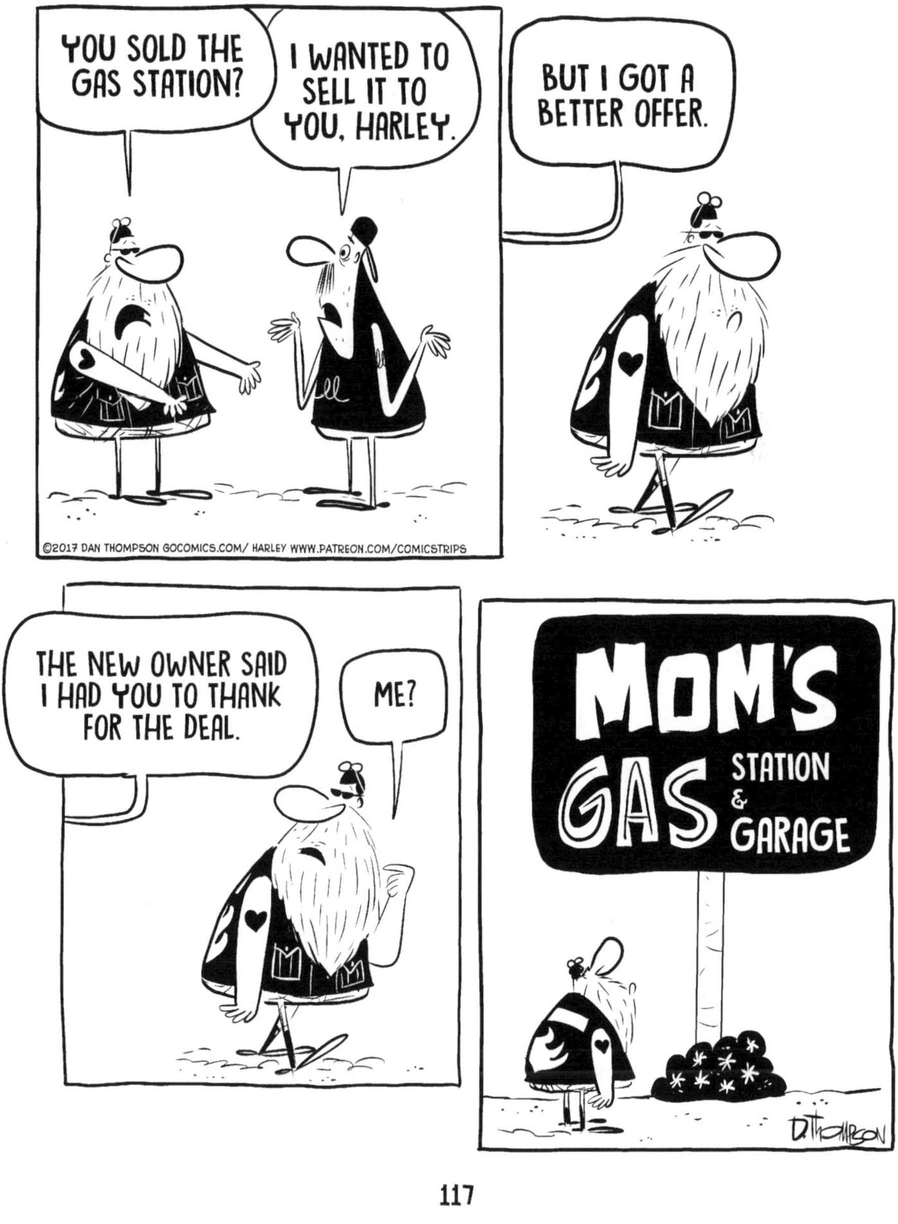

YOU SOLD THE GAS STATION?
I WANTED TO SELL IT TO YOU, HARLEY.
©2017 DAN THOMPSON GOCOMICS.COM/ HARLEY WWW.PATREON.COM/COMICSTRIPS
BUT I GOT A BETTER OFFER.
THE NEW OWNER SAID I HAD YOU TO THANK FOR THE DEAL.
ME?
MOM'S
GAS
STATION
&
GARAGE
D.THOMPSON

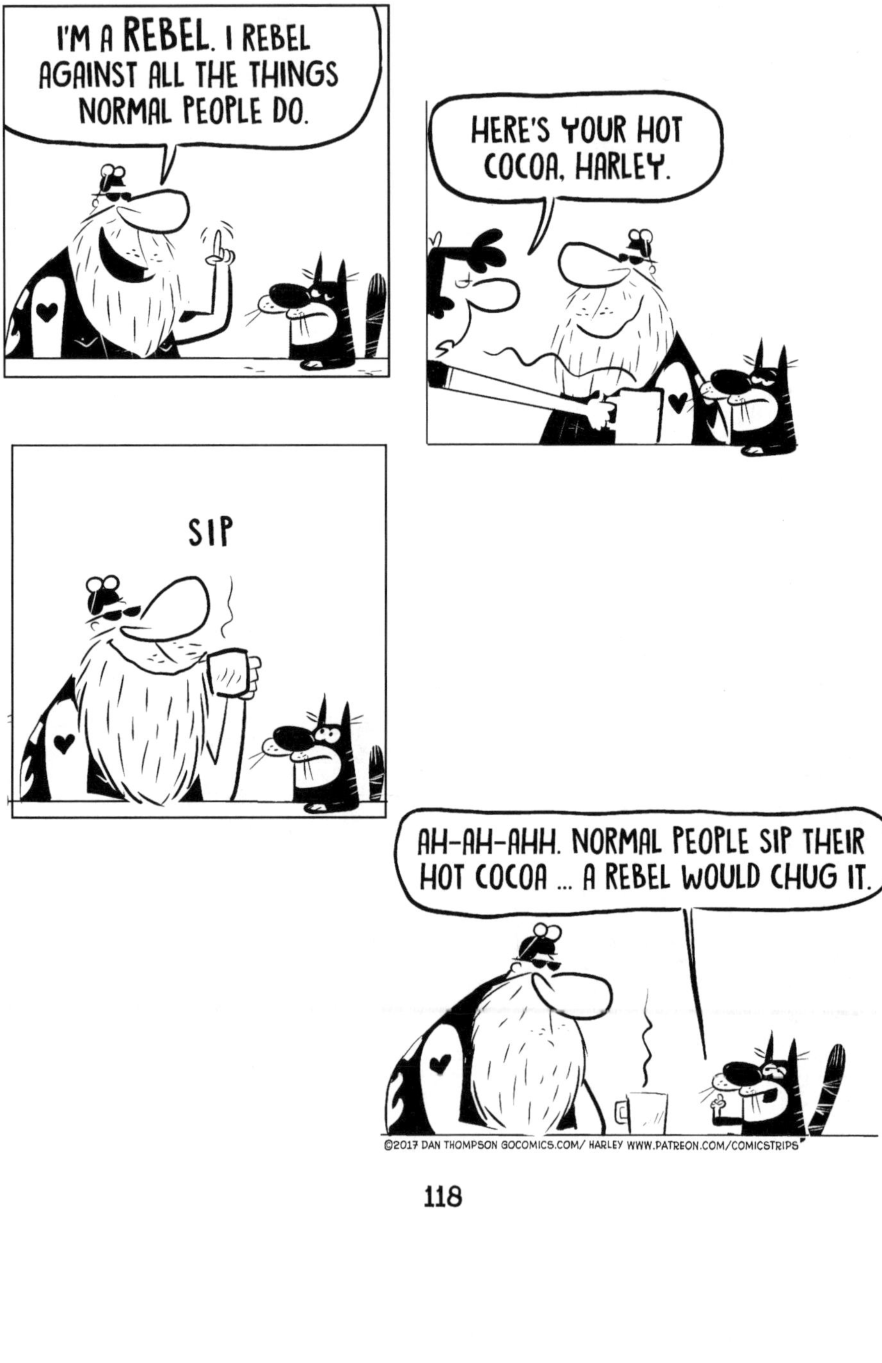
I'M A REBEL. I REBEL AGAINST ALL THE THINGS NORMAL PEOPLE DO.
HERE'S YOUR HOT COCOA, HARLEY.
SIP
AH-AH-AHH. NORMAL PEOPLE SIP THEIR HOT COCOA ... A REBEL WOULD CHUG IT.
©2017 DAN THOMPSON GOCOMICS.COM/ HARLEY WWW.PATREON.COM/COMICSTRIPS

CHUG-CHUG CHUG!

AUGH!

WELL, AT LEAST I PROVED SOMETHING.

YOU CERTAINLY DID.

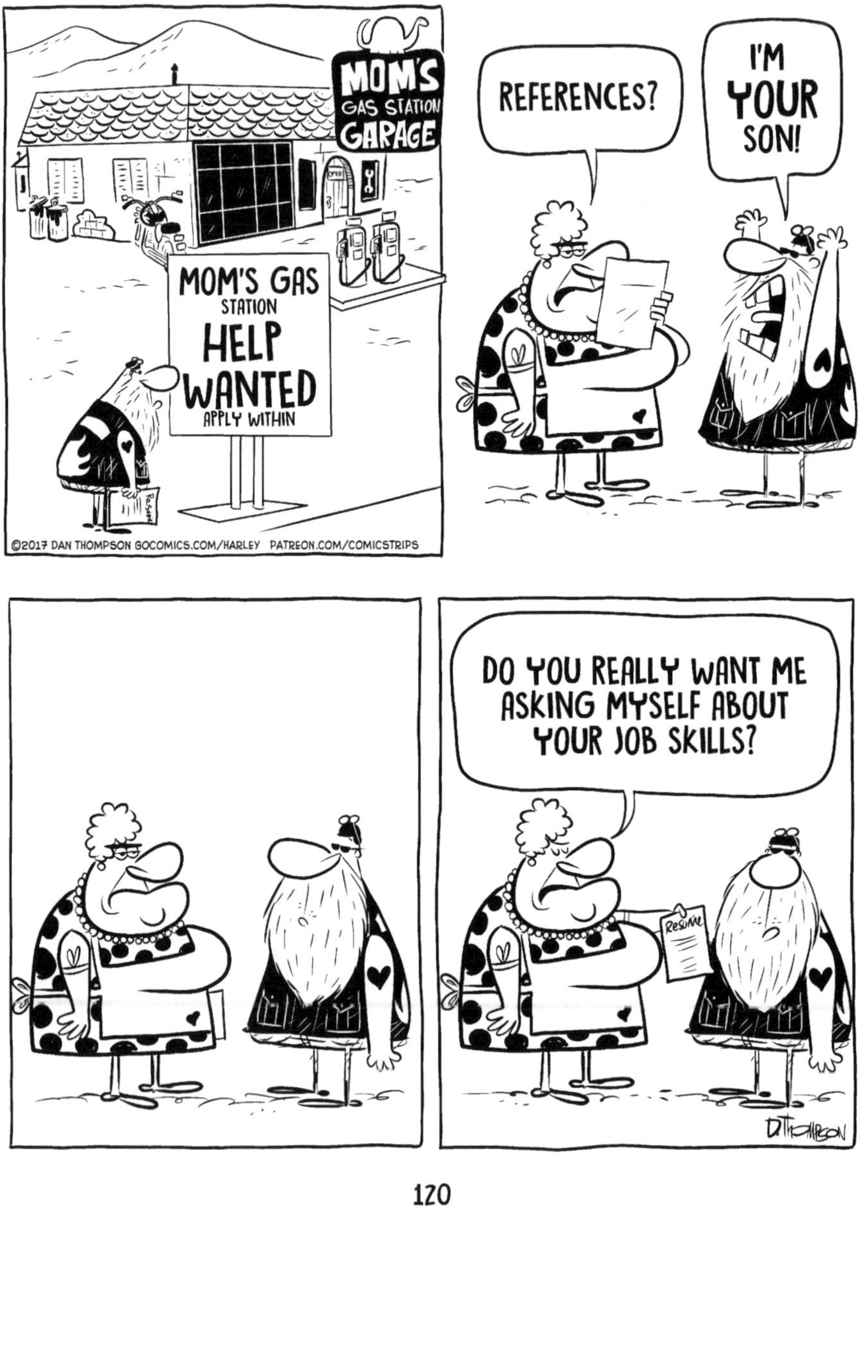
MOM'S
GAS STATION
GARAGE
MOM'S GAS
STATION
HELP
WANTED
APPLY WITHIN
©2017 DAN THOMPSON GOCOMICS.COM/HARLEY PATREON.COM/COMICSTRIPS
REFERENCES?
I'M YOUR SON!
DO YOU REALLY WANT ME ASKING MYSELF ABOUT YOUR JOB SKILLS?
RESUME
D THOMPSON

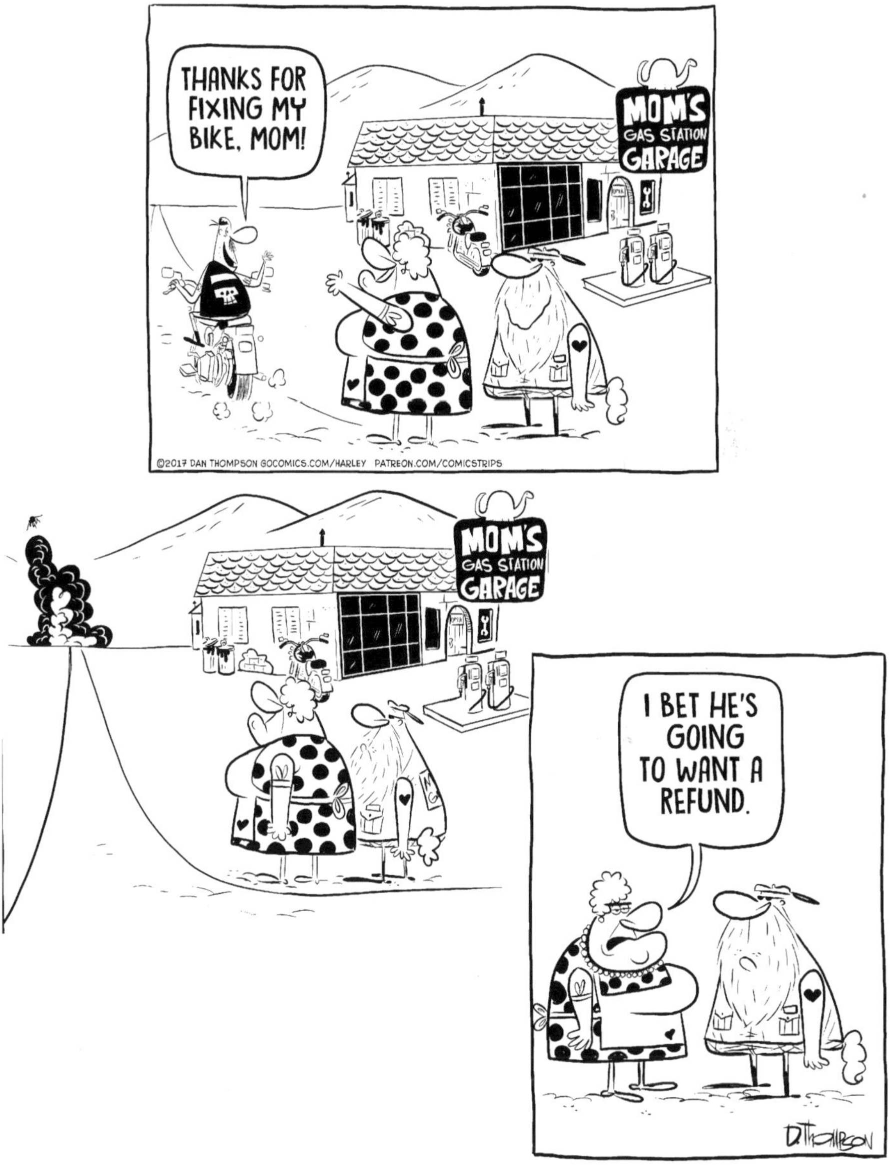
THANKS FOR FIXING MY BIKE, MOM!
MOM'S GAS STATION GARAGE
©2017 DAN THOMPSON GOCOMICS.COM/HARLEY PATREON.COM/COMICSTRIPS
MOM'S GAS STATION GARAGE
I BET HE'S GOING TO WANT A REFUND.
D. THOMPSON

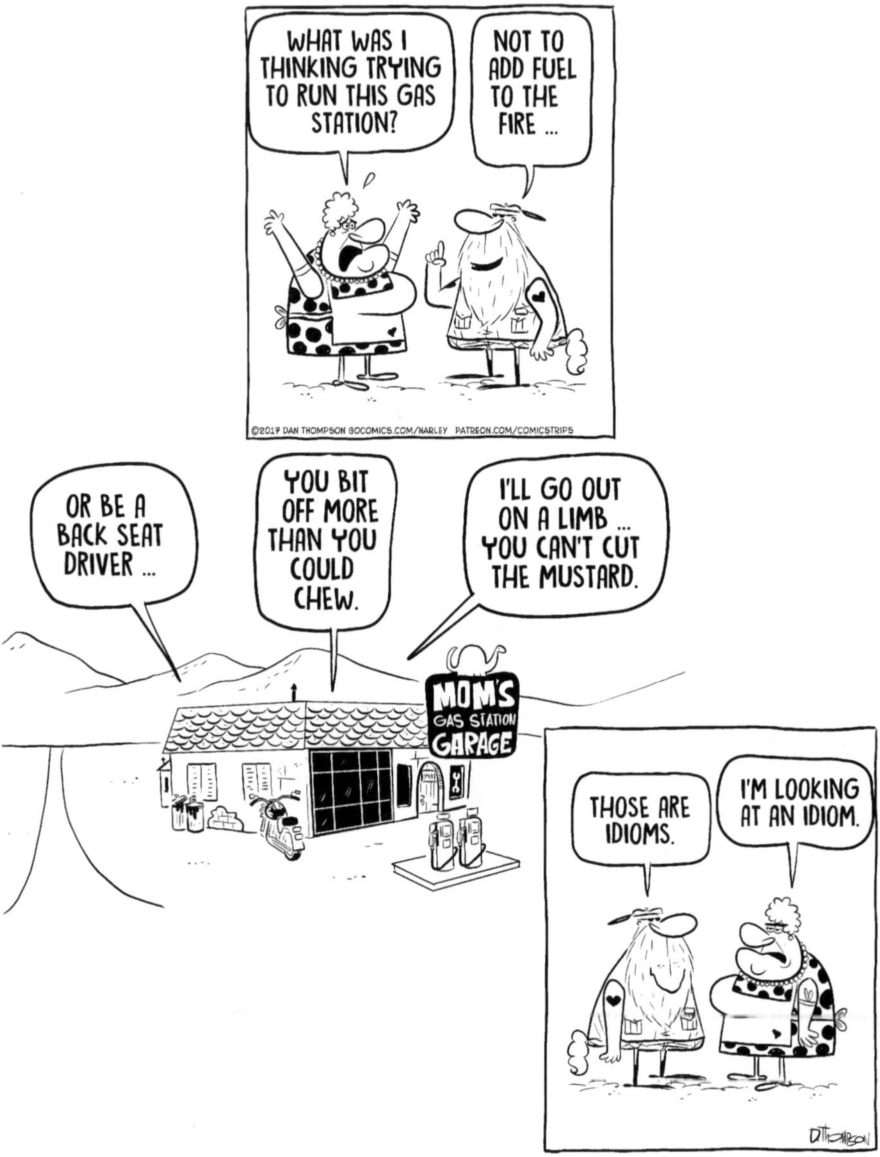
WHAT WAS I THINKING TRYING TO RUN THIS GAS STATION?
NOT TO ADD FUEL TO THE FIRE ...
©2017 DAN THOMPSON GOCOMICS.COM/HARLEY PATREON.COM/COMICSTRIPS
OR BE A BACK SEAT DRIVER ...
YOU BIT OFF MORE THAN YOU COULD CHEW.
I'LL GO OUT ON A LIMB ... YOU CAN'T CUT THE MUSTARD.
MOM'S
GAS STATION
GARAGE
THOSE ARE IDIOMS.
I'M LOOKING AT AN IDIOM.

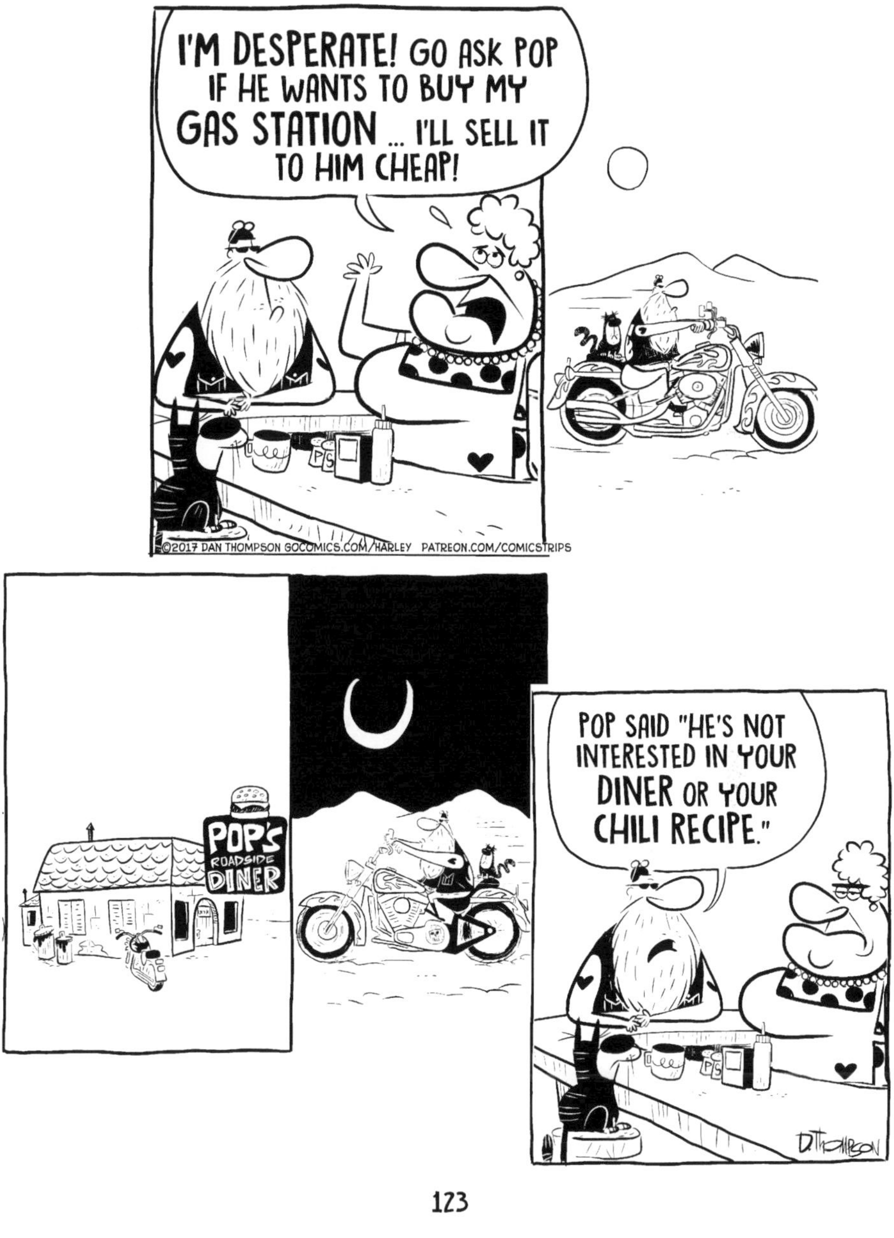
I'M DESPERATE! GO ASK POP IF HE WANTS TO BUY MY GAS STATION ... I'LL SELL IT TO HIM CHEAP!
©2017 DAN THOMPSON GOCOMICS.COM/HARLEY PATREON.COM/COMICSTRIPS
POP'S ROADSIDE DINER
POP SAID "HE'S NOT INTERESTED IN YOUR DINER OR YOUR CHILI RECIPE."
D. THOMPSON

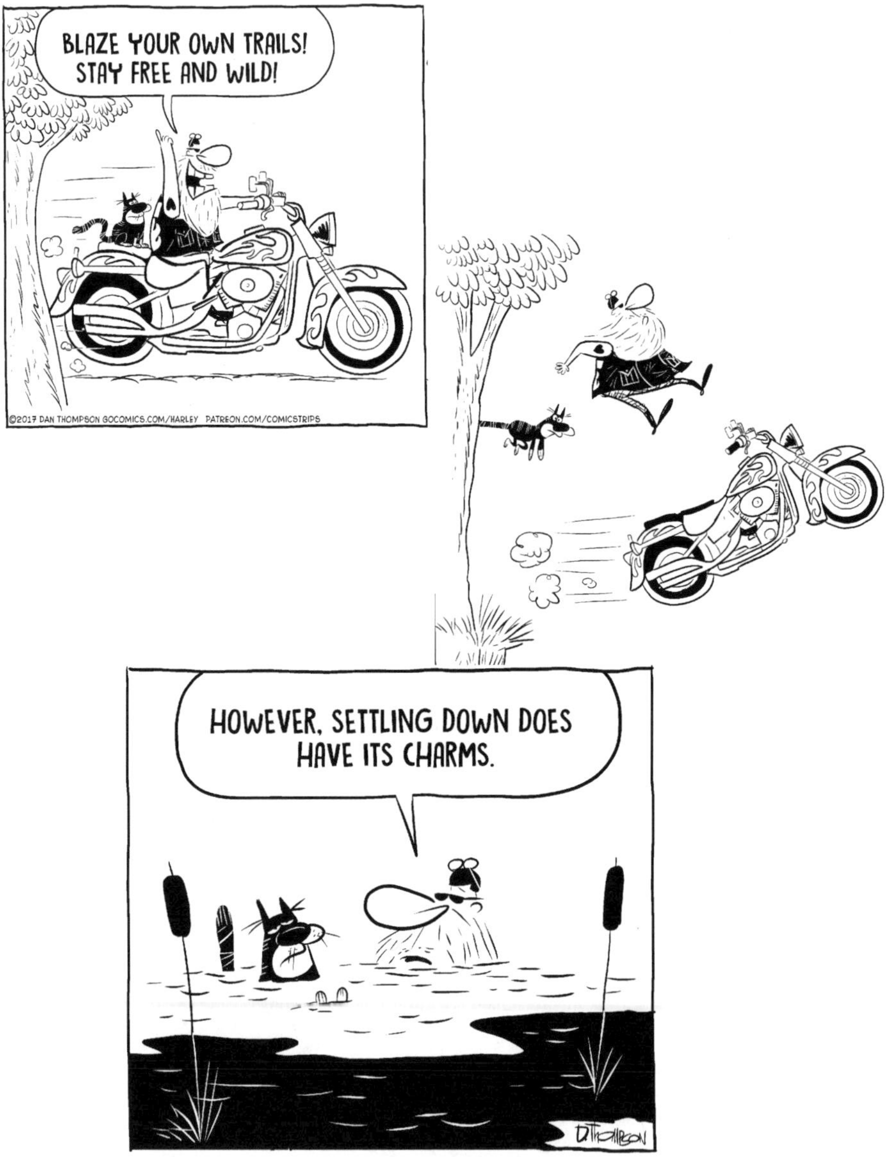
BLAZE YOUR OWN TRAILS! STAY FREE AND WILD!
©2017 DAN THOMPSON GOCOMICS.COM/HARLEY PATREON.COM/COMICSTRIPS
HOWEVER, SETTLING DOWN DOES HAVE ITS CHARMS.
D.THOMPSON

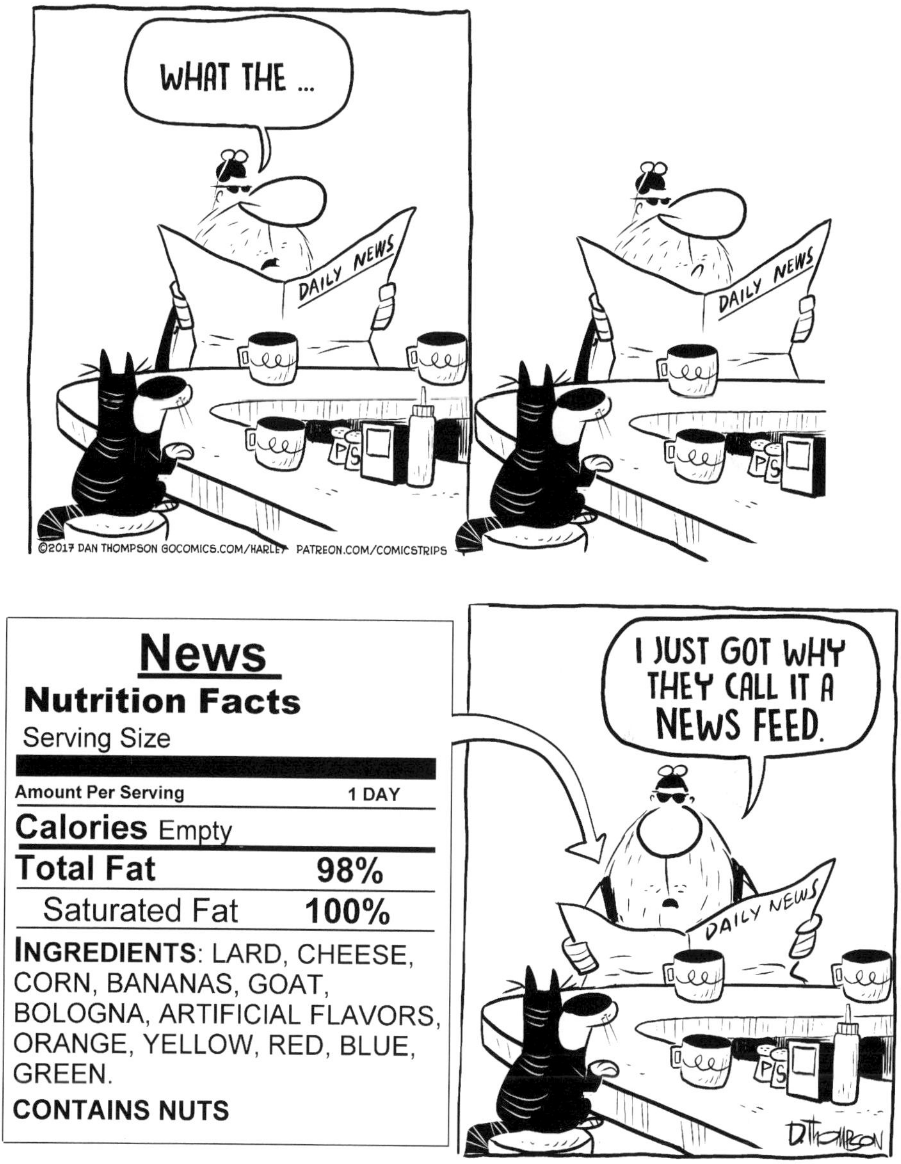
WHAT THE ...
DAILY NEWS
©2017 DAN THOMPSON GOCOMICS.COM/HARLEY PATREON.COM/COMICSTRIPS
DAILY NEWS
News
Nutrition Facts
Serving Size
Amount Per Serving 1 DAY
Calories Empty
Total Fat 98%
Saturated Fat 100%
INGREDIENTS: LARD, CHEESE, CORN, BANANAS, GOAT, BOLOGNA, ARTIFICIAL FLAVORS, ORANGE, YELLOW, RED, BLUE, GREEN.
CONTAINS NUTS
I JUST GOT WHY THEY CALL IT A NEWS FEED.
DAILY NEWS
D. THOMPSON

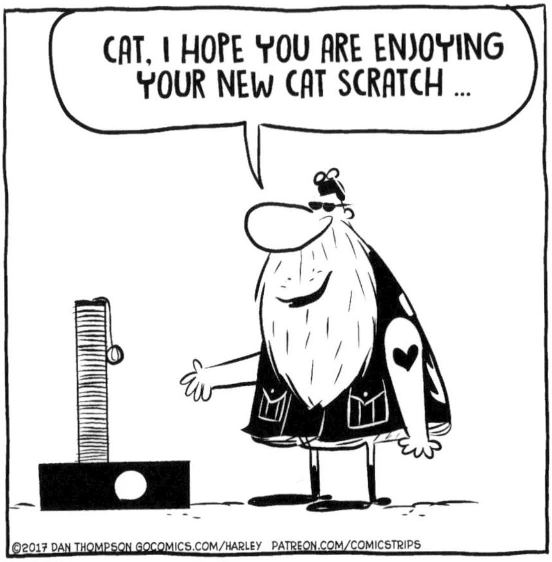
CAT, I HOPE YOU ARE ENJOYING YOUR NEW CAT SCRATCH ...
©2017 DAN THOMPSON GOCOMICS.COM/HARLEY PATREON.COM/COMICSTRIPS

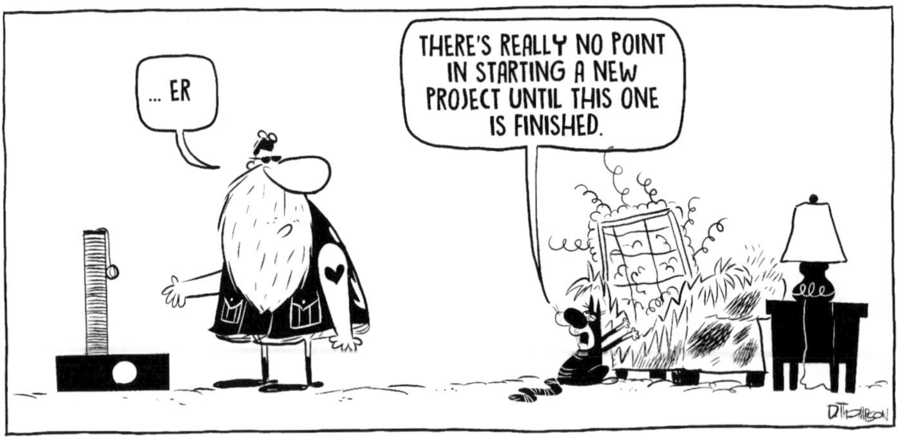
... ER
THERE'S REALLY NO POINT IN STARTING A NEW PROJECT UNTIL THIS ONE IS FINISHED.

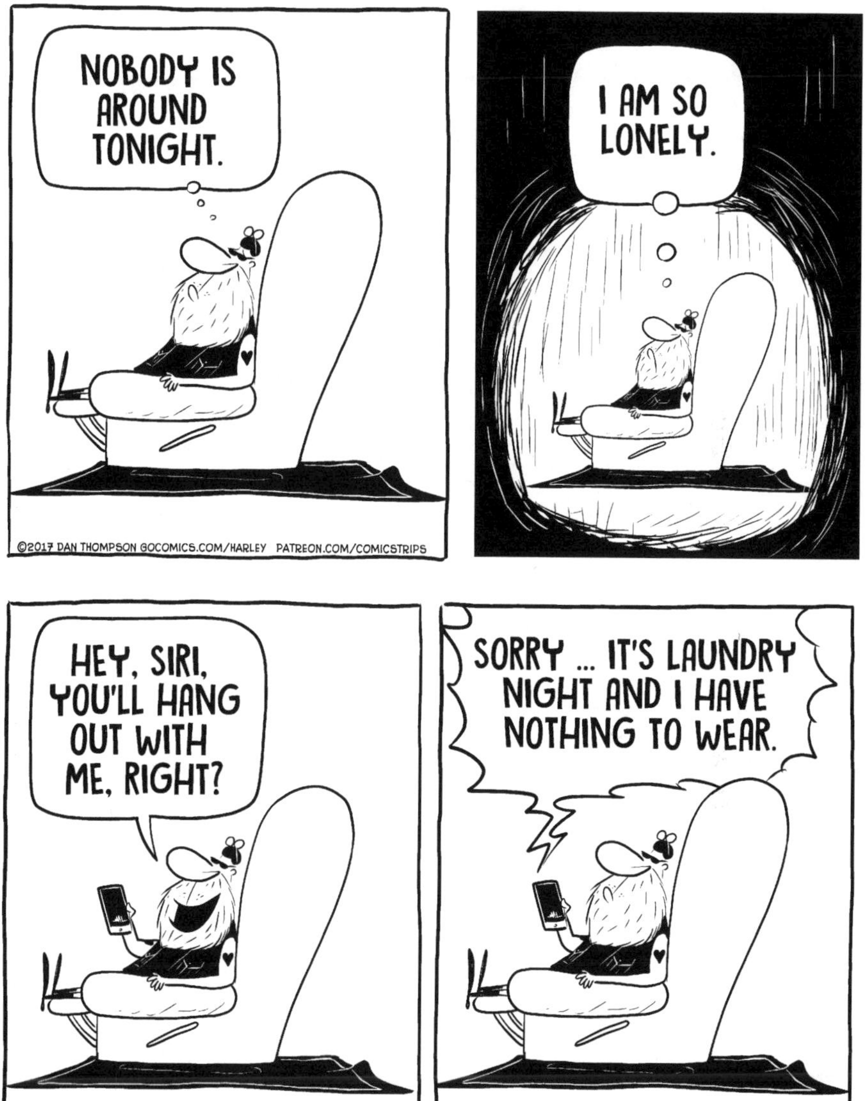
NOBODY IS AROUND TONIGHT.
©2017 DAN THOMPSON GOCOMICS.COM/HARLEY PATREON.COM/COMICSTRIPS
I AM SO LONELY.
HEY, SIRI, YOU'LL HANG OUT WITH ME, RIGHT?
SORRY ... IT'S LAUNDRY NIGHT AND I HAVE NOTHING TO WEAR.
D. THOMPSON

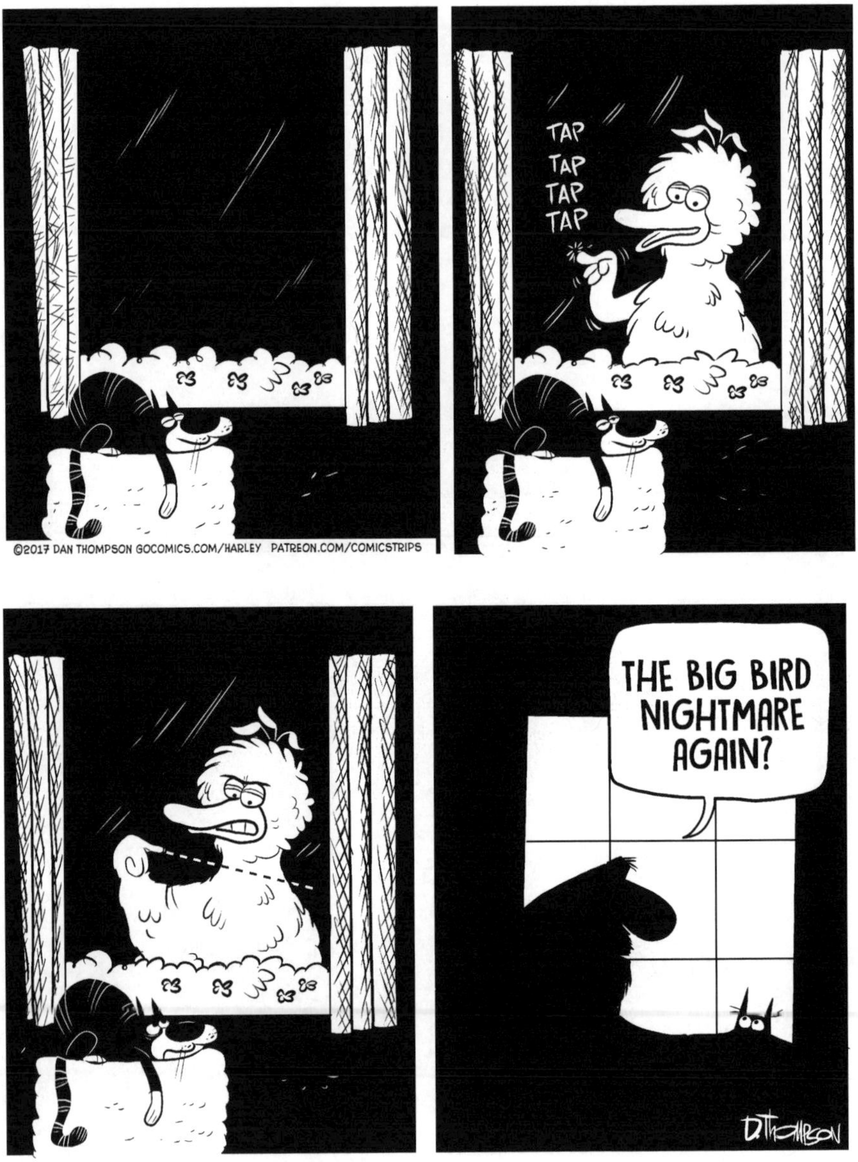
©2017 DAN THOMPSON GOCOMICS.COM/HARLEY PATREON.COM/COMICSTRIPS
TAP
TAP
TAP
TAP
THE BIG BIRD NIGHTMARE AGAIN?
D.THOMPSON

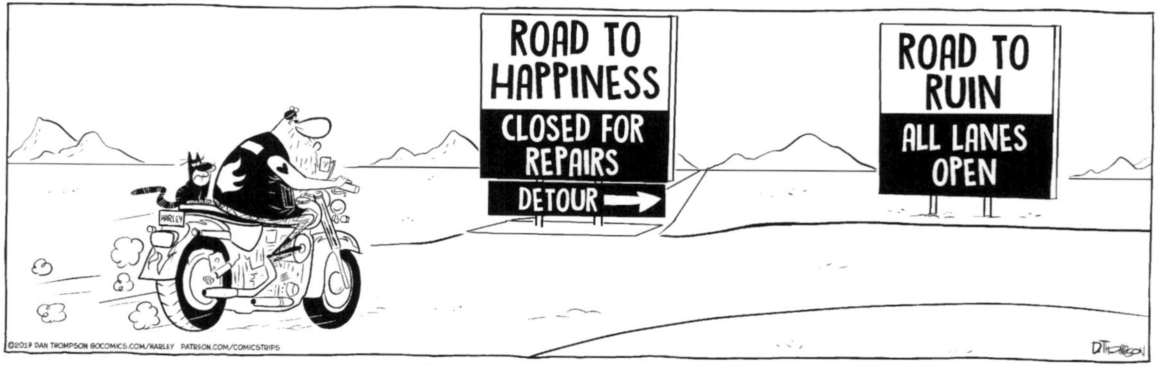
ROAD TO HAPPINESS
CLOSED FOR REPAIRS
DETOUR
ROAD TO RUIN
ALL LANES OPEN
HARLEY
©2017 DAN THOMPSON GOCOMICS.COM/HARLEY PATREON.COM/COMICSTRIPS
DTHOMPSON

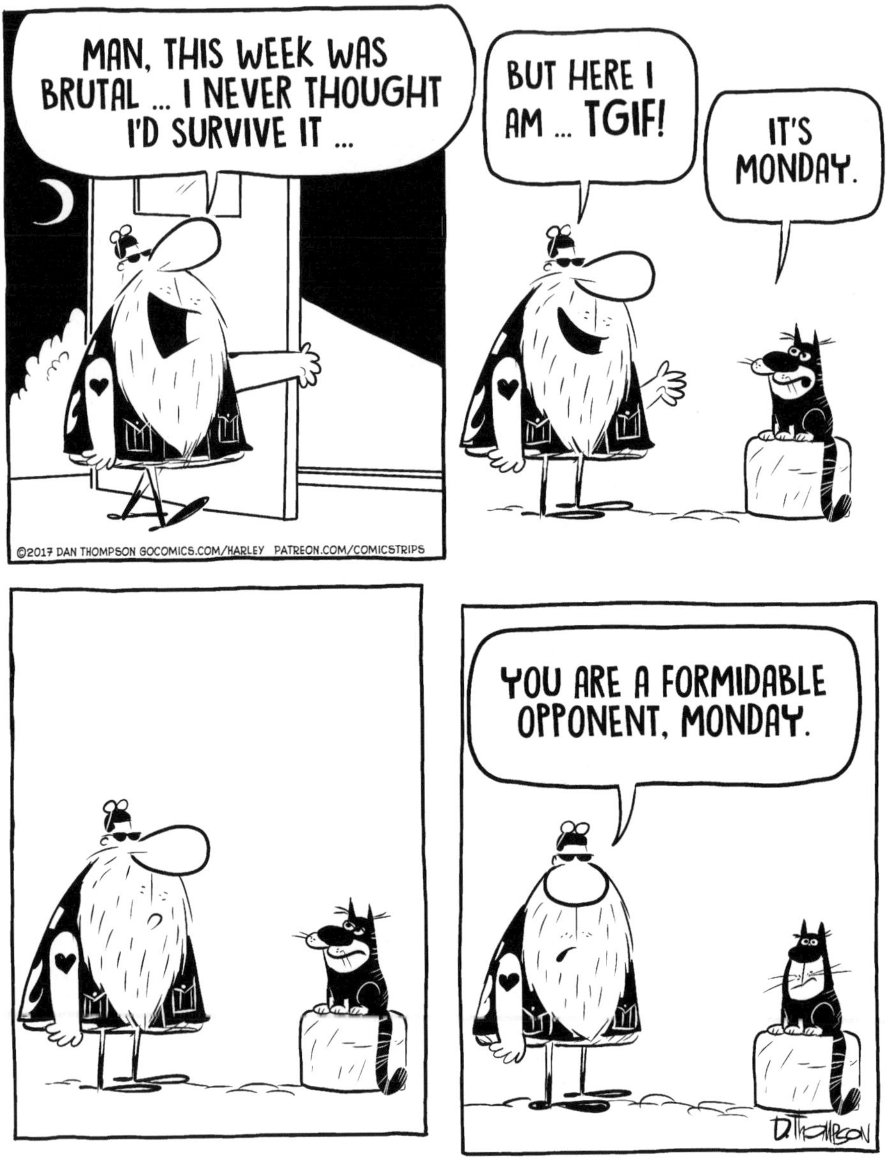
MAN, THIS WEEK WAS BRUTAL ... I NEVER THOUGHT I'D SURVIVE IT ...
BUT HERE I AM ... TGIF!
IT'S MONDAY.
YOU ARE A FORMIDABLE OPPONENT, MONDAY.
©2017 DAN THOMPSON GOCOMICS.COM/HARLEY PATREON.COM/COMICSTRIPS
D. THOMPSON

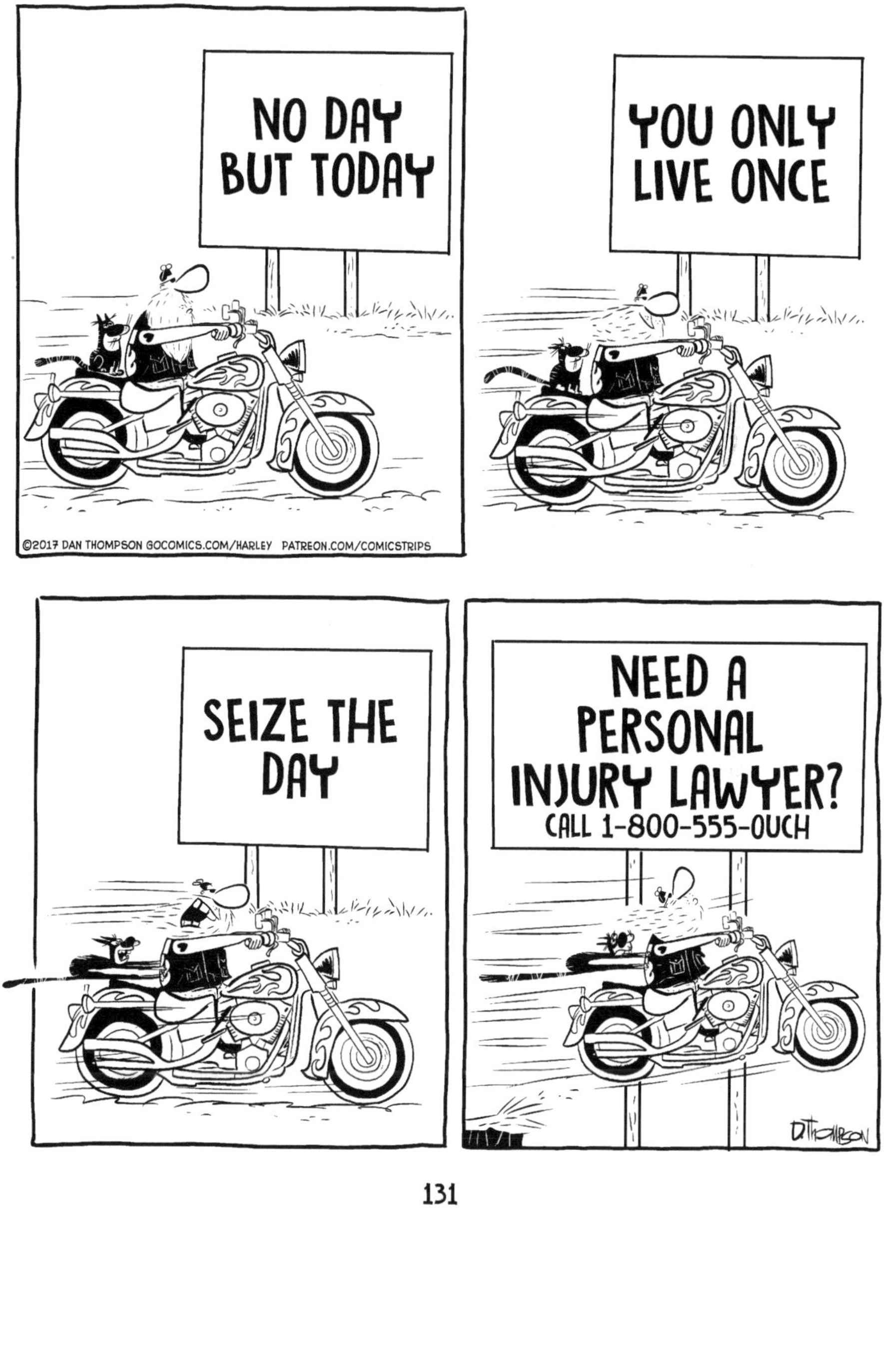
NO DAY BUT TODAY
©2017 DAN THOMPSON GOCOMICS.COM/HARLEY PATREON.COM/COMICSTRIPS
YOU ONLY LIVE ONCE
SEIZE THE DAY
NEED A PERSONAL INJURY LAWYER?
CALL 1-800-555-OUCH
D.THOMPSON

I'VE SCAMMED PEOPLE OUT OF THEIR LIFE SAVINGS.
©2017 DAN THOMPSON GOCOMICS.COM/HARLEY PATREON.COM/COMICSTRIPS
I AM NOT A NICE GUY.
WHAT MADE YOU WANT TO BE A BAD GUY?
I NEVER WANTED TO FINISH LAST.
D.THOMPSON

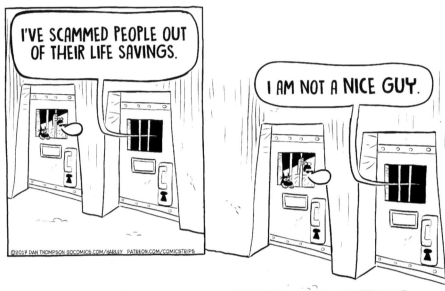

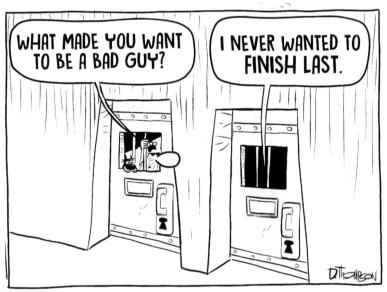

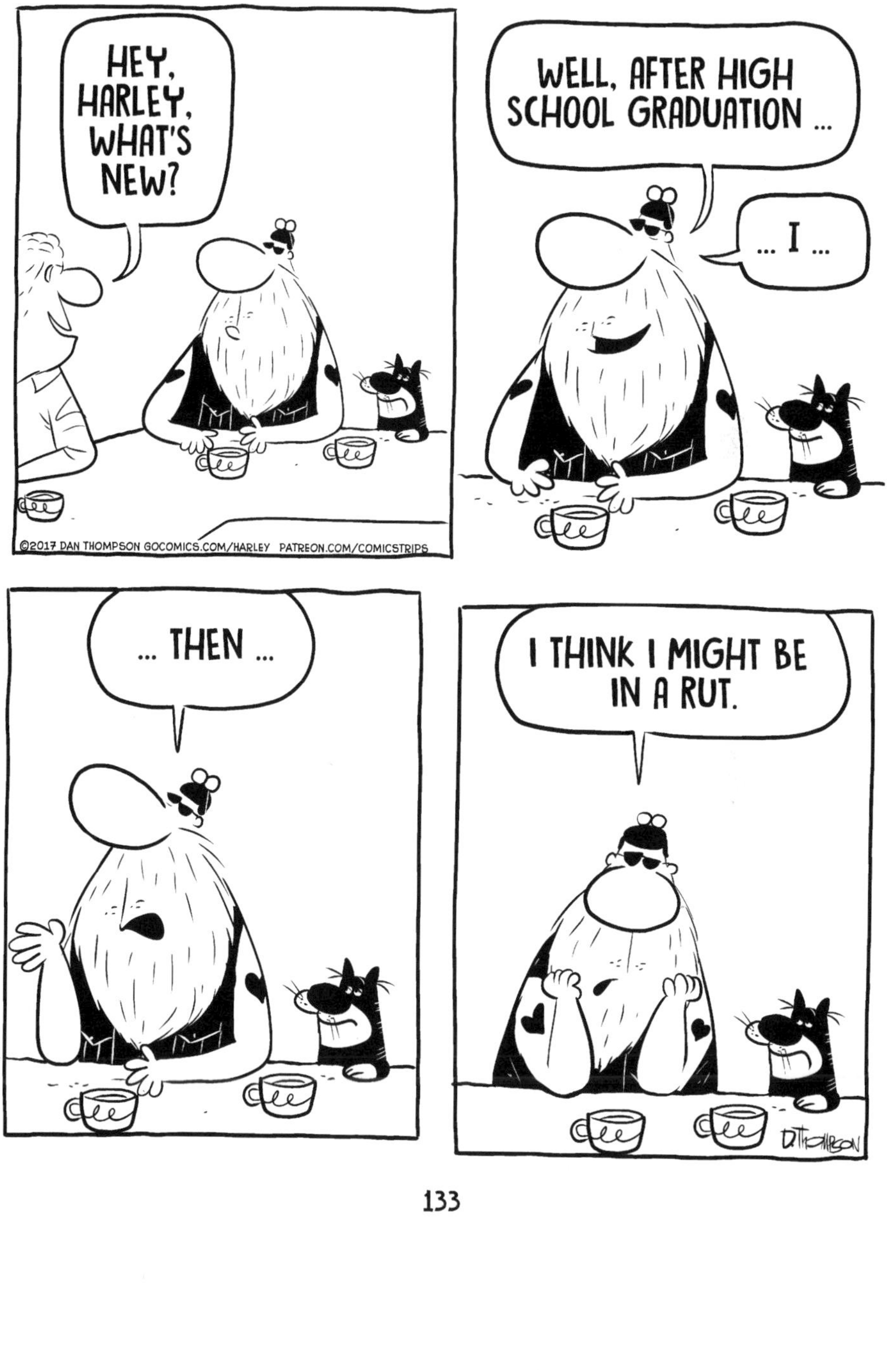
HEY, HARLEY, WHAT'S NEW?
©2017 DAN THOMPSON GOCOMICS.COM/HARLEY PATREON.COM/COMICSTRIPS
WELL, AFTER HIGH SCHOOL GRADUATION ...
... I ...
... THEN ...
I THINK I MIGHT BE IN A RUT.
D.THOMPSON

©2017 DAN THOMPSON GOCOMICS.COM/HARLEY PATREON.COM/COMICSTRIPS
HARLEY
I KNOW I'M OLD WHEN SOMEONE COMPLAINS ABOUT A TOWN THAT HAS NO BARS ...
... AND THEY'RE TALKING ABOUT THEIR SMARTPHONES.
D.THOMPSON

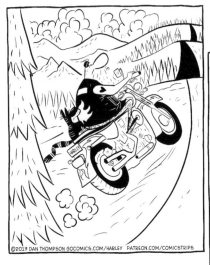

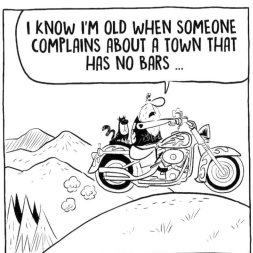

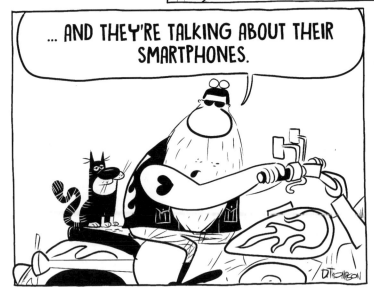

I'D LIKE YOU TO MEET THE DEPARTMENT'S NEWEST K-9 OFFICER, SHERIFF ...
OFFICER BUTTERCUP.
©2017 DAN THOMPSON GOCOMICS.COM/HARLEY PATREON.COM/COMICSTRIPS
SHOULDN'T OUR K-9 OFFICERS HAVE A MENACING LOOK?
THIS IS MY MENACING LOOK.

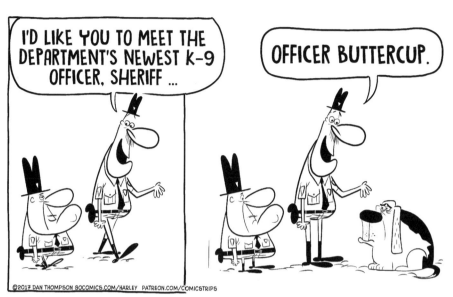

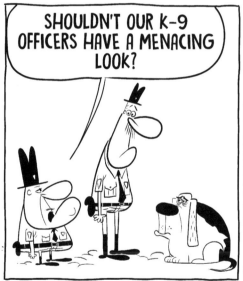

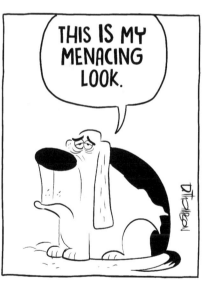

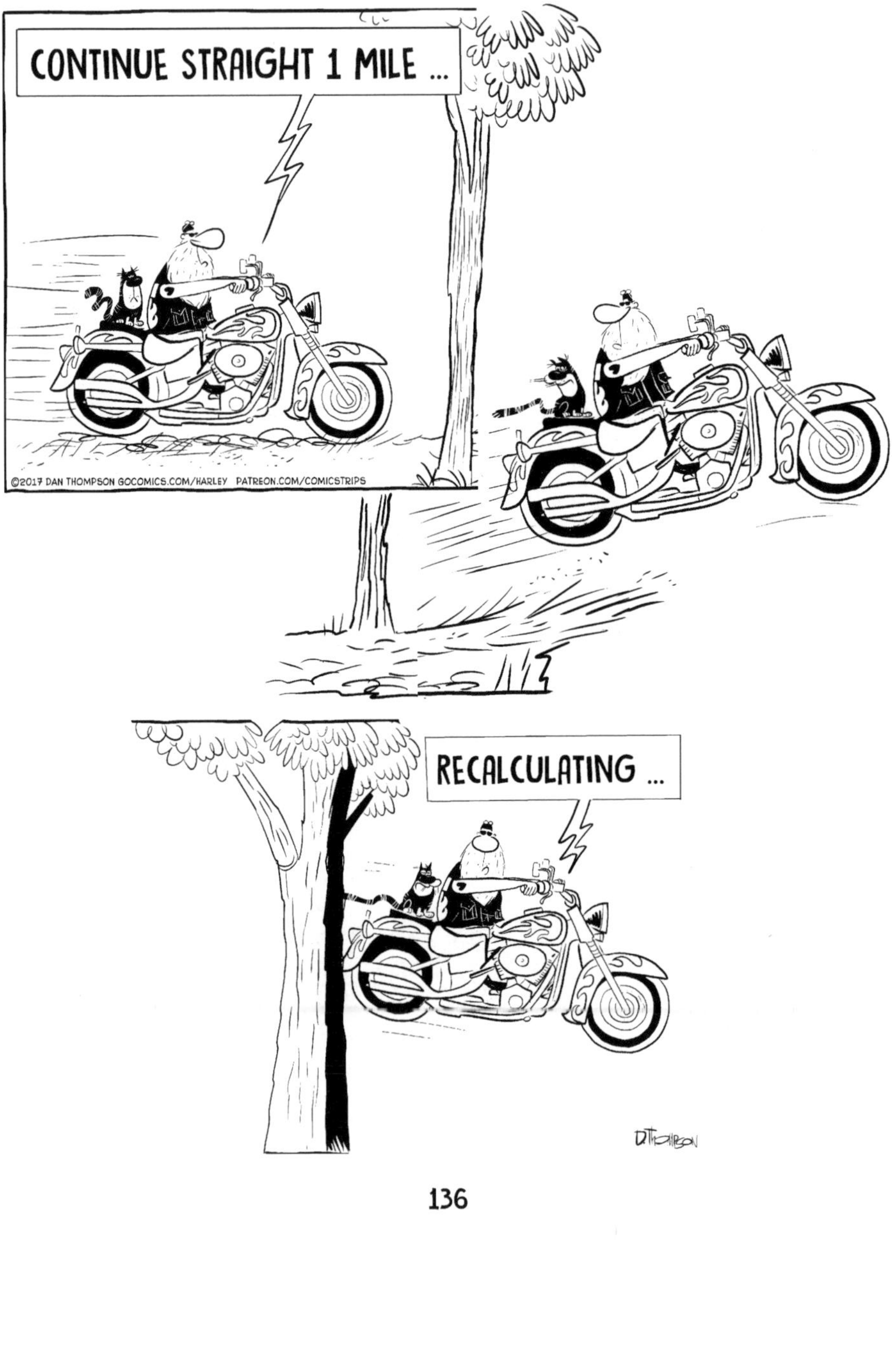
CONTINUE STRAIGHT 1 MILE ...
©2017 DAN THOMPSON GOCOMICS.COM/HARLEY PATREON.COM/COMICSTRIPS
RECALCULATING ...
D THOMPSON

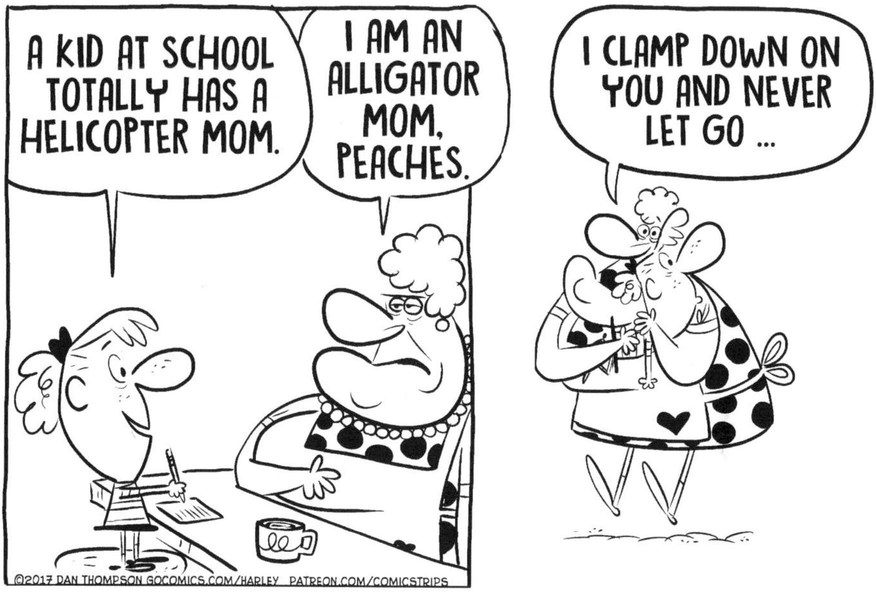
A KID AT SCHOOL TOTALLY HAS A HELICOPTER MOM.
I AM AN ALLIGATOR MOM, PEACHES.
I CLAMP DOWN ON YOU AND NEVER LET GO ...
©2017 DAN THOMPSON GOCOMICS.COM/HARLEY PATREON.COM/COMICSTRIPS

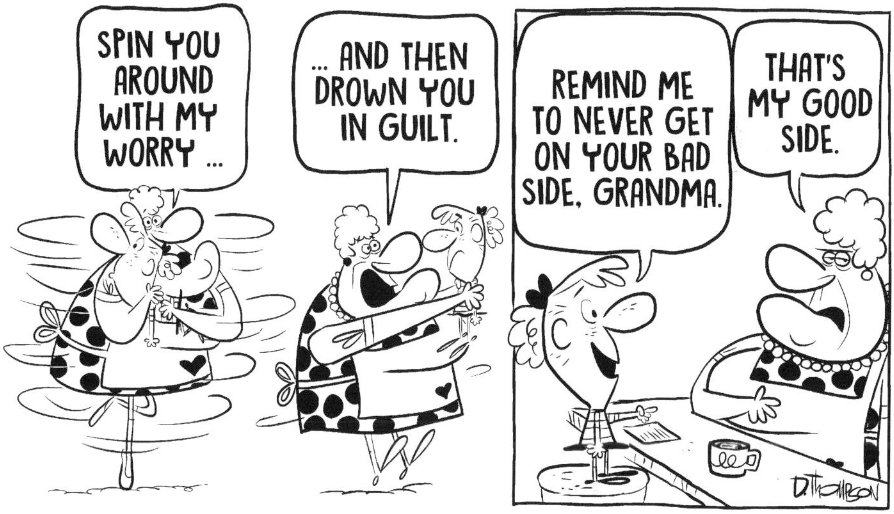
SPIN YOU AROUND WITH MY WORRY ...
... AND THEN DROWN YOU IN GUILT.
REMIND ME TO NEVER GET ON YOUR BAD SIDE, GRANDMA.
THAT'S MY GOOD SIDE.
D. THOMPSON

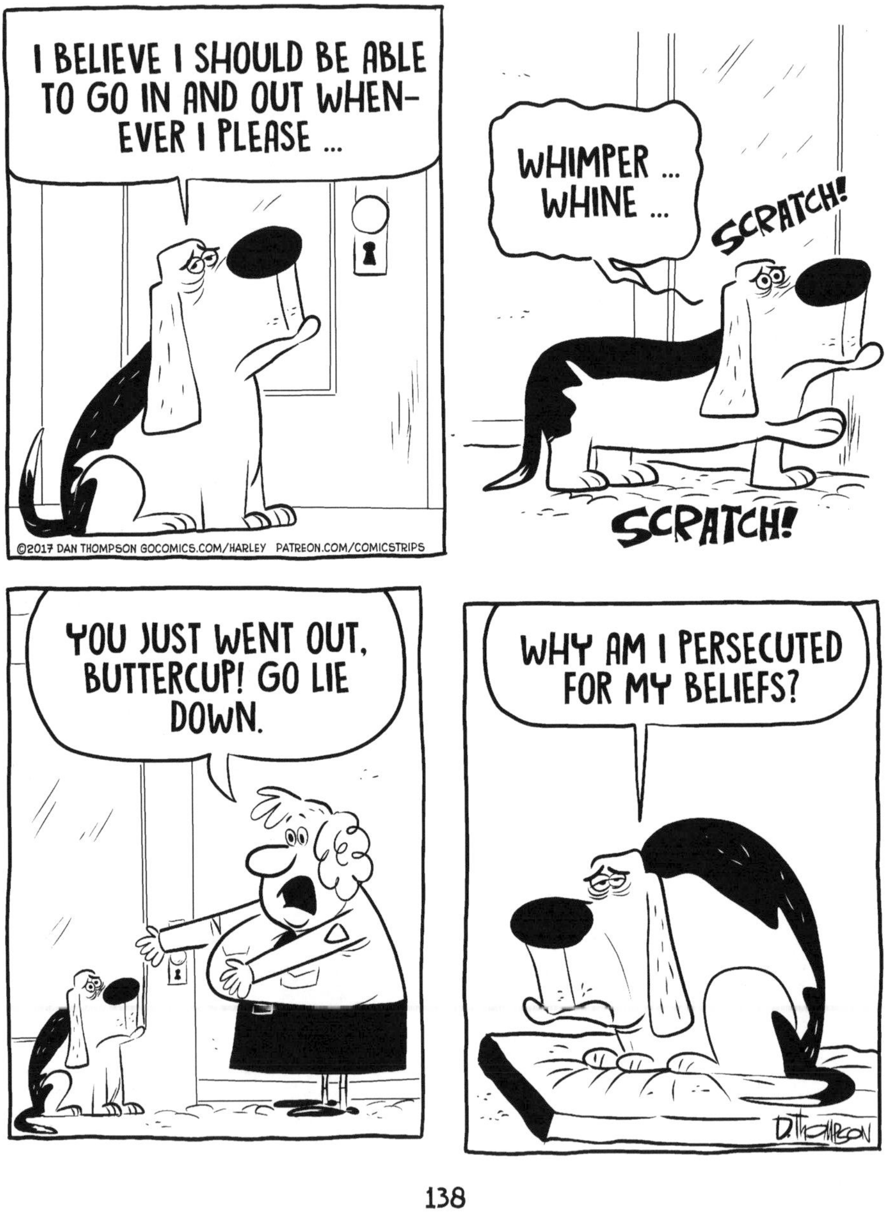
I BELIEVE I SHOULD BE ABLE TO GO IN AND OUT WHEN-EVER I PLEASE ...
©2017 DAN THOMPSON GOCOMICS.COM/HARLEY PATREON.COM/COMICSTRIPS
WHIMPER ... WHINE ...
SCRATCH!
SCRATCH!
YOU JUST WENT OUT, BUTTERCUP! GO LIE DOWN.
WHY AM I PERSECUTED FOR MY BELIEFS?
D.THOMPSON

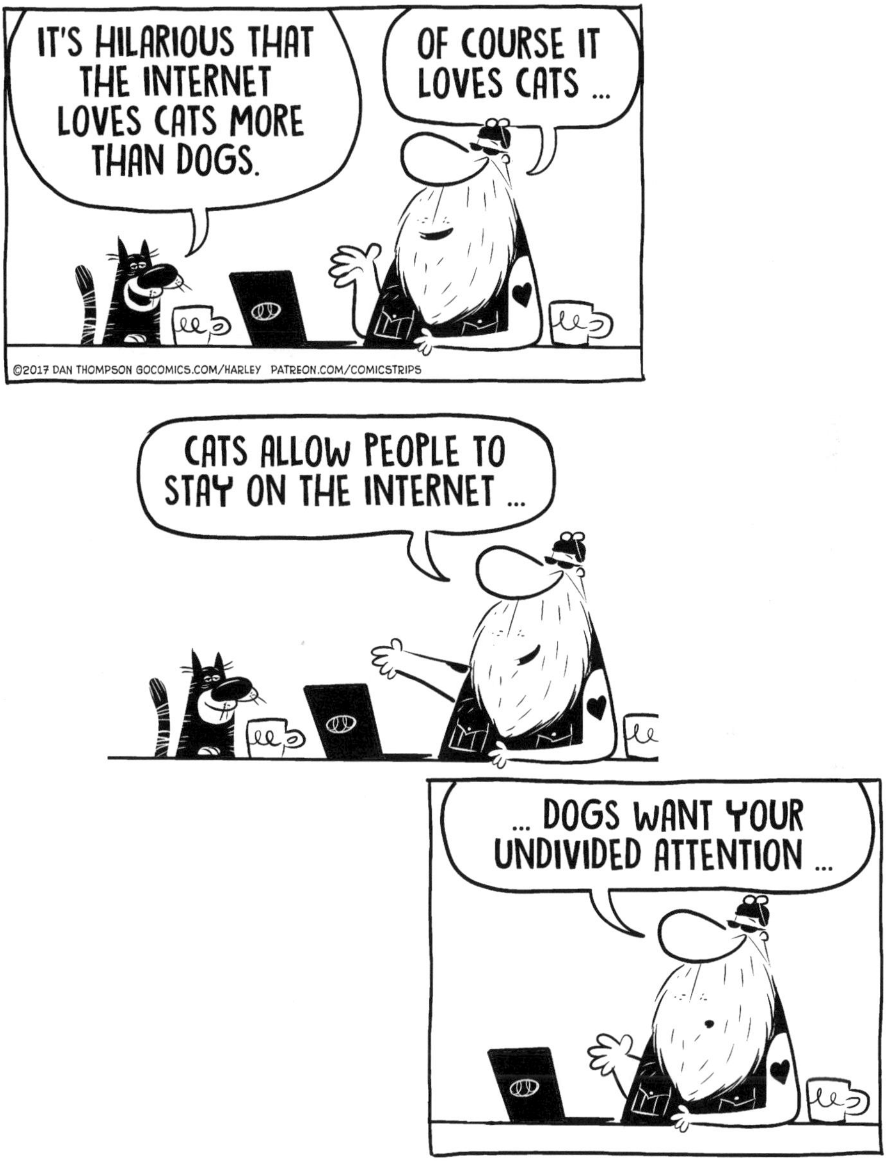
IT'S HILARIOUS THAT THE INTERNET LOVES CATS MORE THAN DOGS.
OF COURSE IT LOVES CATS ...
©2017 DAN THOMPSON GOCOMICS.COM/HARLEY PATREON.COM/COMICSTRIPS
CATS ALLOW PEOPLE TO STAY ON THE INTERNET ...
... DOGS WANT YOUR UNDIVIDED ATTENTION ...

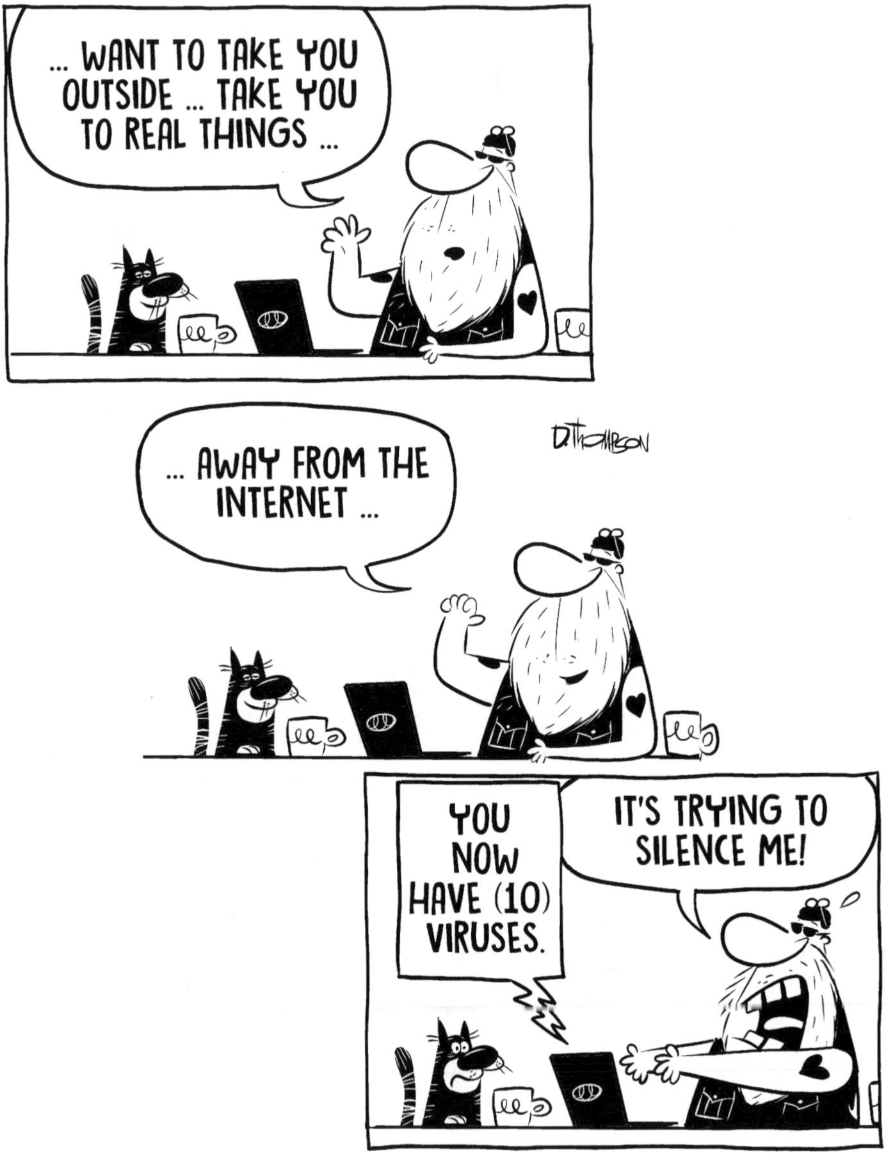
... WANT TO TAKE YOU OUTSIDE ... TAKE YOU TO REAL THINGS ...
D.THOMPSON
... AWAY FROM THE INTERNET ...
YOU NOW HAVE (10) VIRUSES.
IT'S TRYING TO SILENCE ME!

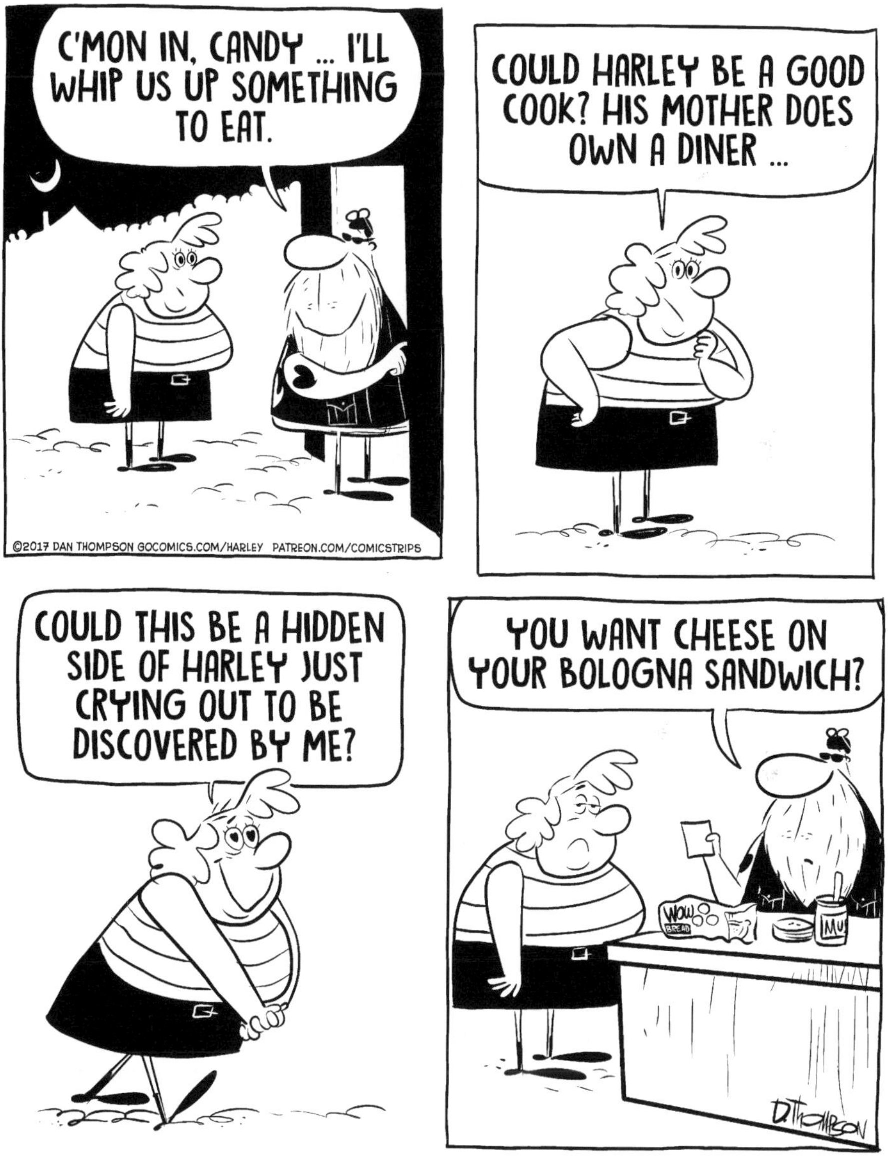
C'MON IN, CANDY ... I'LL WHIP US UP SOMETHING TO EAT.
©2017 DAN THOMPSON GOCOMICS.COM/HARLEY PATREON.COM/COMICSTRIPS
COULD HARLEY BE A GOOD COOK? HIS MOTHER DOES OWN A DINER ...
COULD THIS BE A HIDDEN SIDE OF HARLEY JUST CRYING OUT TO BE DISCOVERED BY ME?
YOU WANT CHEESE ON YOUR BOLOGNA SANDWICH?
WOW BREAD
D. THOMPSON

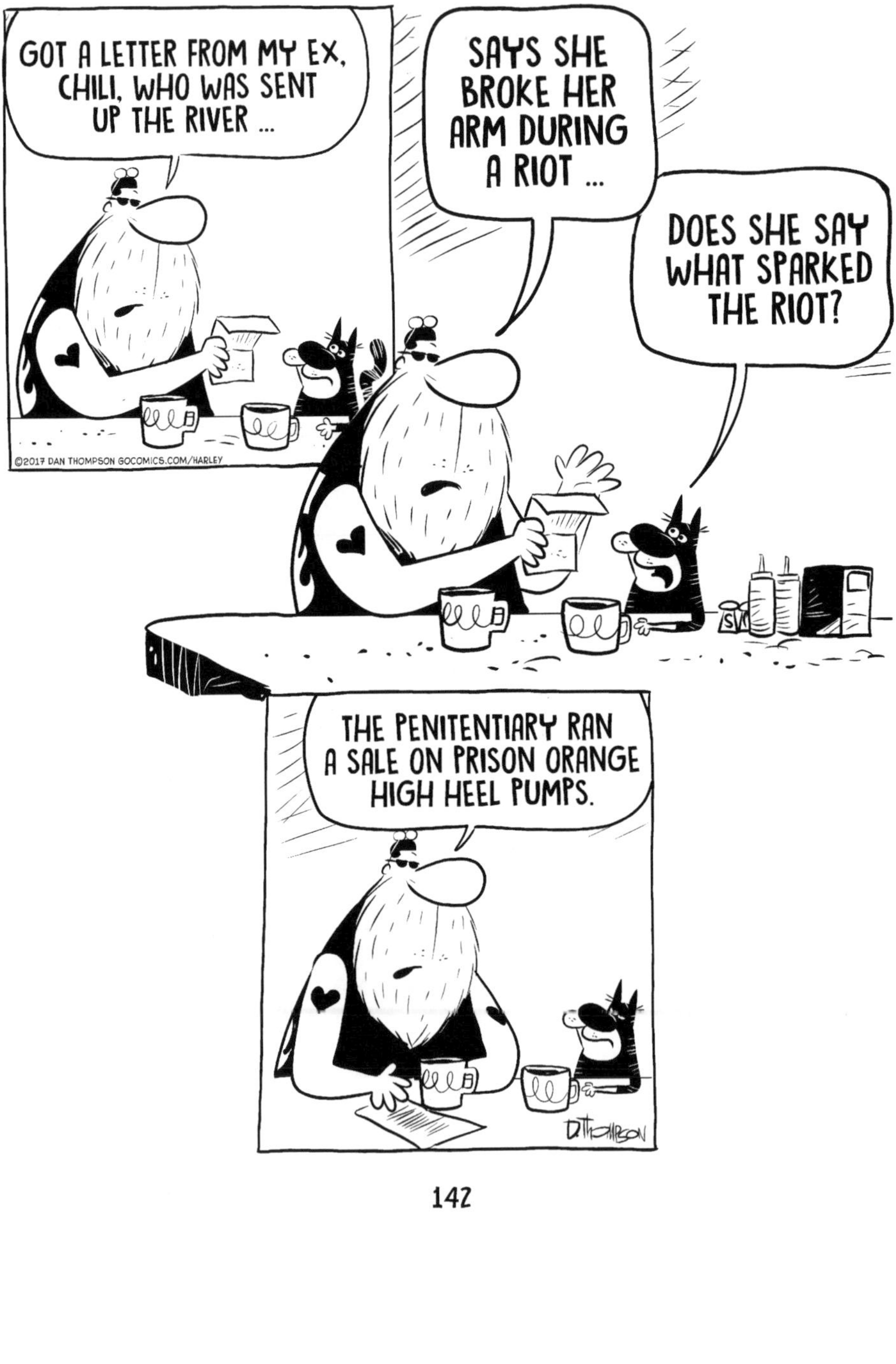
GOT A LETTER FROM MY EX, CHILI, WHO WAS SENT UP THE RIVER ...
©2017 DAN THOMPSON GOCOMICS.COM/HARLEY
SAYS SHE BROKE HER ARM DURING A RIOT ...
DOES SHE SAY WHAT SPARKED THE RIOT?
THE PENITENTIARY RAN A SALE ON PRISON ORANGE HIGH HEEL PUMPS.
D. THOMPSON

OLD HOGS BAR
NEXT LEFT
HARLEY
©2017 DAN THOMPSON GOCOMICS.COM/HARLEY PATREON.COM/COMICSTRIPS
THEY SAY YOU'VE TRAVELED ALL OVER THE WORLD.
BAR
I'VE BEEN EVERY-WHERE.
RTE 66
SWEDISH LAPLAND.
IT'S NOT WHAT IT SOUNDS LIKE.
D. THOMPSON

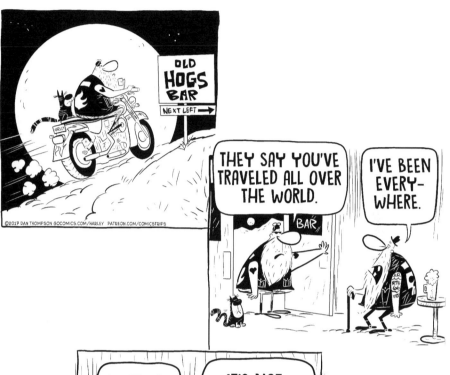

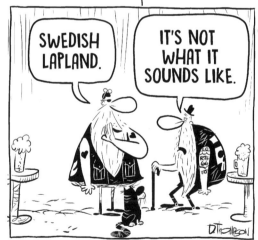

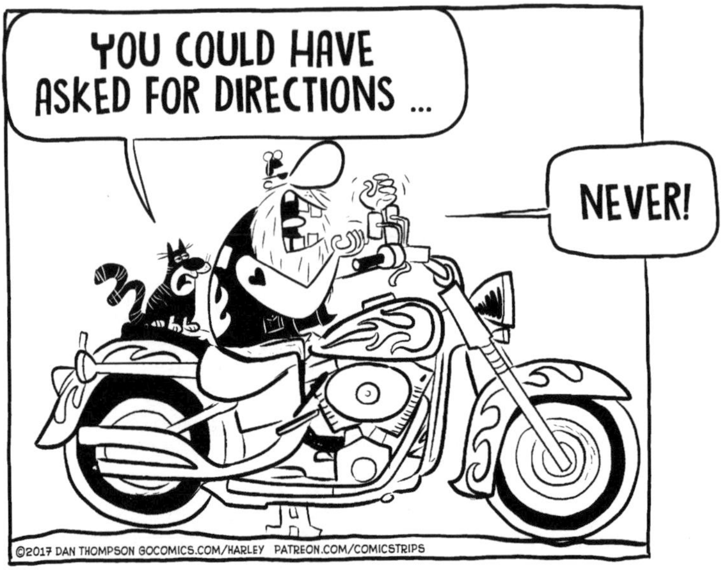
YOU COULD HAVE ASKED FOR DIRECTIONS ...
NEVER!
©2017 DAN THOMPSON GOCOMICS.COM/HARLEY PATREON.COM/COMICSTRIPS

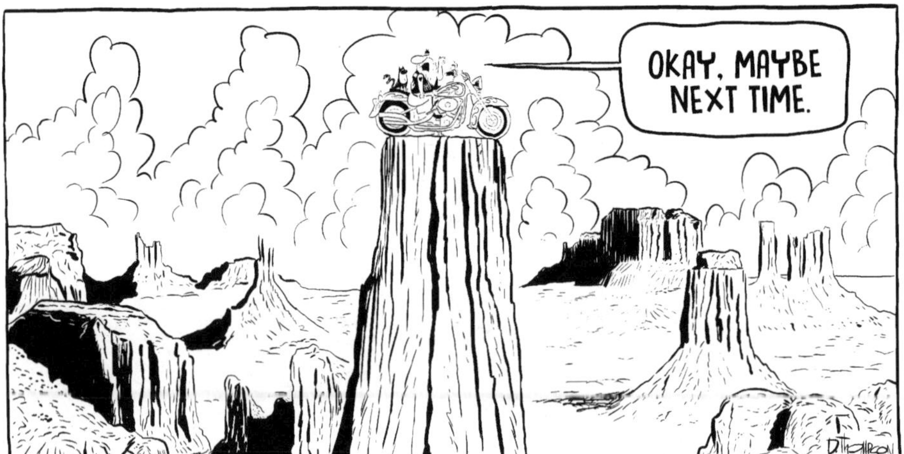
OKAY, MAYBE NEXT TIME.

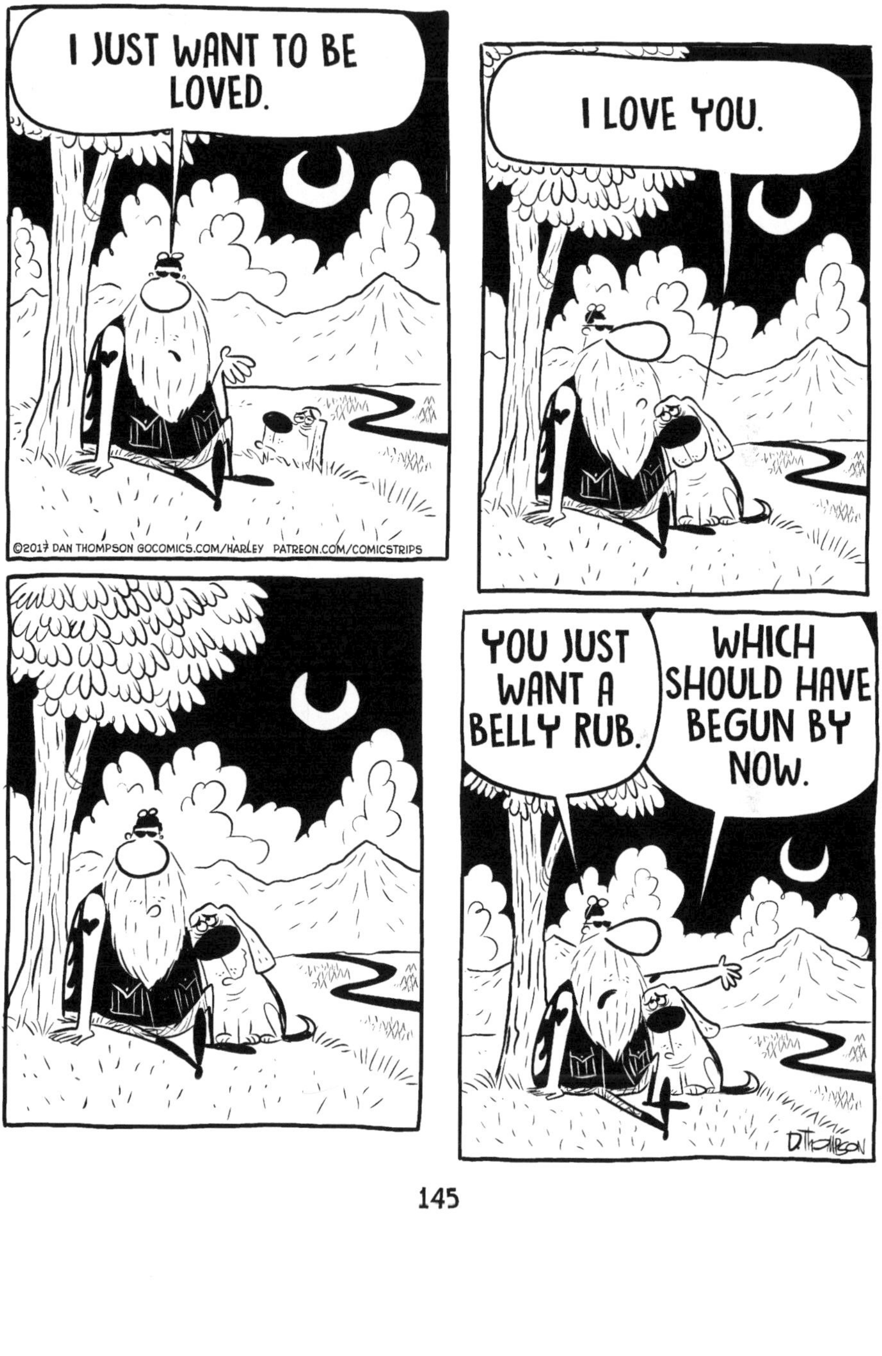
I JUST WANT TO BE LOVED.
©2017 DAN THOMPSON GOCOMICS.COM/HARLEY PATREON.COM/COMICSTRIPS
I LOVE YOU.
YOU JUST WANT A BELLY RUB.
WHICH SHOULD HAVE BEGUN BY NOW.
D.THOMPSON

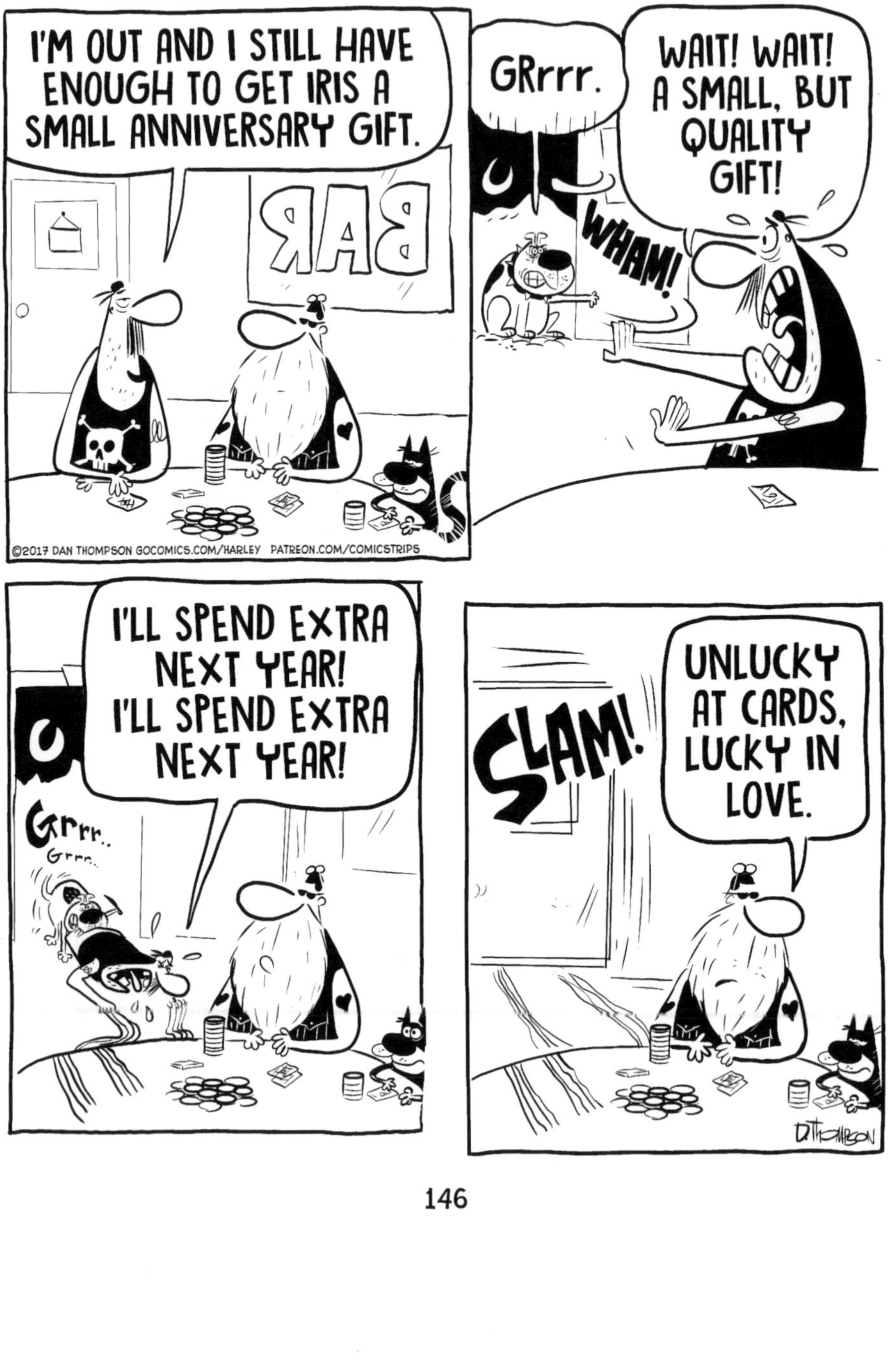
I'M OUT AND I STILL HAVE ENOUGH TO GET IRIS A SMALL ANNIVERSARY GIFT.
BAR
©2017 DAN THOMPSON GOCOMICS.COM/HARLEY PATREON.COM/COMICSTRIPS
GRrrr.
WAIT! WAIT! A SMALL, BUT QUALITY GIFT!
WHAM!
I'LL SPEND EXTRA NEXT YEAR! I'LL SPEND EXTRA NEXT YEAR!
Grrr..
Grrr..
SLAM!
UNLUCKY AT CARDS, LUCKY IN LOVE.
D THOMPSON

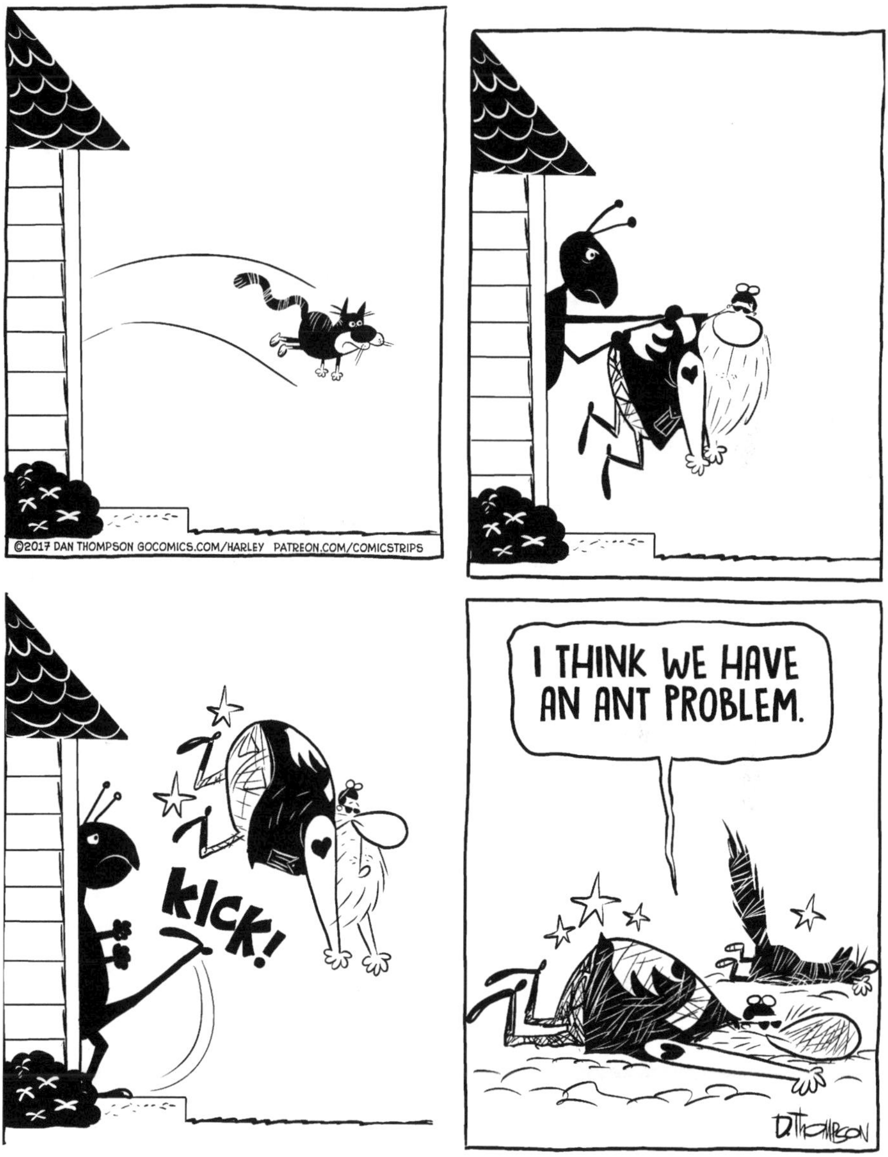
©2017 DAN THOMPSON GOCOMICS.COM/HARLEY PATREON.COM/COMICSTRIPS
KICK!
I THINK WE HAVE AN ANT PROBLEM.
D.THOMPSON

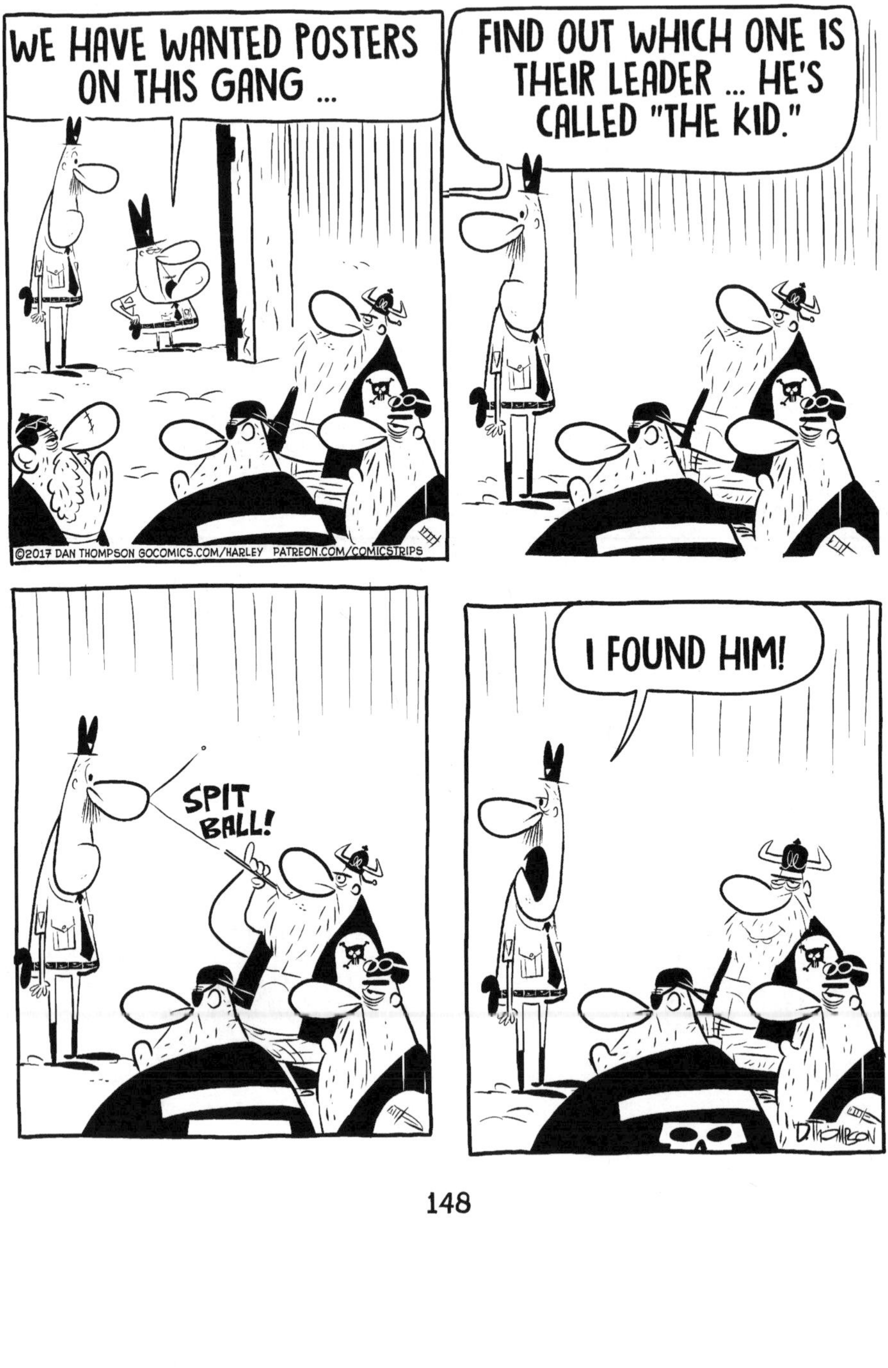
WE HAVE WANTED POSTERS ON THIS GANG ...
©2017 DAN THOMPSON GOCOMICS.COM/HARLEY PATREON.COM/COMICSTRIPS
FIND OUT WHICH ONE IS THEIR LEADER ... HE'S CALLED "THE KID."
SPIT BALL!
I FOUND HIM!
D. THOMPSON

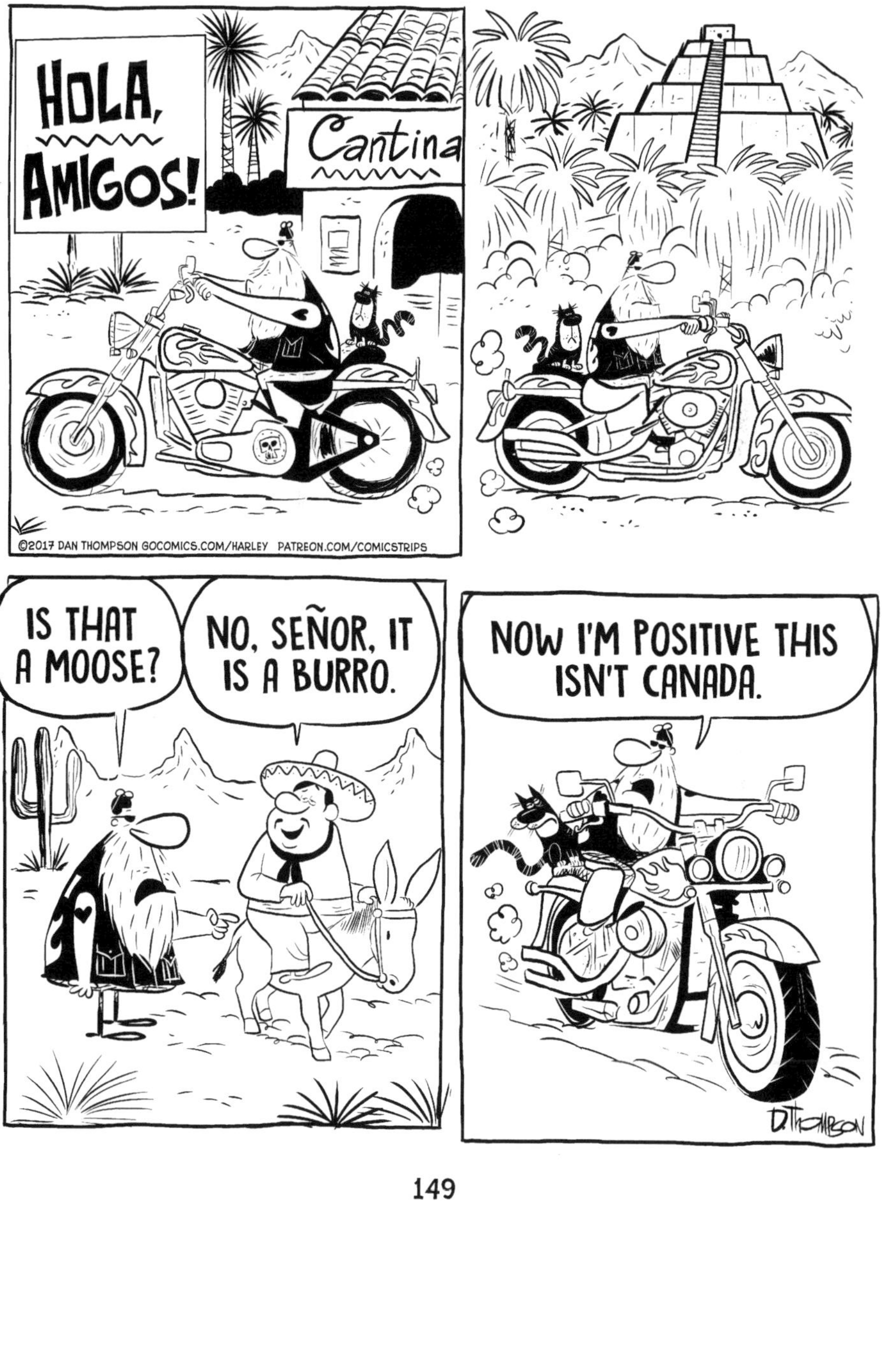
HOLA, AMIGOS!
Cantina
©2017 DAN THOMPSON GOCOMICS.COM/HARLEY PATREON.COM/COMICSTRIPS
IS THAT A MOOSE?
NO, SEÑOR, IT IS A BURRO.
NOW I'M POSITIVE THIS ISN'T CANADA.
D. THOMPSON

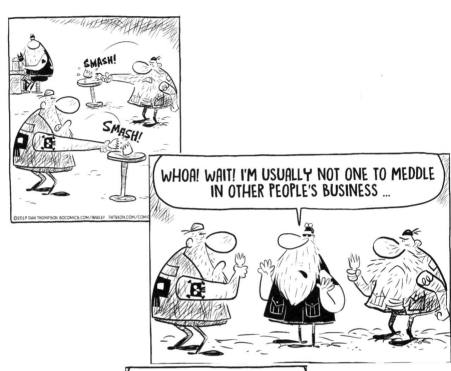

SMASH!
SMASH!
©2017 DAN THOMPSON GOCOMICS.COM/HARLEY PATREON.COM/COMIC
WHOA! WAIT! I'M USUALLY NOT ONE TO MEDDLE IN OTHER PEOPLE'S BUSINESS ...
BUT THERE WAS A 5 CENT DEPOSIT ON EACH OF THOSE BOTTLES.
D.THOMPSON

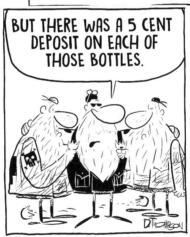

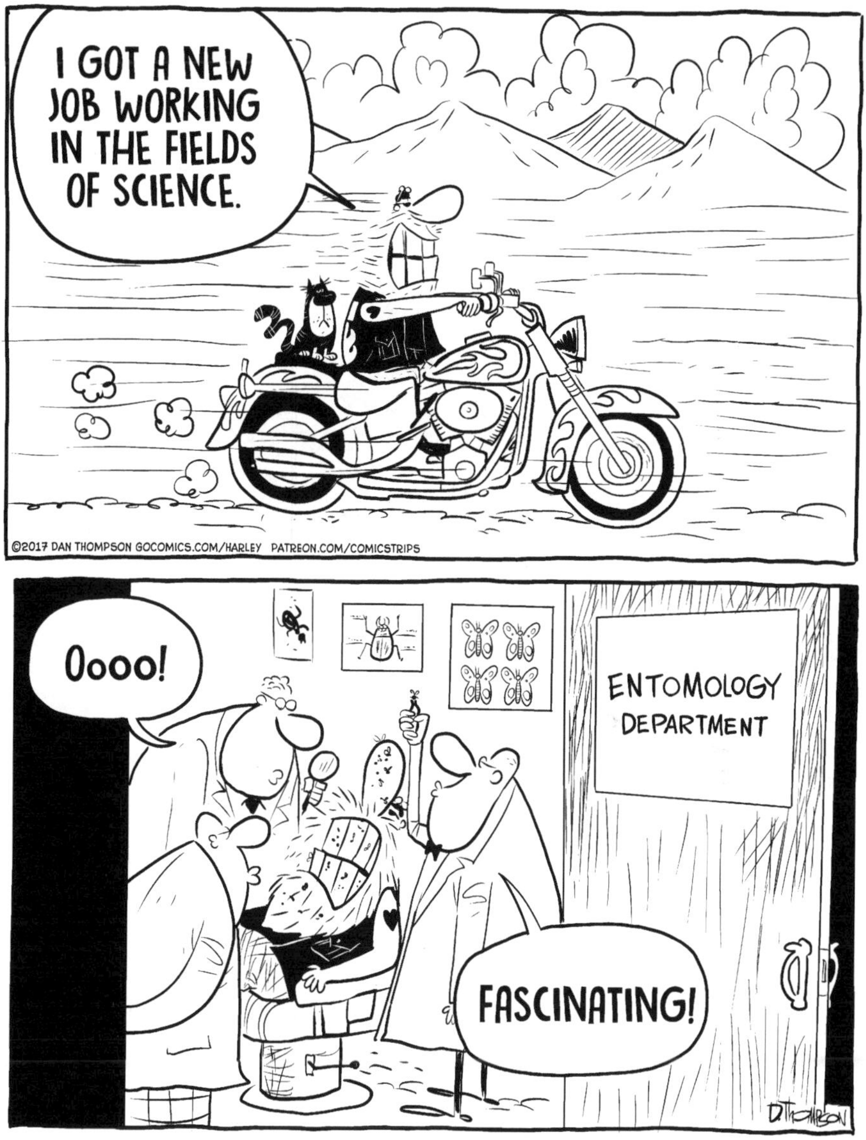
I GOT A NEW JOB WORKING IN THE FIELDS OF SCIENCE.
©2017 DAN THOMPSON GOCOMICS.COM/HARLEY PATREON.COM/COMICSTRIPS
Oooo!
ENTOMOLOGY DEPARTMENT
FASCINATING!
D.THOMPSON

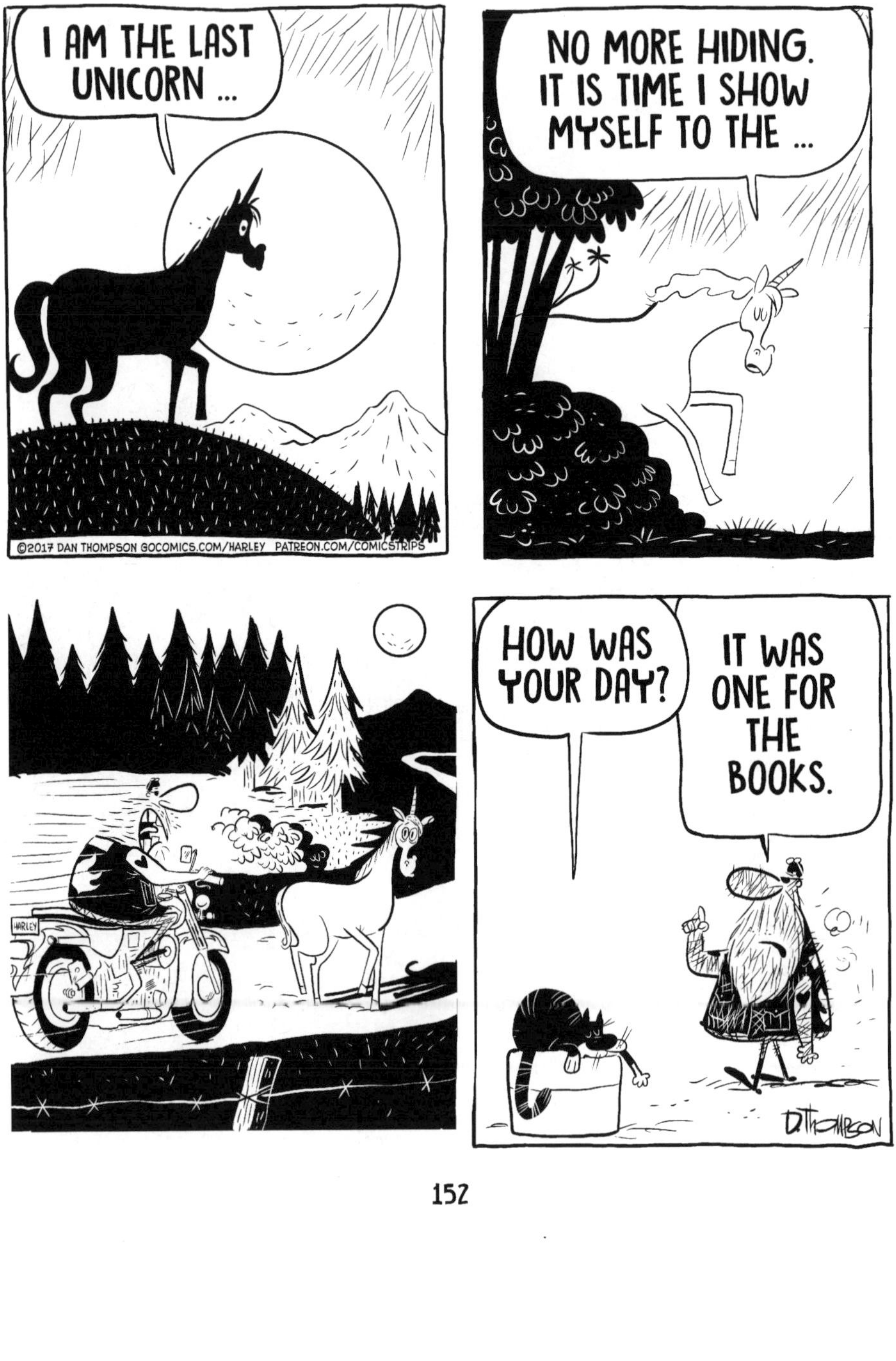
I AM THE LAST UNICORN ...
©2017 DAN THOMPSON GOCOMICS.COM/HARLEY PATREON.COM/COMICSTRIPS
NO MORE HIDING. IT IS TIME I SHOW MYSELF TO THE ...
HARLEY
HOW WAS YOUR DAY?
IT WAS ONE FOR THE BOOKS.
D. THOMPSON

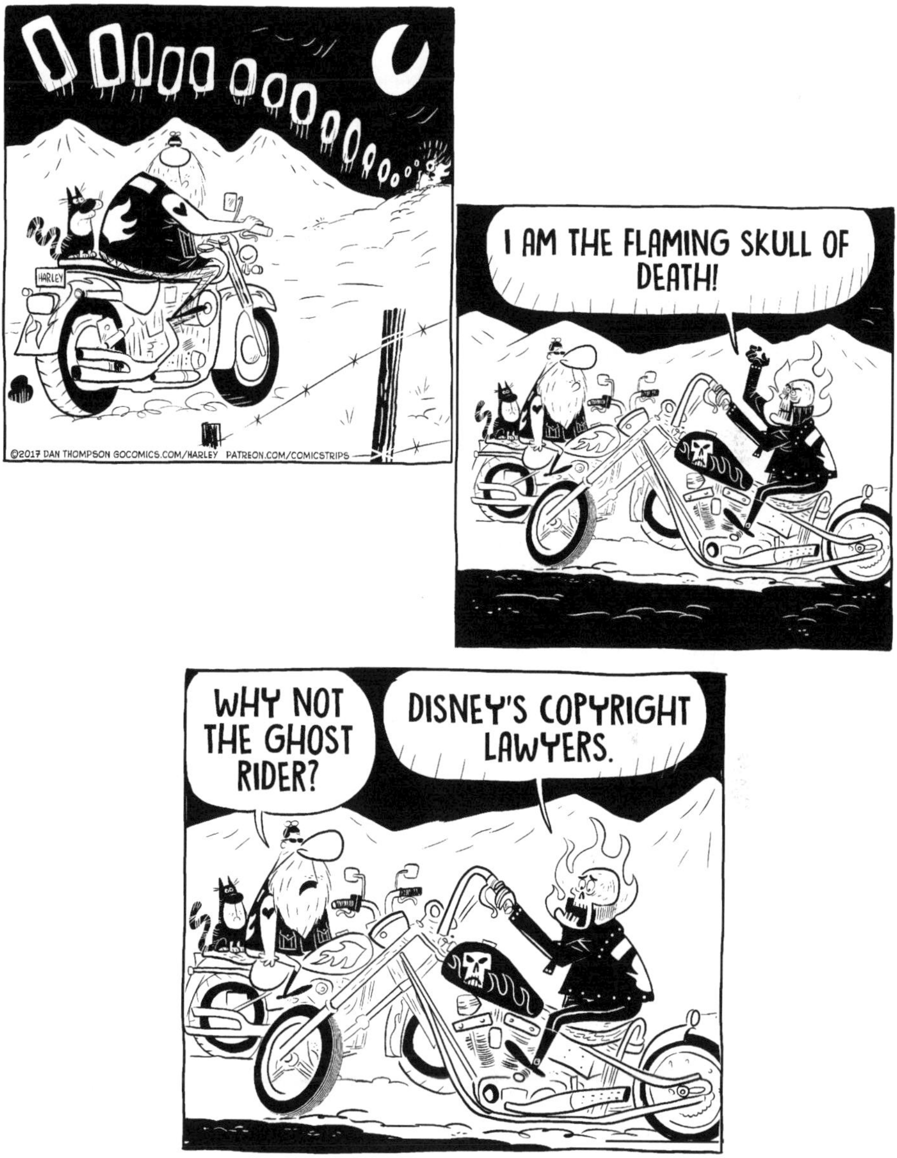
OOOOOOOOOOOOOO
©2017 DAN THOMPSON GOCOMICS.COM/HARLEY PATREON.COM/COMICSTRIPS
HARLEY
I AM THE FLAMING SKULL OF DEATH!
WHY NOT THE GHOST RIDER?
DISNEY'S COPYRIGHT LAWYERS.

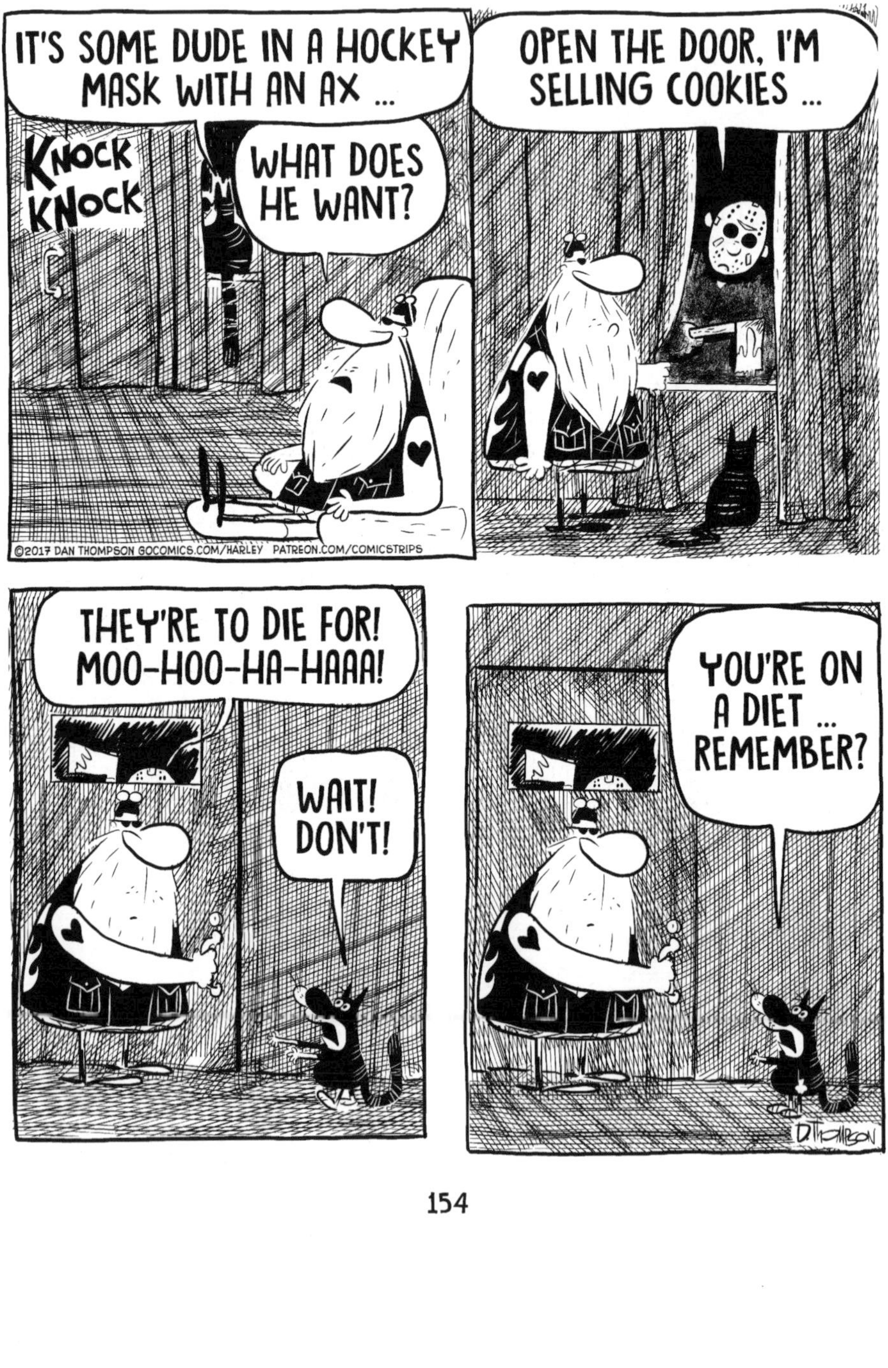
IT'S SOME DUDE IN A HOCKEY MASK WITH AN AX ...
KNOCK KNOCK
WHAT DOES HE WANT?
©2017 DAN THOMPSON GOCOMICS.COM/HARLEY PATREON.COM/COMICSTRIPS
OPEN THE DOOR, I'M SELLING COOKIES ...
THEY'RE TO DIE FOR! MOO-HOO-HA-HAAA!
WAIT! DON'T!
YOU'RE ON A DIET ... REMEMBER?
D. THOMPSON

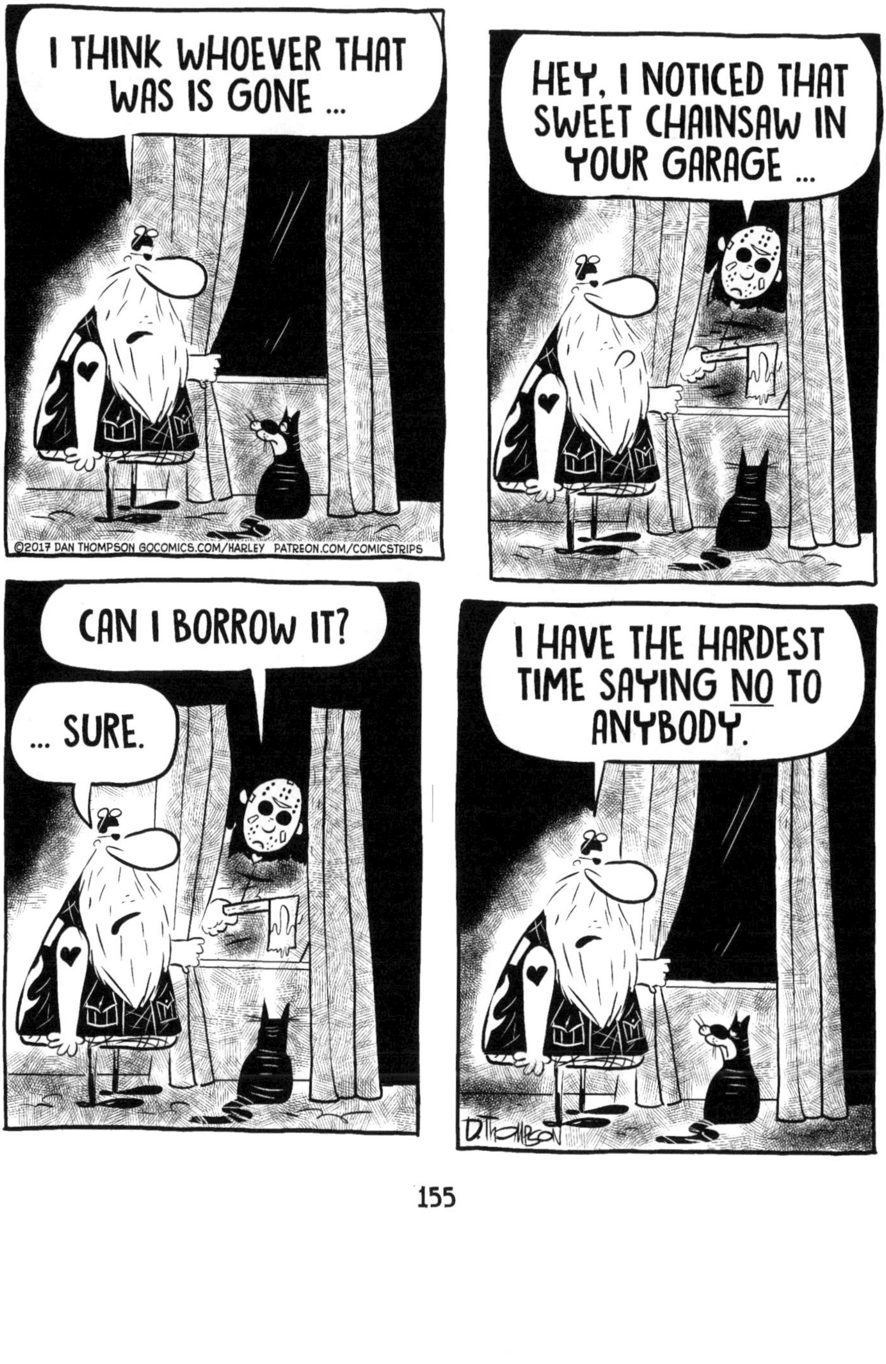
I THINK WHOEVER THAT WAS IS GONE ...
©2017 DAN THOMPSON GOCOMICS.COM/HARLEY PATREON.COM/COMICSTRIPS
HEY, I NOTICED THAT SWEET CHAINSAW IN YOUR GARAGE ...
CAN I BORROW IT?
... SURE.
I HAVE THE HARDEST TIME SAYING NO TO ANYBODY.
D. THOMPSON

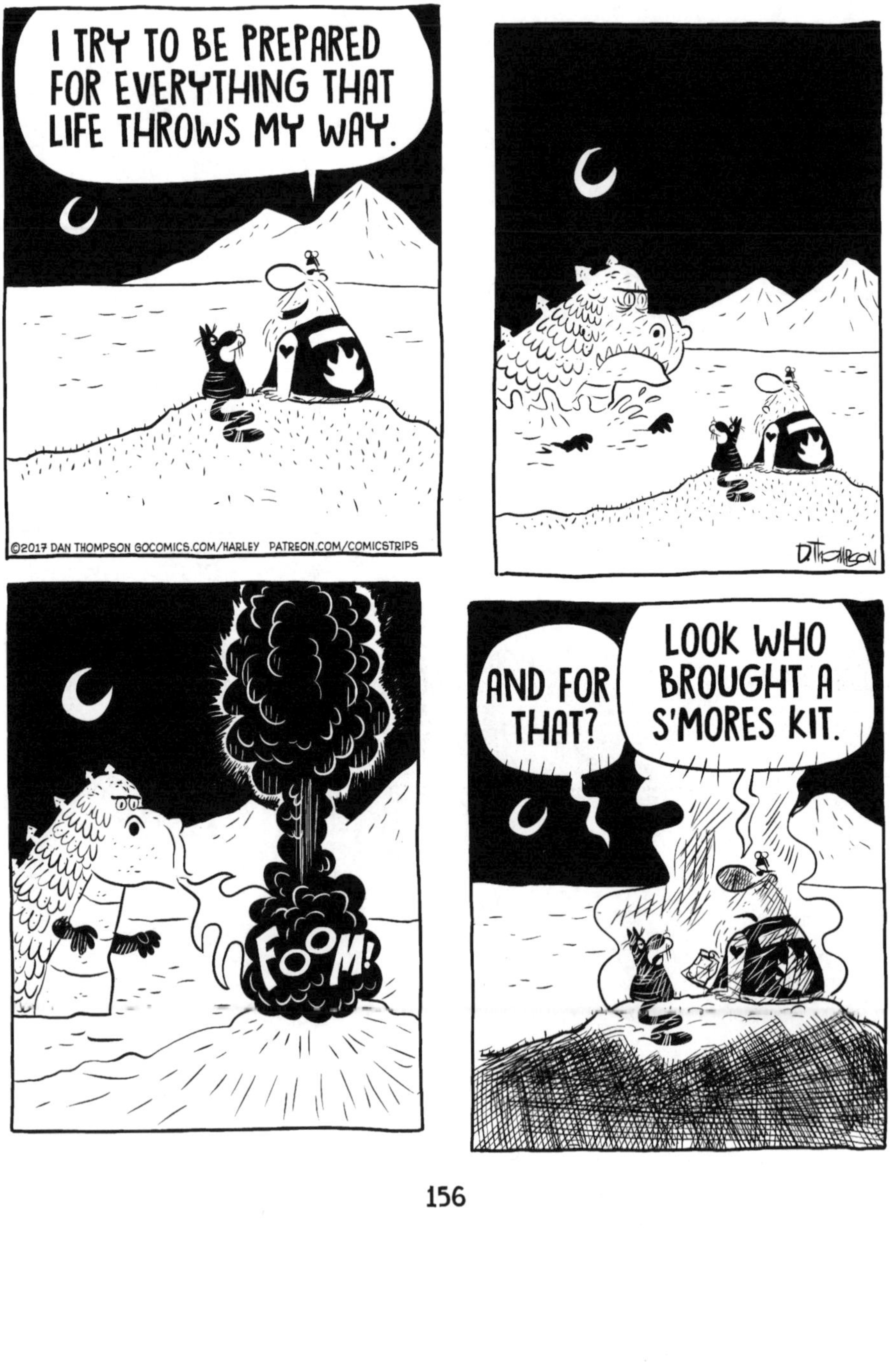
I TRY TO BE PREPARED FOR EVERYTHING THAT LIFE THROWS MY WAY.
©2017 DAN THOMPSON GOCOMICS.COM/HARLEY PATREON.COM/COMICSTRIPS
D.THOMPSON
FOOM!
AND FOR THAT?
LOOK WHO BROUGHT A S'MORES KIT.

NO MATTER HOW BAD YOU THINK YOU HAVE IT ...
©2017 DAN THOMPSON GOCOMICS.COM/HARLEY PATREON.COM/COMICSTRIPS
SOMEBODY ALWAYS HAS IT WORSE ...
GIVE ME AN EXAMPLE.
D. THOMPSON

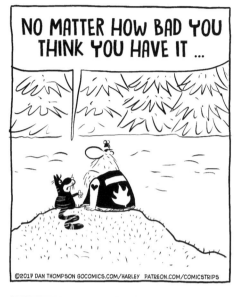

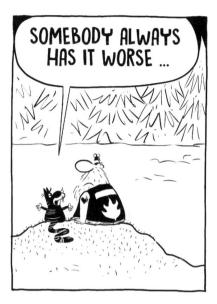

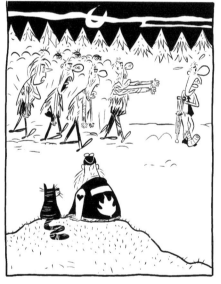

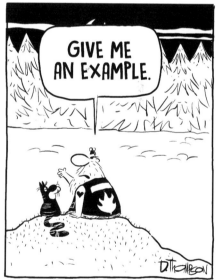

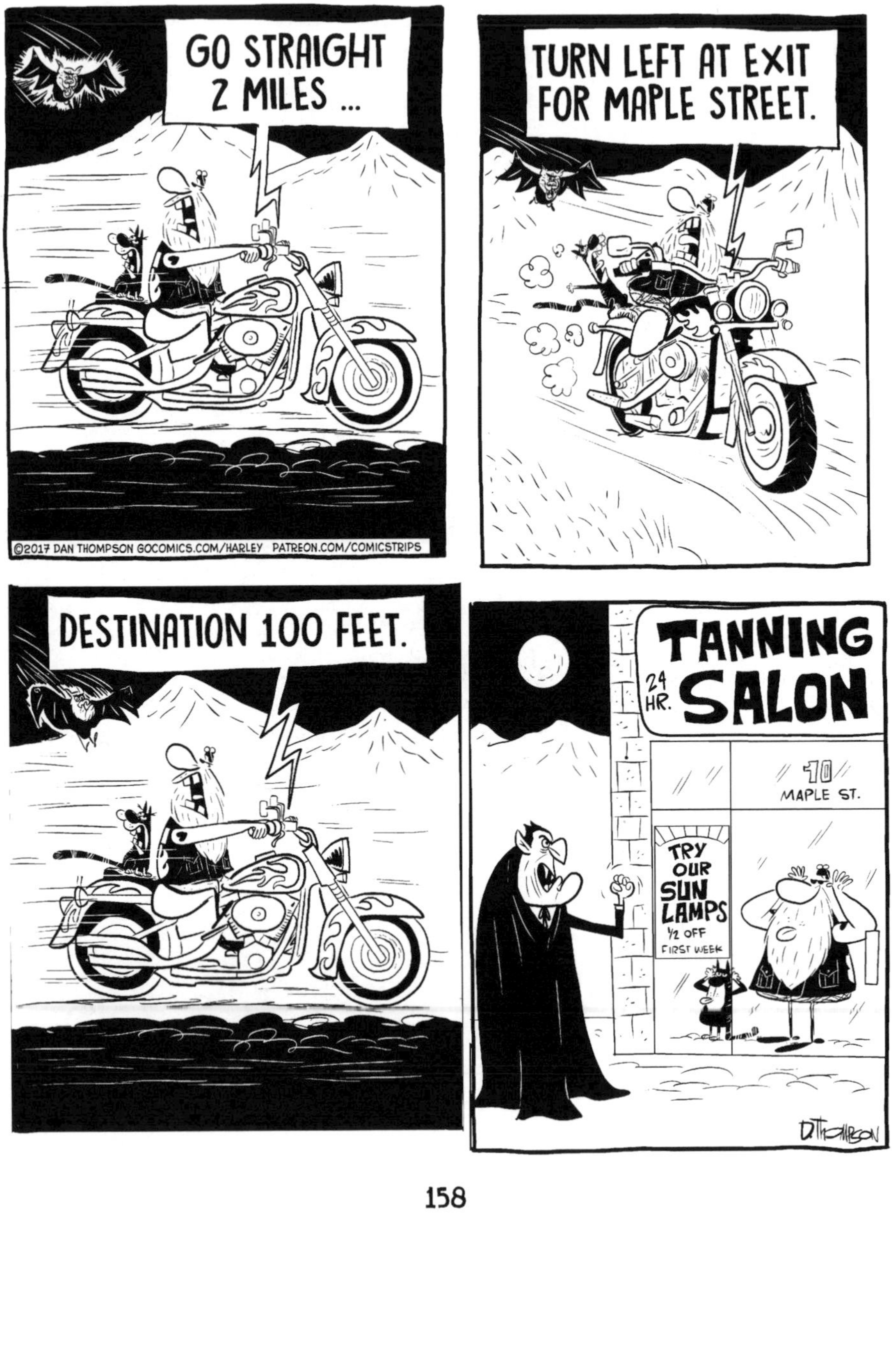
GO STRAIGHT 2 MILES ...
©2017 DAN THOMPSON GOCOMICS.COM/HARLEY PATREON.COM/COMICSTRIPS
TURN LEFT AT EXIT FOR MAPLE STREET.
DESTINATION 100 FEET.
TANNING
24 HR. SALON
10
MAPLE ST.
TRY OUR SUN LAMPS
1/2 OFF FIRST WEEK
D. THOMPSON

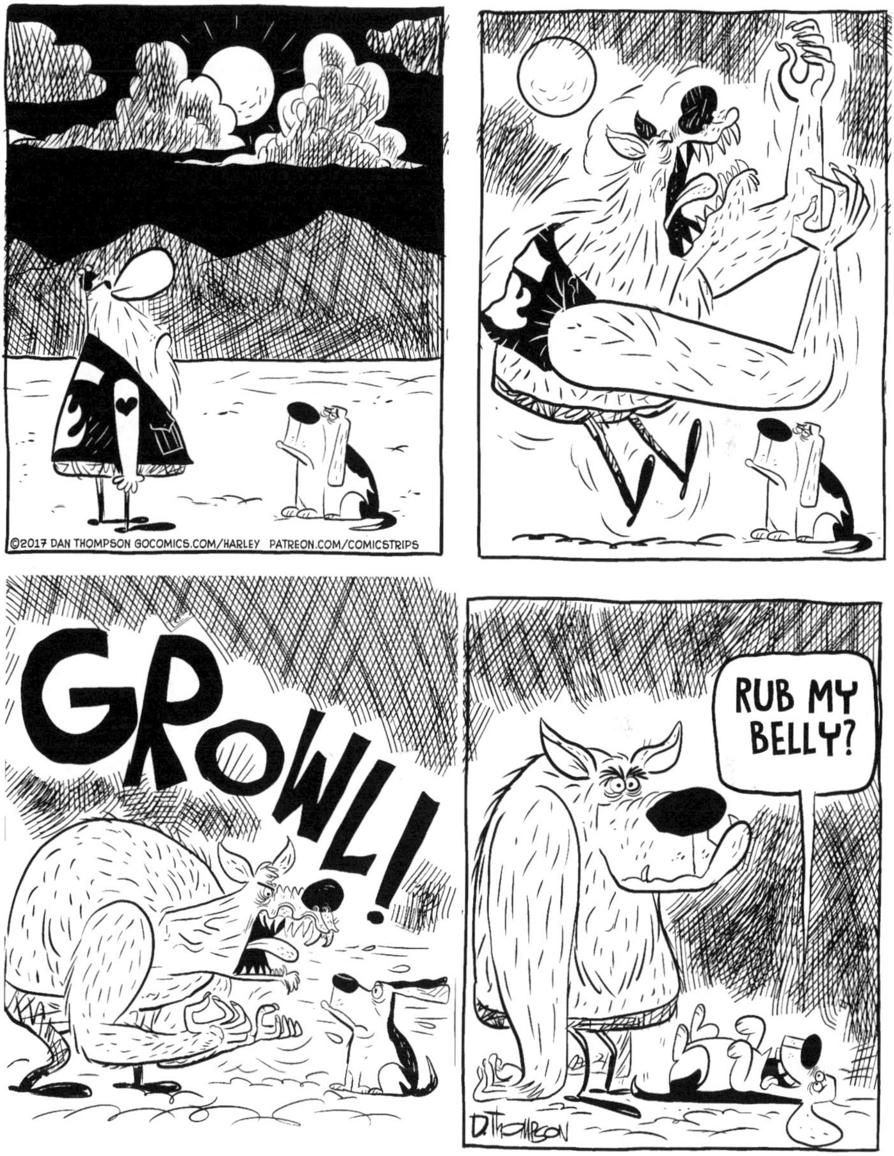
©2017 DAN THOMPSON GOCOMICS.COM/HARLEY PATREON.COM/COMICSTRIPS
GROWL!
RUB MY BELLY?
D. THOMPSON

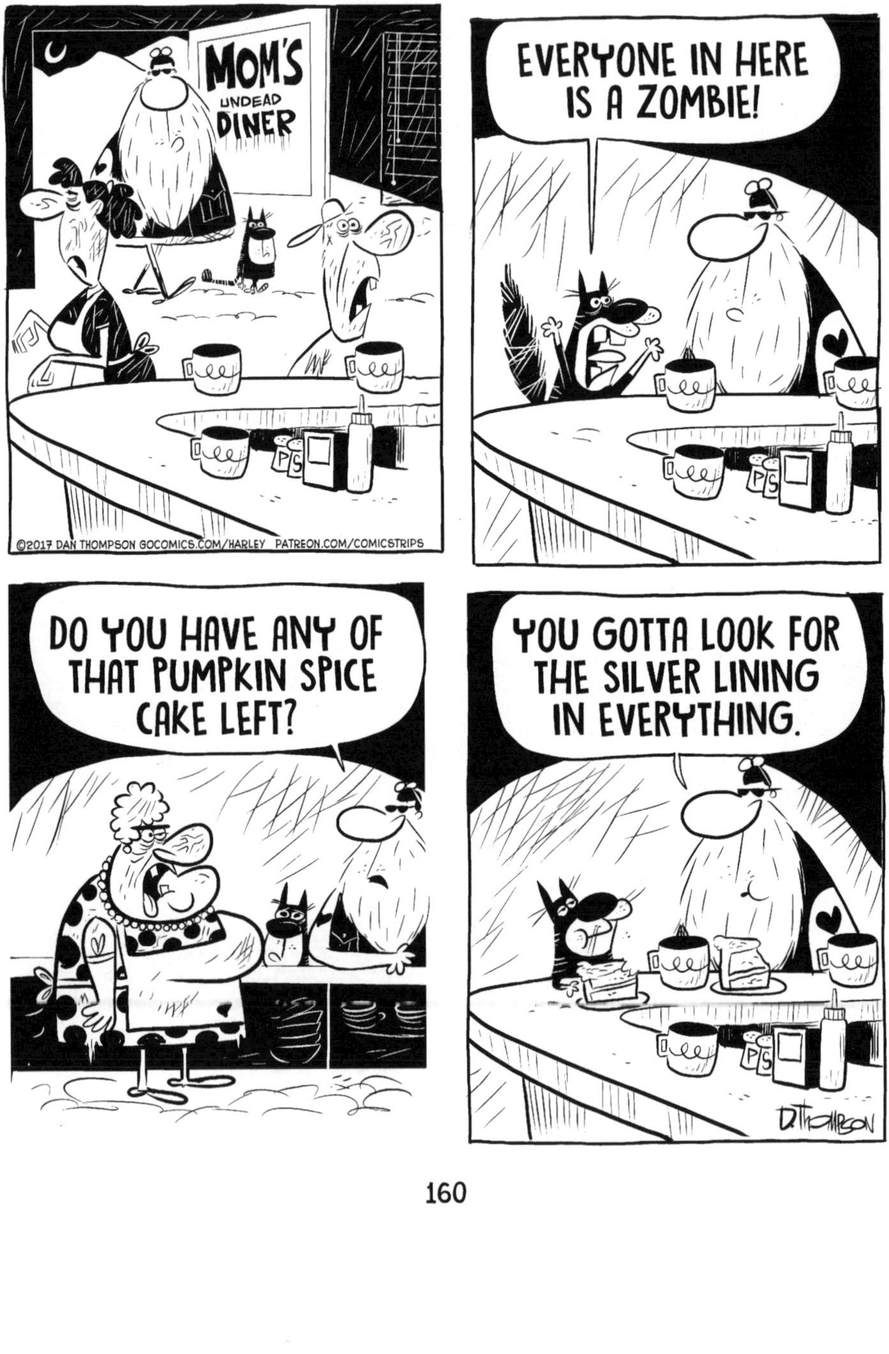
MOM'S
UNDEAD
DINER
©2017 DAN THOMPSON GOCOMICS.COM/HARLEY PATREON.COM/COMICSTRIPS
EVERYONE IN HERE IS A ZOMBIE!
DO YOU HAVE ANY OF THAT PUMPKIN SPICE CAKE LEFT?
YOU GOTTA LOOK FOR THE SILVER LINING IN EVERYTHING.
D. THOMPSON

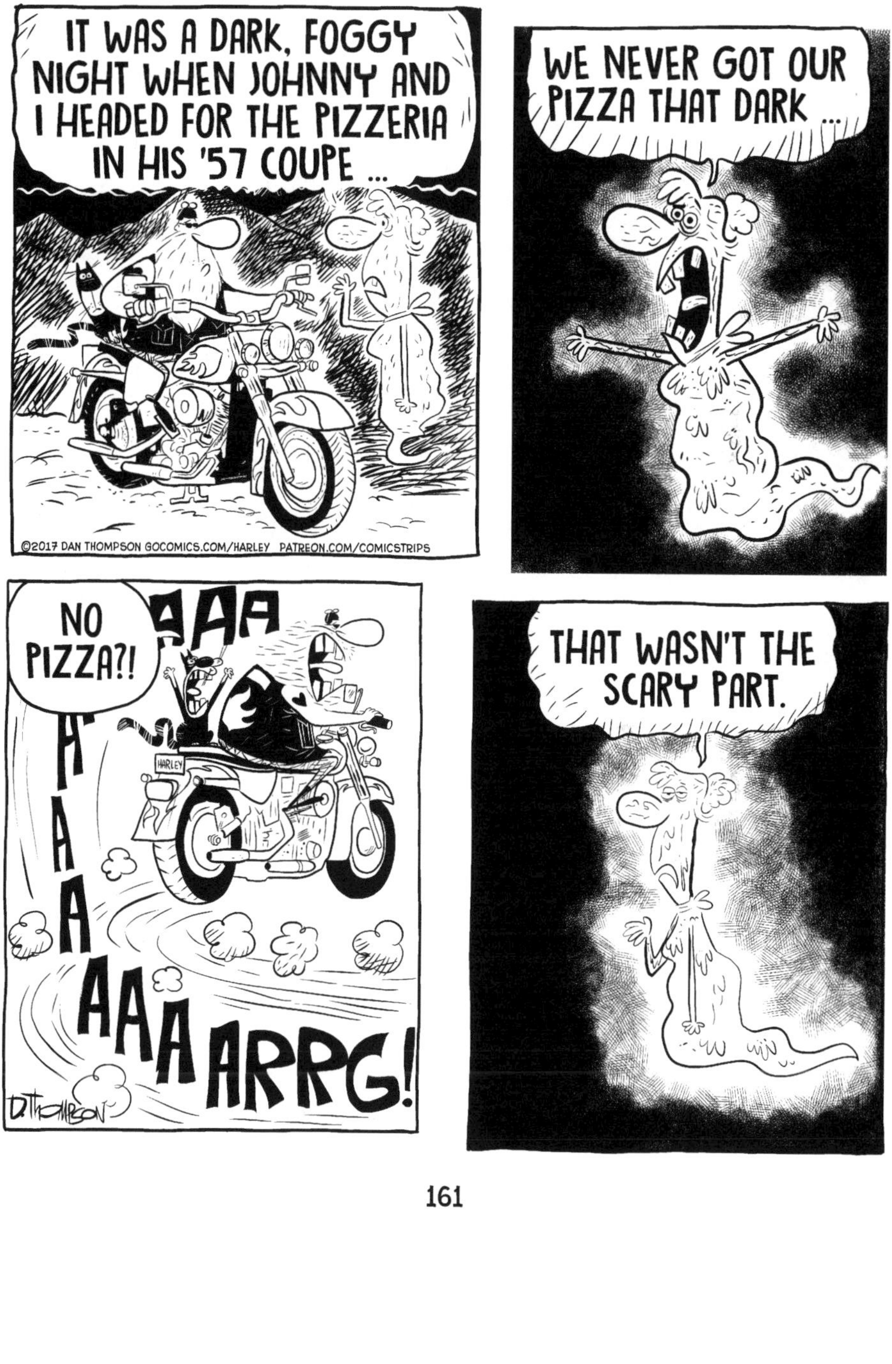
IT WAS A DARK, FOGGY NIGHT WHEN JOHNNY AND I HEADED FOR THE PIZZERIA IN HIS '57 COUPE ...
©2017 DAN THOMPSON GOCOMICS.COM/HARLEY PATREON.COM/COMICSTRIPS
WE NEVER GOT OUR PIZZA THAT DARK ...
NO PIZZA?!
AAAAAAAAAAAARRG!
HARLEY
D. THOMPSON
THAT WASN'T THE SCARY PART.

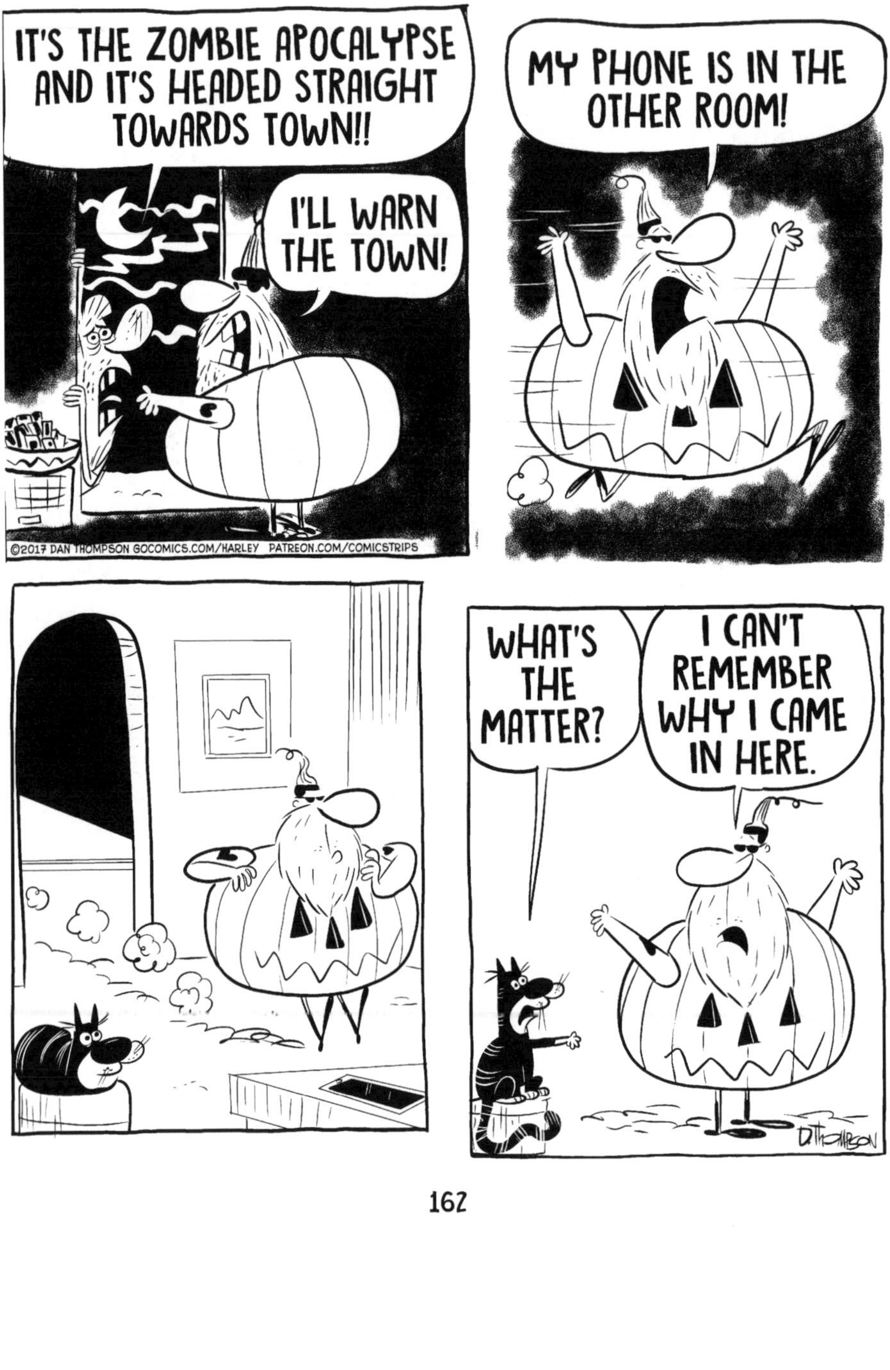
IT'S THE ZOMBIE APOCALYPSE AND IT'S HEADED STRAIGHT TOWARDS TOWN!!
I'LL WARN THE TOWN!
©2017 DAN THOMPSON GOCOMICS.COM/HARLEY PATREON.COM/COMICSTRIPS
MY PHONE IS IN THE OTHER ROOM!
WHAT'S THE MATTER?
I CAN'T REMEMBER WHY I CAME IN HERE.
D THOMPSON

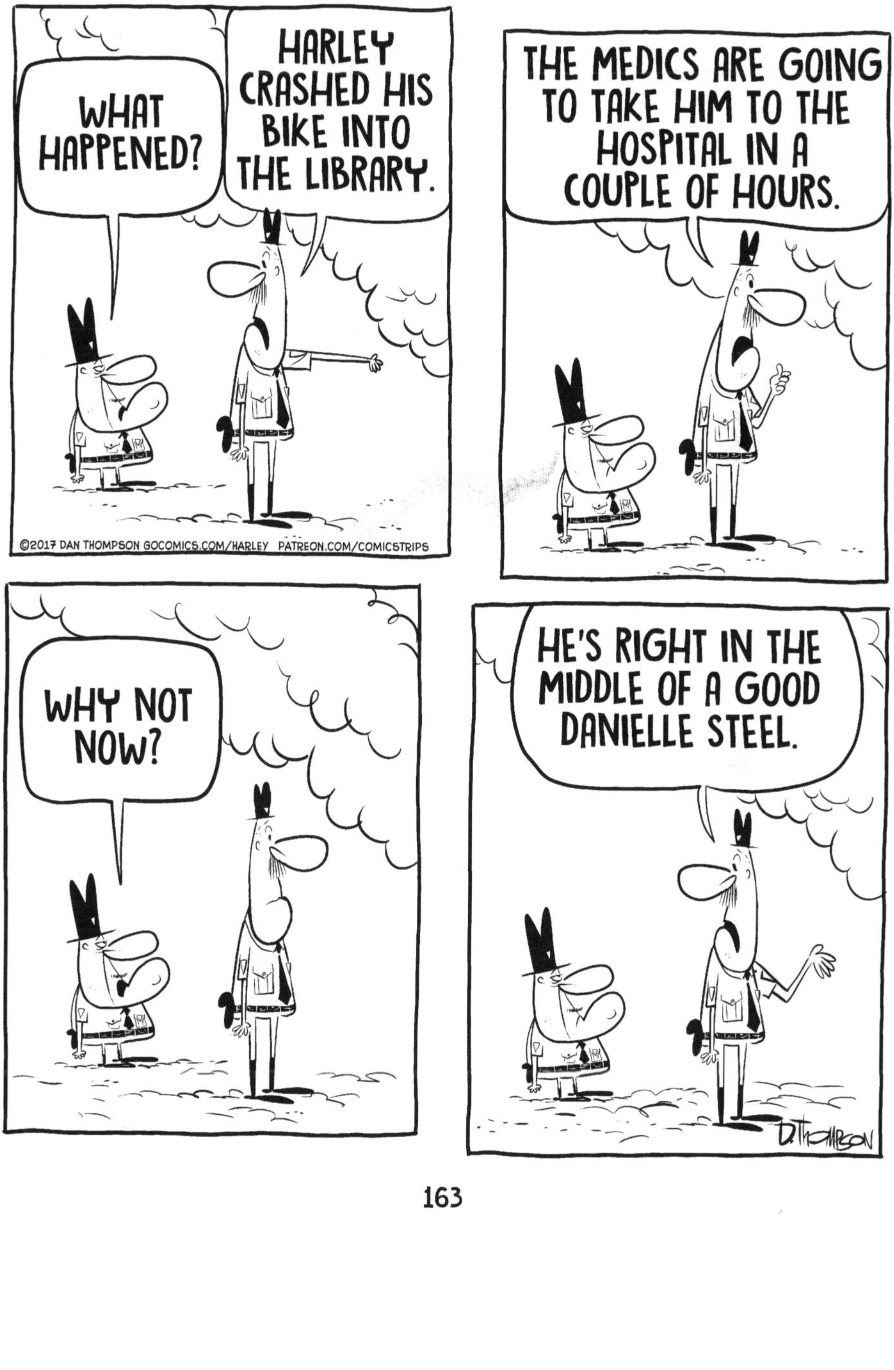
WHAT HAPPENED?
HARLEY CRASHED HIS BIKE INTO THE LIBRARY.
©2017 DAN THOMPSON GOCOMICS.COM/HARLEY PATREON.COM/COMICSTRIPS
THE MEDICS ARE GOING TO TAKE HIM TO THE HOSPITAL IN A COUPLE OF HOURS.
WHY NOT NOW?
HE'S RIGHT IN THE MIDDLE OF A GOOD DANIELLE STEEL.
D. THOMPSON

WHO'S THERE?
©2017 DAN THOMPSON GOCOMICS.COM/HARLEY PATREON.COM/COMICSTRIPS
'TIS I, THE PIZZA YOU WANTED SO BADLY, BUT POLITELY ASKED IF ANYBODY ELSE WANTED THE LAST SLICE.
I WAS DELICIOUS!
SOB
WHY? WHY DID I LET YOU GO...
SAD. PROBABLY DREAMING ABOUT THE GIRL WHO GOT AWAY.
D. THOMPSON

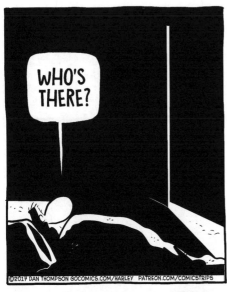

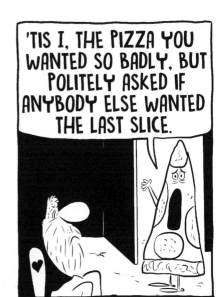

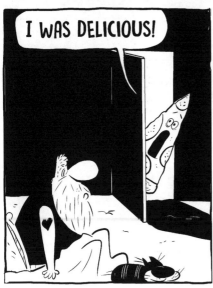

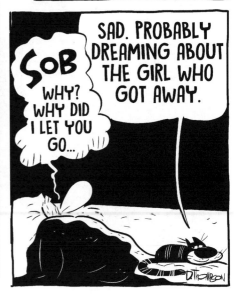

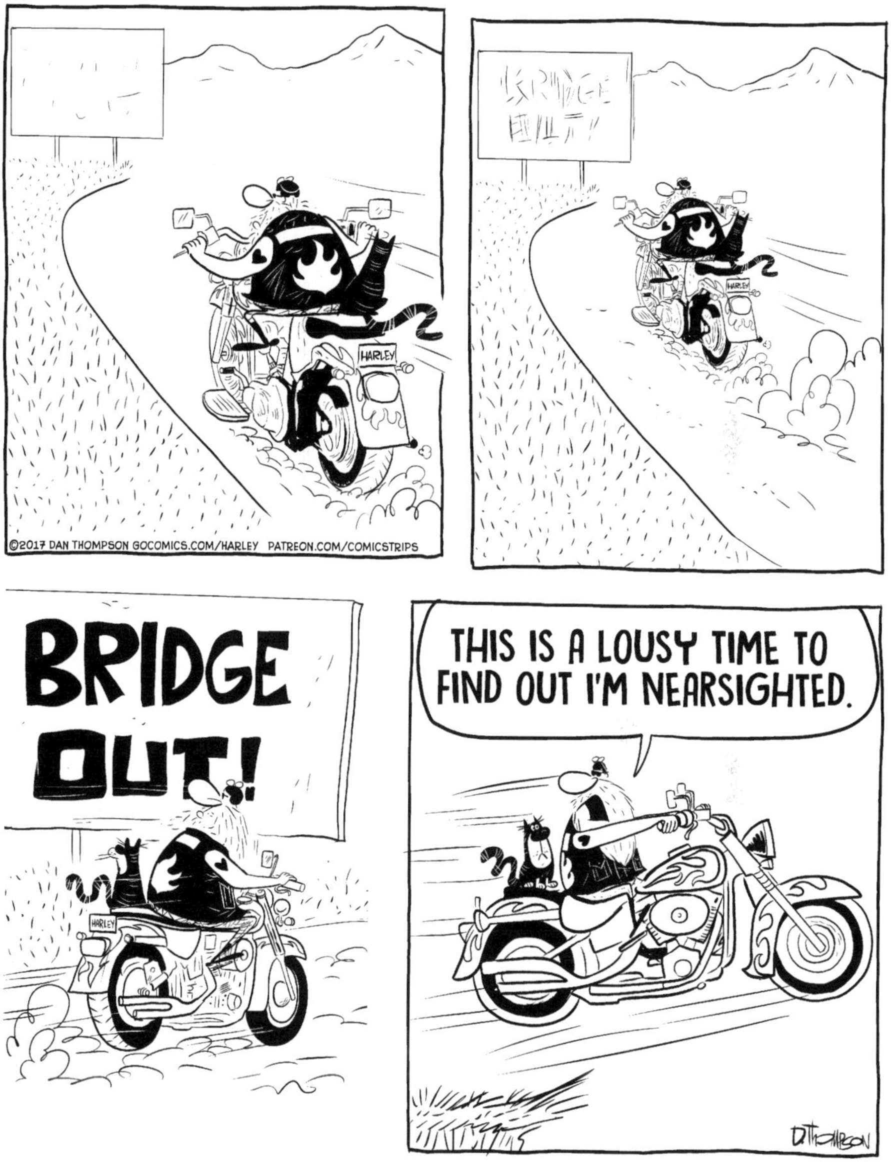
©2017 DAN THOMPSON GOCOMICS.COM/HARLEY PATREON.COM/COMICSTRIPS
HARLEY
BRIDGE OUT!
THIS IS A LOUSY TIME TO FIND OUT I'M NEARSIGHTED.
D. THOMPSON

MOM CALLED AND WANTED ME TO LOOK AFTER YOU, PEACHES ...
©2017 DAN THOMPSON GOCOMICS.COM/HARLEY PATREON.COM/COMICSTRIPS
WHILE YOU STAY HOME SICK FROM SCHOOL .
I USED TO STAY HOME FROM SCHOOL ALL THE TIME WHEN I WAS A KID.
SICK?
SICK OF SCHOOL.
D.THOMPSON

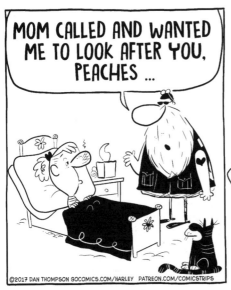

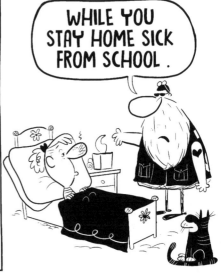

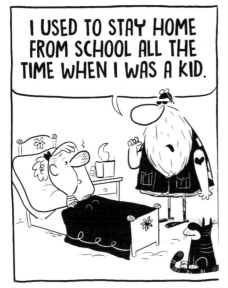

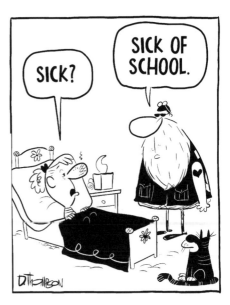

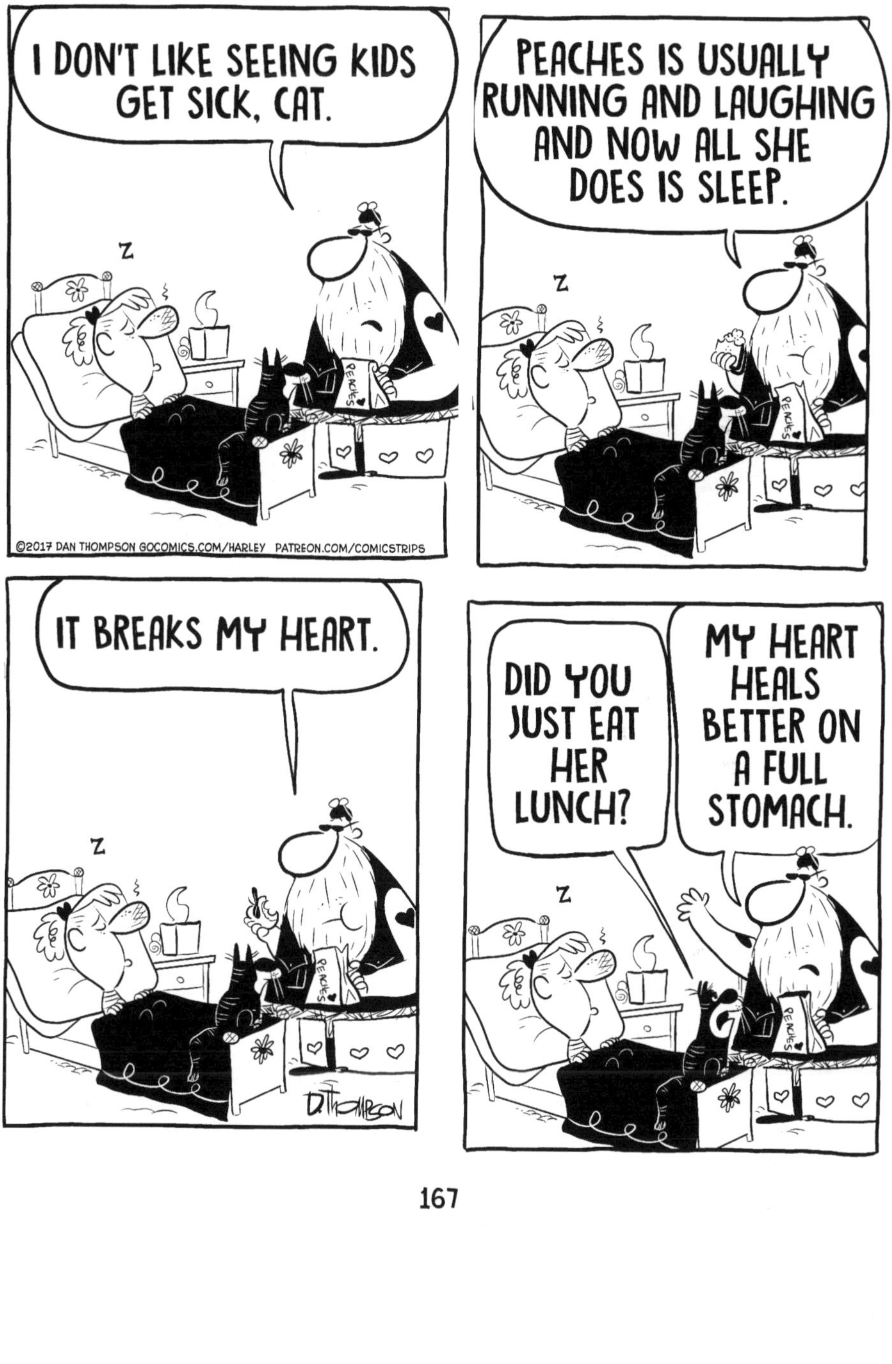
I DON'T LIKE SEEING KIDS GET SICK, CAT.
Z
PEACHES
©2017 DAN THOMPSON GOCOMICS.COM/HARLEY PATREON.COM/COMICSTRIPS
PEACHES IS USUALLY RUNNING AND LAUGHING AND NOW ALL SHE DOES IS SLEEP.
Z
PEACHES
IT BREAKS MY HEART.
Z
PEACHES
D. THOMPSON
DID YOU JUST EAT HER LUNCH?
MY HEART HEALS BETTER ON A FULL STOMACH.
Z
PEACHES

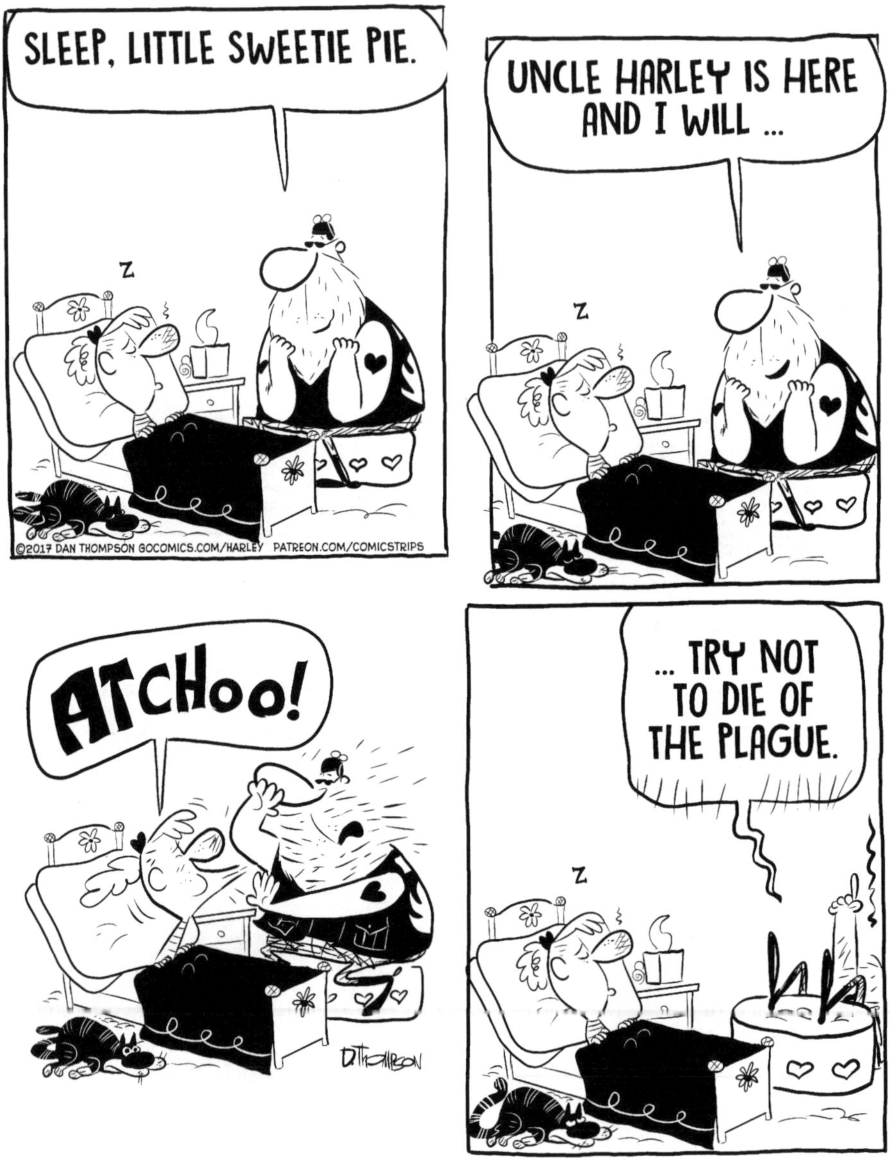
SLEEP, LITTLE SWEETIE PIE.
Z
©2017 DAN THOMPSON GOCOMICS.COM/HARLEY PATREON.COM/COMICSTRIPS
UNCLE HARLEY IS HERE AND I WILL ...
Z
ATCHOO!
D. THOMPSON
... TRY NOT TO DIE OF THE PLAGUE.
Z

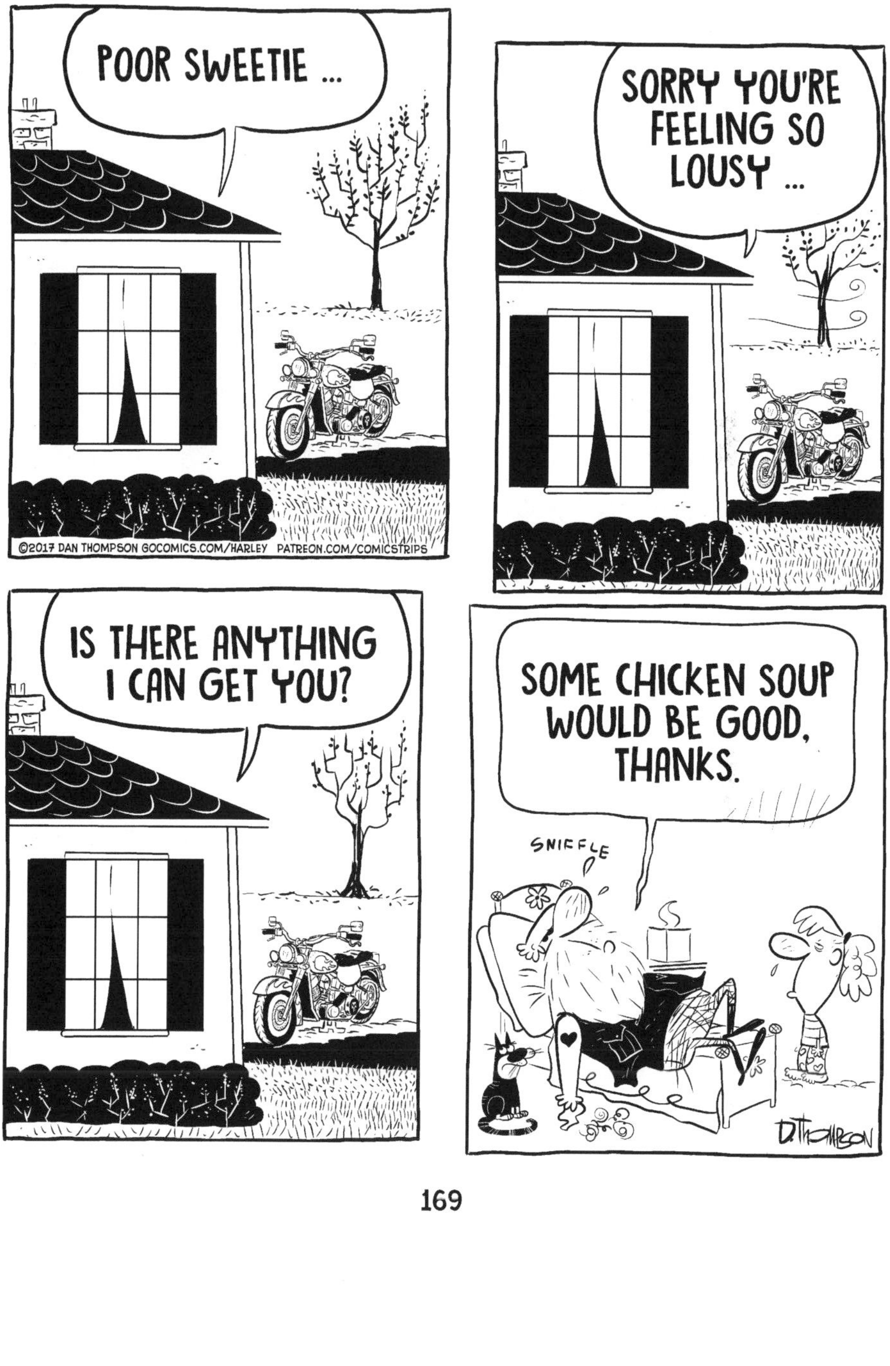
POOR SWEETIE ...
©2017 DAN THOMPSON GOCOMICS.COM/HARLEY PATREON.COM/COMICSTRIPS
SORRY YOU'RE FEELING SO LOUSY ...
IS THERE ANYTHING I CAN GET YOU?
SOME CHICKEN SOUP WOULD BE GOOD, THANKS.
SNIFFLE
D. THOMPSON

DEARLY BELOVED, WE ARE GATHERED HERE TODAY ...
©2017 DAN THOMPSON GOCOMICS.COM/HARLEY PATREON.COM/COMICSTRIPS
DO WE HAVE TO DO THIS EVERY TIME HE PUTS HIS BIKE AWAY FOR THE WINTER?
WEEP!
D.THOMPSON

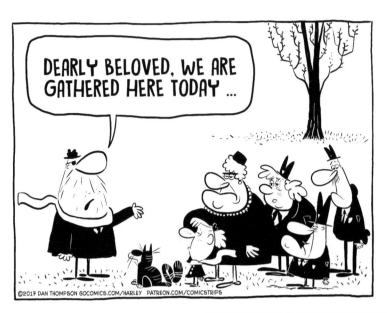

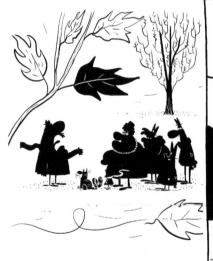

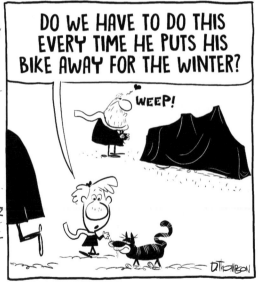

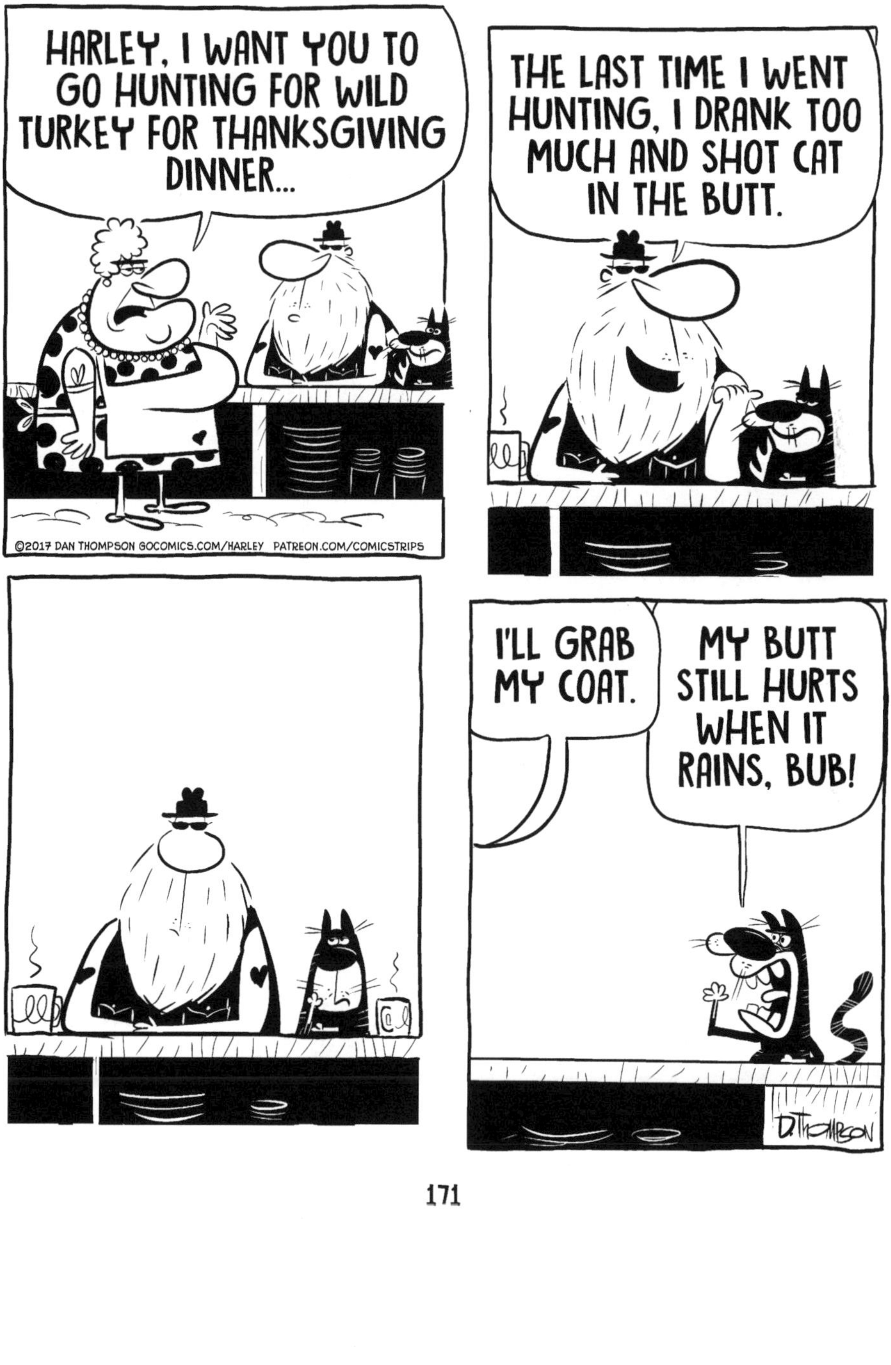
HARLEY, I WANT YOU TO GO HUNTING FOR WILD TURKEY FOR THANKSGIVING DINNER...
©2017 DAN THOMPSON GOCOMICS.COM/HARLEY PATREON.COM/COMICSTRIPS
THE LAST TIME I WENT HUNTING, I DRANK TOO MUCH AND SHOT CAT IN THE BUTT.
I'LL GRAB MY COAT.
MY BUTT STILL HURTS WHEN IT RAINS, BUB!
D. THOMPSON

YOU ARE SO LUCKY I CAME ON THE HUNT WITH YOU, HARLEY ...
©2017 DAN THOMPSON GOCOMICS.COM/HARLEY PATREON.COM/COMICSTRIPS
HUNTING BIRDS IS IN MY BLOOD ...
I CAN PICK UP THEIR SCENT FROM MILES AWAY ...
SOMETIMES IT'S EMBARRASSING HOW GOOD I AM.
D.THOMPSON

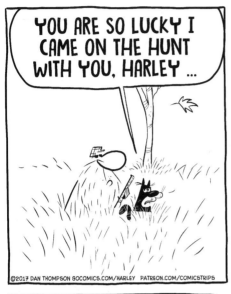

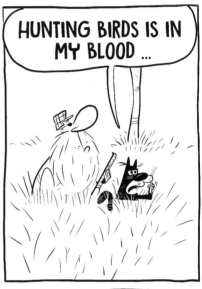

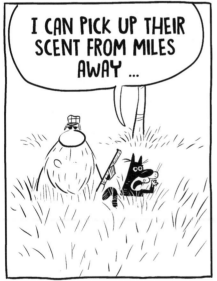

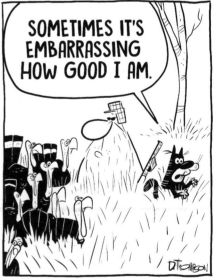

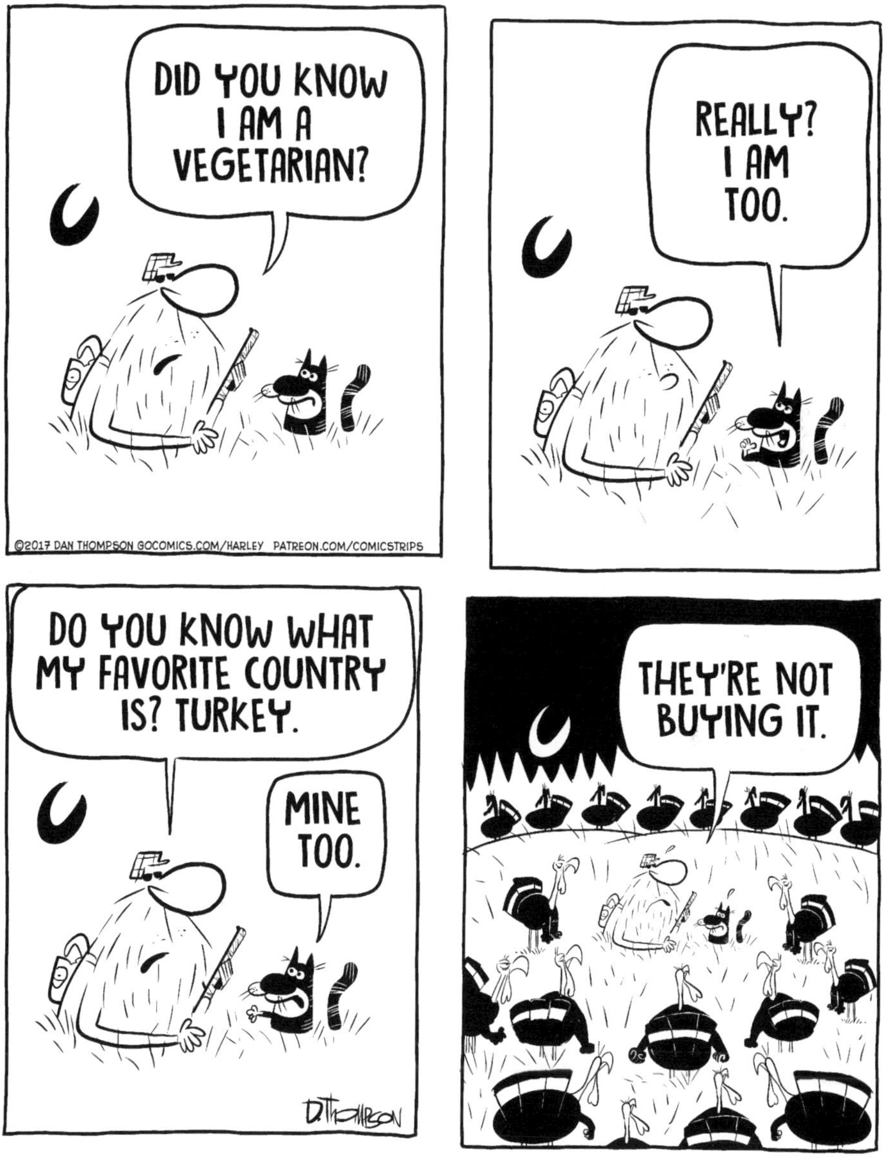
DID YOU KNOW I AM A VEGETARIAN?
©2017 DAN THOMPSON GOCOMICS.COM/HARLEY PATREON.COM/COMICSTRIPS
REALLY? I AM TOO.
DO YOU KNOW WHAT MY FAVORITE COUNTRY IS? TURKEY.
MINE TOO.
D. THOMPSON
THEY'RE NOT BUYING IT.

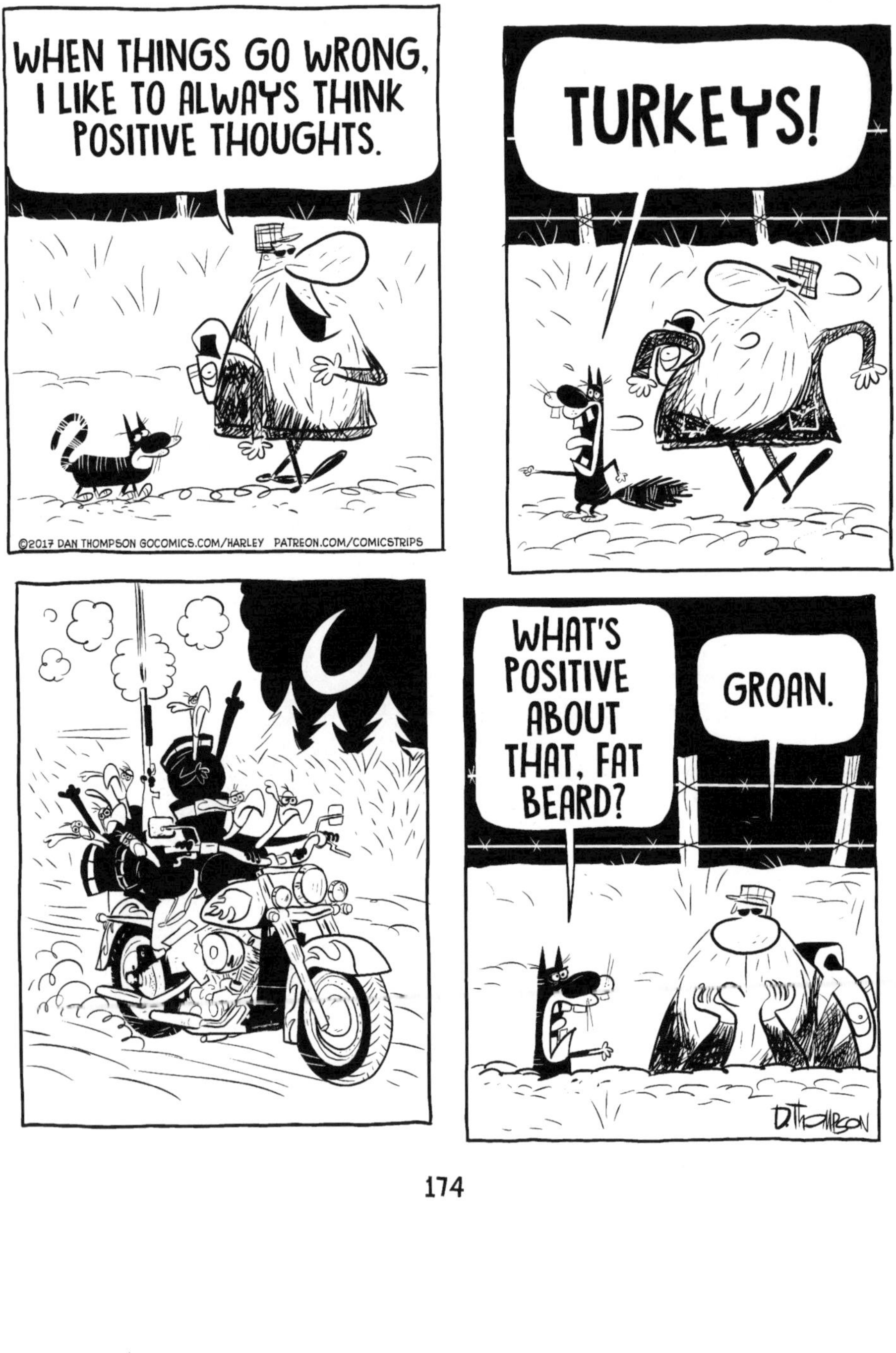
WHEN THINGS GO WRONG, I LIKE TO ALWAYS THINK POSITIVE THOUGHTS.
©2017 DAN THOMPSON GOCOMICS.COM/HARLEY PATREON.COM/COMICSTRIPS
TURKEYS!
WHAT'S POSITIVE ABOUT THAT, FAT BEARD?
GROAN.
D.THOMPSON

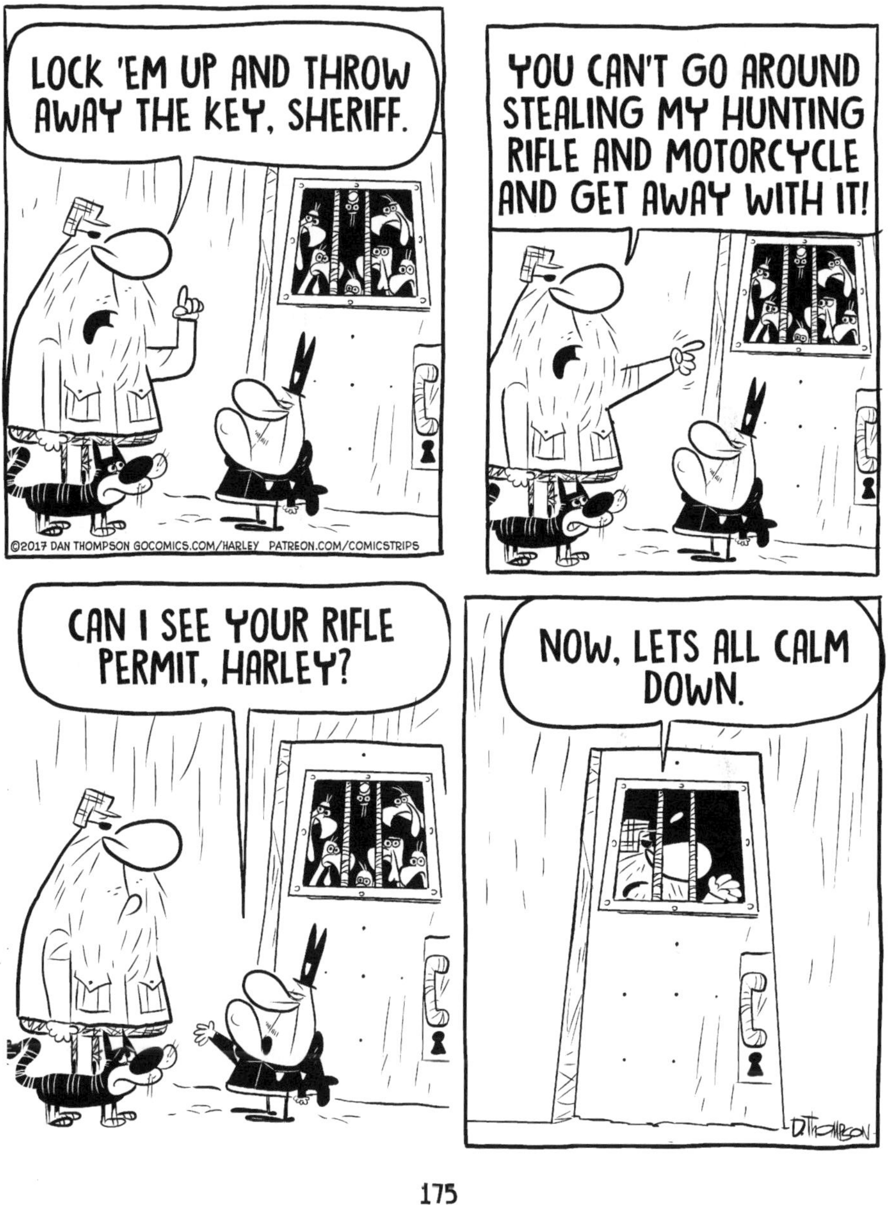
LOCK 'EM UP AND THROW AWAY THE KEY, SHERIFF.
©2017 DAN THOMPSON GOCOMICS.COM/HARLEY PATREON.COM/COMICSTRIPS
YOU CAN'T GO AROUND STEALING MY HUNTING RIFLE AND MOTORCYCLE AND GET AWAY WITH IT!
CAN I SEE YOUR RIFLE PERMIT, HARLEY?
NOW, LETS ALL CALM DOWN.
D. THOMPSON

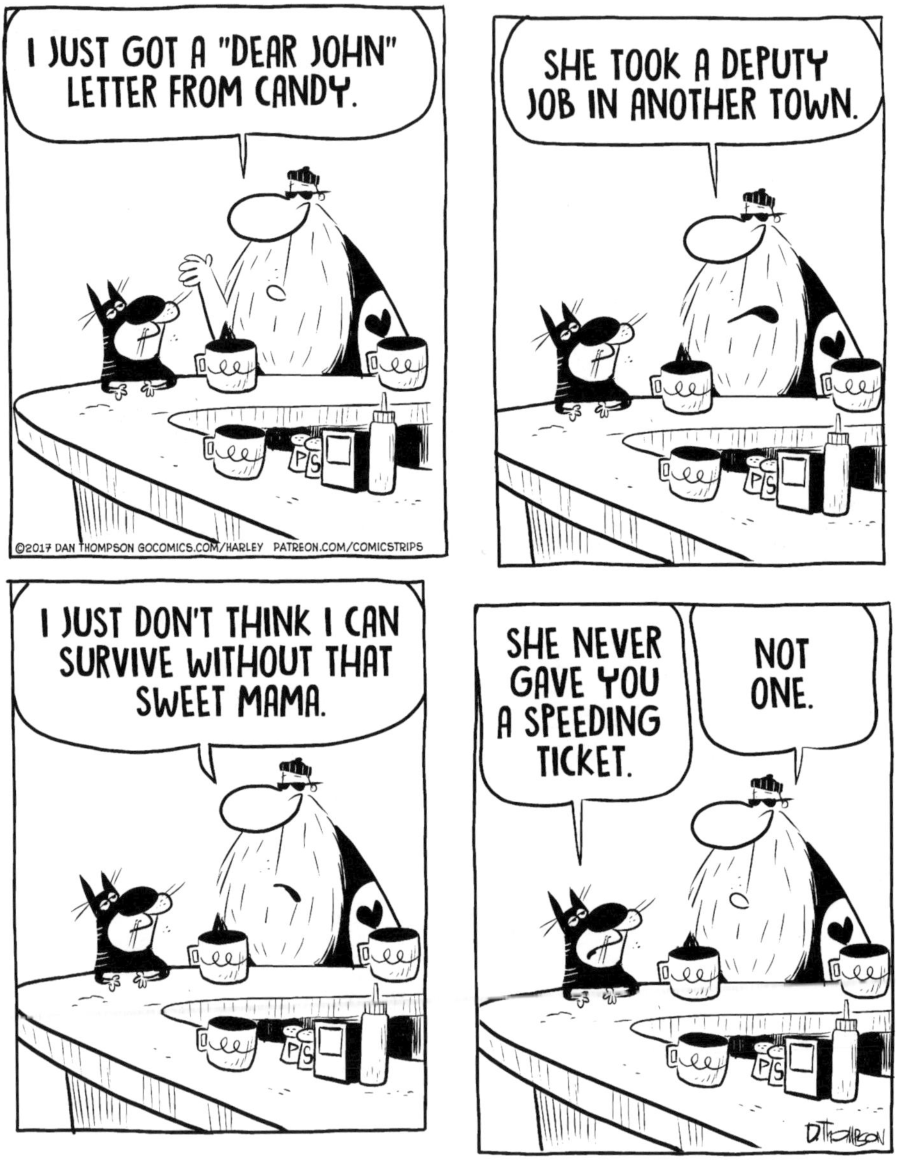
I JUST GOT A "DEAR JOHN" LETTER FROM CANDY.
©2017 DAN THOMPSON GOCOMICS.COM/HARLEY PATREON.COM/COMICSTRIPS
SHE TOOK A DEPUTY JOB IN ANOTHER TOWN.
I JUST DON'T THINK I CAN SURVIVE WITHOUT THAT SWEET MAMA.
SHE NEVER GAVE YOU A SPEEDING TICKET.
NOT ONE.
D. THOMPSON

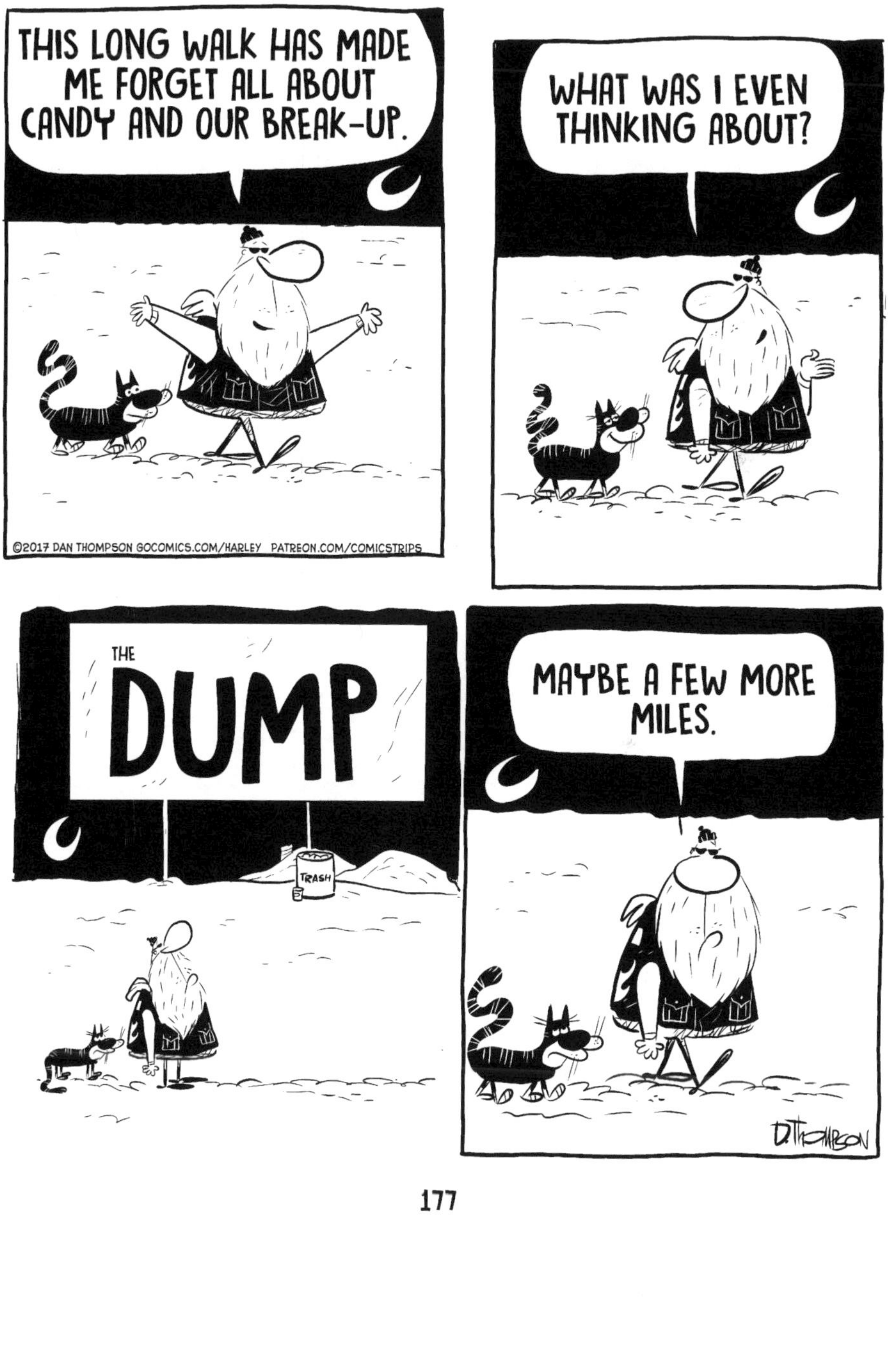
THIS LONG WALK HAS MADE ME FORGET ALL ABOUT CANDY AND OUR BREAK-UP.
©2017 DAN THOMPSON GOCOMICS.COM/HARLEY PATREON.COM/COMICSTRIPS
WHAT WAS I EVEN THINKING ABOUT?
THE DUMP
TRASH
MAYBE A FEW MORE MILES.
D. THOMPSON

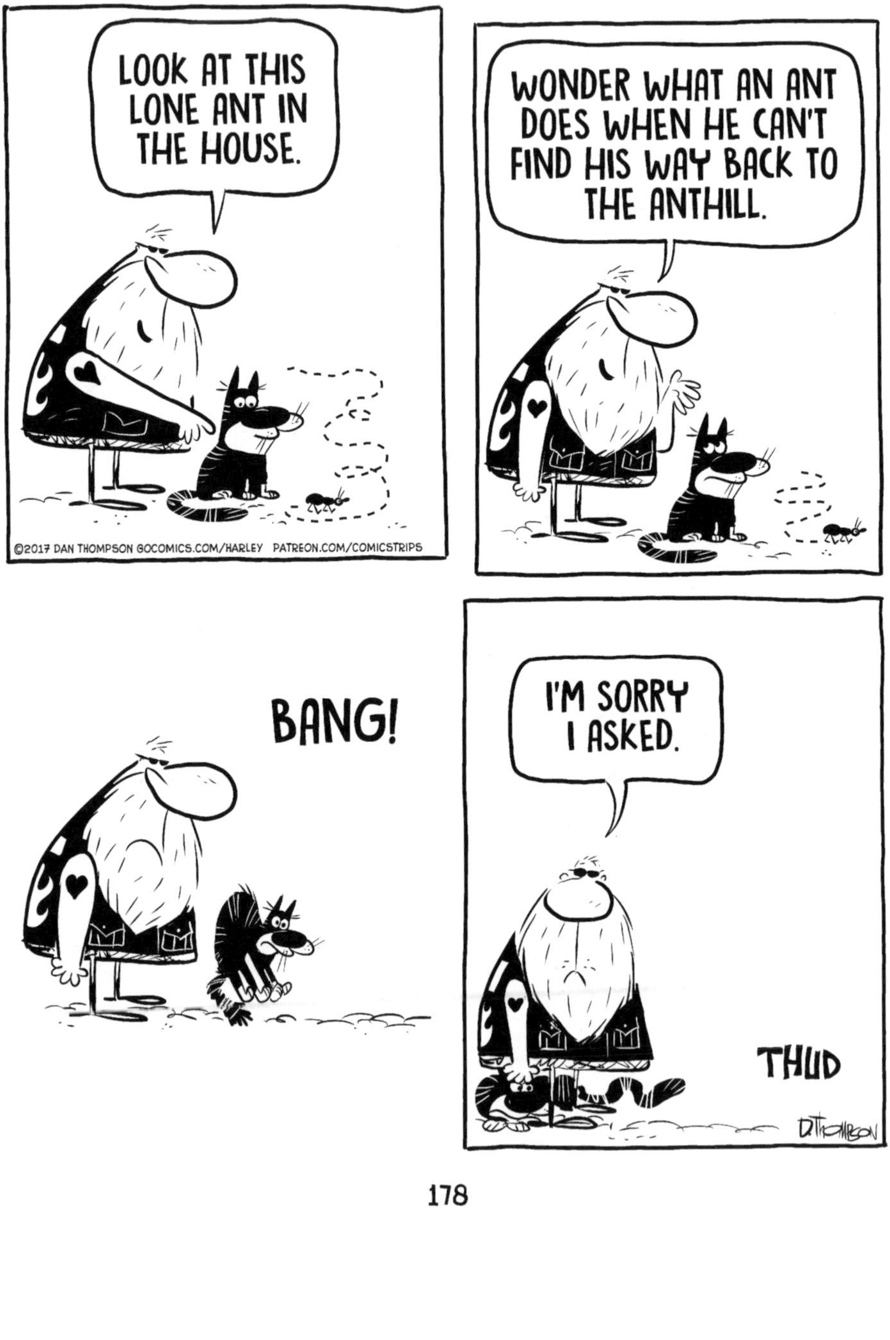
LOOK AT THIS LONE ANT IN THE HOUSE.
©2017 DAN THOMPSON GOCOMICS.COM/HARLEY PATREON.COM/COMICSTRIPS
WONDER WHAT AN ANT DOES WHEN HE CAN'T FIND HIS WAY BACK TO THE ANTHILL.
BANG!
I'M SORRY I ASKED.
THUD
D.THOMPSON

©2017 DAN THOMPSON GOCOMICS.COM/HARLEY PATREON.COM/COMICSTRIPS
TRUMP...
SOMETIMES I DON'T THINK BEFORE I SPEAK.
D. THOMPSON

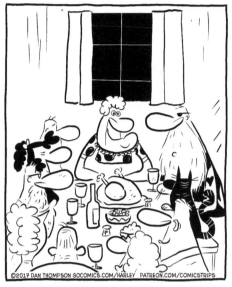

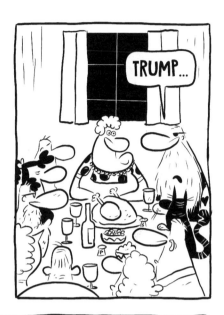

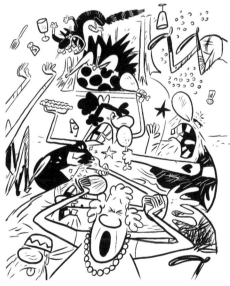

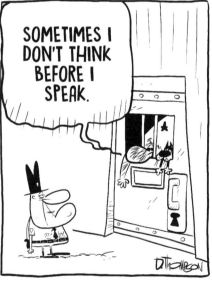

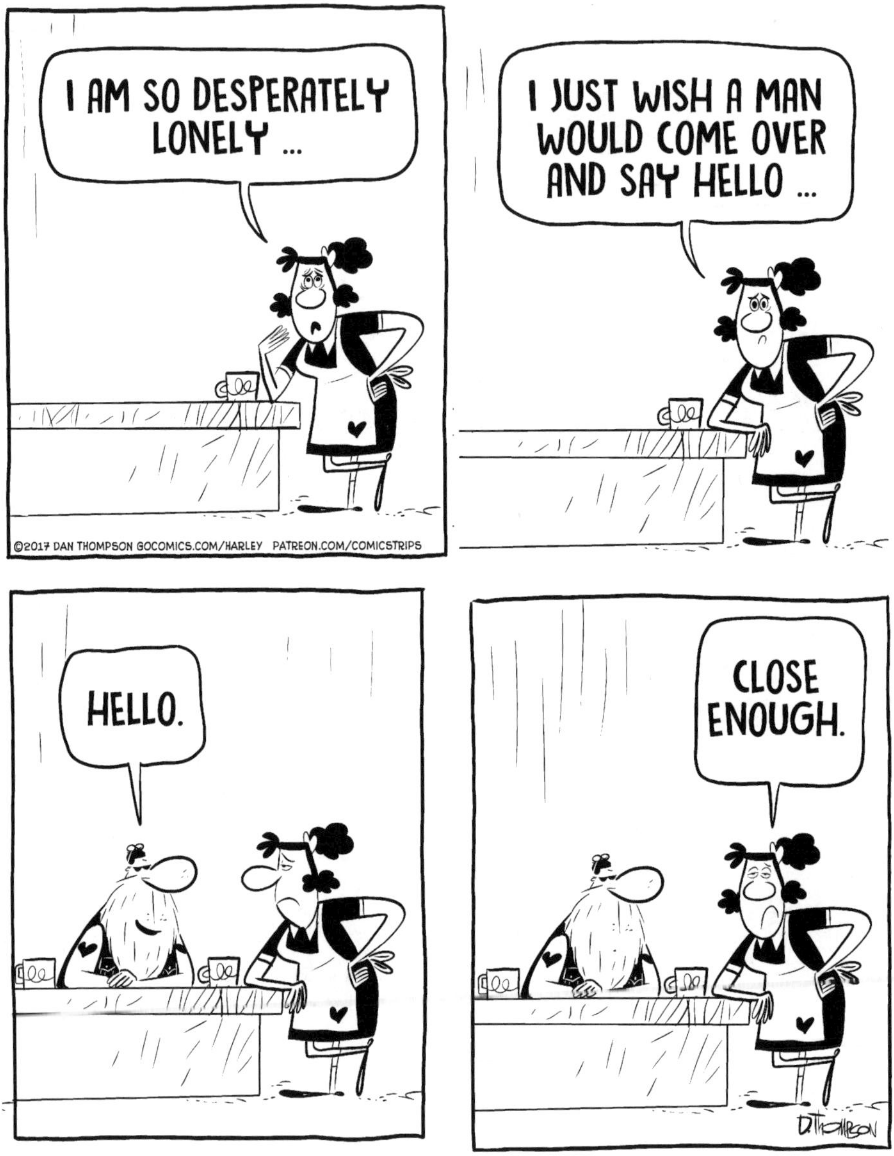
I AM SO DESPERATELY LONELY ...
©2017 DAN THOMPSON GOCOMICS.COM/HARLEY PATREON.COM/COMICSTRIPS
I JUST WISH A MAN WOULD COME OVER AND SAY HELLO ...
HELLO.
CLOSE ENOUGH.
D. THOMPSON

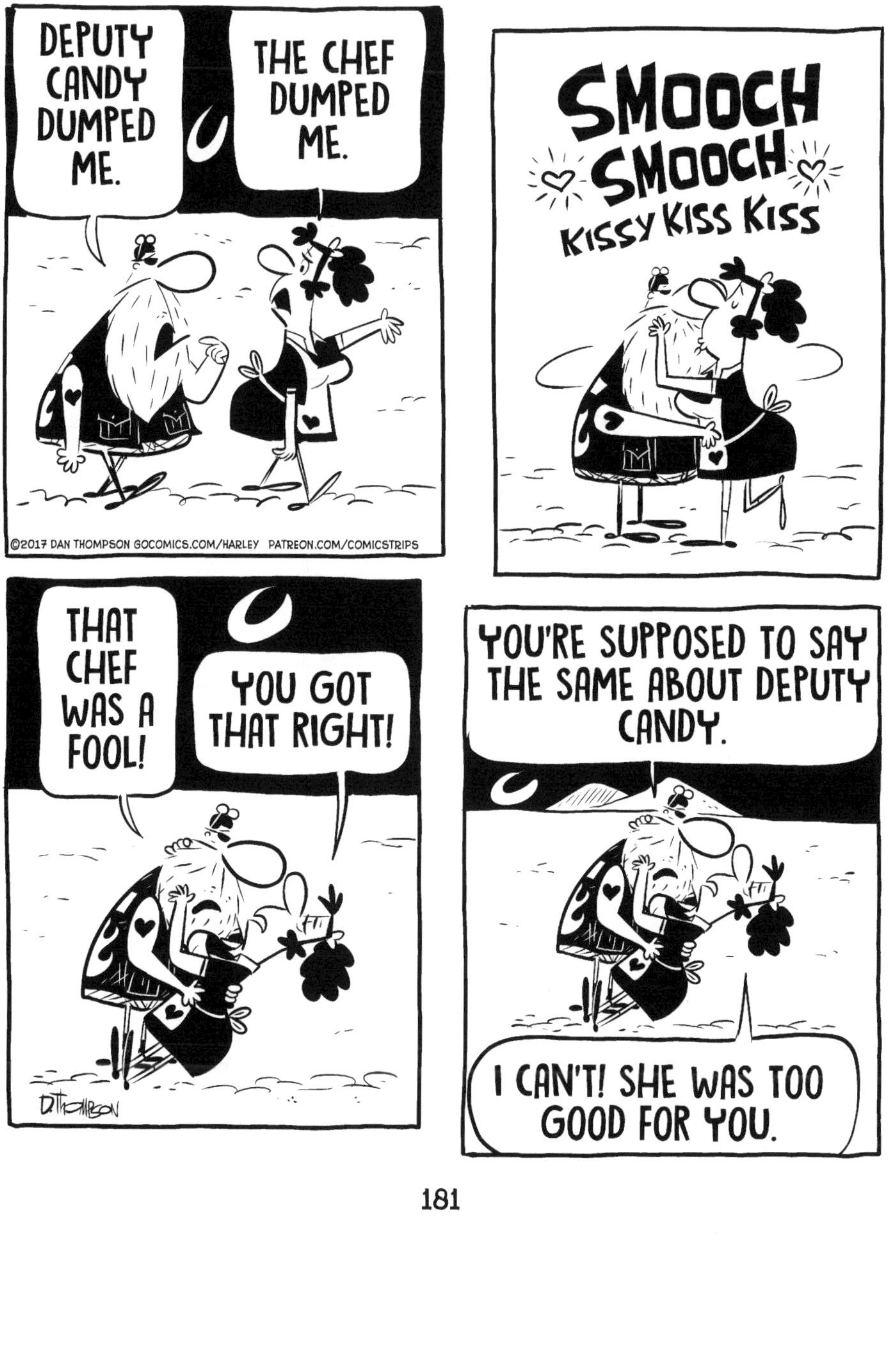
DEPUTY CANDY DUMPED ME.
THE CHEF DUMPED ME.
©2017 DAN THOMPSON GOCOMICS.COM/HARLEY PATREON.COM/COMICSTRIPS
SMOOCH SMOOCH KISSY KISS KISS
THAT CHEF WAS A FOOL!
YOU GOT THAT RIGHT!
D.THOMPSON
YOU'RE SUPPOSED TO SAY THE SAME ABOUT DEPUTY CANDY.
I CAN'T! SHE WAS TOO GOOD FOR YOU.

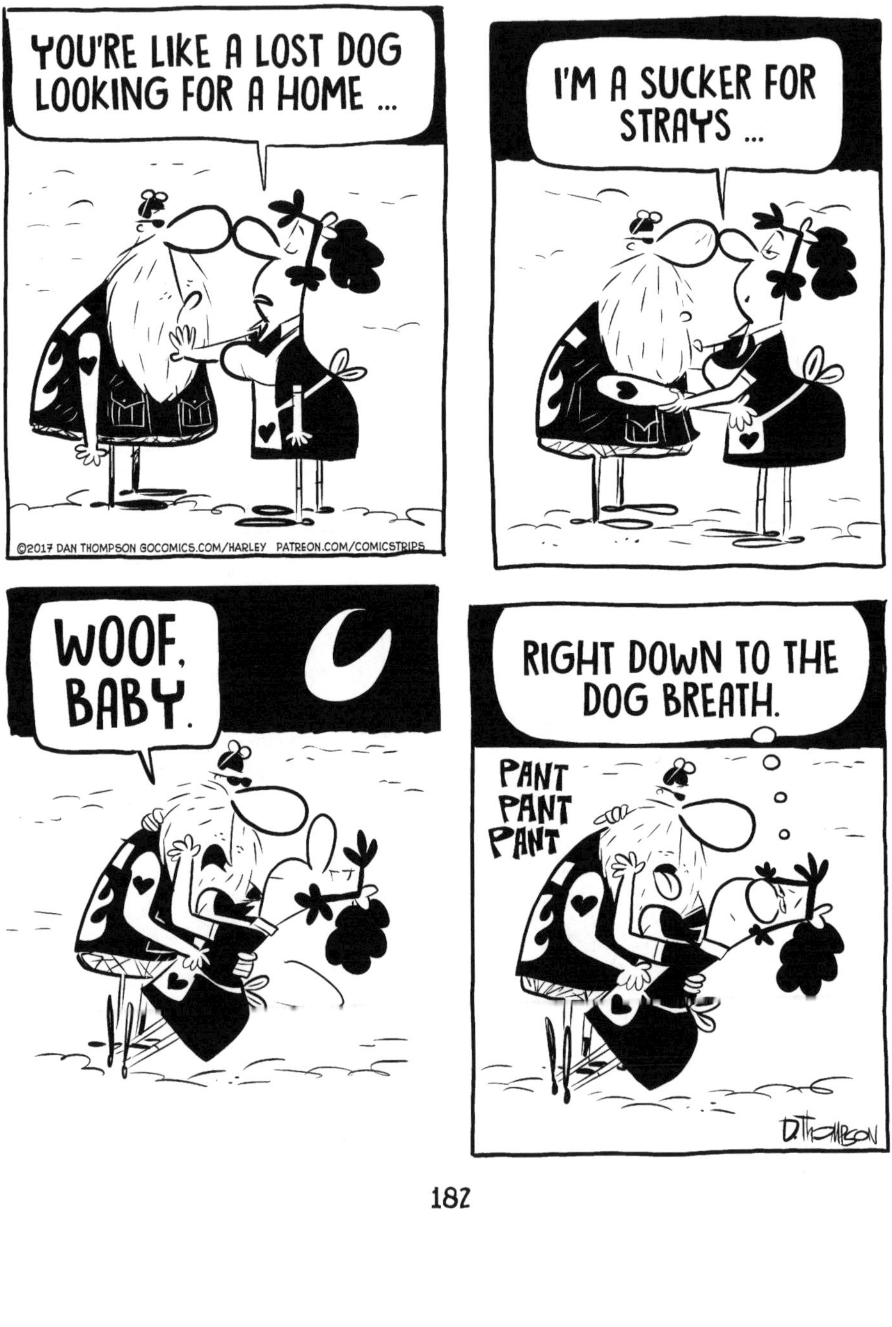
YOU'RE LIKE A LOST DOG LOOKING FOR A HOME ...
©2017 DAN THOMPSON GOCOMICS.COM/HARLEY PATREON.COM/COMICSTRIPS
I'M A SUCKER FOR STRAYS ...
WOOF, BABY.
RIGHT DOWN TO THE DOG BREATH.
PANT PANT PANT
D. THOMPSON

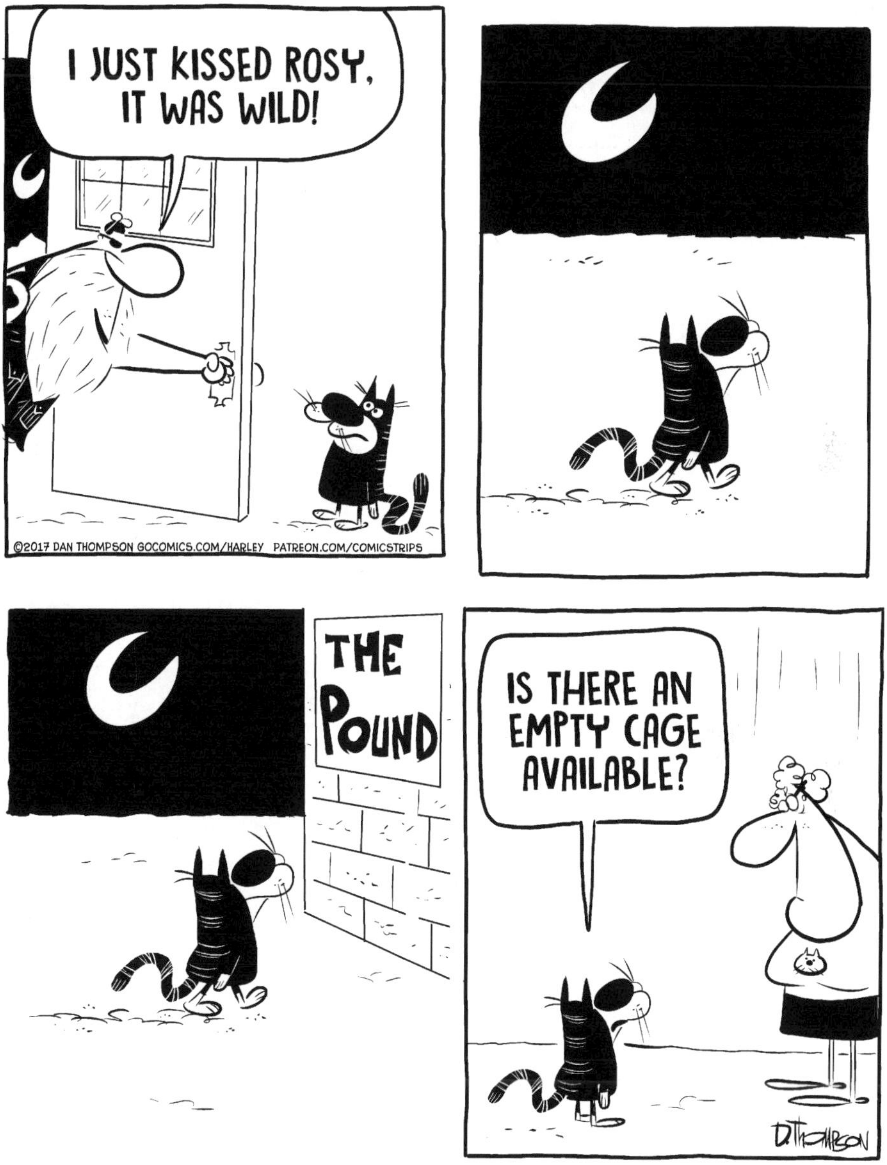
I JUST KISSED ROSY, IT WAS WILD!
©2017 DAN THOMPSON GOCOMICS.COM/HARLEY PATREON.COM/COMICSTRIPS
THE POUND
IS THERE AN EMPTY CAGE AVAILABLE?
D. THOMPSON

WHEN DOGS SLEEP ...
D. THOMPSON
©2017 DAN THOMPSON GOCOMICS.COM/HARLEY PATREON.COM/COMICSTRIPS
THEY'RE MEAN, THEY YELL, THEY'RE SO HARD TO GET ALONG WITH!
DON'T GIVE UP! YOU JUST DON'T KNOW HOW MUCH GOOD YOU'RE DOING FOR THEM!
I'M GLAD YOU'RE HERE ... I NEEDED A FRIEND TODAY.

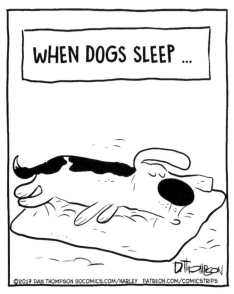

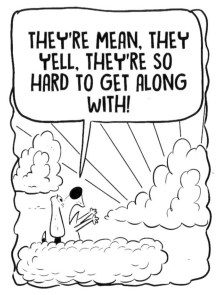

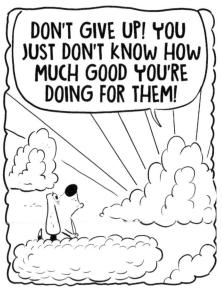

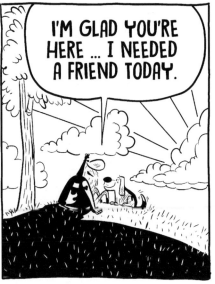

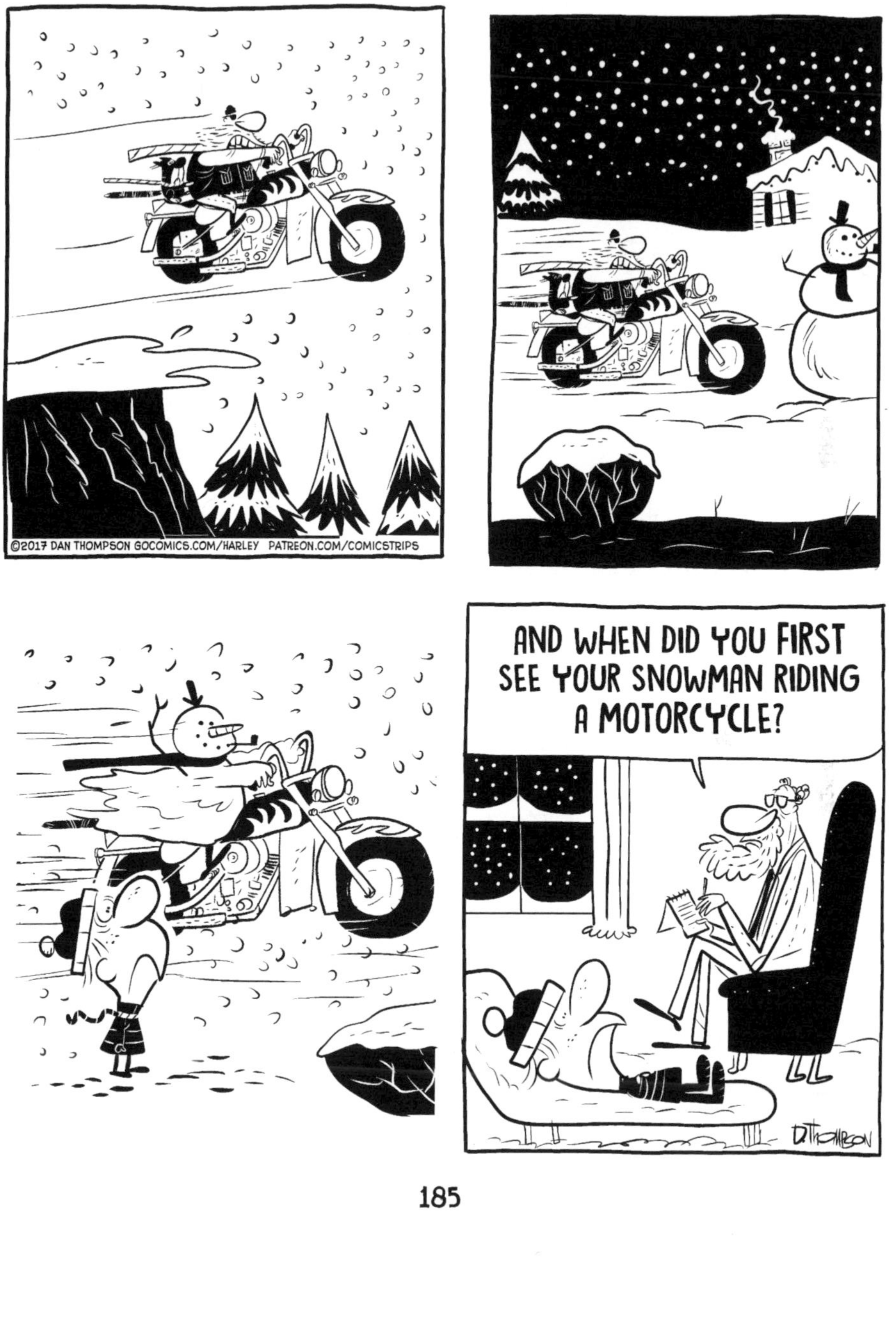
©2017 DAN THOMPSON GOCOMICS.COM/HARLEY PATREON.COM/COMICSTRIPS
AND WHEN DID YOU FIRST SEE YOUR SNOWMAN RIDING A MOTORCYCLE?
D.THOMPSON

TIPPY TIPPY TOE
TIPPY TIPPY TOE!
©2017 DAN THOMPSON GOCOMICS.COM/HARLEY PATREON.COM/COMICSTRIPS
CLAP CLAP CLAP CLAP CLAP CLAP
CLAP CLAP CLAP CLAP CLAP CLAP
A BIG CHUNK OF SNOW WENT DOWN MY BACK.
D. THOMPSON

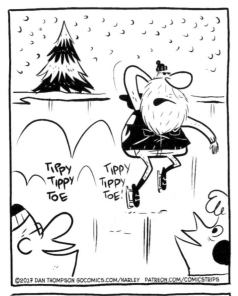

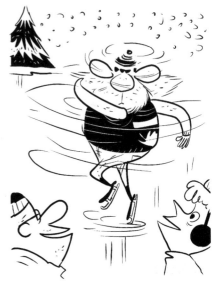

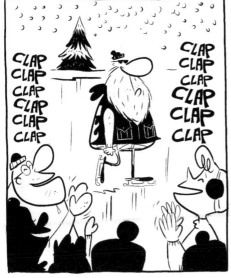

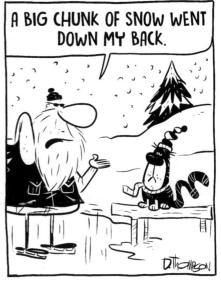

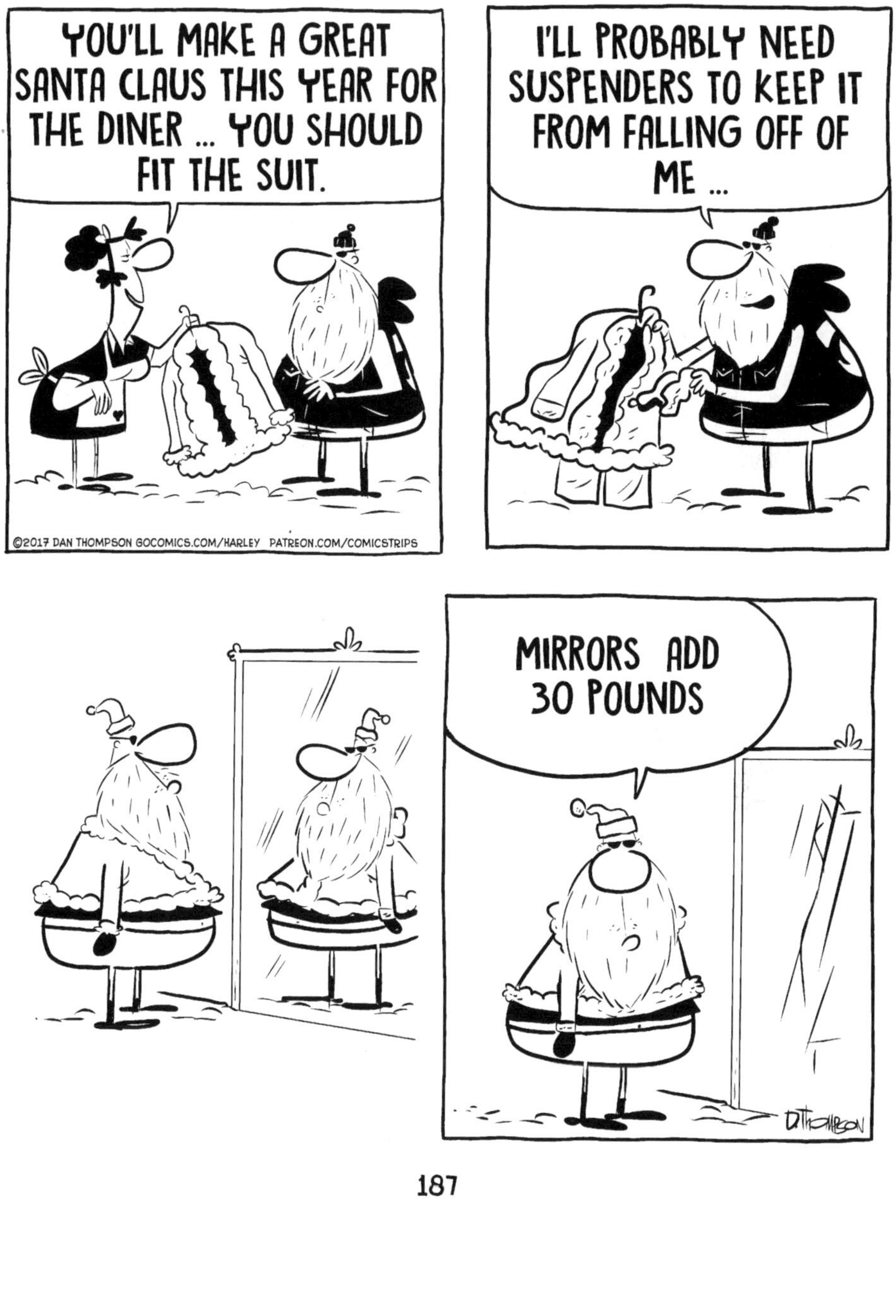
YOU'LL MAKE A GREAT SANTA CLAUS THIS YEAR FOR THE DINER ... YOU SHOULD FIT THE SUIT.
©2017 DAN THOMPSON GOCOMICS.COM/HARLEY PATREON.COM/COMICSTRIPS
I'LL PROBABLY NEED SUSPENDERS TO KEEP IT FROM FALLING OFF OF ME ...
MIRRORS ADD 30 POUNDS
D. THOMPSON

HERE COMES THE SNOW PLOW.

V·ROOM
SPLASH
SLUDGE
ICE
FREEZE

©2017 DAN THOMPSON GOCOMICS.COM/HARLEY PATREON.COM/COMICSTRIPS

I'M FROZEN ... I CAN'T MOVE!

HEY, KID! HELP ME BEFORE I FREEZE TO DEATH!

AND TELL ME WHEN YOU FIRST STARTED HEARING SNOWMEN TALK.

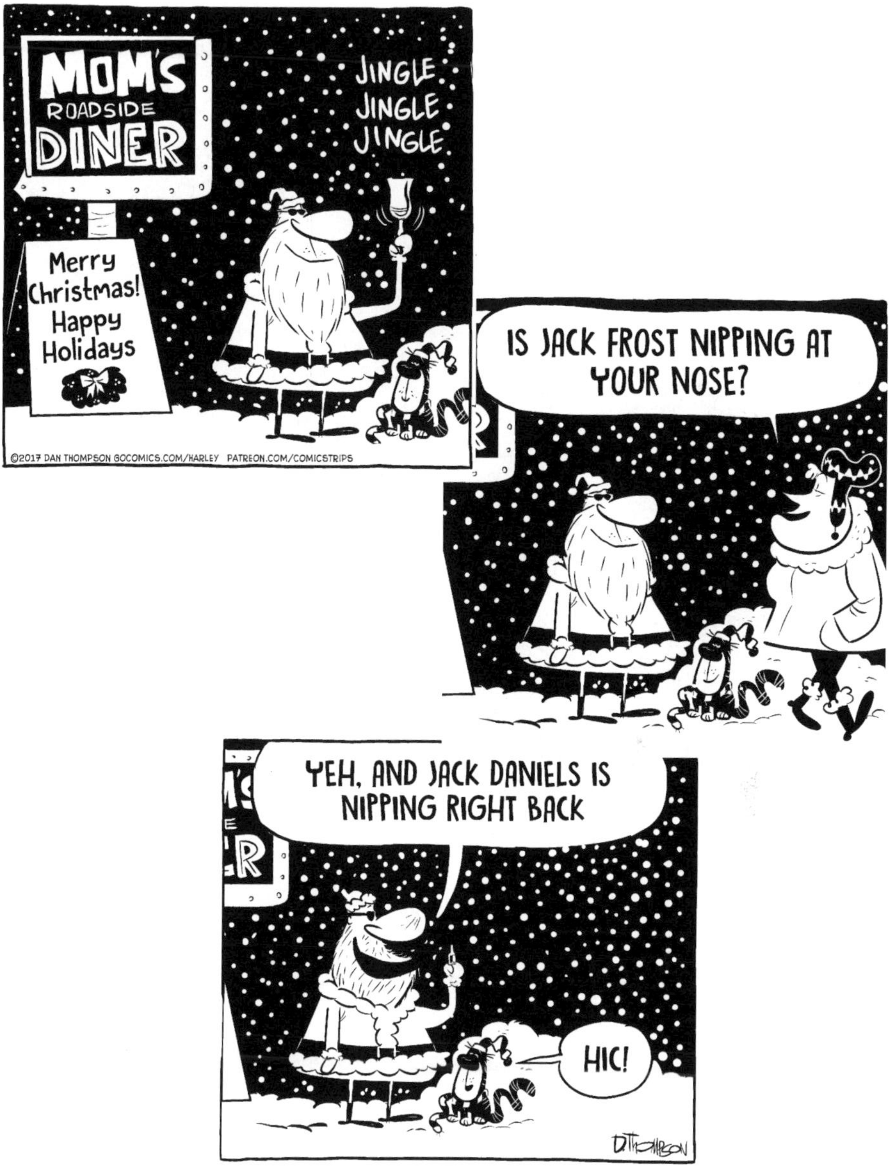
MOM'S ROADSIDE DINER
JINGLE JINGLE JINGLE
Merry Christmas! Happy Holidays
©2017 DAN THOMPSON GOCOMICS.COM/HARLEY PATREON.COM/COMICSTRIPS
IS JACK FROST NIPPING AT YOUR NOSE?
YEH, AND JACK DANIELS IS NIPPING RIGHT BACK
HIC!
D.THOMPSON

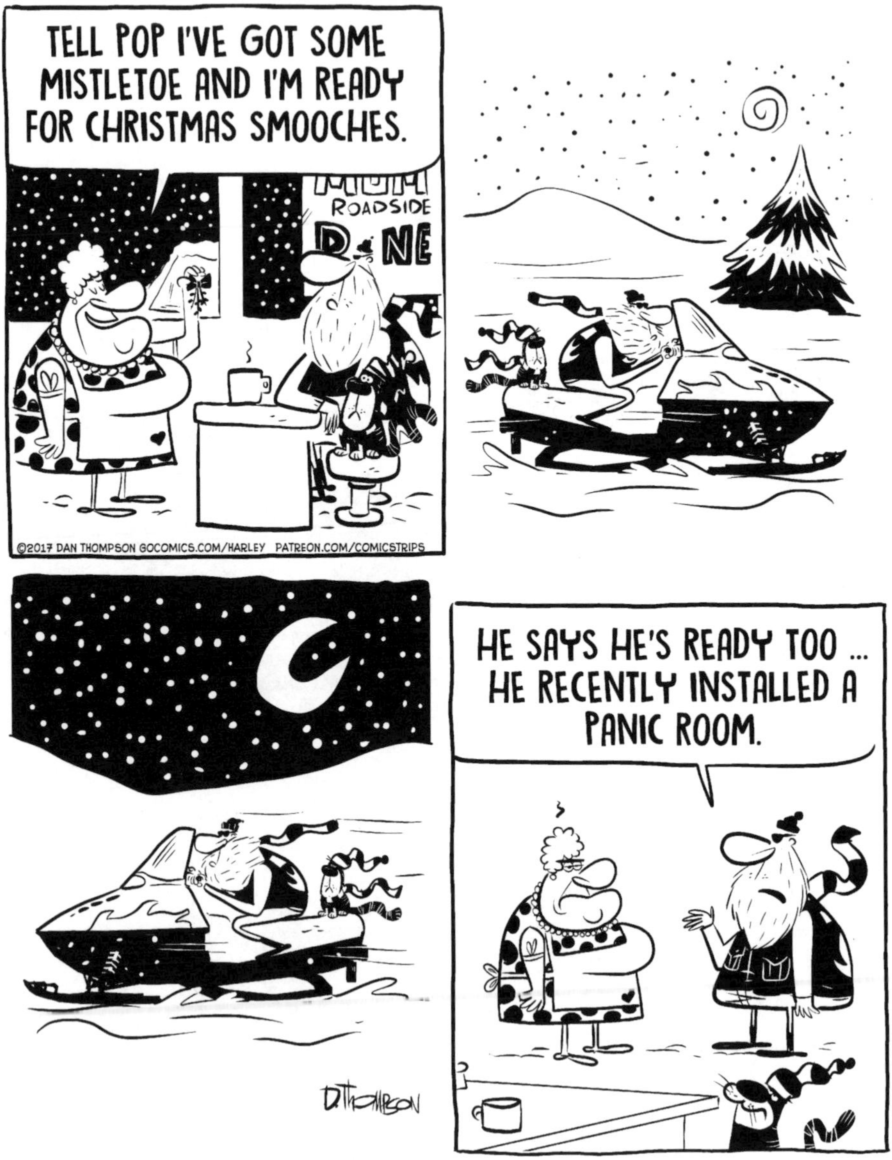
TELL POP I'VE GOT SOME MISTLETOE AND I'M READY FOR CHRISTMAS SMOOCHES.
ROADSIDE
©2017 DAN THOMPSON GOCOMICS.COM/HARLEY PATREON.COM/COMICSTRIPS
HE SAYS HE'S READY TOO ... HE RECENTLY INSTALLED A PANIC ROOM.
D. THOMPSON

I LOVE CRASHING HOLIDAY OFFICE PARTIES.
Consolidated Global Merge UNLIMITED X-MAS PARTY
©2017 DAN THOMPSON GOCOMICS.COM/HARLEY PATREON.COM/COMICSTRIPS
LET'S BE LOW-KEY ... NOT TO AROUSE SUSPICION.
I THINK THEY'RE SUSPICIOUS.
D THOMPSON

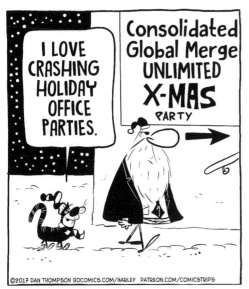

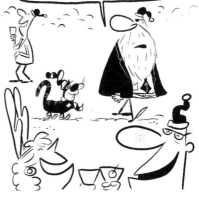

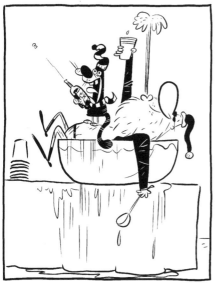

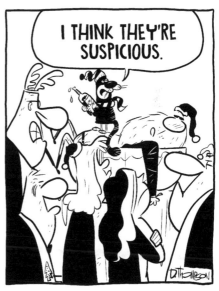

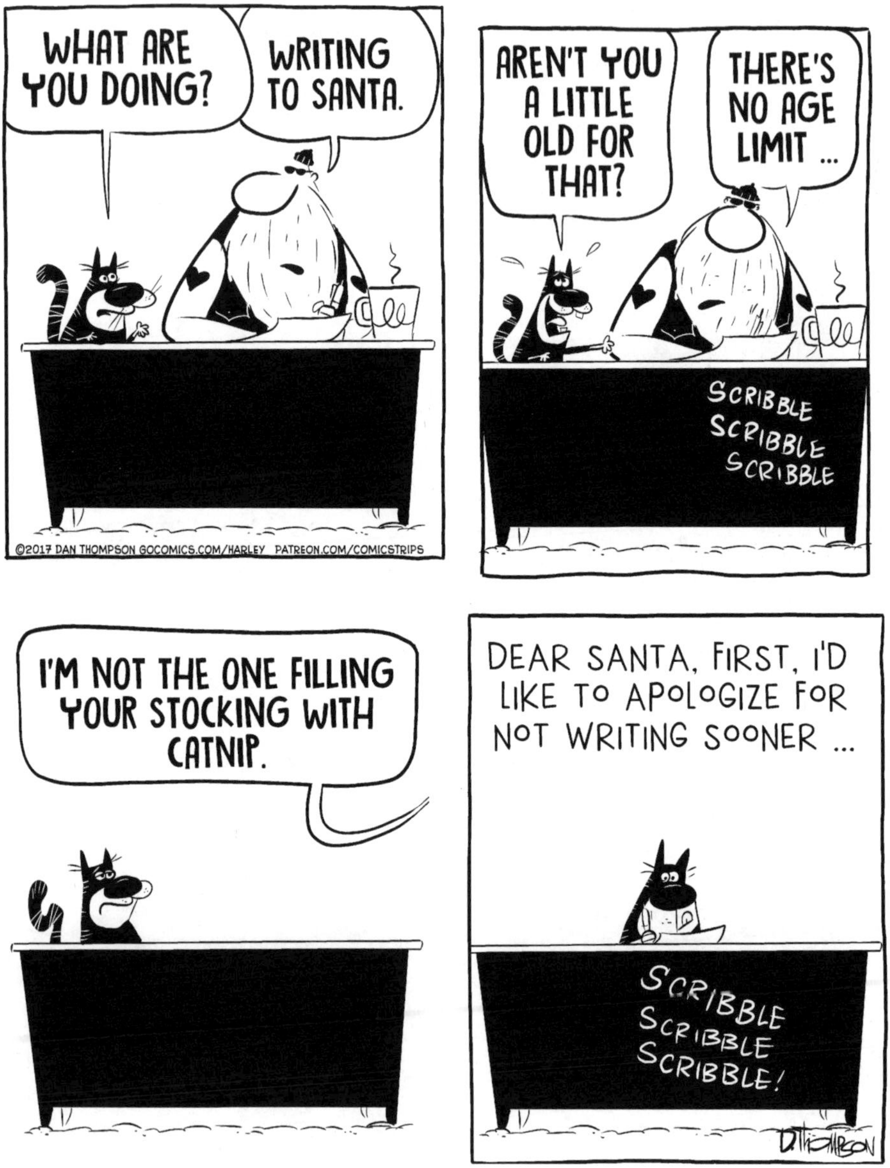
WHAT ARE YOU DOING?
WRITING TO SANTA.
©2017 DAN THOMPSON GOCOMICS.COM/HARLEY PATREON.COM/COMICSTRIPS
AREN'T YOU A LITTLE OLD FOR THAT?
THERE'S NO AGE LIMIT ...
SCRIBBLE SCRIBBLE SCRIBBLE
I'M NOT THE ONE FILLING YOUR STOCKING WITH CATNIP.
DEAR SANTA, FIRST, I'D LIKE TO APOLOGIZE FOR NOT WRITING SOONER ...
SCRIBBLE SCRIBBLE SCRIBBLE!
D. THOMPSON

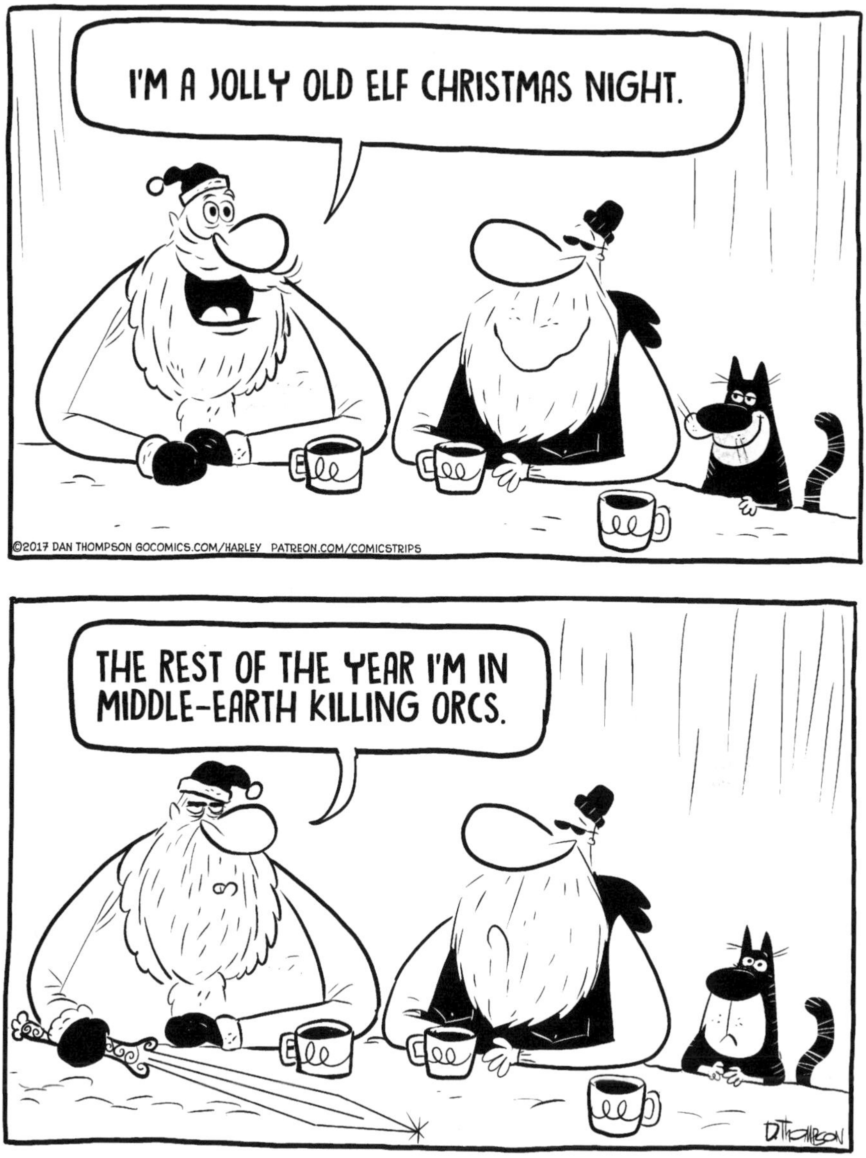
I'M A JOLLY OLD ELF CHRISTMAS NIGHT.
©2017 DAN THOMPSON GOCOMICS.COM/HARLEY PATREON.COM/COMICSTRIPS
THE REST OF THE YEAR I'M IN MIDDLE-EARTH KILLING ORCS.
D. THOMPSON

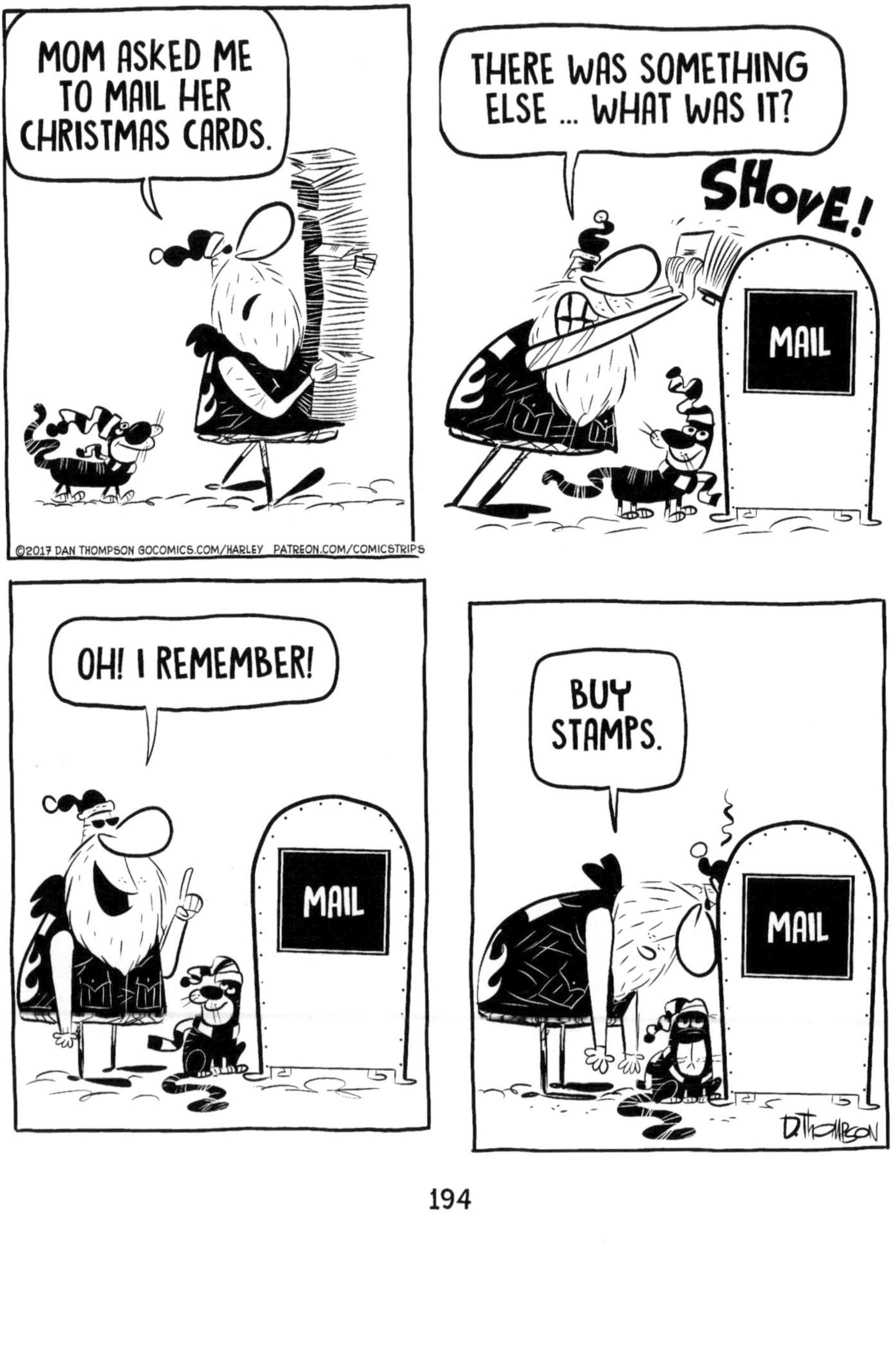
MOM ASKED ME TO MAIL HER CHRISTMAS CARDS.
©2017 DAN THOMPSON GOCOMICS.COM/HARLEY PATREON.COM/COMICSTRIPS
THERE WAS SOMETHING ELSE ... WHAT WAS IT?
SHOVE!
MAIL
OH! I REMEMBER!
MAIL
BUY STAMPS.
MAIL
D.THOMPSON

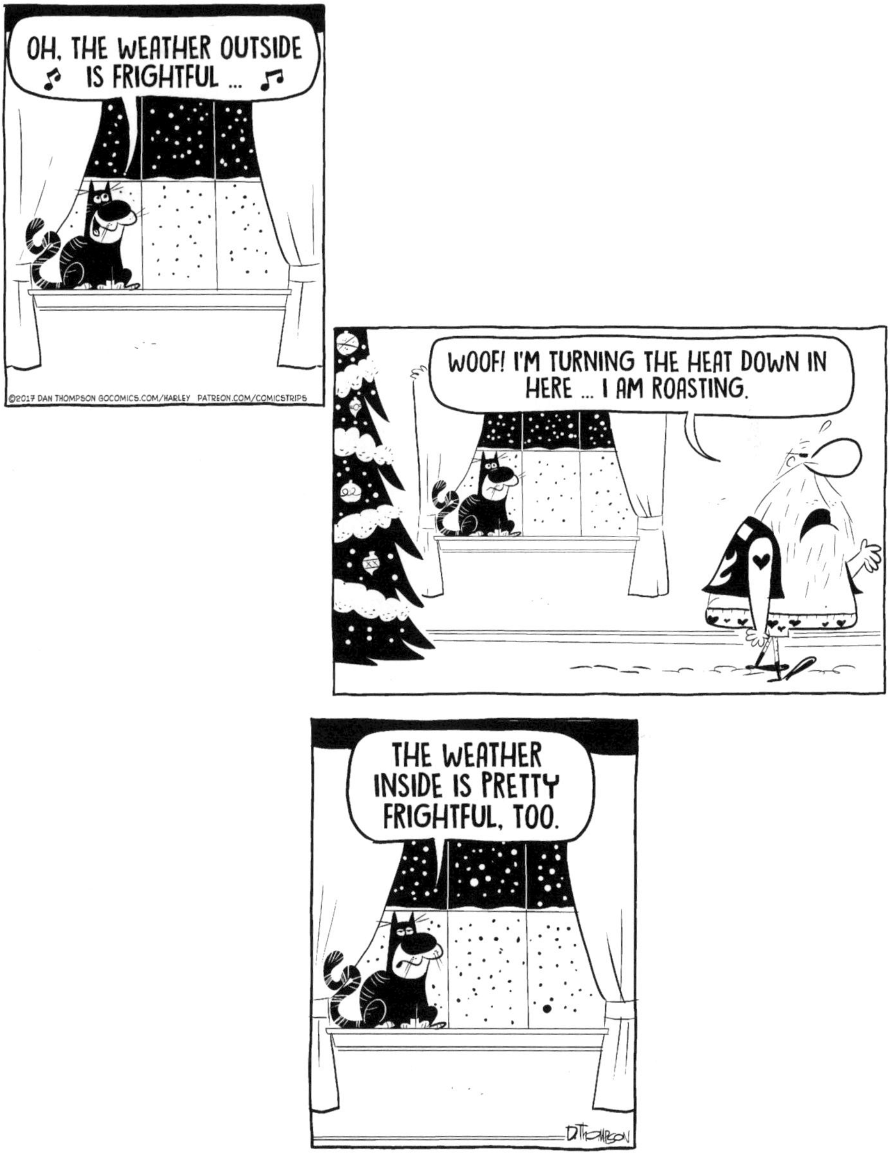
OH, THE WEATHER OUTSIDE IS FRIGHTFUL ...
©2017 DAN THOMPSON GOCOMICS.COM/HARLEY PATREON.COM/COMICSTRIPS
WOOF! I'M TURNING THE HEAT DOWN IN HERE ... I AM ROASTING.
THE WEATHER INSIDE IS PRETTY FRIGHTFUL, TOO.
D THOMPSON

MAYBE IT'S MUCH TOO EARLY ♫ IN THE GAME ... ♫
D. THOMPSON
©2017 DAN THOMPSON GOCOMICS.COM/HARLEY PATREON.COM/COMICSTRIPS
OOH, BUT I THOUGHT I'D ASK YOU JUST THE SAME ... ♫ ♫
WHAT ARE YOU DOING NEW YEAR'S ... NEW ♫ YEAR'S EVE? ♫
NOTHING. PICK ME UP AROUND 8.

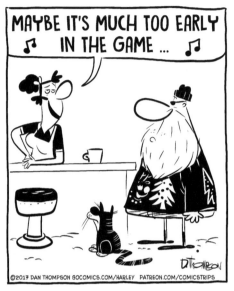

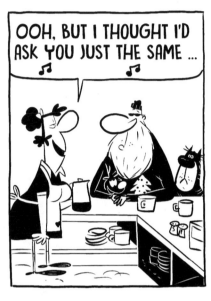

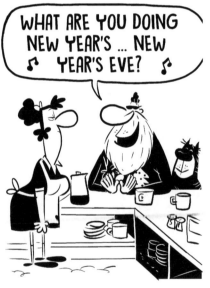

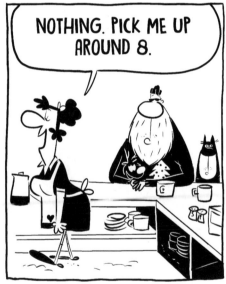

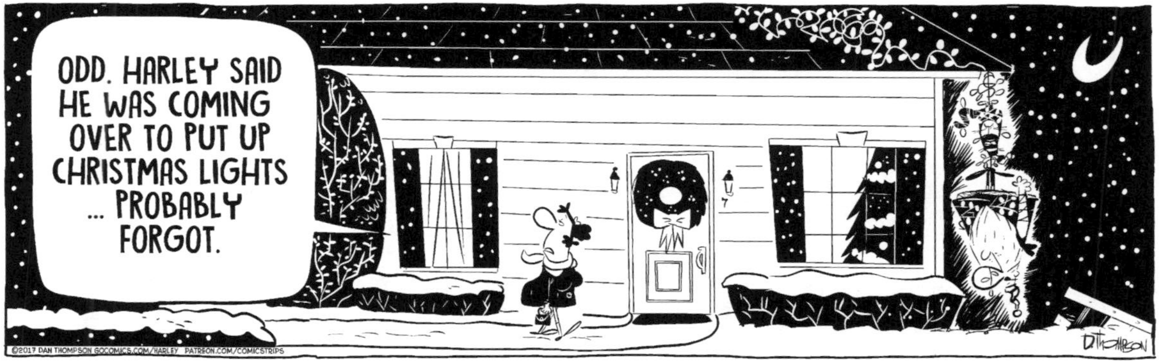
ODD. HARLEY SAID HE WAS COMING OVER TO PUT UP CHRISTMAS LIGHTS ... PROBABLY FORGOT.
©2017 DAN THOMPSON GOCOMICS.COM/HARLEY PATREON.COM/COMICSTRIPS
D. THOMPSON

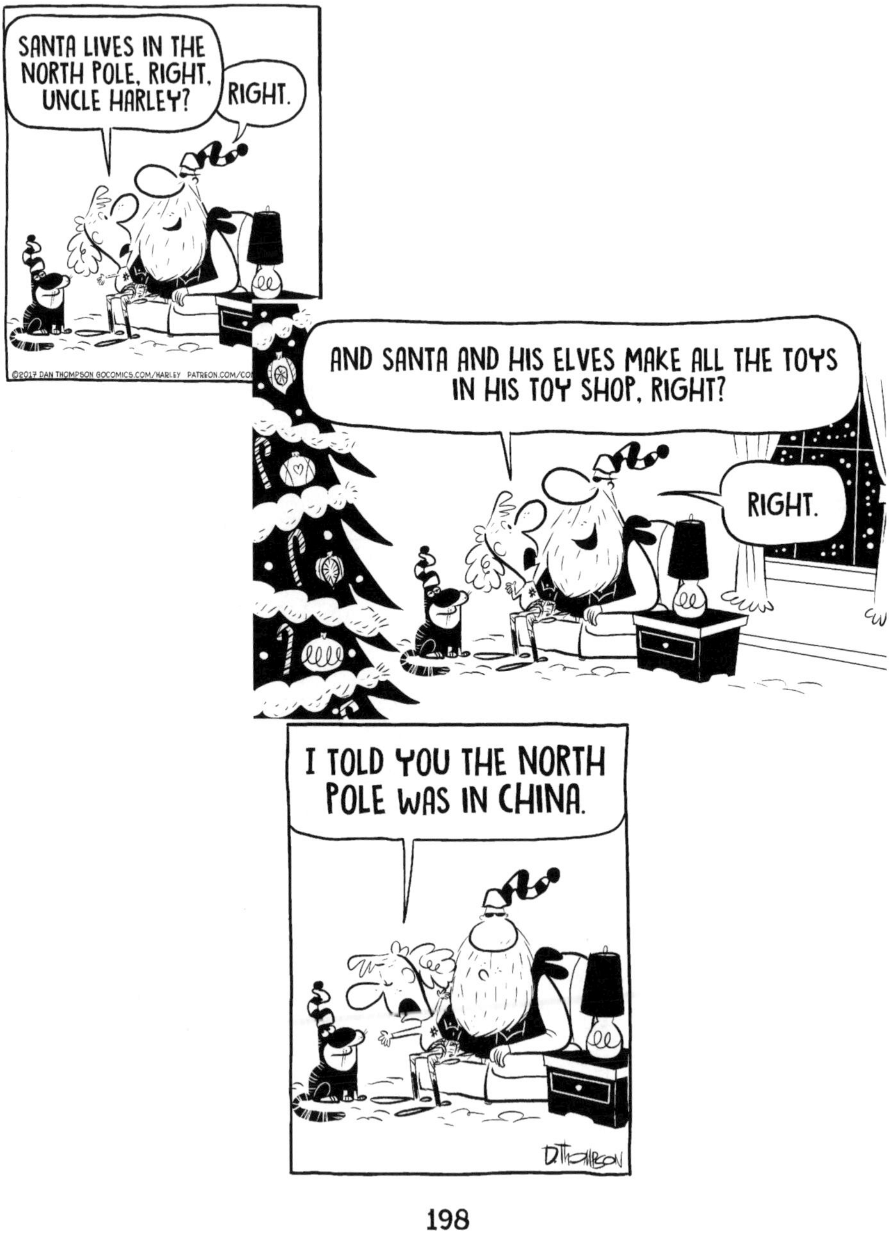
SANTA LIVES IN THE NORTH POLE, RIGHT, UNCLE HARLEY?
RIGHT.
©2017 DAN THOMPSON GOCOMICS.COM/HARLEY
AND SANTA AND HIS ELVES MAKE ALL THE TOYS IN HIS TOY SHOP, RIGHT?
RIGHT.
I TOLD YOU THE NORTH POLE WAS IN CHINA.
D. THOMPSON

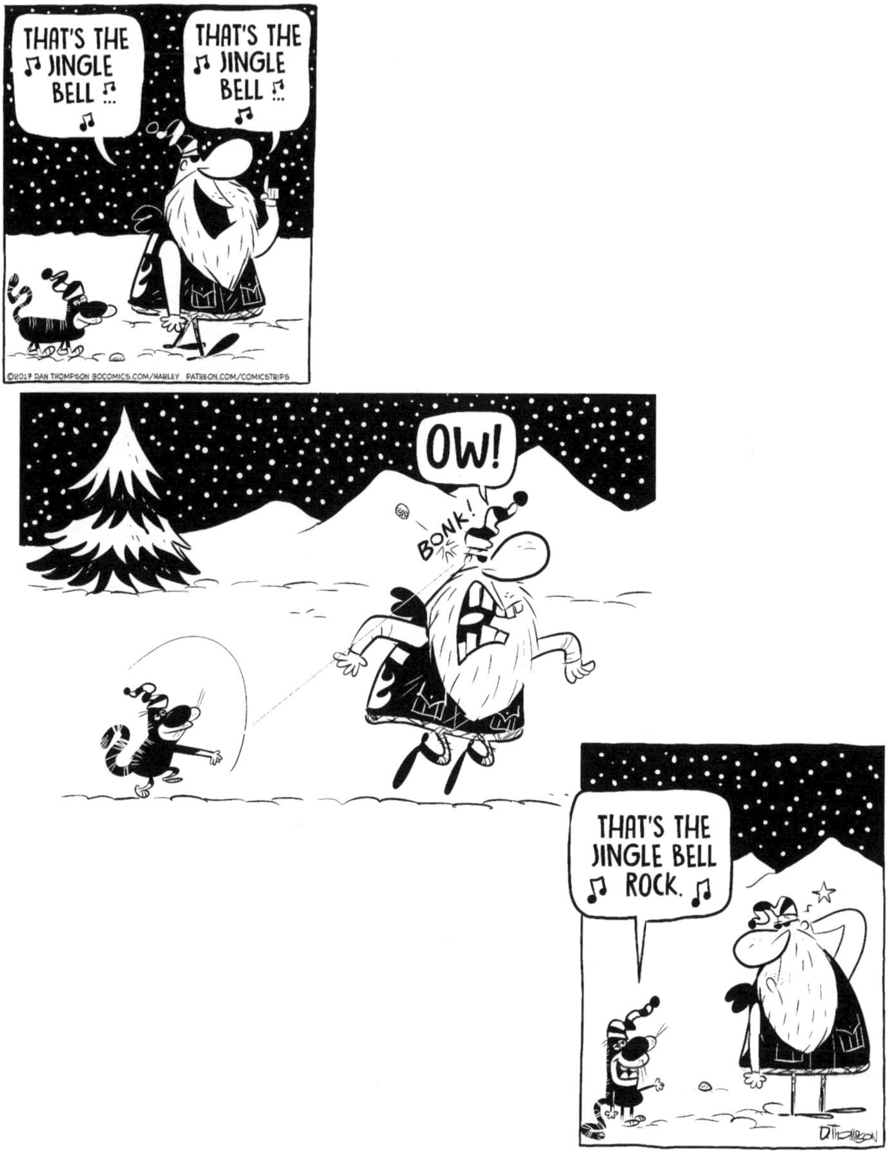
THAT'S THE JINGLE BELL ...
THAT'S THE JINGLE BELL ...
©2017 DAN THOMPSON GOCOMICS.COM/HARLEY PATREON.COM/COMICSTRIPS
OW!
BONK!
THAT'S THE JINGLE BELL ROCK.
D THOMPSON

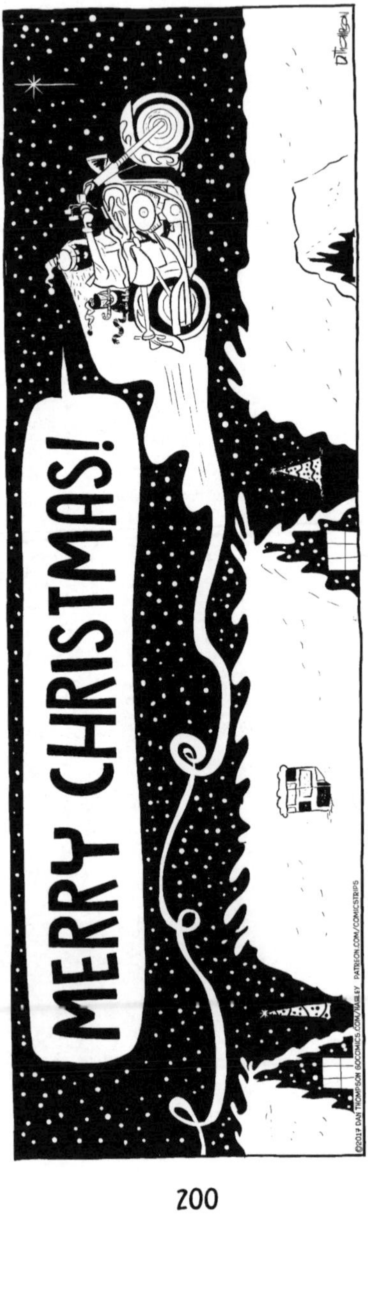
MERRY CHRISTMAS!
©2017 DAN THOMPSON GOCOMICS.COM/HARLEY PATREON.COM/COMICSTRIPS

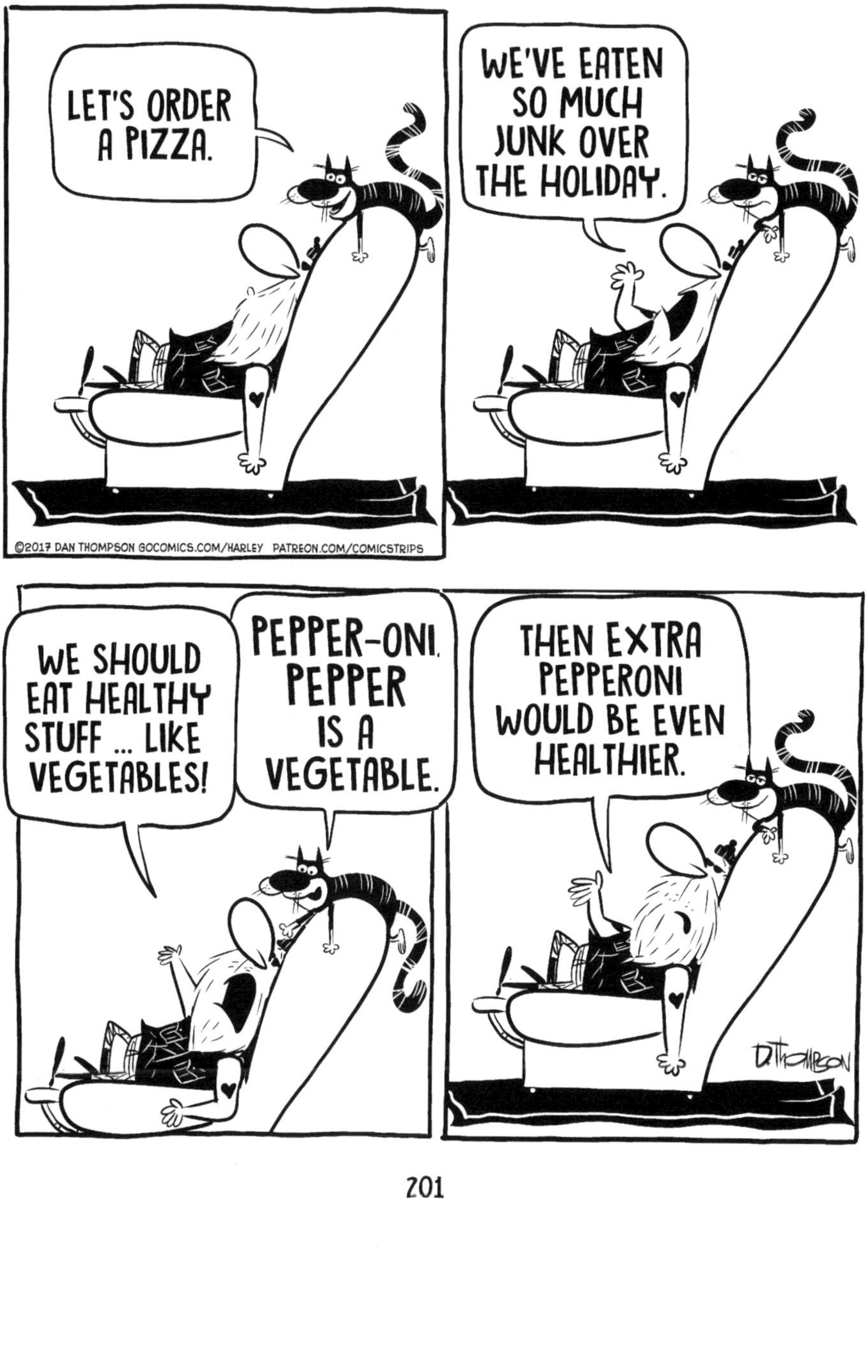
LET'S ORDER A PIZZA.
WE'VE EATEN SO MUCH JUNK OVER THE HOLIDAY.
©2017 DAN THOMPSON GOCOMICS.COM/HARLEY PATREON.COM/COMICSTRIPS
WE SHOULD EAT HEALTHY STUFF ... LIKE VEGETABLES!
PEPPER-ONI. PEPPER IS A VEGETABLE.
THEN EXTRA PEPPERONI WOULD BE EVEN HEALTHIER.
D.THOMPSON

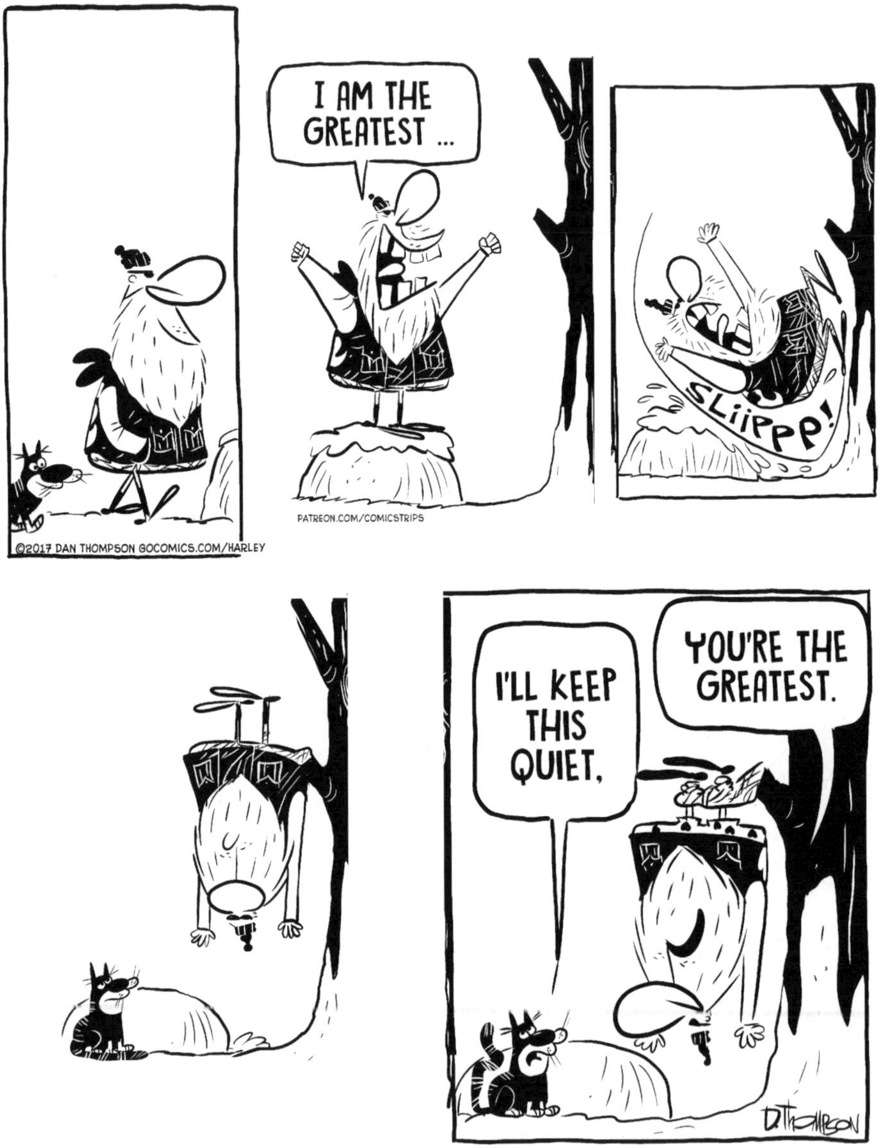
©2017 DAN THOMPSON GOCOMICS.COM/HARLEY
I AM THE GREATEST ...
PATREON.COM/COMICSTRIPS
SLiiPPP!
I'LL KEEP THIS QUIET,
YOU'RE THE GREATEST.
D.THOMPSON

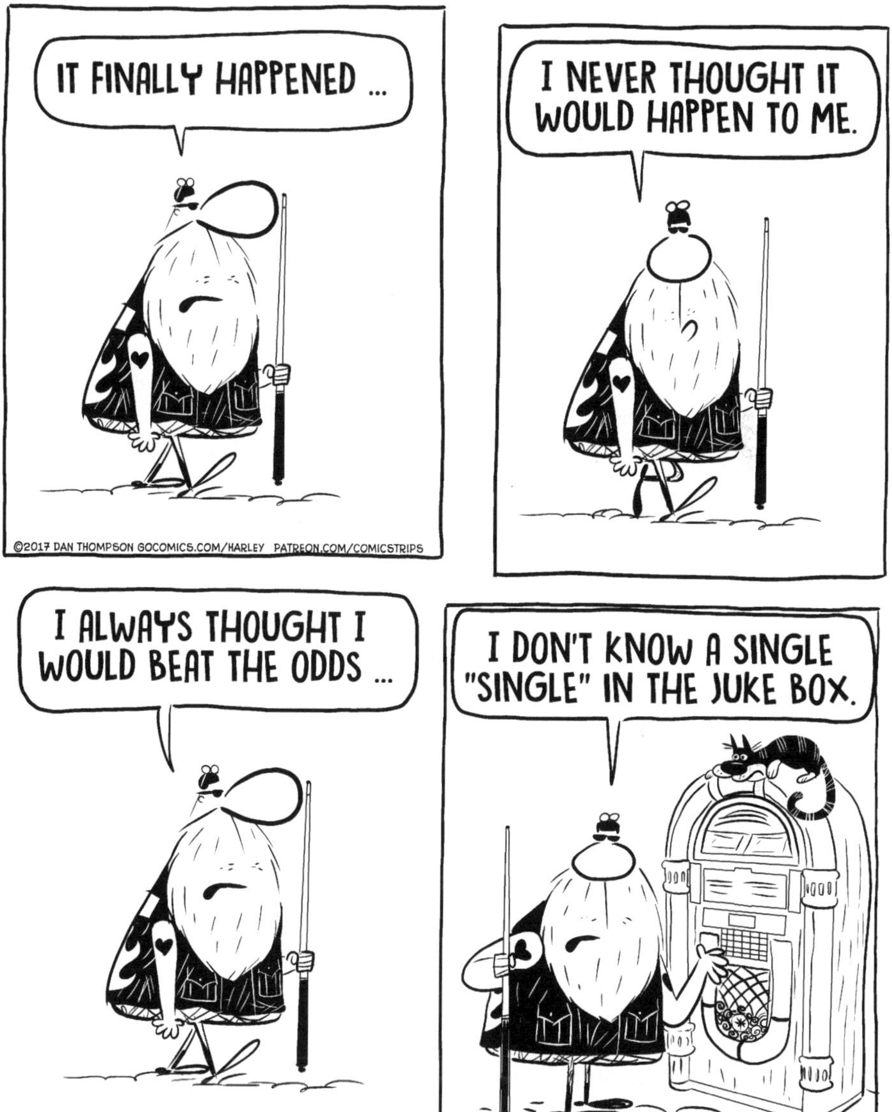
IT FINALLY HAPPENED ...
©2017 DAN THOMPSON GOCOMICS.COM/HARLEY PATREON.COM/COMICSTRIPS
I NEVER THOUGHT IT WOULD HAPPEN TO ME.
I ALWAYS THOUGHT I WOULD BEAT THE ODDS ...
I DON'T KNOW A SINGLE "SINGLE" IN THE JUKE BOX.
D. THOMPSON

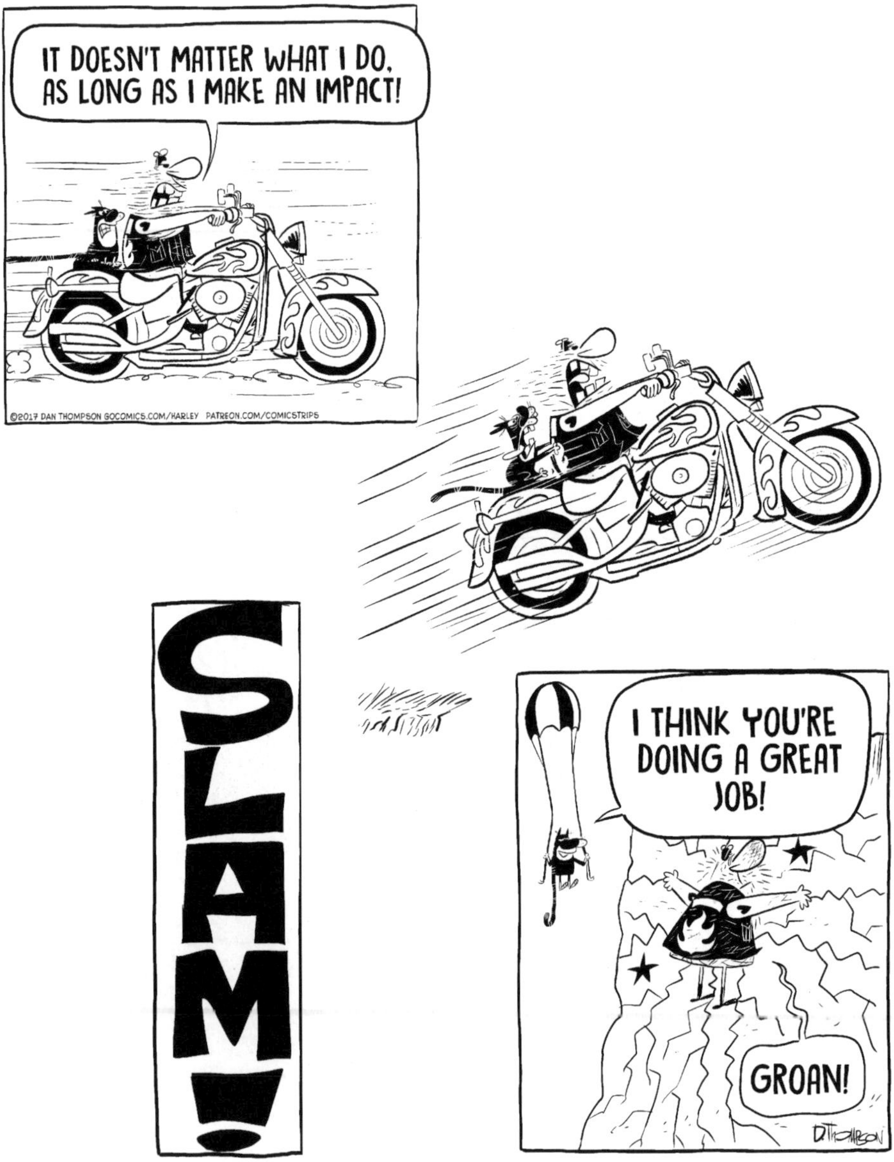
IT DOESN'T MATTER WHAT I DO, AS LONG AS I MAKE AN IMPACT!
©2017 DAN THOMPSON GOCOMICS.COM/HARLEY PATREON.COM/COMICSTRIPS
SLAM!
I THINK YOU'RE DOING A GREAT JOB!
GROAN!
D.THOMPSON

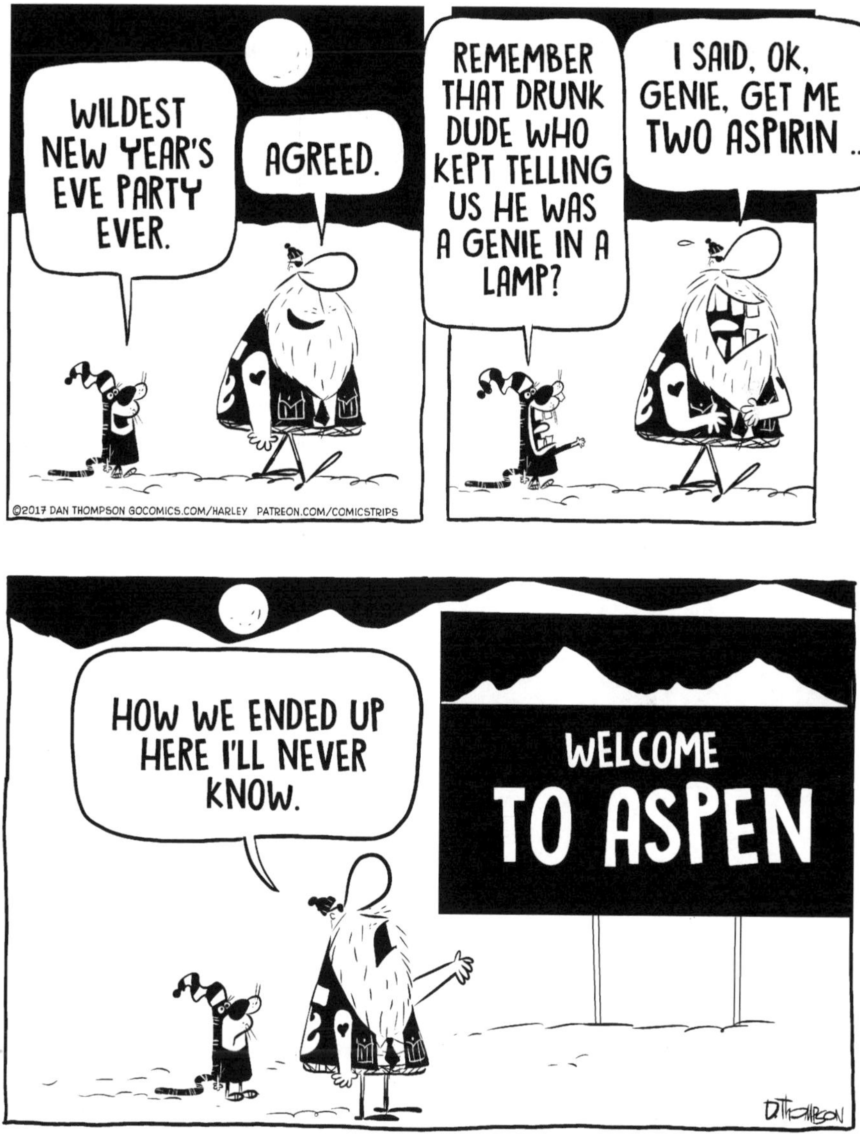
WILDEST NEW YEAR'S EVE PARTY EVER.
AGREED.
©2017 DAN THOMPSON GOCOMICS.COM/HARLEY PATREON.COM/COMICSTRIPS
REMEMBER THAT DRUNK DUDE WHO KEPT TELLING US HE WAS A GENIE IN A LAMP?
I SAID, OK, GENIE, GET ME TWO ASPIRIN ...
HOW WE ENDED UP HERE I'LL NEVER KNOW.
WELCOME TO ASPEN
D. THOMPSON

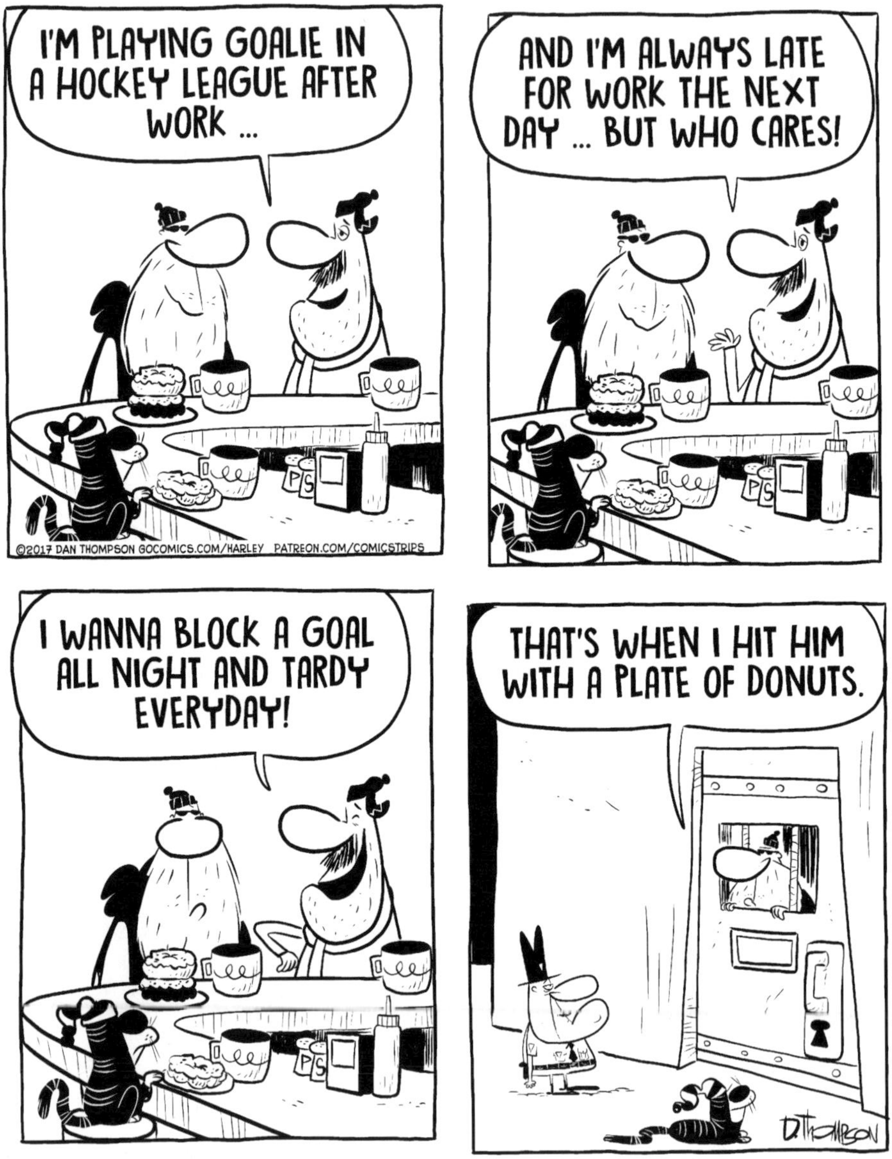
I'M PLAYING GOALIE IN A HOCKEY LEAGUE AFTER WORK ...
©2017 DAN THOMPSON GOCOMICS.COM/HARLEY PATREON.COM/COMICSTRIPS
AND I'M ALWAYS LATE FOR WORK THE NEXT DAY ... BUT WHO CARES!
I WANNA BLOCK A GOAL ALL NIGHT AND TARDY EVERYDAY!
THAT'S WHEN I HIT HIM WITH A PLATE OF DONUTS.
D. THOMPSON

COFFEE IS GREAT ...
IT GIVES YOU A BURST
OF ENERGY ...

©2017 DAN THOMPSON GOCOMICS.COM/HARLEY PATREON.COM/COMICSTRIPS

SOMETIMES IT CAN MAKE
YOU BOUNCE OFF THE
WALLS ...

THEN WHEN YOU
STOP DRINKING
IT, YOU CRASH.

SO, THIS STUFF
TURNS YOU
INTO A CAT?

207

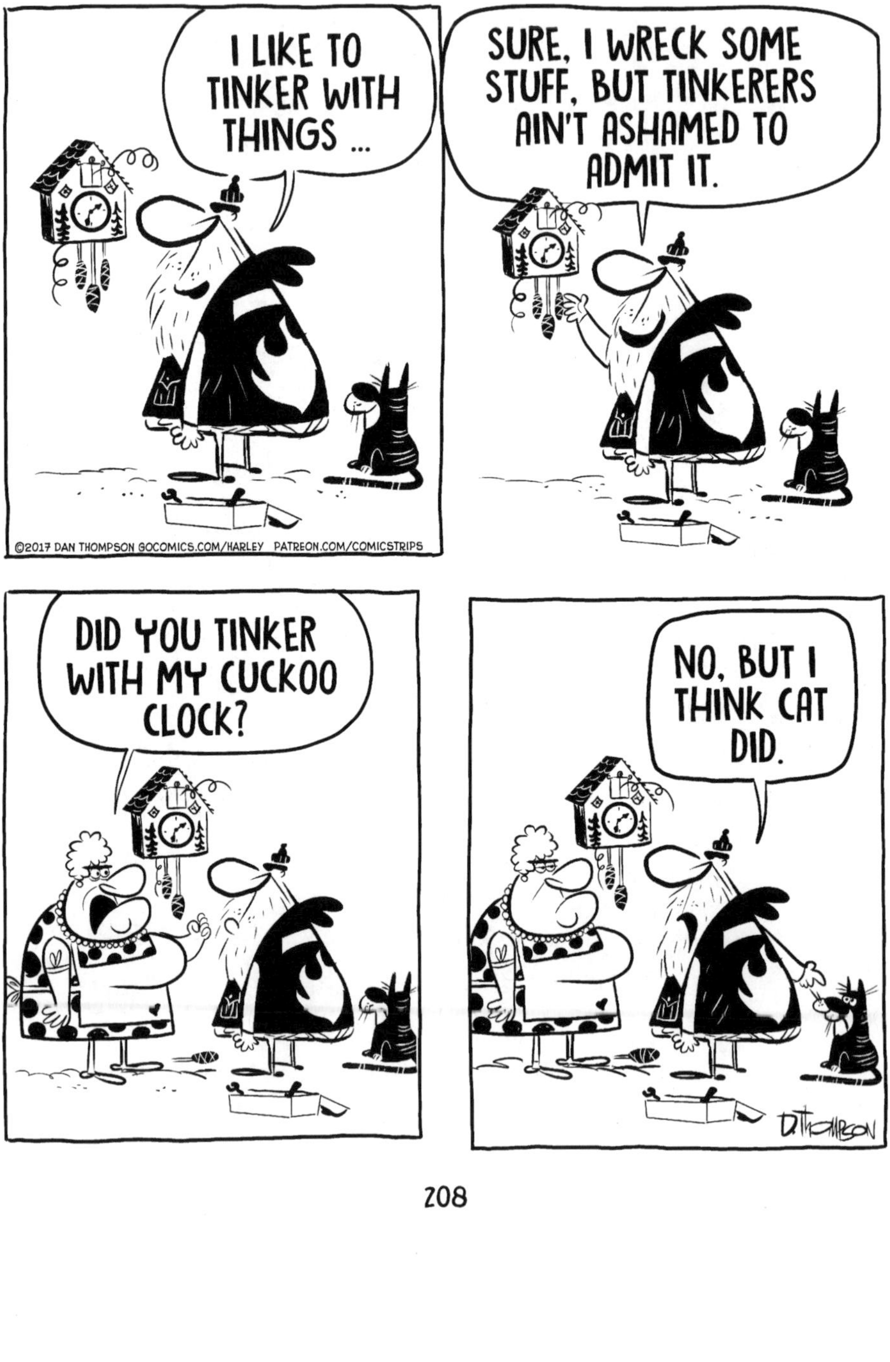
I LIKE TO TINKER WITH THINGS ...
SURE, I WRECK SOME STUFF, BUT TINKERERS AIN'T ASHAMED TO ADMIT IT.
DID YOU TINKER WITH MY CUCKOO CLOCK?
NO, BUT I THINK CAT DID.
©2017 DAN THOMPSON GOCOMICS.COM/HARLEY PATREON.COM/COMICSTRIPS
D. THOMPSON

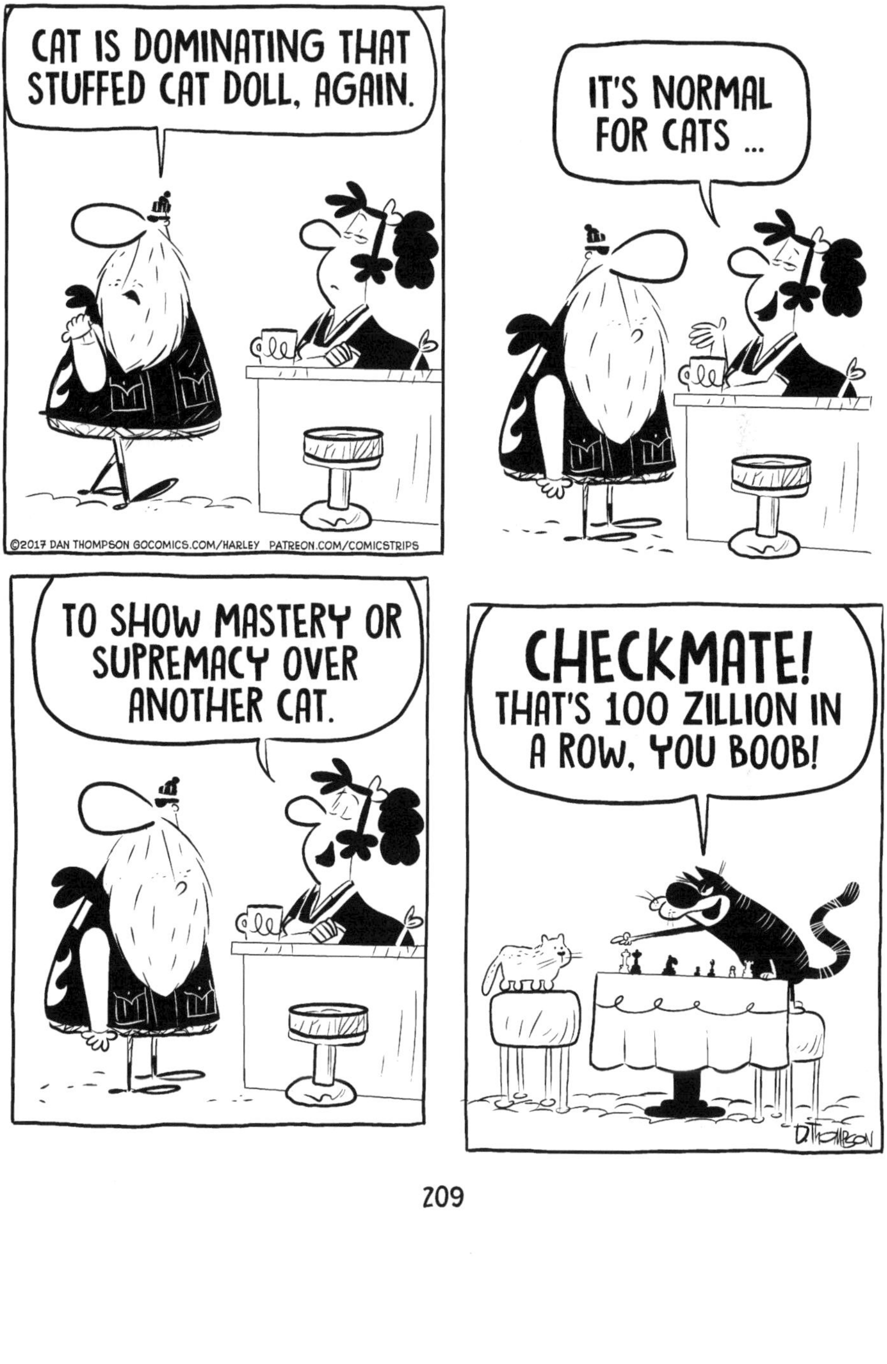
CAT IS DOMINATING THAT STUFFED CAT DOLL, AGAIN.
©2017 DAN THOMPSON GOCOMICS.COM/HARLEY PATREON.COM/COMICSTRIPS
IT'S NORMAL FOR CATS ...
TO SHOW MASTERY OR SUPREMACY OVER ANOTHER CAT.
CHECKMATE! THAT'S 100 ZILLION IN A ROW, YOU BOOB!
D THOMPSON

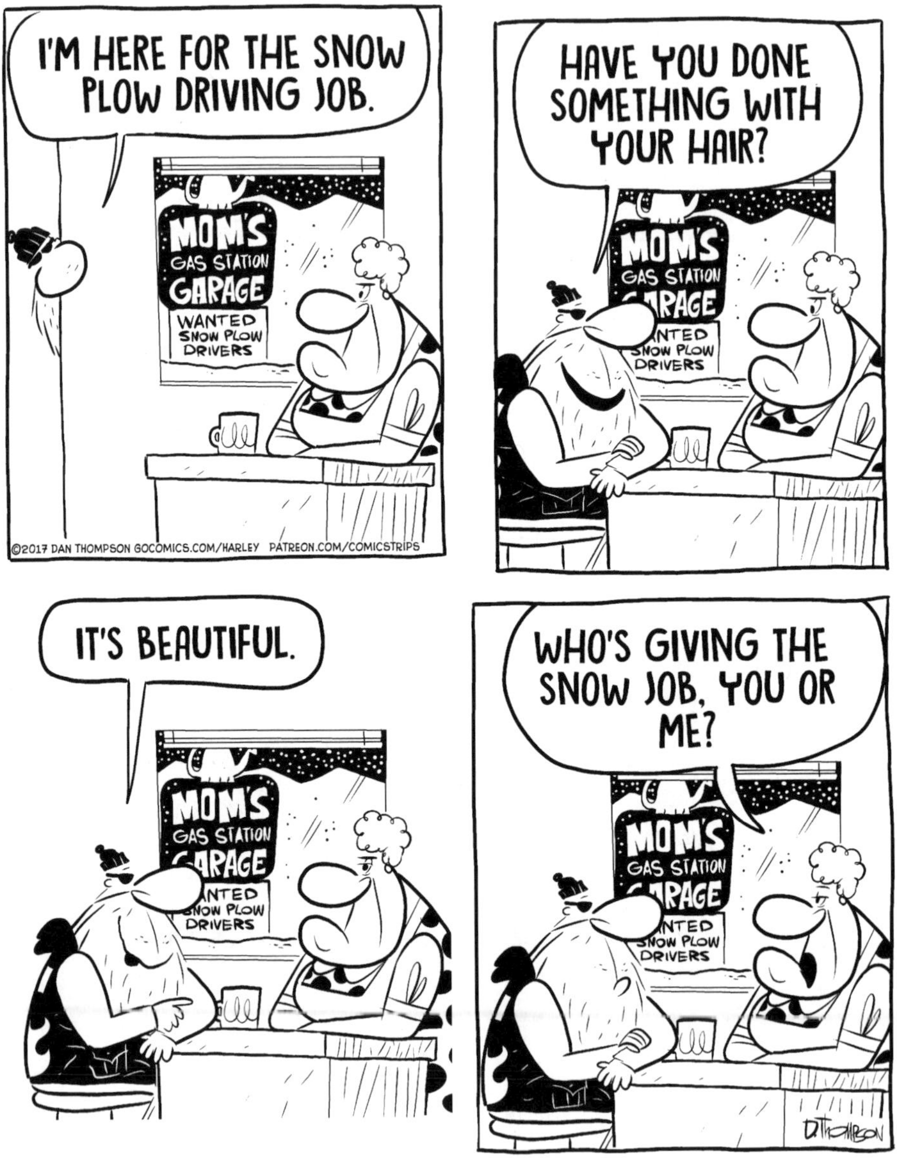
I'M HERE FOR THE SNOW PLOW DRIVING JOB.
MOM'S
GAS STATION
GARAGE
WANTED
SNOW PLOW
DRIVERS
©2017 DAN THOMPSON GOCOMICS.COM/HARLEY PATREON.COM/COMICSTRIPS
HAVE YOU DONE SOMETHING WITH YOUR HAIR?
IT'S BEAUTIFUL.
WHO'S GIVING THE SNOW JOB, YOU OR ME?
D THOMPSON

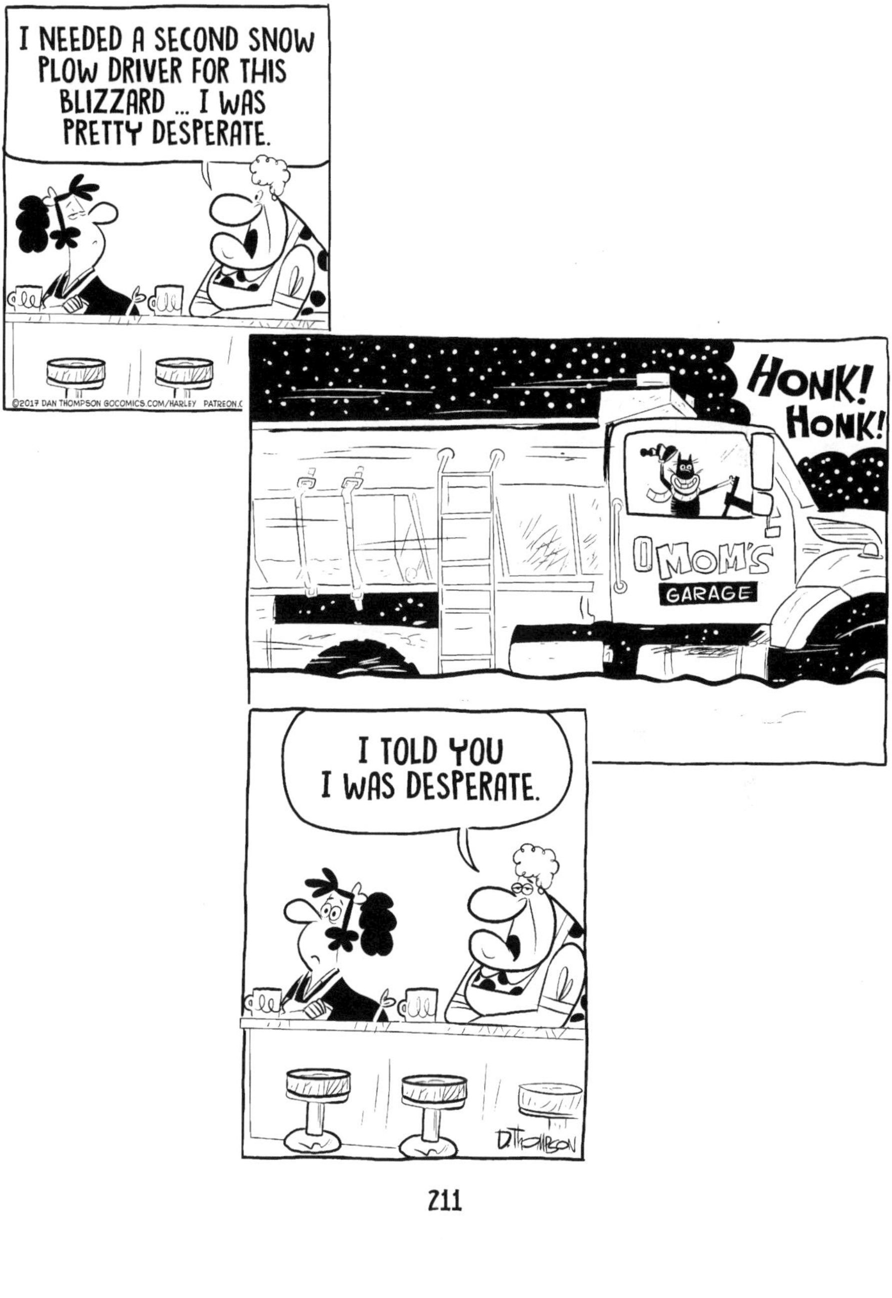
I NEEDED A SECOND SNOW PLOW DRIVER FOR THIS BLIZZARD ... I WAS PRETTY DESPERATE.
©2017 DAN THOMPSON GOCOMICS.COM/HARLEY PATREON.C
HONK! HONK!
MOM'S
GARAGE
I TOLD YOU I WAS DESPERATE.

CAT, THIS BLIZZARD CAUSED ME TO HAVE AN ACCIDENT!
©2017 DAN THOMPSON GOCOMICS.COM/HARLEY PATREON.COM/COMICSTRIPS
CAN YOU HELP ME OUT?
I'M STUCK IN A JAM.
CAN DO.
THANKS, CAT.
JONES FRUIT SPREAD CO.
D.THOMPSON

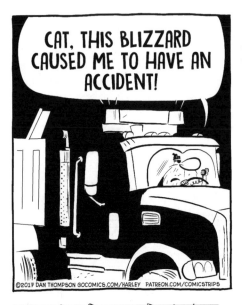

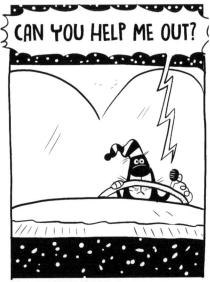

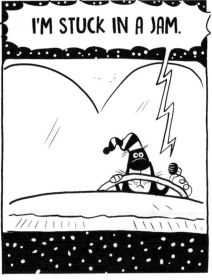

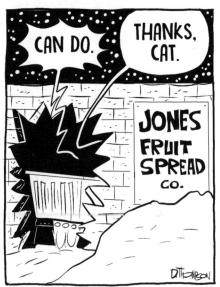

THE PLOW GUY IS A HERO WHO IS ALWAYS LOOKING OUT FOR THE LITTLE GUY, CAT ...
©2017 DAN THOMPSON GOCOMICS.COM/HARLEY PATREON.COM/COMICSTRIPS
THE FORGOTTEN WHO CRY OUT, "GIMMIE SWEET RELIEF!"
ARE YOU PLOWING TO THE COFFEE SHOP?
COFFEE Shop
DON'T SPOIL MY MOMENT.
D. THOMPSON

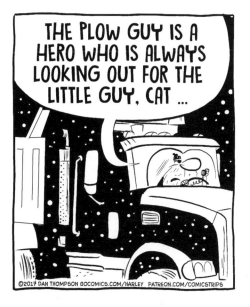

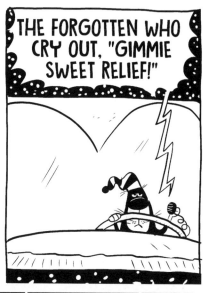

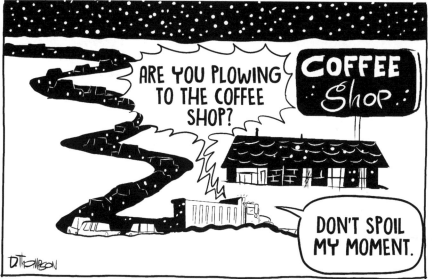

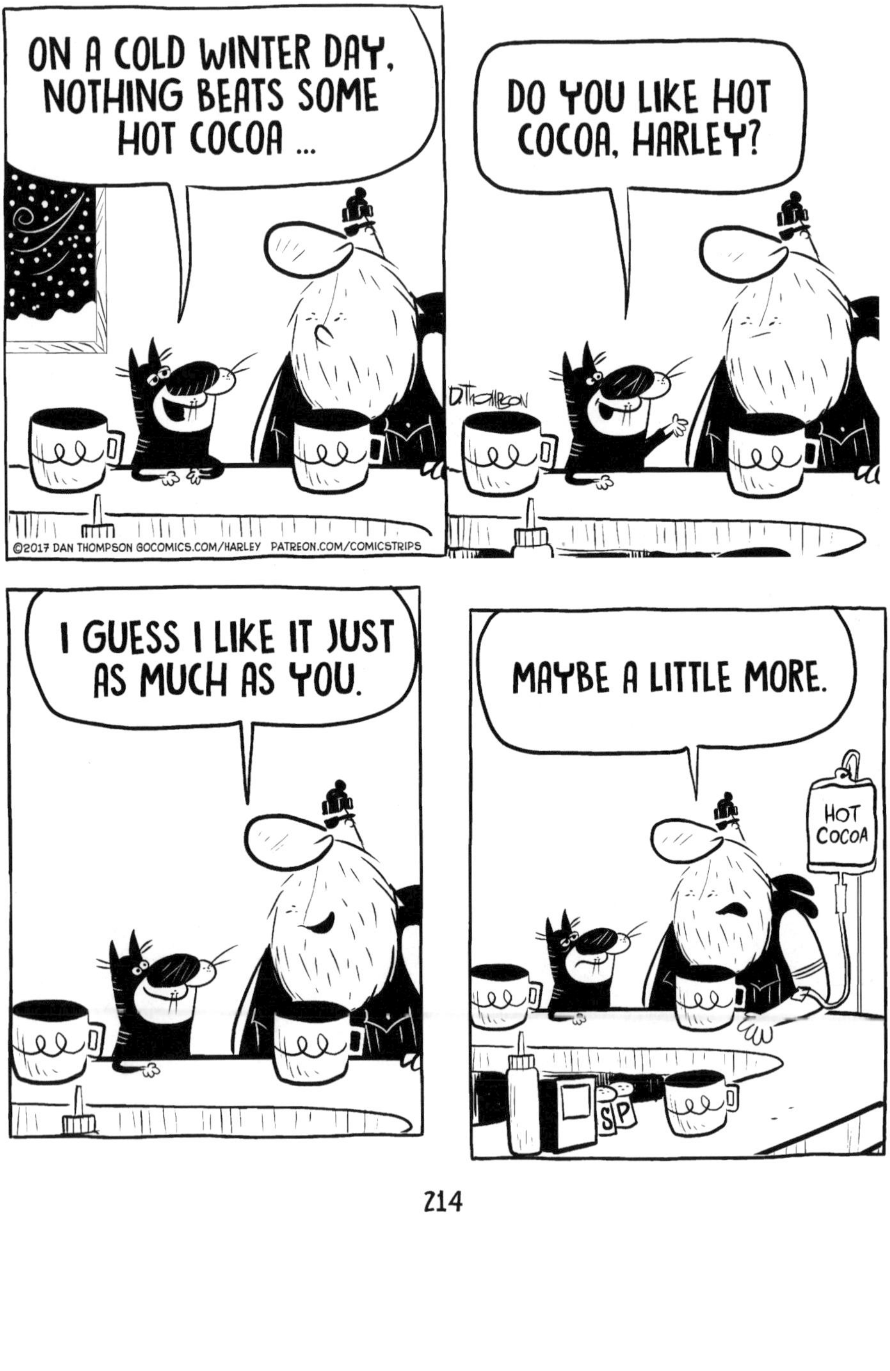
ON A COLD WINTER DAY, NOTHING BEATS SOME HOT COCOA ...
©2017 DAN THOMPSON GOCOMICS.COM/HARLEY PATREON.COM/COMICSTRIPS
DO YOU LIKE HOT COCOA, HARLEY?
D THOMPSON
I GUESS I LIKE IT JUST AS MUCH AS YOU.
MAYBE A LITTLE MORE.
HOT COCOA
S P

I TOLD YOU OVER AN HOUR AGO TO PICK ME UP!
SORRY, I CAN'T ALWAYS BE AT YOUR BACK AND CALL.
IT'S BECK AND CALL!
DON'T TURN YOUR BECK ON ME.
©2017 DAN THOMPSON GOCOMICS.COM/HARLEY PATREON.COM/COMICSTRIPS
D. THOMPSON

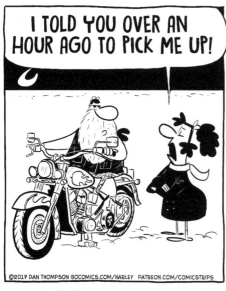

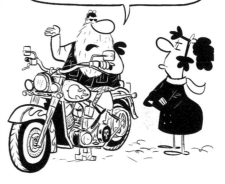

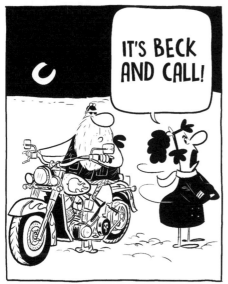

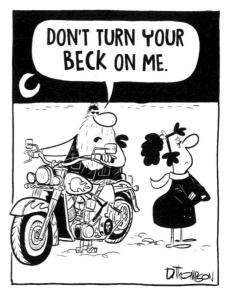

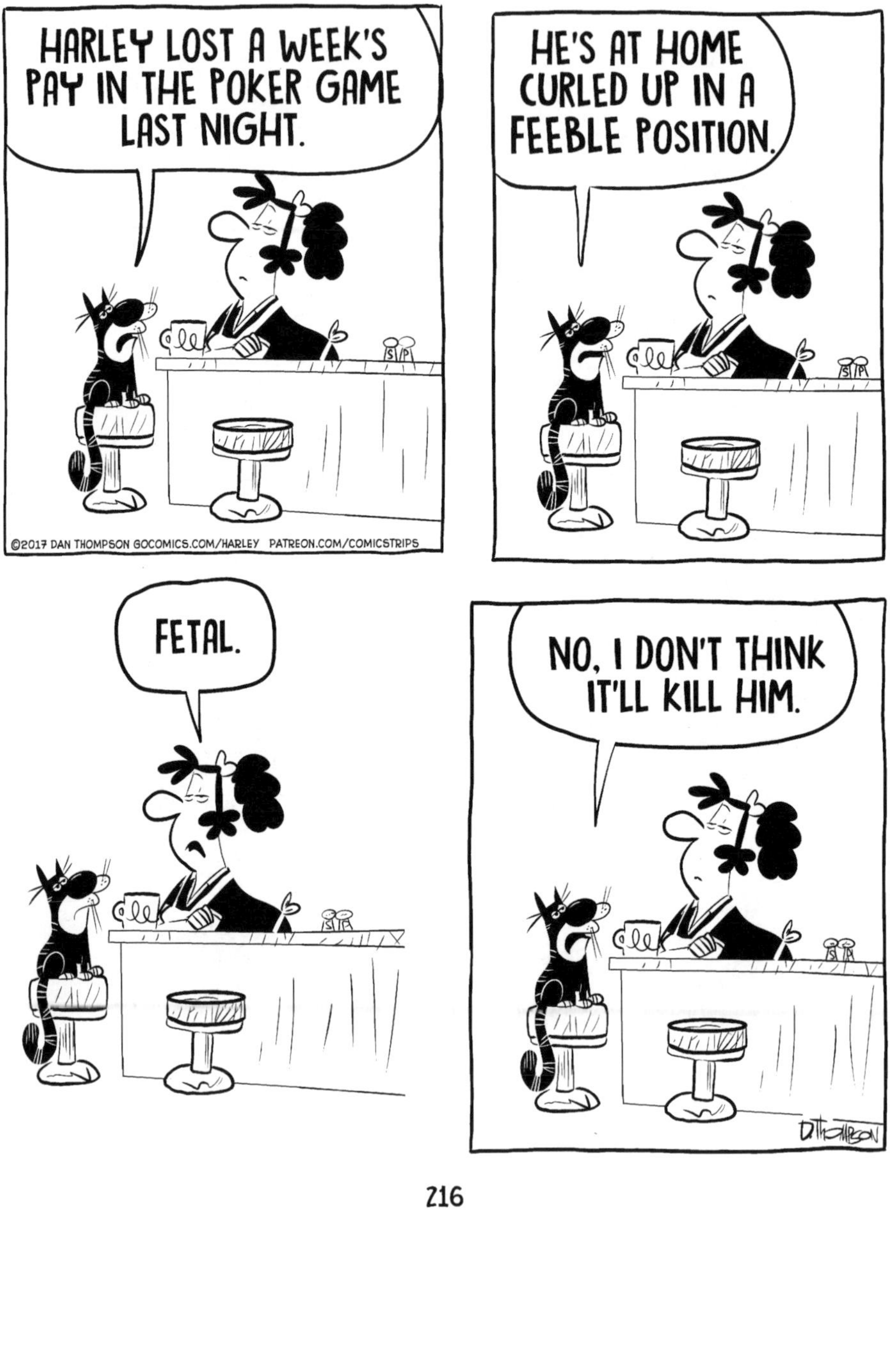
HARLEY LOST A WEEK'S PAY IN THE POKER GAME LAST NIGHT.
©2017 DAN THOMPSON GOCOMICS.COM/HARLEY PATREON.COM/COMICSTRIPS
S P
HE'S AT HOME CURLED UP IN A FEEBLE POSITION.
S P
FETAL.
NO, I DON'T THINK IT'LL KILL HIM.
D.THOMPSON

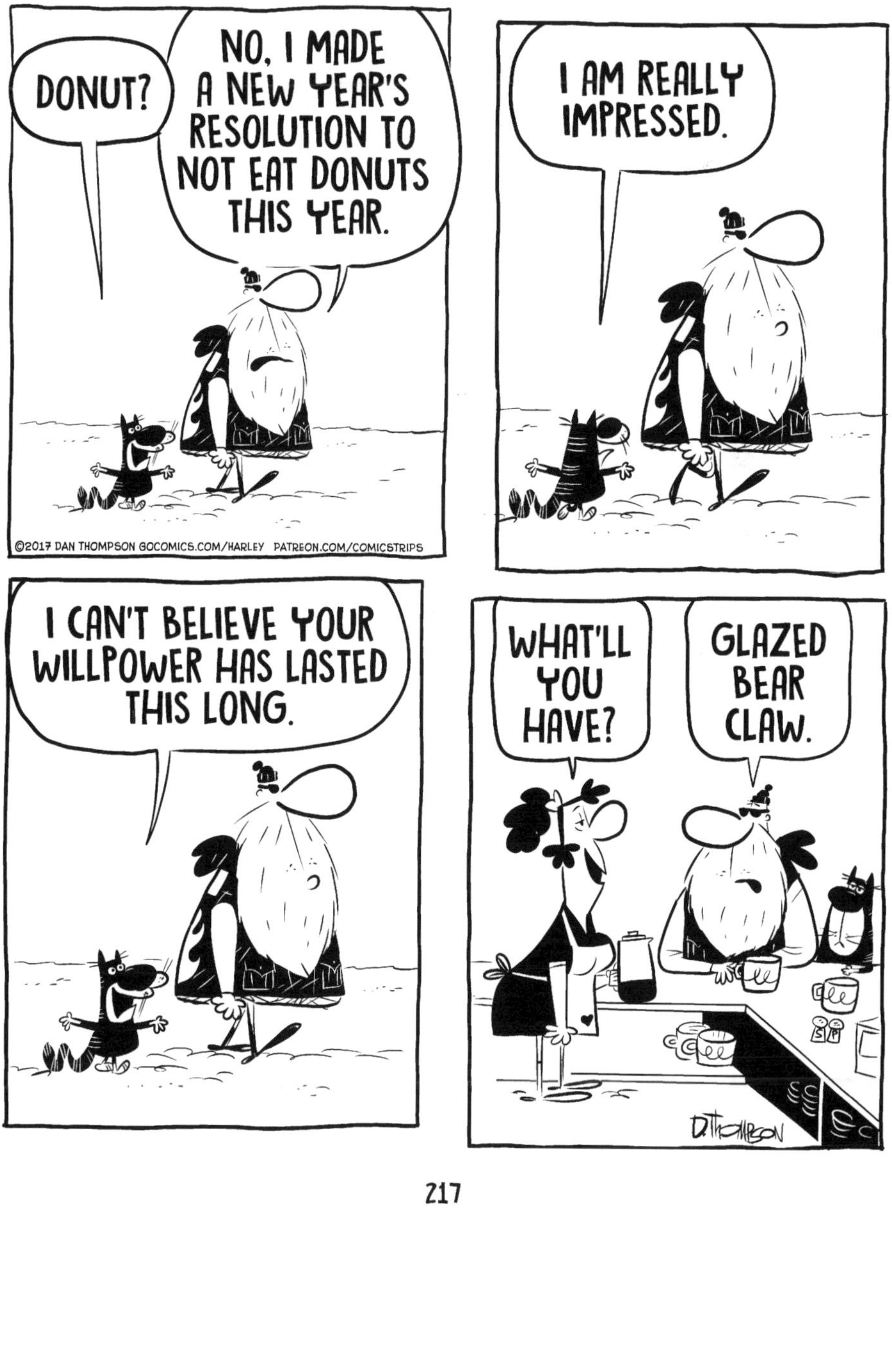
DONUT?
NO, I MADE A NEW YEAR'S RESOLUTION TO NOT EAT DONUTS THIS YEAR.
©2017 DAN THOMPSON GOCOMICS.COM/HARLEY PATREON.COM/COMICSTRIPS
I AM REALLY IMPRESSED.
I CAN'T BELIEVE YOUR WILLPOWER HAS LASTED THIS LONG.
WHAT'LL YOU HAVE?
GLAZED BEAR CLAW.
D. THOMPSON

OOOoh, MY ACHING HEAD. WHERE ARE WE?
©2017 DAN THOMPSON GOCOMICS.COM/HARLEY PATREON.COM/COMICSTRIPS
AT YOUR NEIGHBORS HOUSE! YOU STUMBLED IN HERE LAST NIGHT ...
AND FELL ASLEEP ON TOP OF US ...
D. THOMPSON
SO, NOBODY MADE COFFEE?

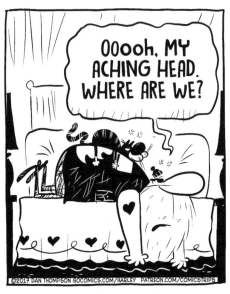

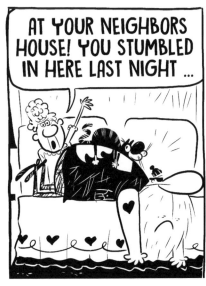

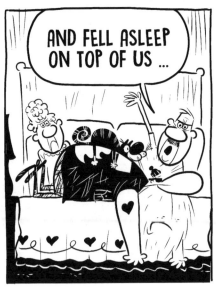

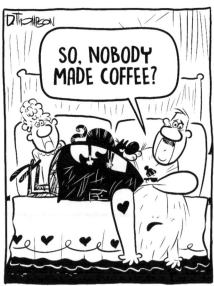

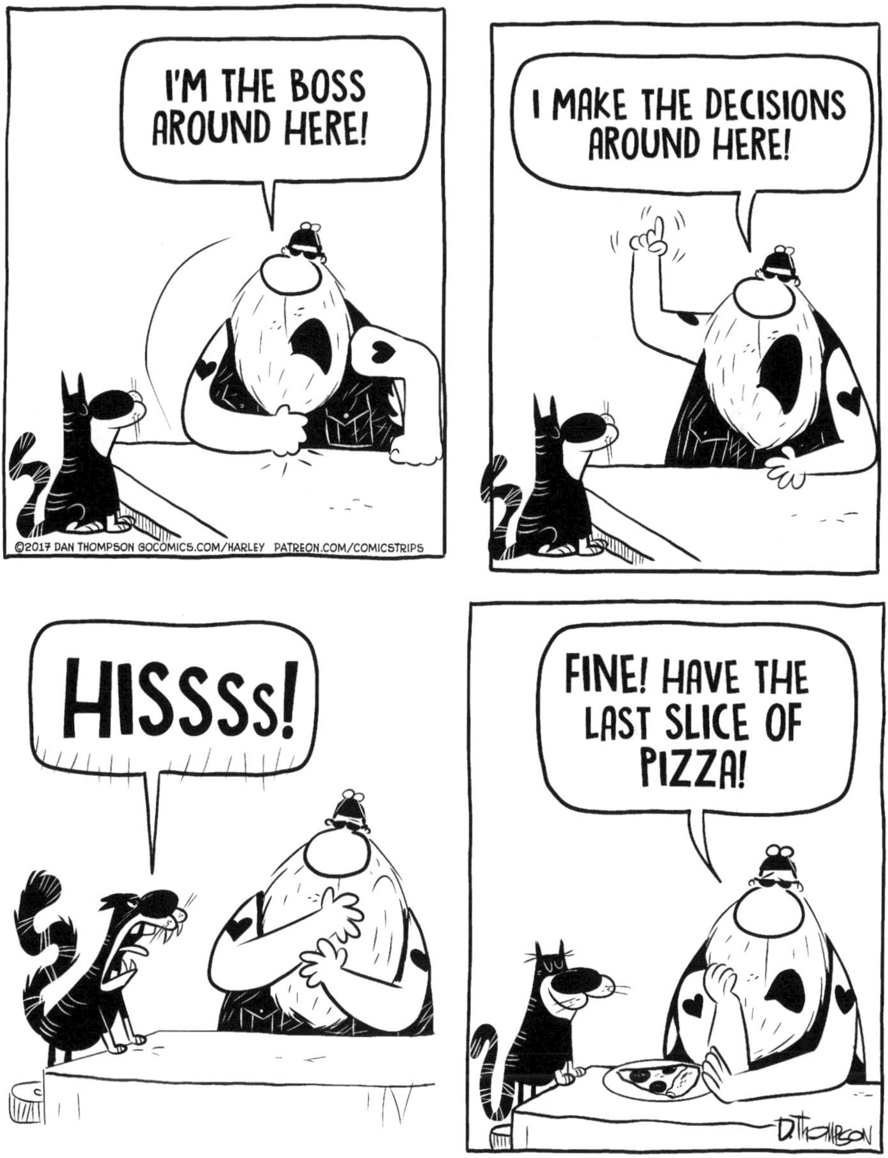
I'M THE BOSS AROUND HERE!
©2017 DAN THOMPSON GOCOMICS.COM/HARLEY PATREON.COM/COMICSTRIPS
I MAKE THE DECISIONS AROUND HERE!
HISSSs!
FINE! HAVE THE LAST SLICE OF PIZZA!
D. THOMPSON

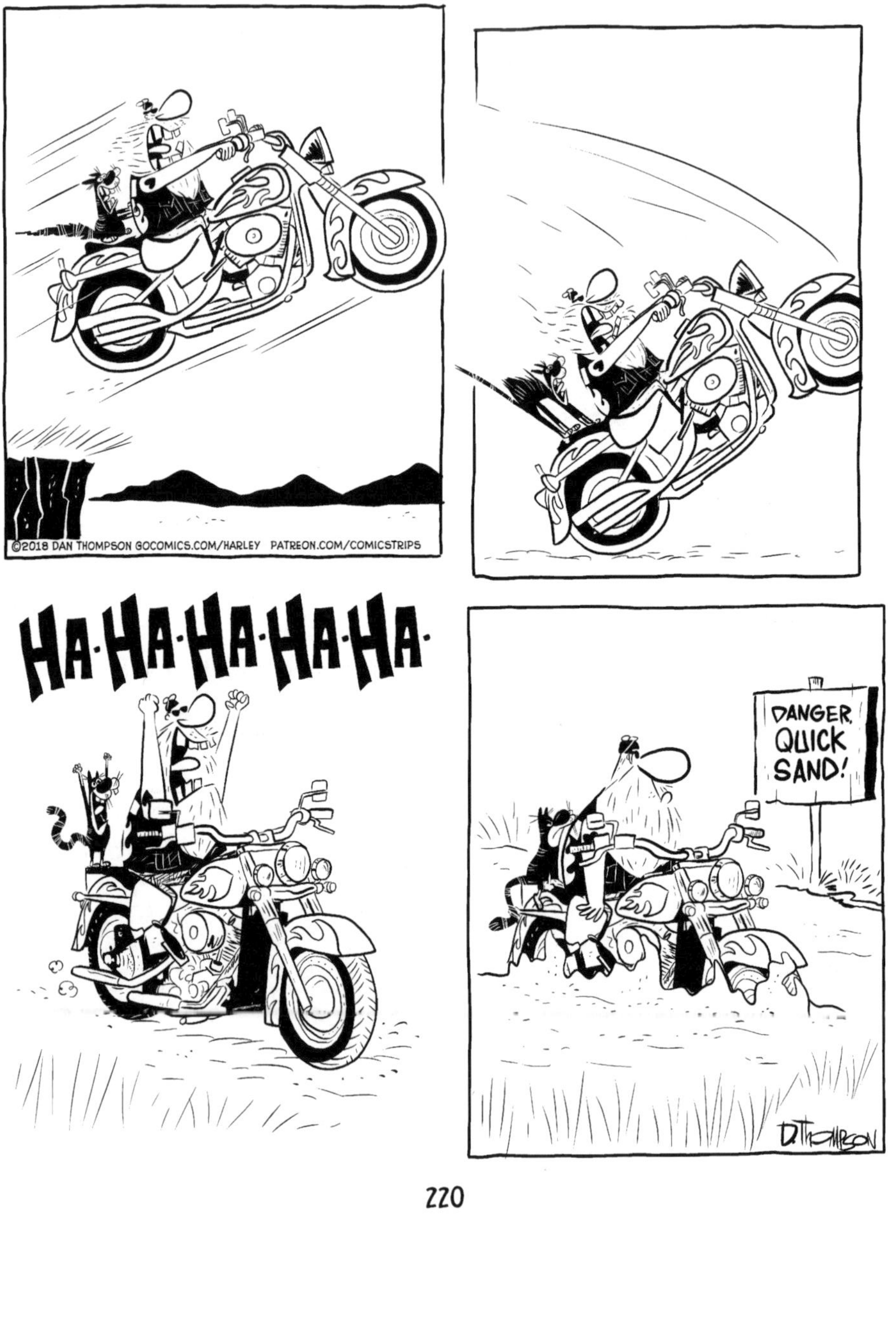
©2018 DAN THOMPSON GOCOMICS.COM/HARLEY PATREON.COM/COMICSTRIPS
HA-HA-HA-HA-HA-
DANGER, QUICK SAND!
D. THOMPSON

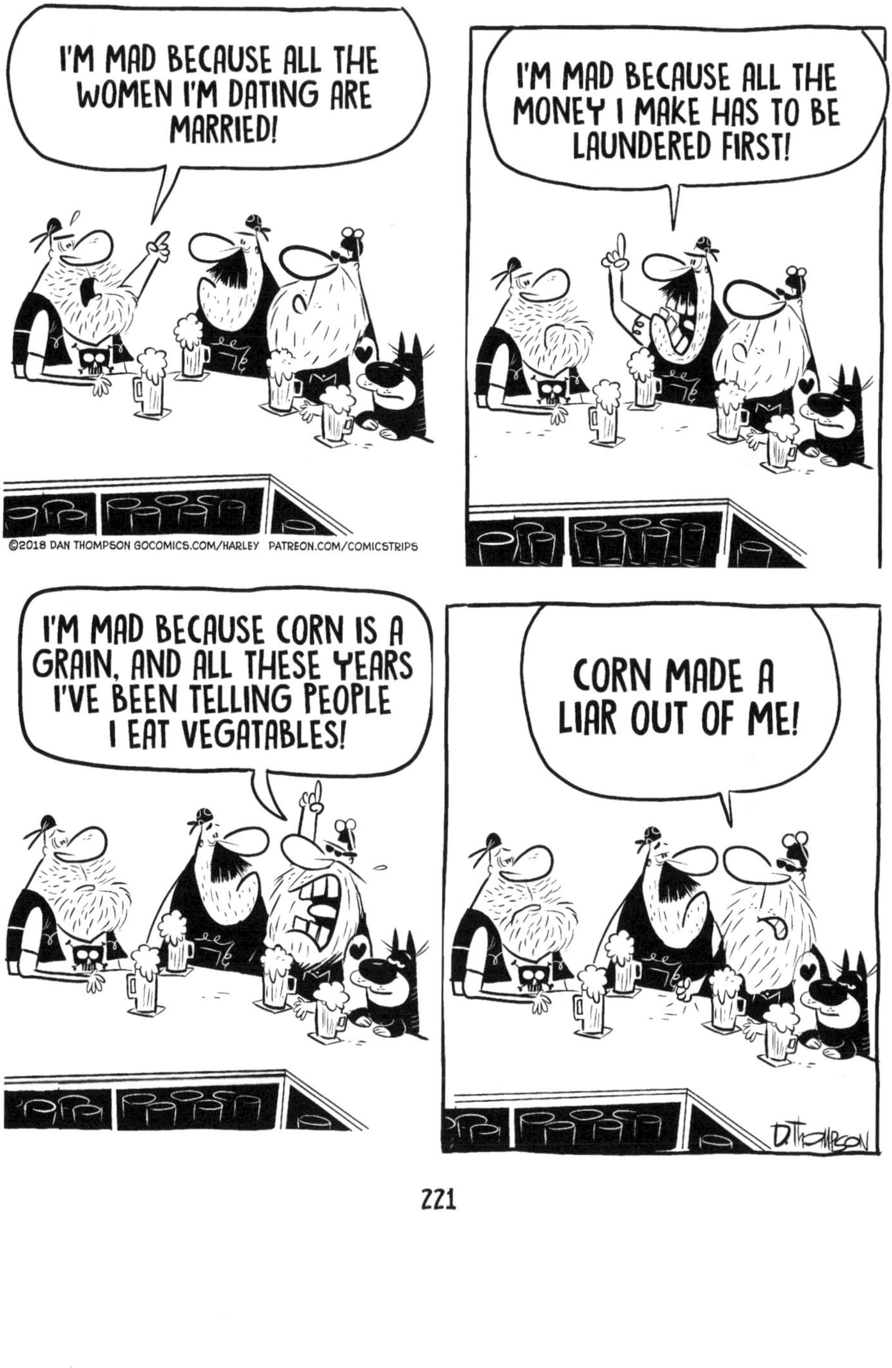
I'M MAD BECAUSE ALL THE WOMEN I'M DATING ARE MARRIED!
©2018 DAN THOMPSON GOCOMICS.COM/HARLEY PATREON.COM/COMICSTRIPS
I'M MAD BECAUSE ALL THE MONEY I MAKE HAS TO BE LAUNDERED FIRST!
I'M MAD BECAUSE CORN IS A GRAIN, AND ALL THESE YEARS I'VE BEEN TELLING PEOPLE I EAT VEGATABLES!
CORN MADE A LIAR OUT OF ME!
D. THOMPSON

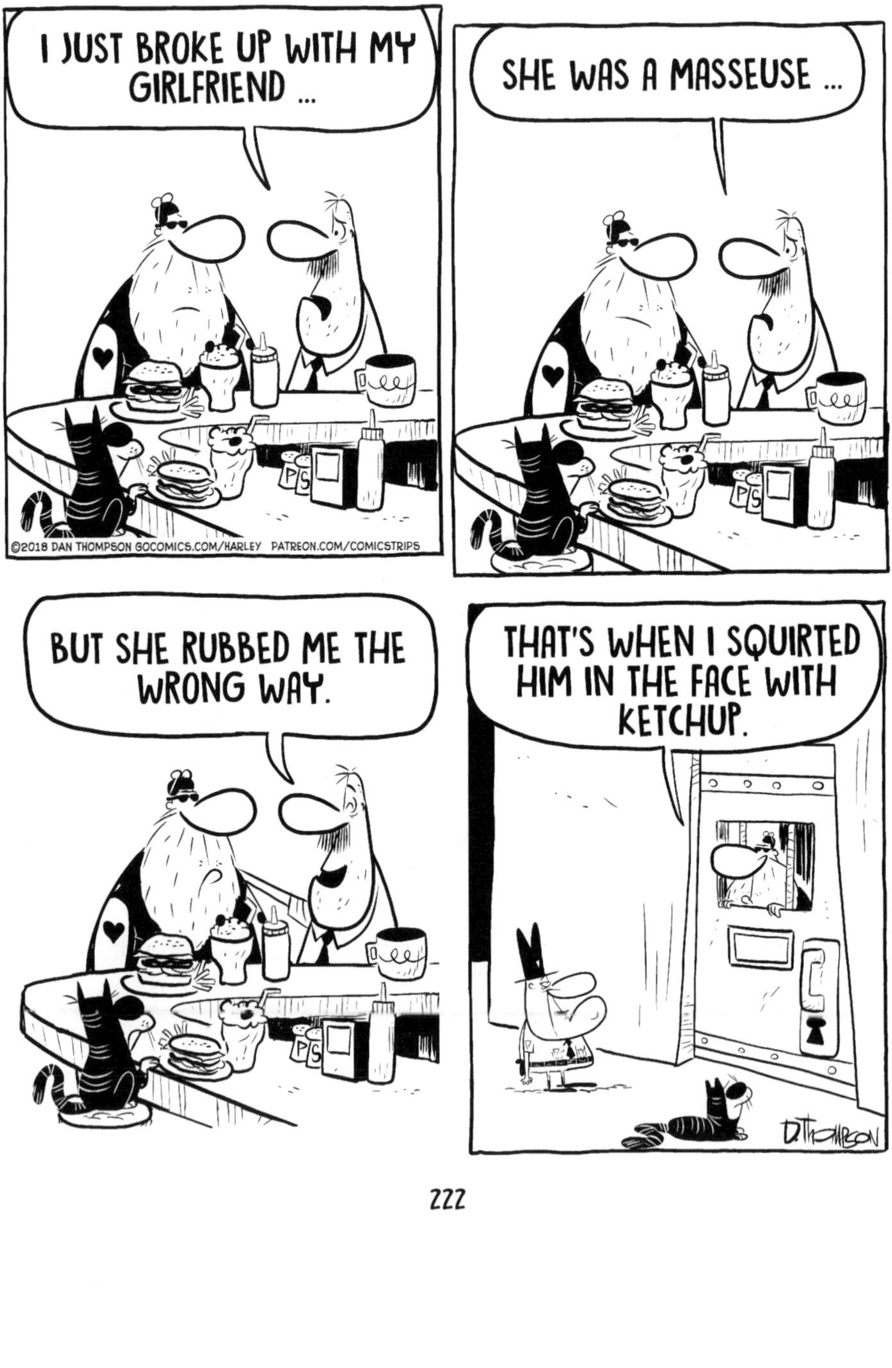
I JUST BROKE UP WITH MY GIRLFRIEND ...
©2018 DAN THOMPSON GOCOMICS.COM/HARLEY PATREON.COM/COMICSTRIPS
SHE WAS A MASSEUSE ...
BUT SHE RUBBED ME THE WRONG WAY.
THAT'S WHEN I SQUIRTED HIM IN THE FACE WITH KETCHUP.
D.THOMPSON

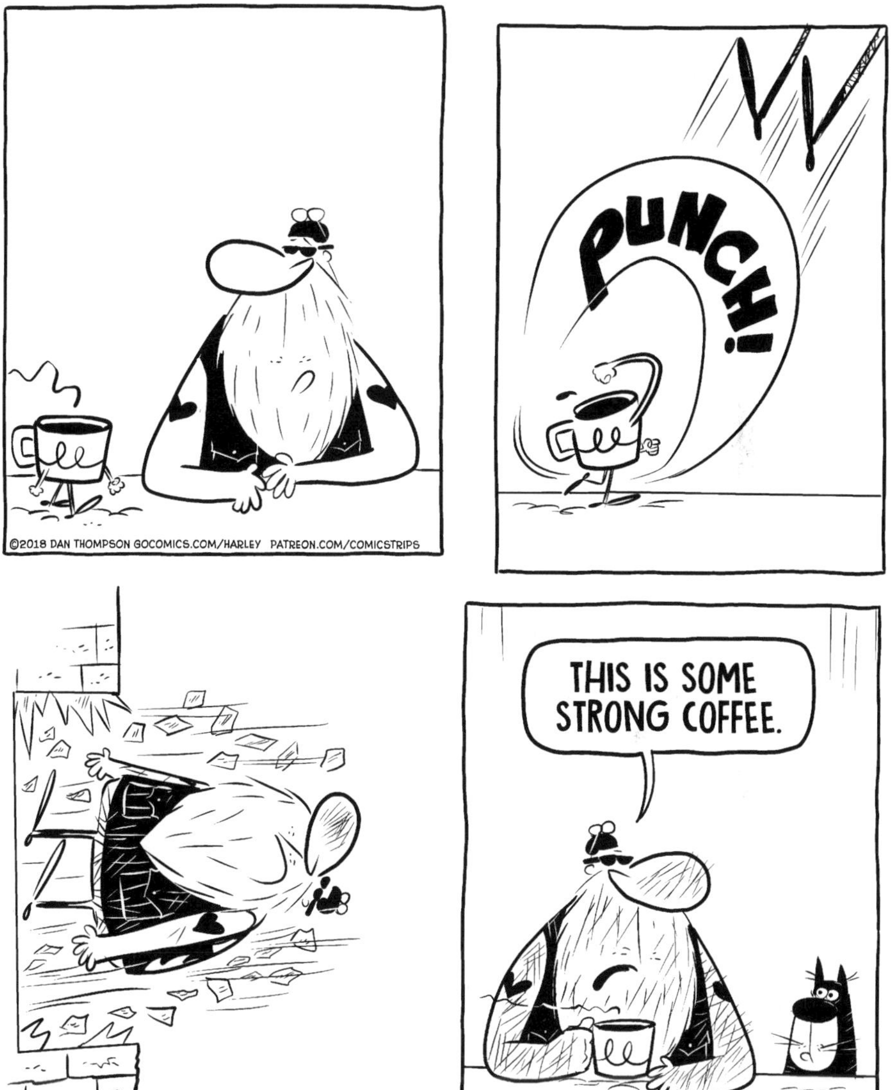
©2018 DAN THOMPSON GOCOMICS.COM/HARLEY PATREON.COM/COMICSTRIPS
PUNCH!
THIS IS SOME STRONG COFFEE.
D. THOMPSON

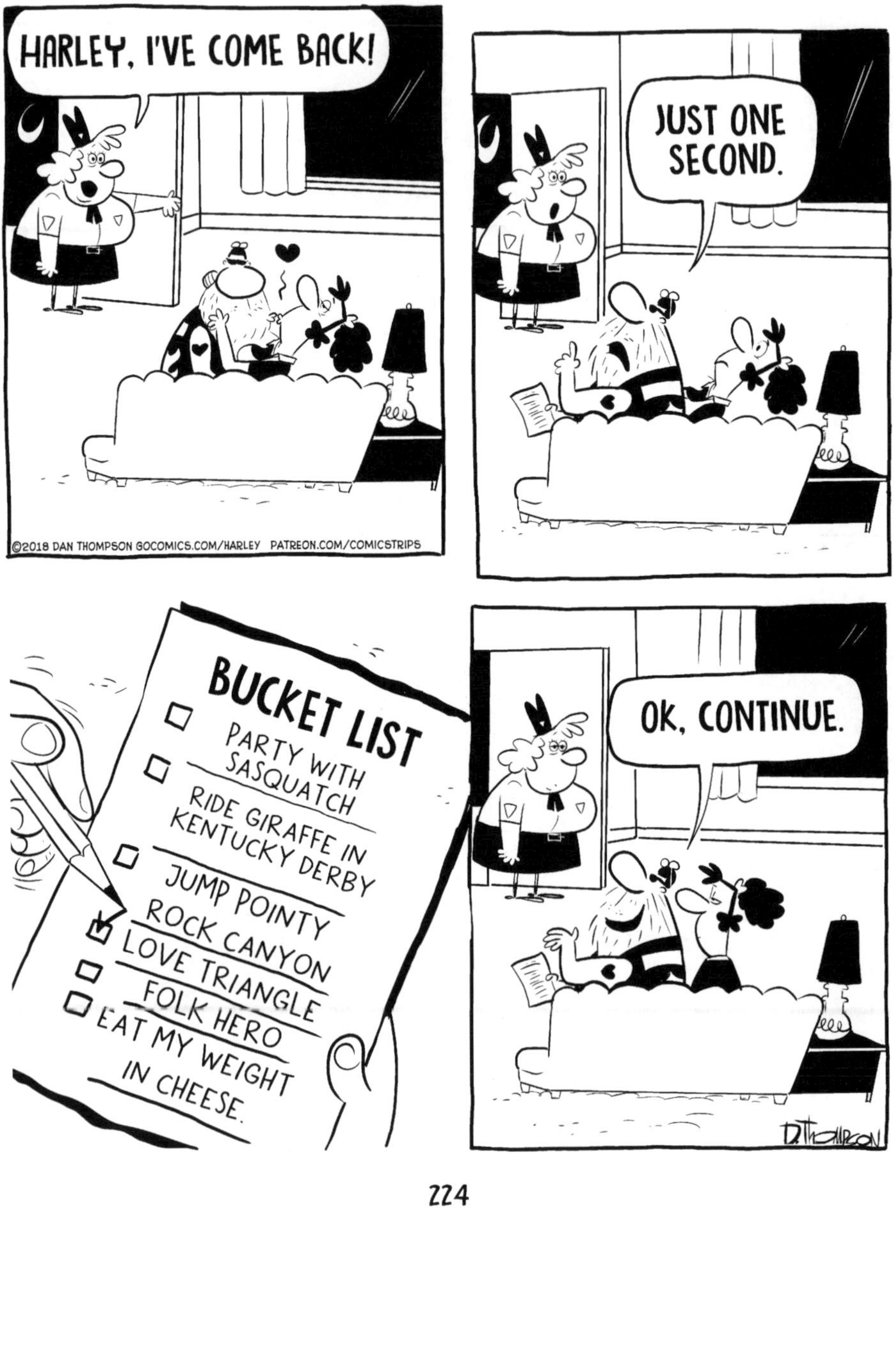
HARLEY, I'VE COME BACK!
©2018 DAN THOMPSON GOCOMICS.COM/HARLEY PATREON.COM/COMICSTRIPS
JUST ONE SECOND.
BUCKET LIST
PARTY WITH SASQUATCH
RIDE GIRAFFE IN KENTUCKY DERBY
JUMP POINTY ROCK CANYON
LOVE TRIANGLE
FOLK HERO
EAT MY WEIGHT IN CHEESE.
OK, CONTINUE.
D. THOMPSON

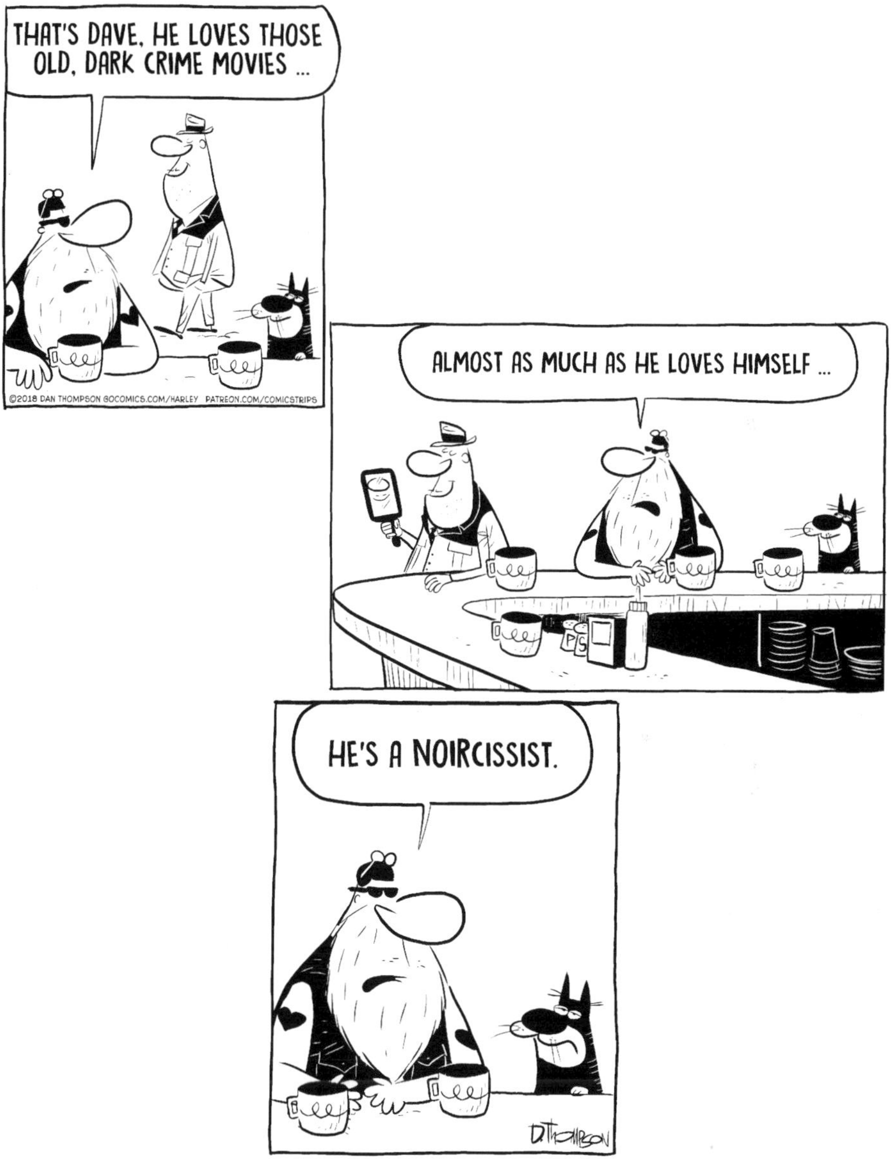
THAT'S DAVE, HE LOVES THOSE OLD, DARK CRIME MOVIES ...
©2018 DAN THOMPSON GOCOMICS.COM/HARLEY PATREON.COM/COMICSTRIPS
ALMOST AS MUCH AS HE LOVES HIMSELF ...
HE'S A NOIRCISSIST.
D.THOMPSON

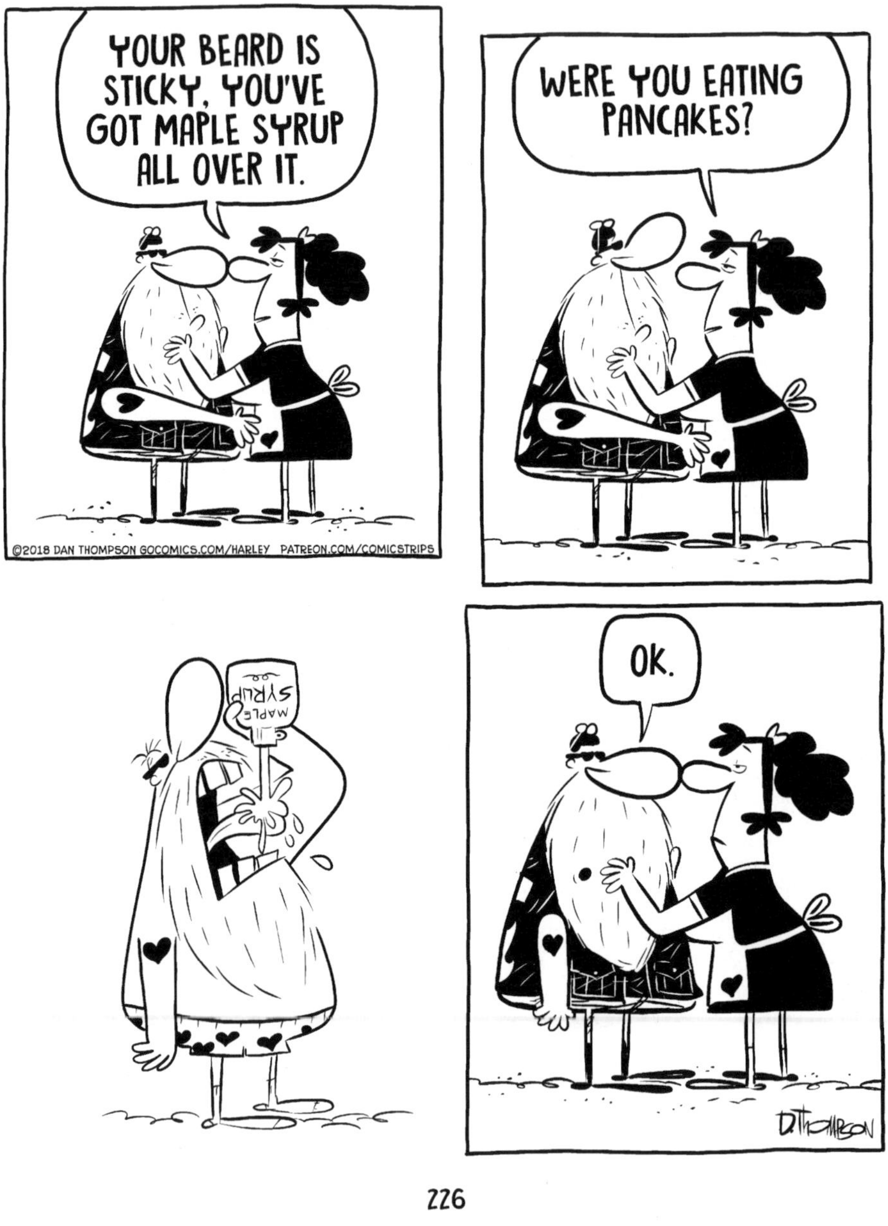
YOUR BEARD IS STICKY, YOU'VE GOT MAPLE SYRUP ALL OVER IT.
©2018 DAN THOMPSON GOCOMICS.COM/HARLEY PATREON.COM/COMICSTRIPS
WERE YOU EATING PANCAKES?
MAPLE SYRUP
OK.
D. THOMPSON

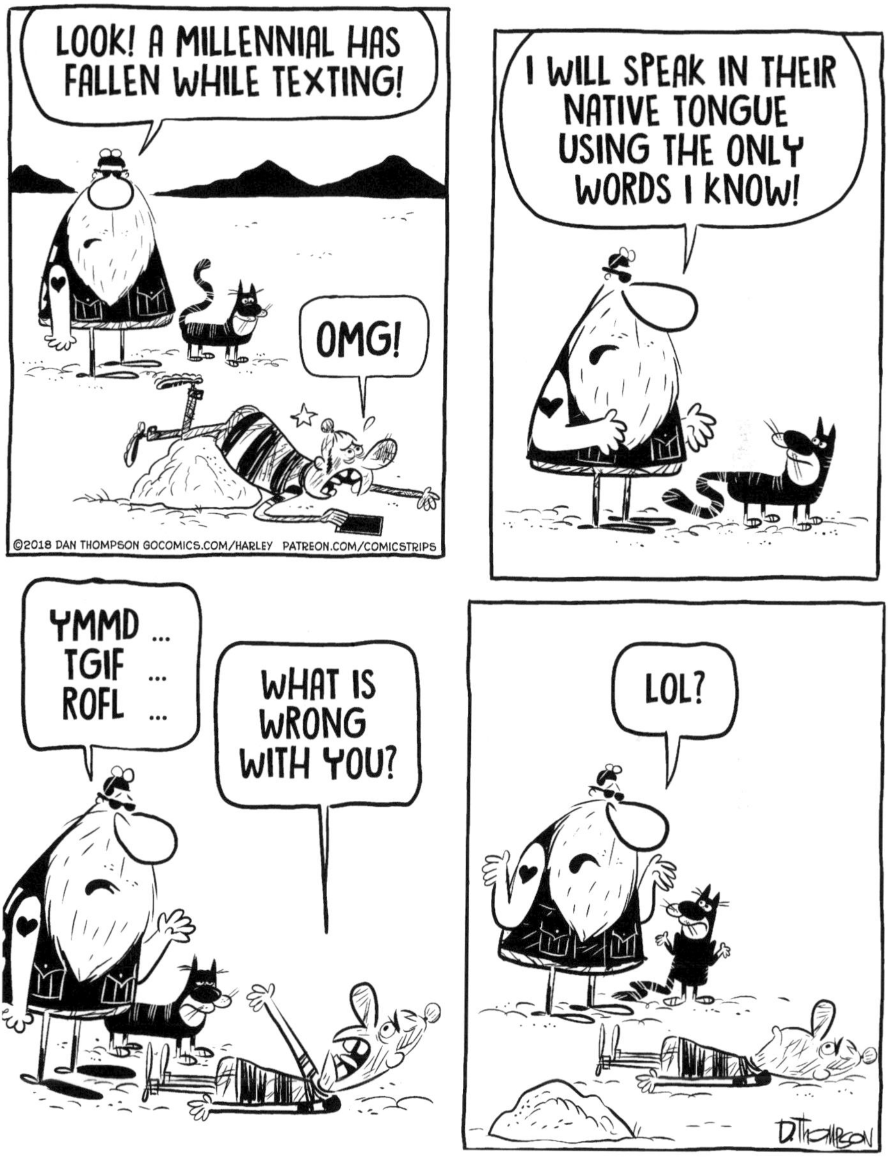
LOOK! A MILLENNIAL HAS FALLEN WHILE TEXTING!
OMG!
©2018 DAN THOMPSON GOCOMICS.COM/HARLEY PATREON.COM/COMICSTRIPS
I WILL SPEAK IN THEIR NATIVE TONGUE USING THE ONLY WORDS I KNOW!
YMMD ... TGIF ... ROFL ...
WHAT IS WRONG WITH YOU?
LOL?
D. THOMPSON

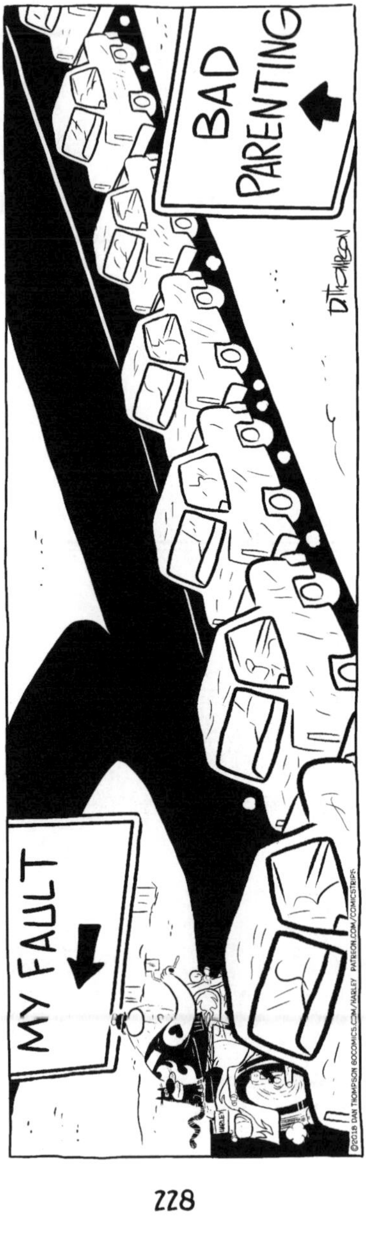
BAD PARENTING
MY FAULT

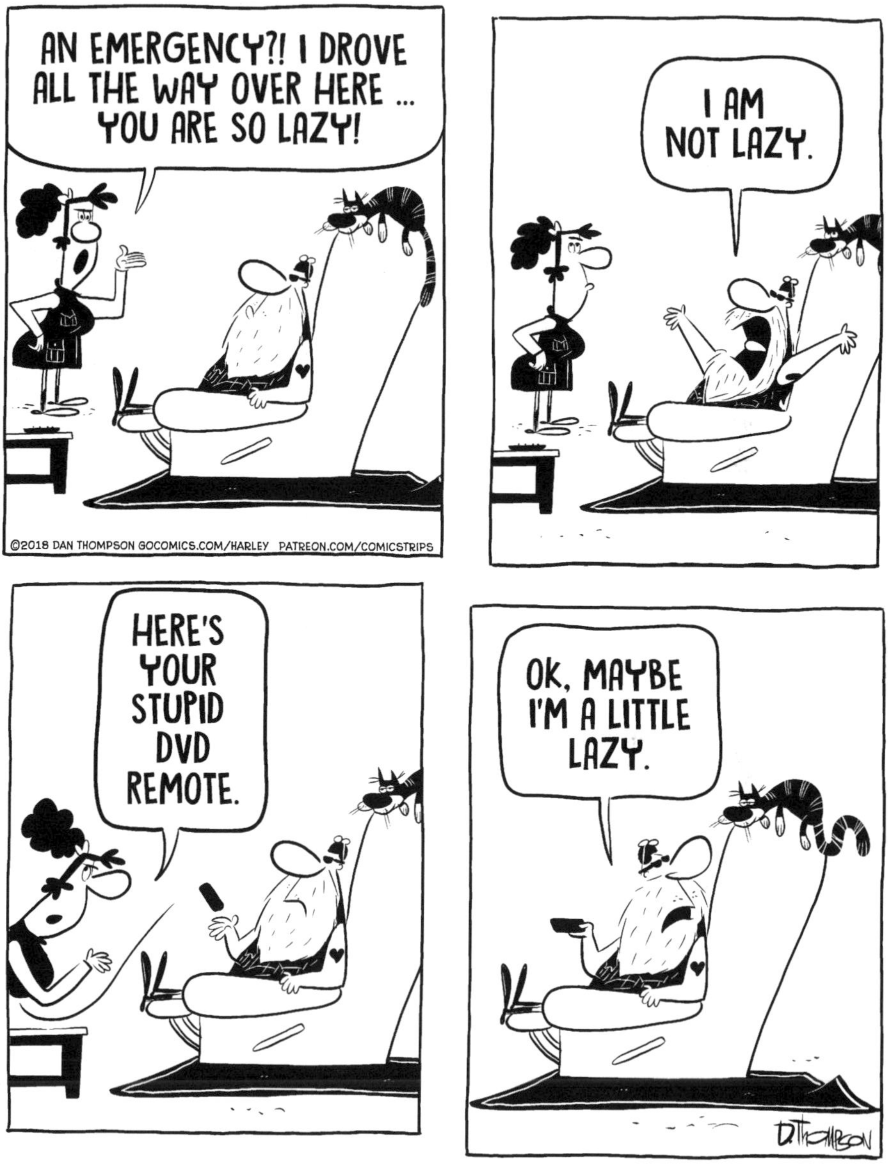
AN EMERGENCY?! I DROVE ALL THE WAY OVER HERE ... YOU ARE SO LAZY!
©2018 DAN THOMPSON GOCOMICS.COM/HARLEY PATREON.COM/COMICSTRIPS
I AM NOT LAZY.
HERE'S YOUR STUPID DVD REMOTE.
OK, MAYBE I'M A LITTLE LAZY.
D.THOMPSON

TWO ROADS DIVERGED IN A WOOD, AND I–
HARLEY
©2017 DAN THOMPSON GOCOMICS.COM/HARLEY PATREON.COM/COMICSTRIPS
I TOOK THE ONE LESS TRAVELED BY,
AND THAT HAS MADE ALL THE DIFFERENCE.
OF COURSE, THERE'S A GOOD REASON NOBODY TRAVELS THIS ROAD A LOT.
D.THOMPSON

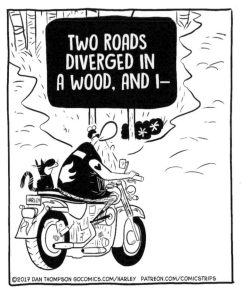

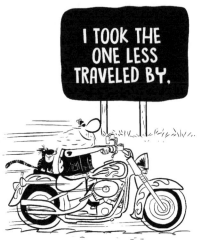

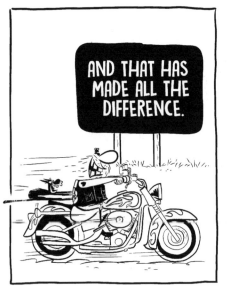

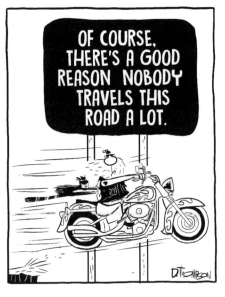

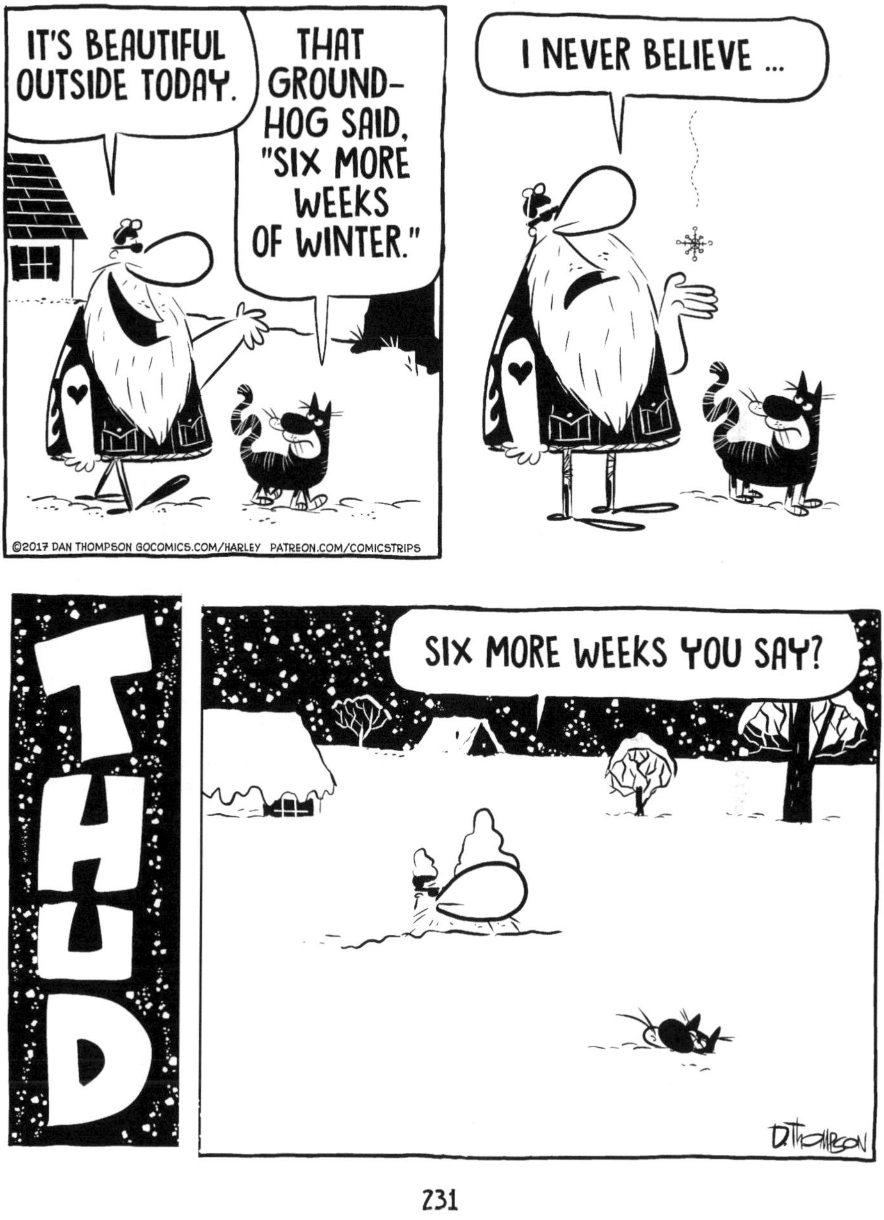
IT'S BEAUTIFUL OUTSIDE TODAY.
THAT GROUND-HOG SAID, "SIX MORE WEEKS OF WINTER."
©2017 DAN THOMPSON GOCOMICS.COM/HARLEY PATREON.COM/COMICSTRIPS
I NEVER BELIEVE ...
THUD
SIX MORE WEEKS YOU SAY?
D. THOMPSON

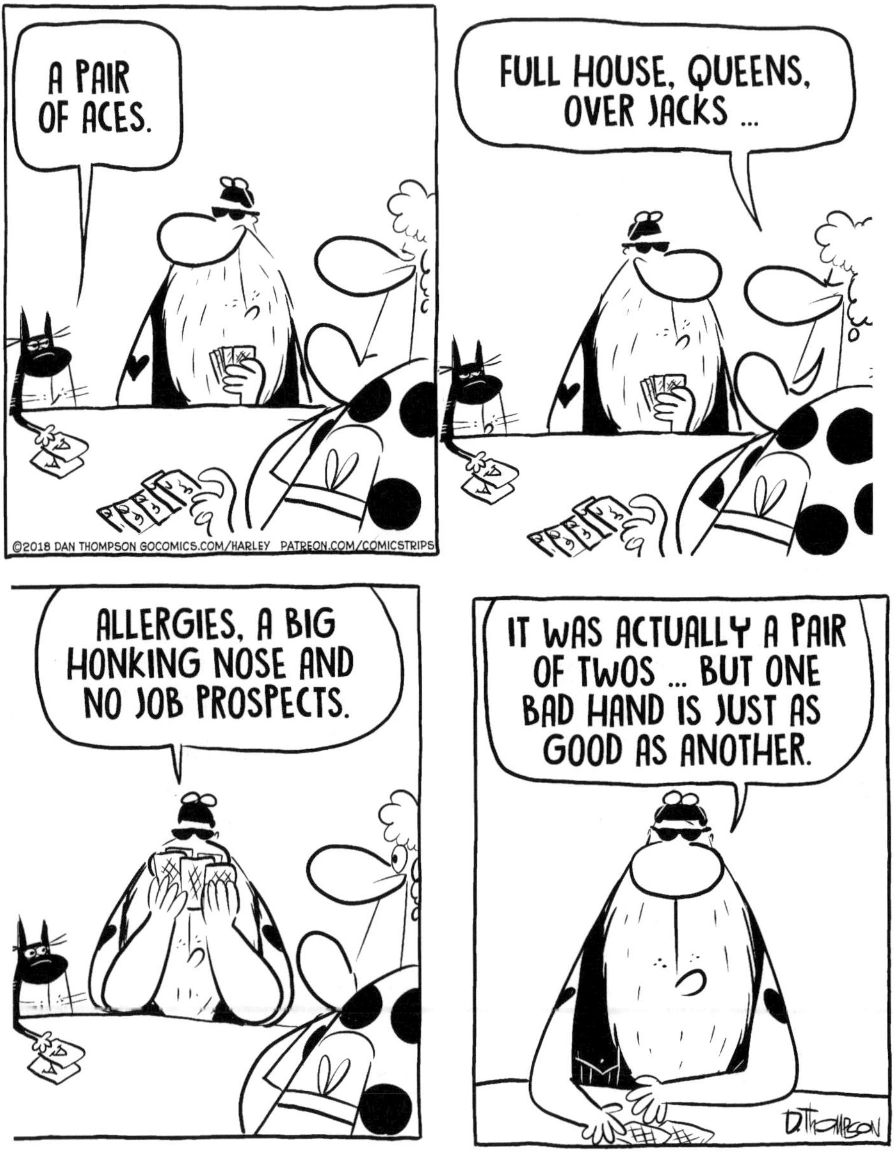
A PAIR OF ACES.
©2018 DAN THOMPSON GOCOMICS.COM/HARLEY PATREON.COM/COMICSTRIPS
FULL HOUSE, QUEENS, OVER JACKS ...
ALLERGIES, A BIG HONKING NOSE AND NO JOB PROSPECTS.
IT WAS ACTUALLY A PAIR OF TWOS ... BUT ONE BAD HAND IS JUST AS GOOD AS ANOTHER.
D.THOMPSON

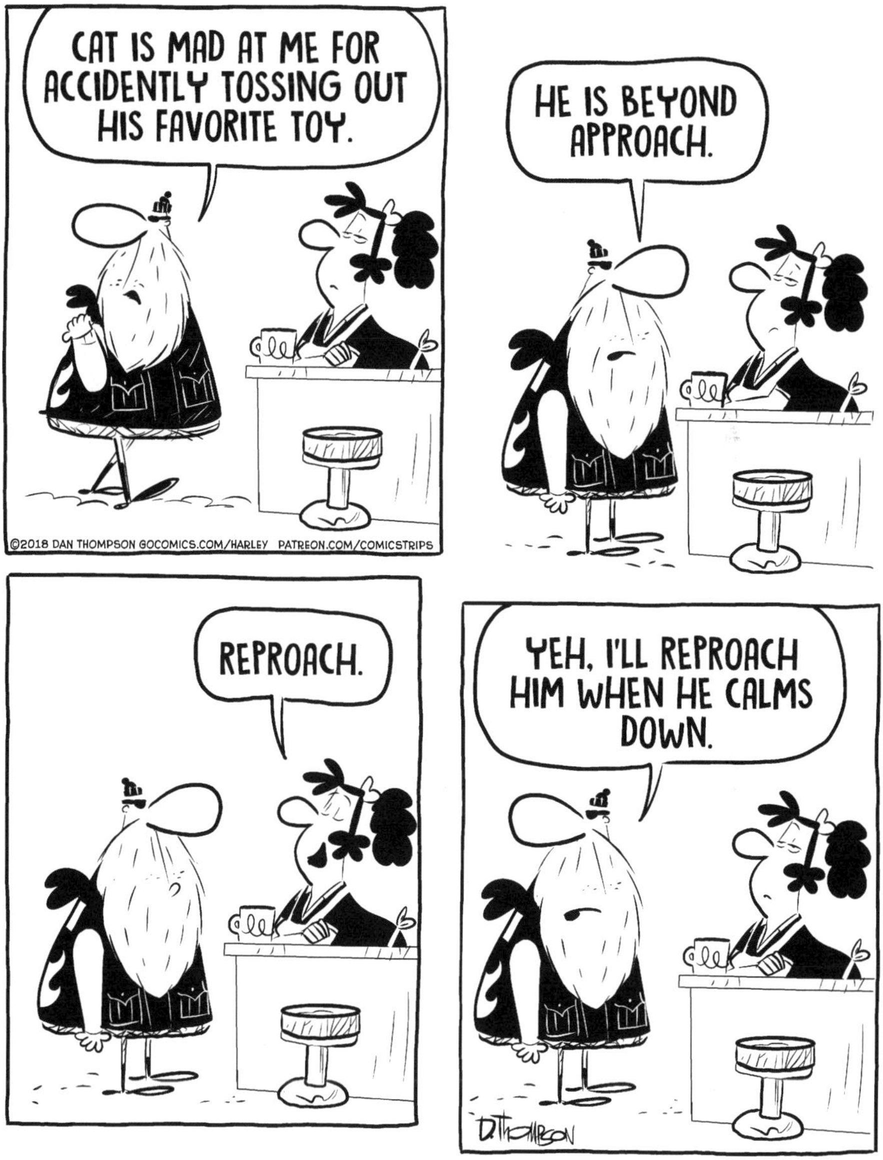
CAT IS MAD AT ME FOR ACCIDENTLY TOSSING OUT HIS FAVORITE TOY.
©2018 DAN THOMPSON GOCOMICS.COM/HARLEY PATREON.COM/COMICSTRIPS
HE IS BEYOND APPROACH.
REPROACH.
YEH, I'LL REPROACH HIM WHEN HE CALMS DOWN.
D. THOMPSON

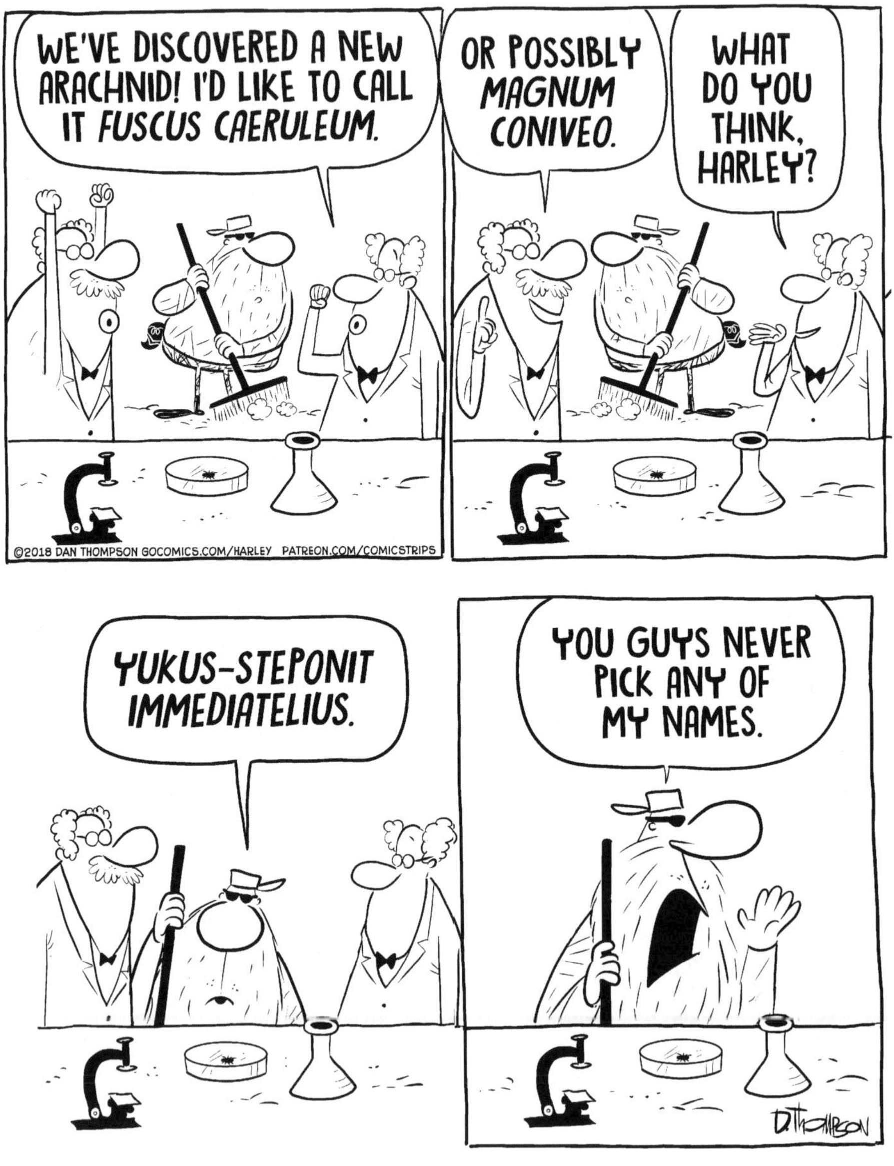
WE'VE DISCOVERED A NEW ARACHNID! I'D LIKE TO CALL IT *FUSCUS CAERULEUM.*
©2018 DAN THOMPSON GOCOMICS.COM/HARLEY PATREON.COM/COMICSTRIPS
OR POSSIBLY *MAGNUM CONIVEO.*
WHAT DO YOU THINK, HARLEY?
YUKUS-STEPONIT IMMEDIATELIUS.
YOU GUYS NEVER PICK ANY OF MY NAMES.
D. THOMPSON

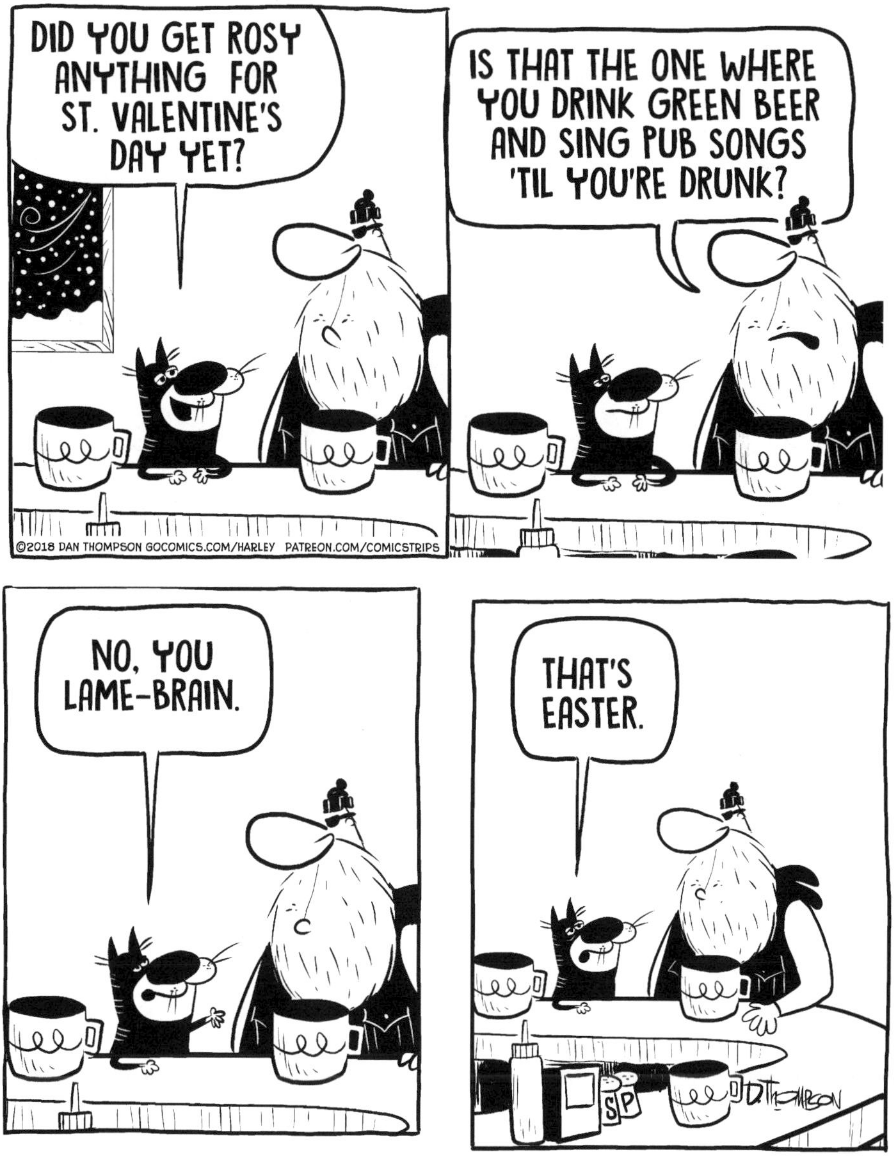
DID YOU GET ROSY ANYTHING FOR ST. VALENTINE'S DAY YET?
©2018 DAN THOMPSON GOCOMICS.COM/HARLEY PATREON.COM/COMICSTRIPS
IS THAT THE ONE WHERE YOU DRINK GREEN BEER AND SING PUB SONGS 'TIL YOU'RE DRUNK?
NO, YOU LAME-BRAIN.
THAT'S EASTER.
SP
D. THOMPSON

HAPPY VALENTINE'S DAY! I BROUGHT PIZZA AND CHOCOLATES.
YOU DON'T WANT TO GO OUT?
©2018 DAN THOMPSON GOCOMICS.COM/HARLEY PATREON.COM/COMICSTRIPS
NAH. YOU'RE AN INTROVERT AND WOULDN'T HAVE ANY FUN.
SMOOCH!
SMACK! SMACK!
SMOOCH!
MARRY ME AND HAVE MY SPAWN.
D. THOMPSON

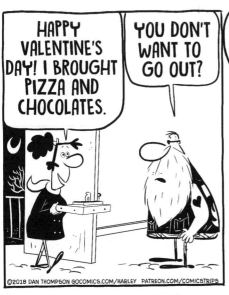

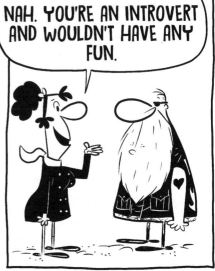

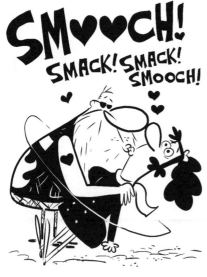

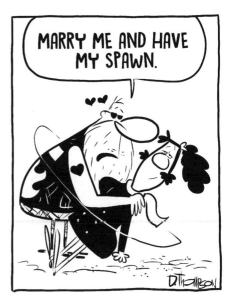

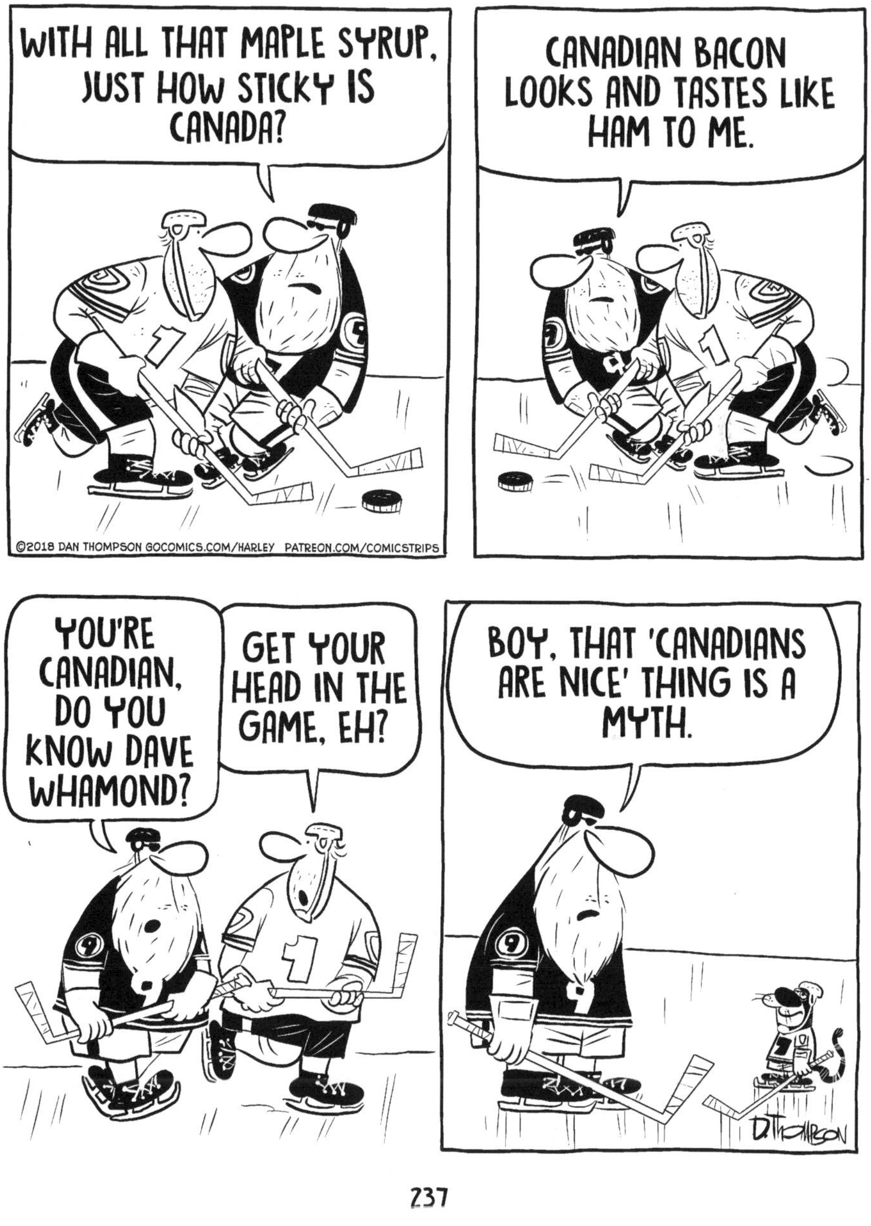
WITH ALL THAT MAPLE SYRUP, JUST HOW STICKY IS CANADA?
©2018 DAN THOMPSON GOCOMICS.COM/HARLEY PATREON.COM/COMICSTRIPS
CANADIAN BACON LOOKS AND TASTES LIKE HAM TO ME.
YOU'RE CANADIAN, DO YOU KNOW DAVE WHAMOND?
GET YOUR HEAD IN THE GAME, EH?
BOY, THAT 'CANADIANS ARE NICE' THING IS A MYTH.
D. THOMPSON

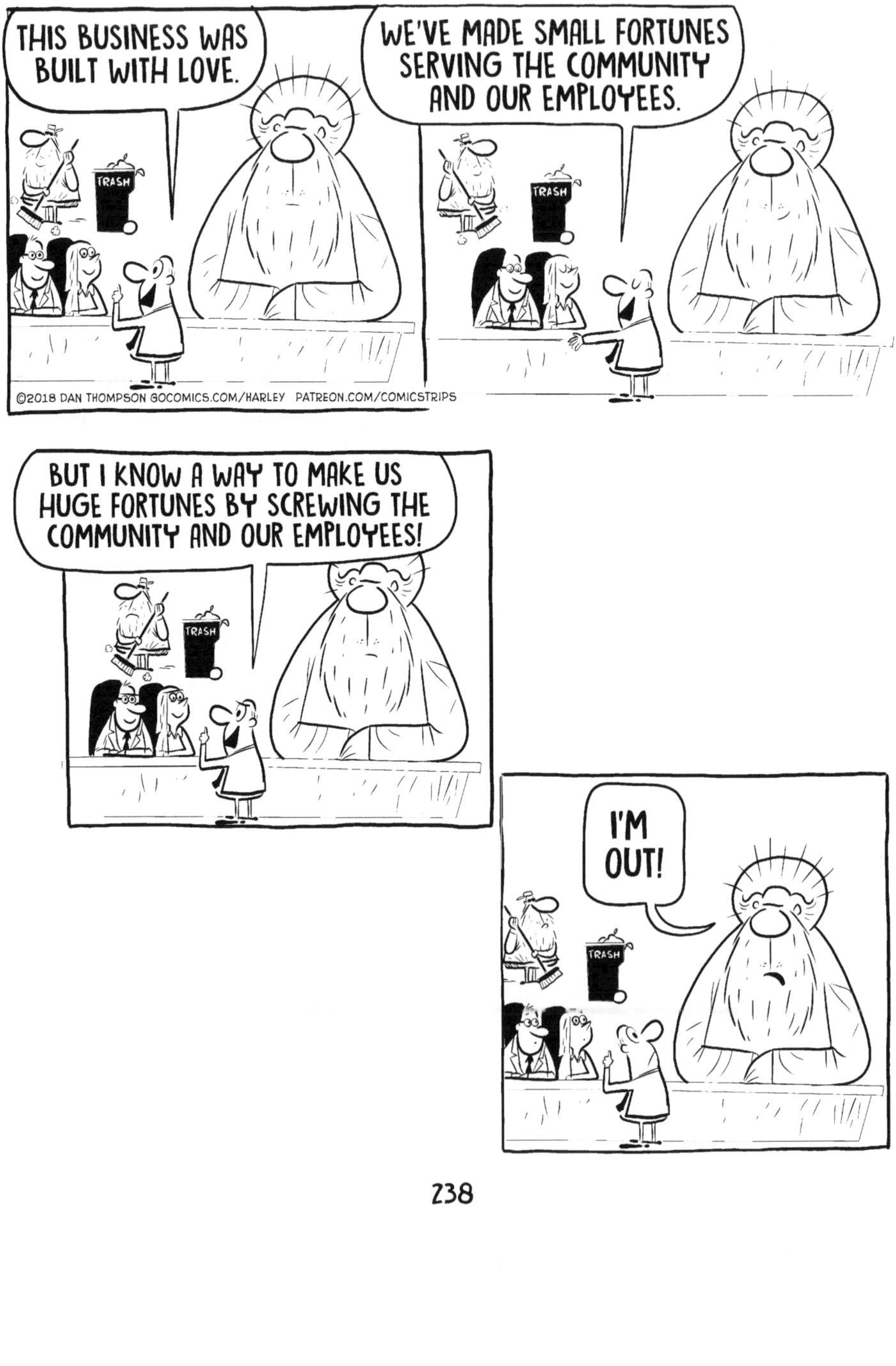
THIS BUSINESS WAS BUILT WITH LOVE.
©2018 DAN THOMPSON GOCOMICS.COM/HARLEY PATREON.COM/COMICSTRIPS
TRASH
WE'VE MADE SMALL FORTUNES SERVING THE COMMUNITY AND OUR EMPLOYEES.
TRASH
BUT I KNOW A WAY TO MAKE US HUGE FORTUNES BY SCREWING THE COMMUNITY AND OUR EMPLOYEES!
TRASH
I'M OUT!
TRASH

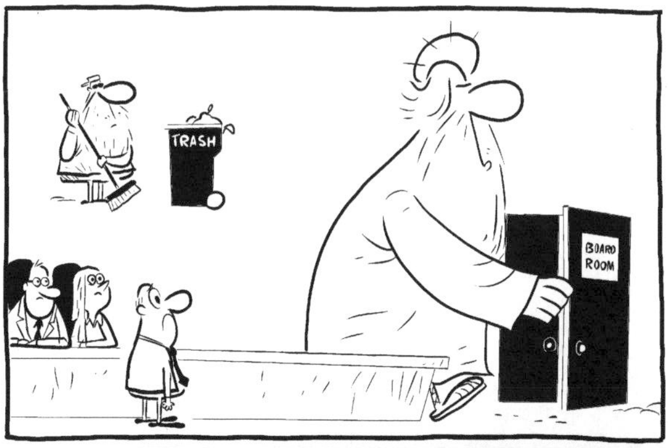
TRASH
BOARD ROOM

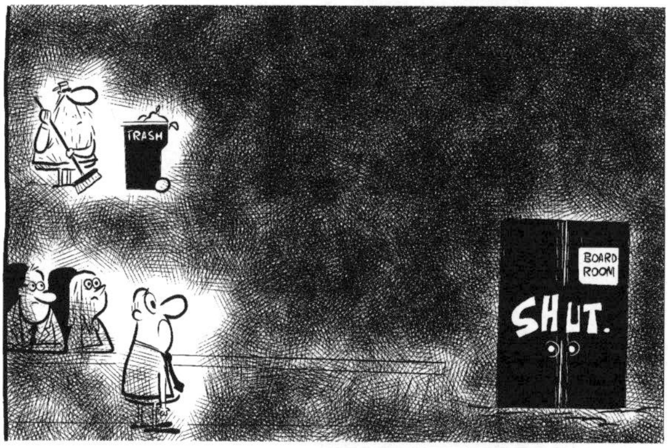
TRASH
BOARD ROOM
SHUT.

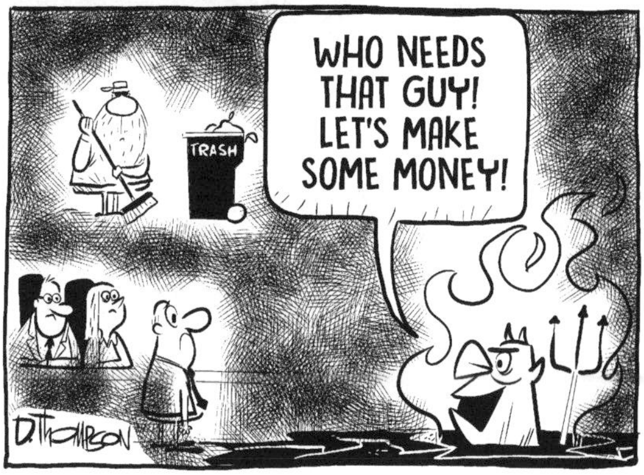
TRASH
WHO NEEDS THAT GUY! LET'S MAKE SOME MONEY!
D. THOMPSON

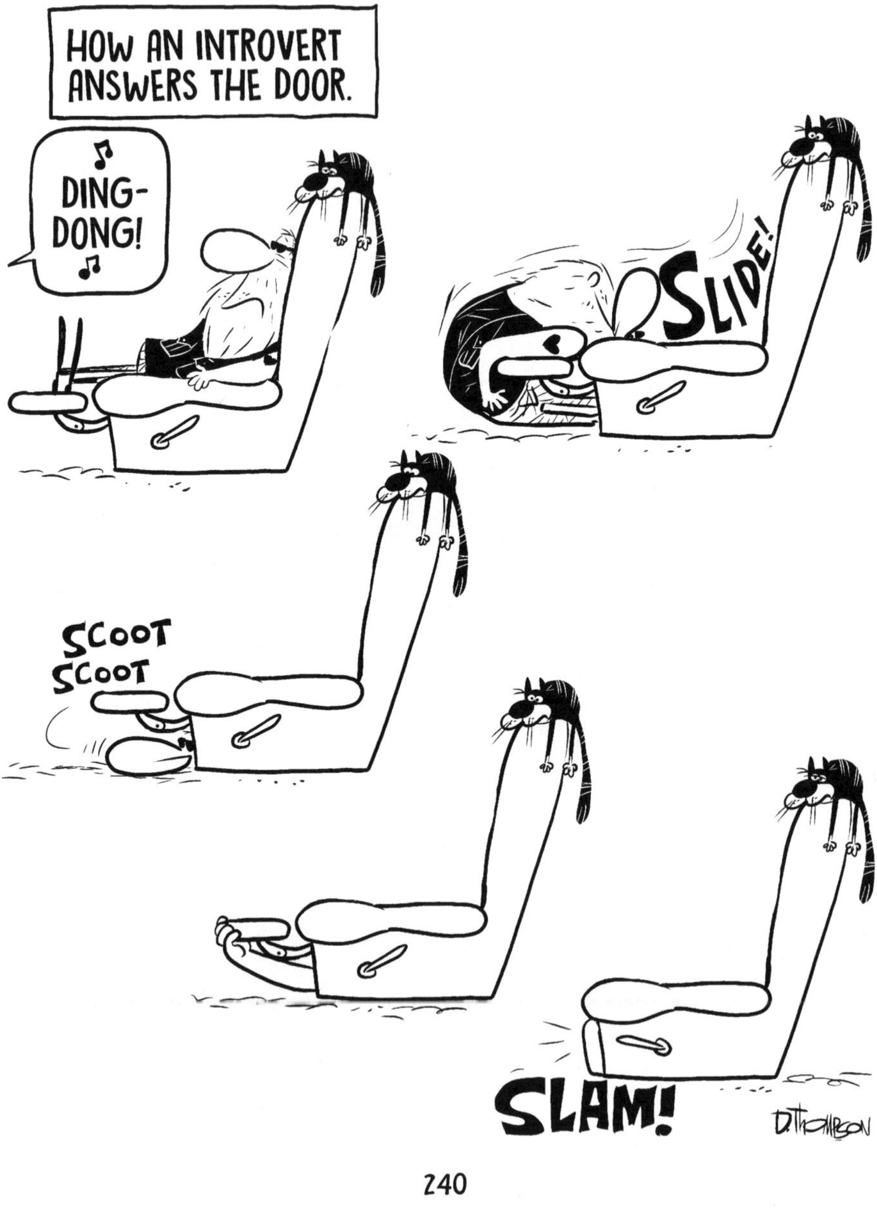
HOW AN INTROVERT ANSWERS THE DOOR.
DING-DONG!
SLIDE!
SCOOT SCOOT
SLAM!
D. THOMPSON

I KNOW YOU! YOU'RE THAT GUY!
©2018 DAN THOMPSON GOCOMICS.COM/HARLEY PATREON.COM/COMICSTRIPS
NOTHING BUT PIZZA AND BEER FOR TEN YEARS STRAIGHT. WOW!
AAAH! %!$$ OFF!
NEVER MEET YOUR HEROES.
D.THOMPSON

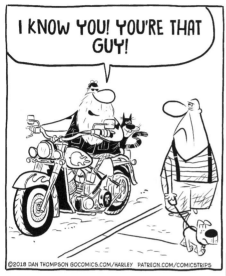

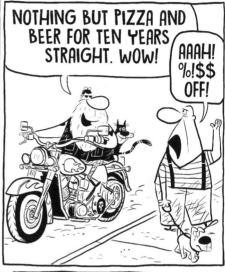

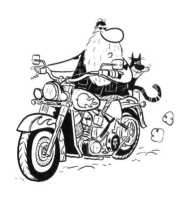

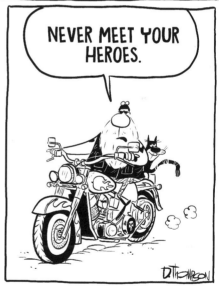

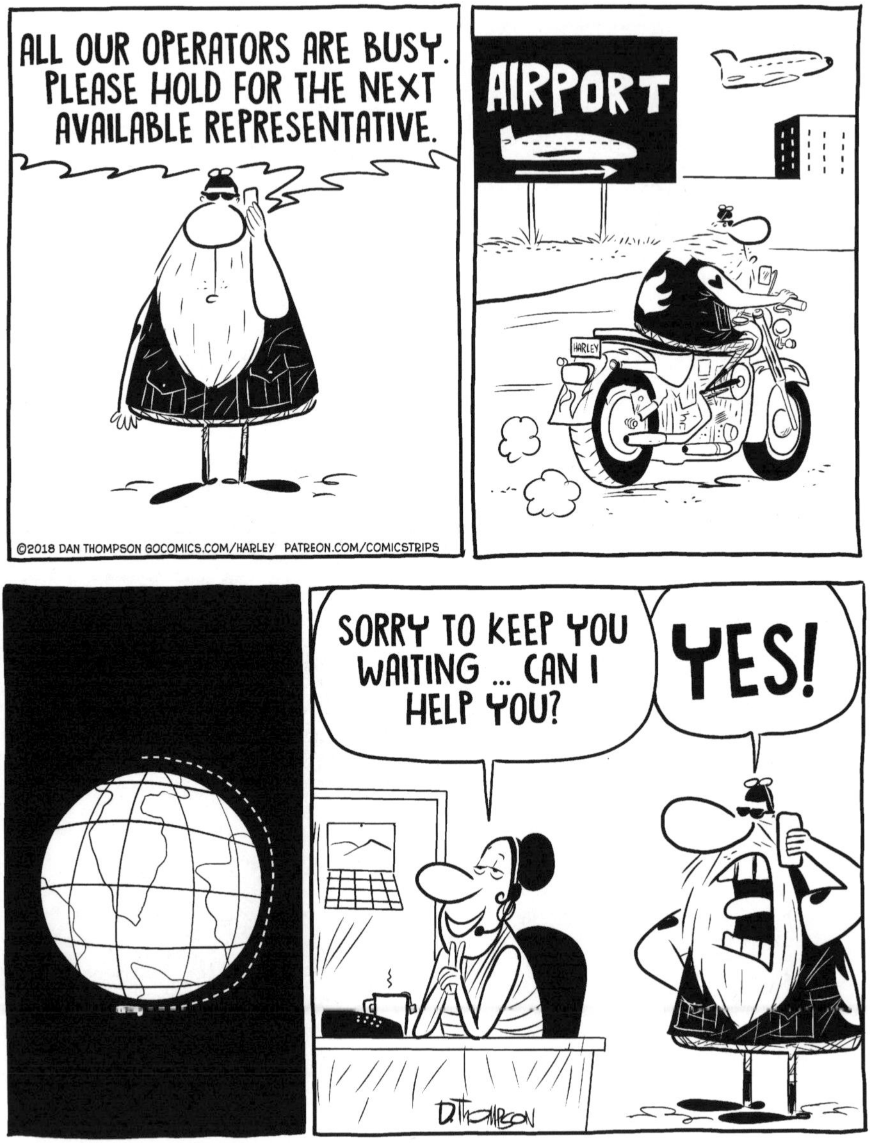
ALL OUR OPERATORS ARE BUSY. PLEASE HOLD FOR THE NEXT AVAILABLE REPRESENTATIVE.
©2018 DAN THOMPSON GOCOMICS.COM/HARLEY PATREON.COM/COMICSTRIPS
AIRPORT
HARLEY
SORRY TO KEEP YOU WAITING ... CAN I HELP YOU?
YES!
D. THOMPSON

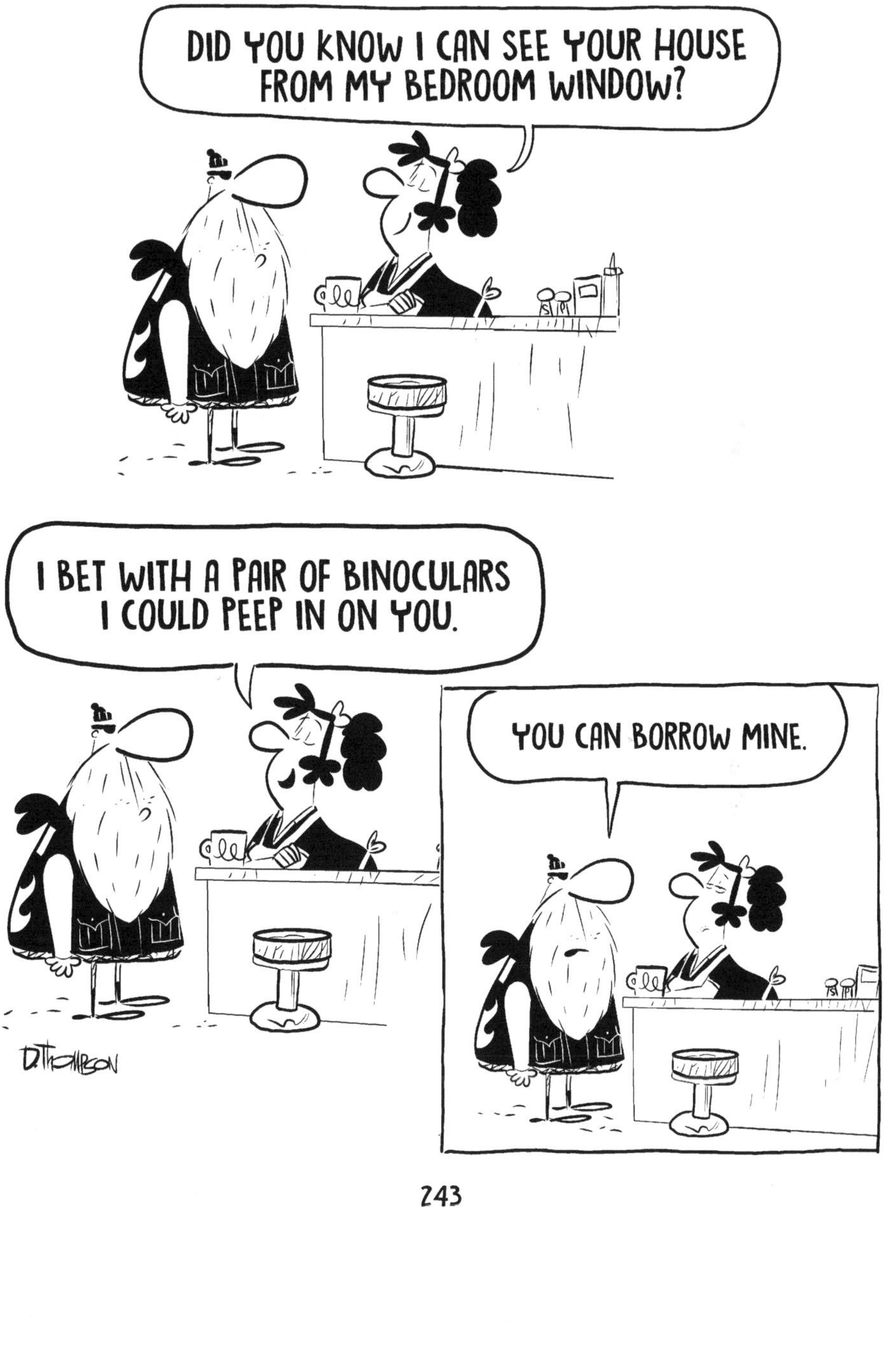
DID YOU KNOW I CAN SEE YOUR HOUSE FROM MY BEDROOM WINDOW?
I BET WITH A PAIR OF BINOCULARS I COULD PEEP IN ON YOU.
YOU CAN BORROW MINE.
D. THOMPSON

I'M PLANNING ON CROSSING DELAWARE STREET ...
©2018 DAN THOMPSON GOCOMICS.COM/HARLEY PATREON.COM/COMICSTRIPS
THEN CHOPPING DOWN A PINT OF CHERRY GARCIA.
USING ONLY ONE DOLLAR BILLS.
THAT'S A FUN WAY TO CELEBRATE WASHINGTON'S BIRTHDAY.
WHOSE BIRTH-DAY?
D. THOMPSON

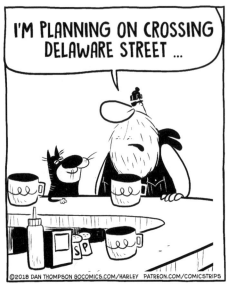

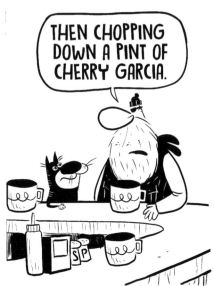

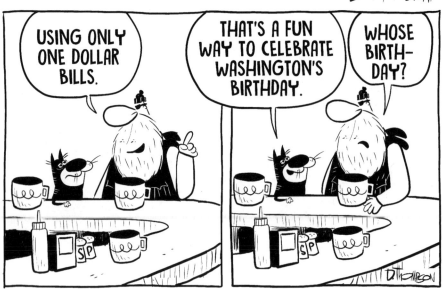

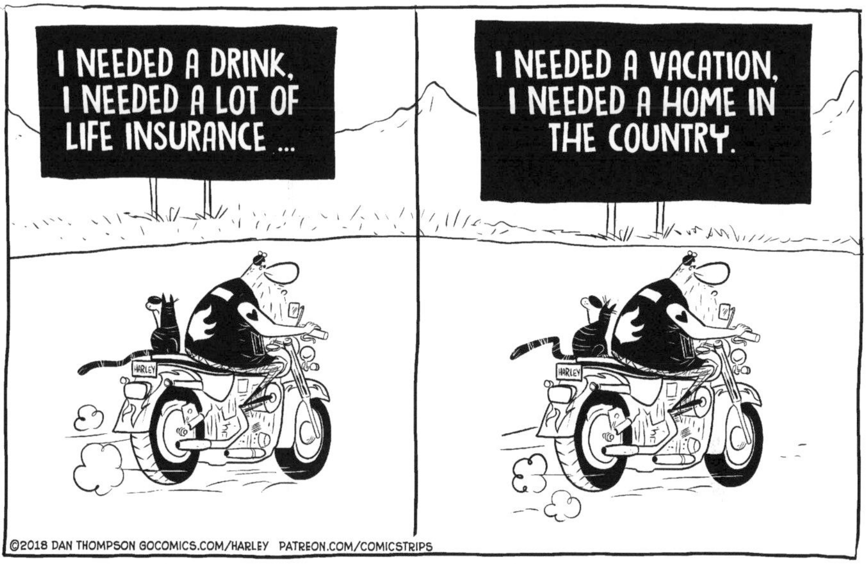
I NEEDED A DRINK, I NEEDED A LOT OF LIFE INSURANCE ...
I NEEDED A VACATION, I NEEDED A HOME IN THE COUNTRY.
HARLEY
HARLEY
©2018 DAN THOMPSON GOCOMICS.COM/HARLEY PATREON.COM/COMICSTRIPS

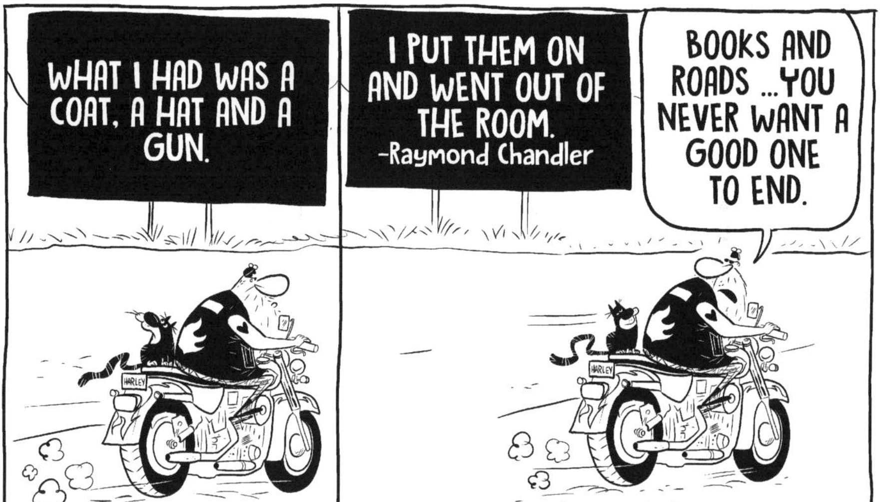
WHAT I HAD WAS A COAT, A HAT AND A GUN.
I PUT THEM ON AND WENT OUT OF THE ROOM.
-Raymond Chandler
BOOKS AND ROADS ...YOU NEVER WANT A GOOD ONE TO END.
HARLEY
HARLEY
D. THOMPSON

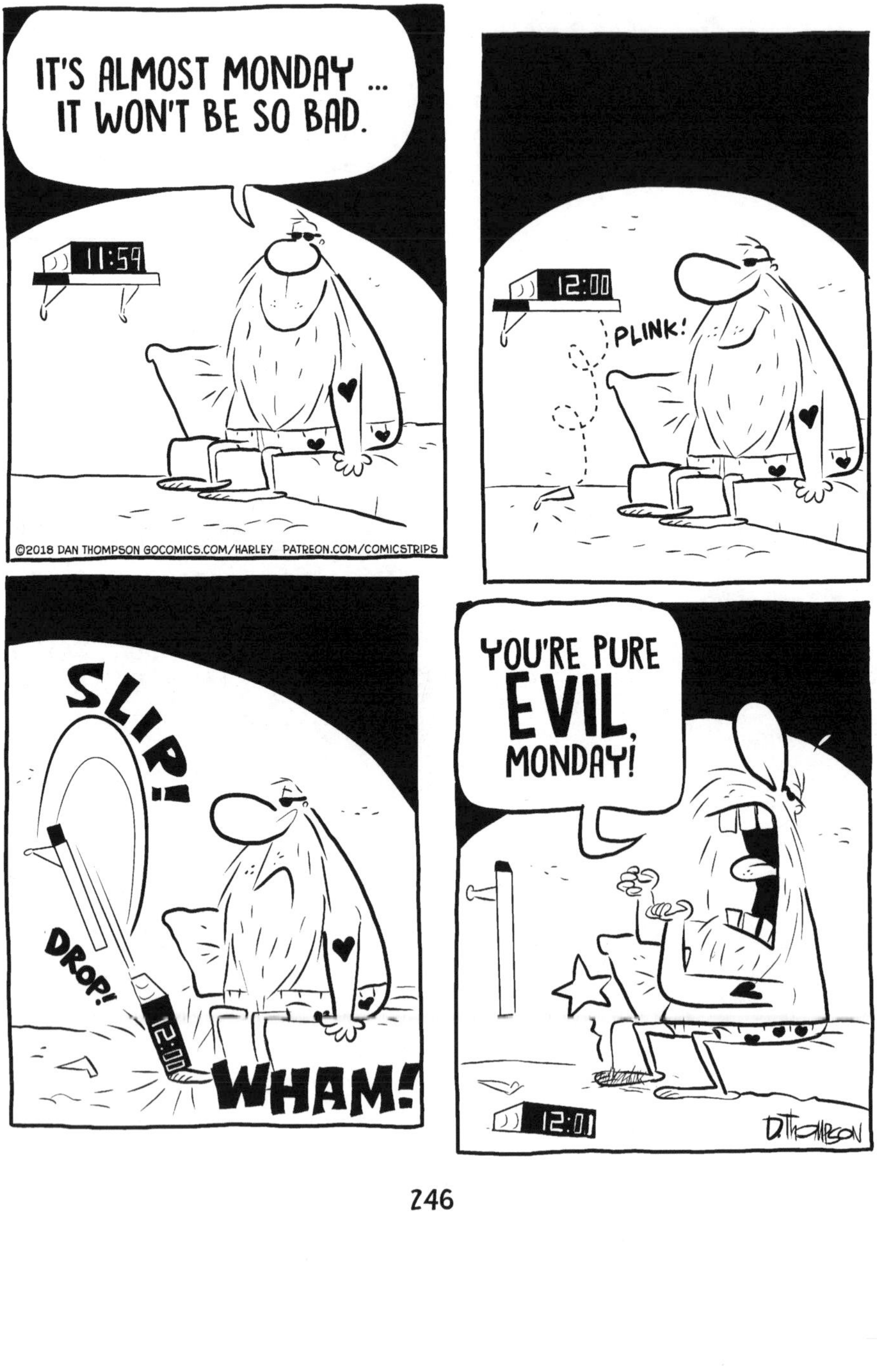
IT'S ALMOST MONDAY ... IT WON'T BE SO BAD.
11:59
©2018 DAN THOMPSON GOCOMICS.COM/HARLEY PATREON.COM/COMICSTRIPS
12:00
PLINK!
SLIP!
DROP!
12:00
WHAM!
YOU'RE PURE EVIL, MONDAY!
12:01
D. THOMPSON

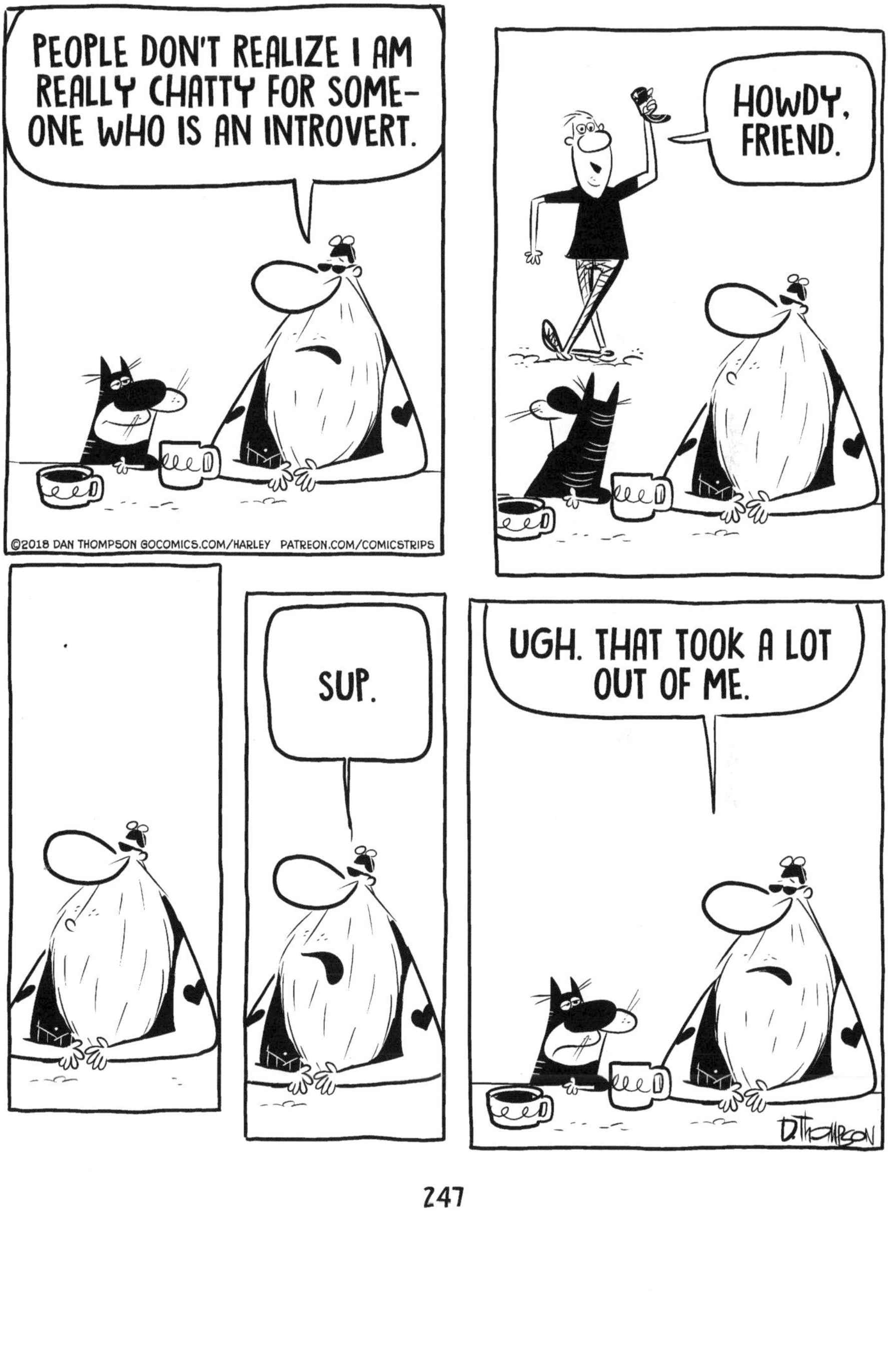
PEOPLE DON'T REALIZE I AM REALLY CHATTY FOR SOME-ONE WHO IS AN INTROVERT.
©2018 DAN THOMPSON GOCOMICS.COM/HARLEY PATREON.COM/COMICSTRIPS
HOWDY, FRIEND.
SUP.
UGH. THAT TOOK A LOT OUT OF ME.
D. THOMPSON

WE'RE WIDE AWAKE IN THE MIDDLE OF THE NIGHT ... KNOW ANY SCARY STORIES?

©2017 DAN THOMPSON GOCOMICS.COM/HARLEY PATREON.COM/COMICSTRIPS

LIKE WHEN GARDEN GNOMES SNEAK INTO HOUSES AND TICKLE YOUR TOES WHILE YOU SLEEP?

HA-HA! NO, I SAID SCARY.

DO YOU REMEMBER IF I LOCKED THE BACK DOOR?

I JUST FEEL LIKE I'M DOING ALL THE WORK IN THIS RELATIONSHIP.
MARRIAGE COUNSELOR
©2018 DAN THOMPSON GOCOMICS.COM/HARLEY PATREON.COM/COMICSTRIPS
HOW DO YOU FEEL ABOUT ROSY'S COMMENT, HARLEY?
MARRIAGE COUNSELOR
WE'RE NOT EVEN MARRIED!
SEE WHAT I HAVE TO PUT UP WITH?
MARRIAGE COUNSELOR
D. THOMPSON

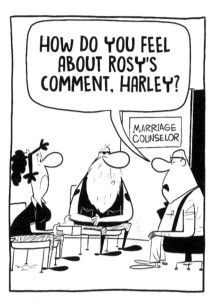

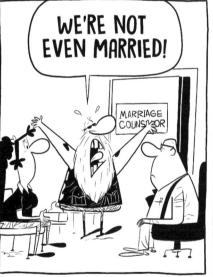

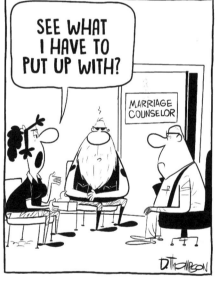

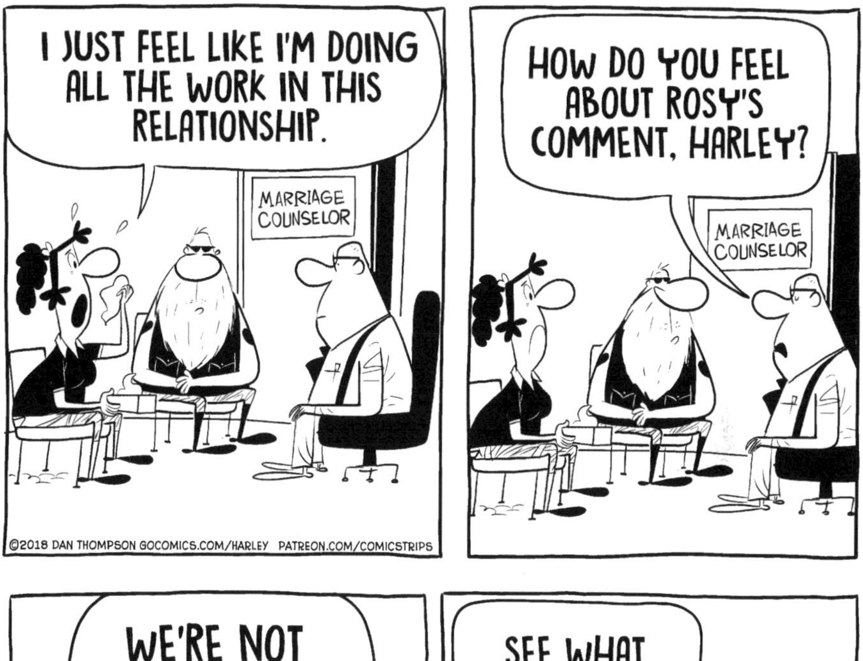

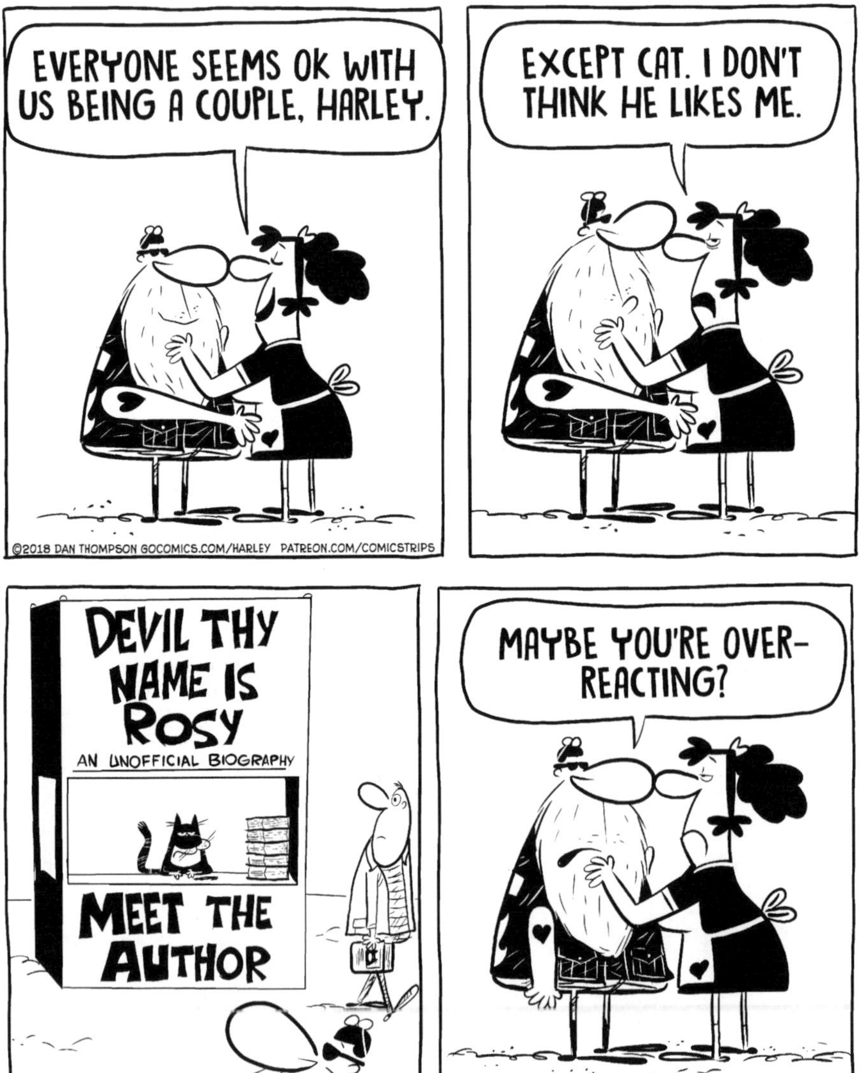
EVERYONE SEEMS OK WITH US BEING A COUPLE, HARLEY.
©2018 DAN THOMPSON GOCOMICS.COM/HARLEY PATREON.COM/COMICSTRIPS
EXCEPT CAT. I DON'T THINK HE LIKES ME.
DEVIL THY NAME IS ROSY
AN UNOFFICIAL BIOGRAPHY
MEET THE AUTHOR
MAYBE YOU'RE OVER-REACTING?
D. THOMPSON

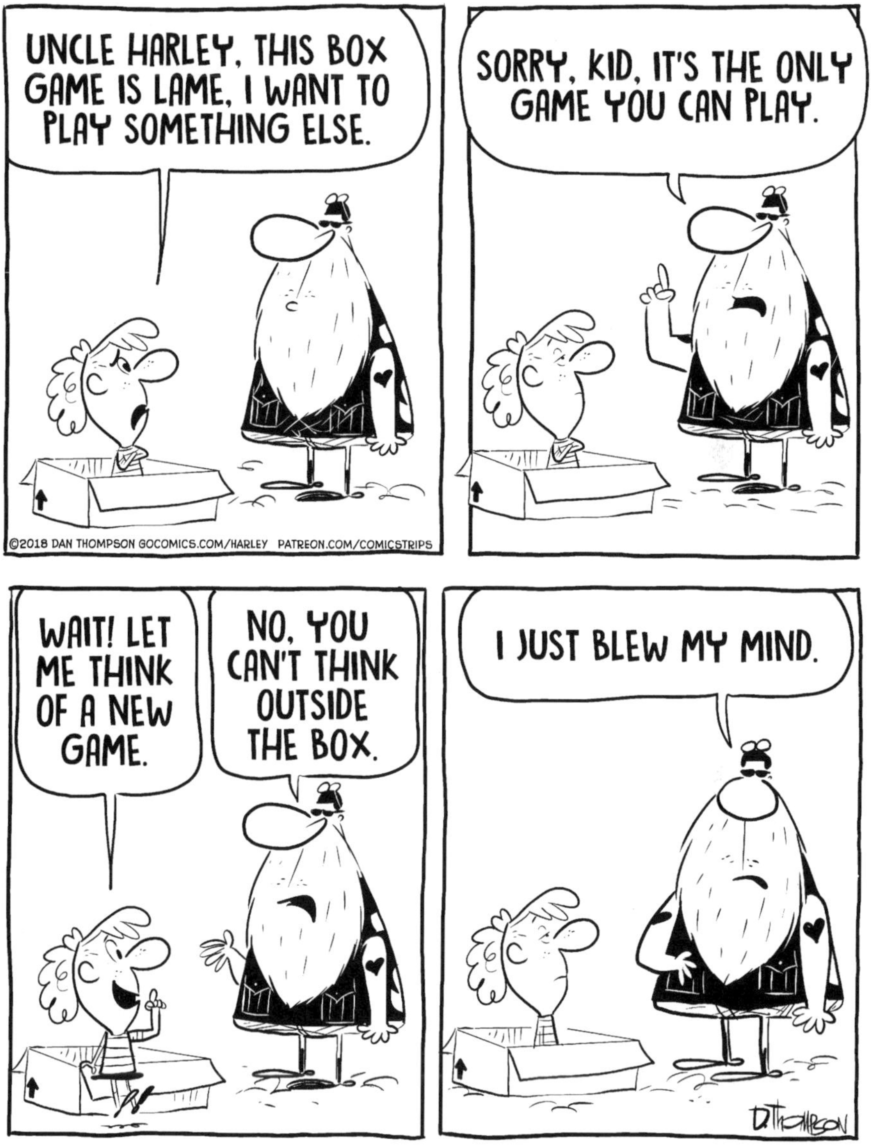
UNCLE HARLEY, THIS BOX GAME IS LAME, I WANT TO PLAY SOMETHING ELSE.
©2018 DAN THOMPSON GOCOMICS.COM/HARLEY PATREON.COM/COMICSTRIPS
SORRY, KID, IT'S THE ONLY GAME YOU CAN PLAY.
WAIT! LET ME THINK OF A NEW GAME.
NO, YOU CAN'T THINK OUTSIDE THE BOX.
I JUST BLEW MY MIND.
D.THOMPSON

39625941R00144

Made in the USA
Middletown, DE
18 March 2019